I0813774

THE SOLDIER'S REWARD

The Soldier's Reward

LOVE AND WAR IN THE AGE OF THE FRENCH REVOLUTION AND NAPOLEON

Jennifer Ngaire Heuer

PRINCETON UNIVERSITY PRESS
PRINCETON & OXFORD

Published by Princeton University Press
41 William Street, Princeton, New Jersey 08540
99 Banbury Road, Oxford OX2 6JX

press.princeton.edu

Library of Congress Cataloging-in-Publication Data

Names: Heuer, Jennifer Ngaire, 1969- author.
Title: The soldier's reward : love and war in the age of the French Revolution and Napoleon / Jennifer Ngaire Heuer.
Other titles: Love and war in the age of the French Revolution and Napoleon
Description: Princeton : Princeton University Press, [2024] | Includes bibliographical references and index.
Identifiers: LCCN 2024019956 (print) | LCCN 2024019957 (ebook) | ISBN 9780691262574 (hardcover) | ISBN 9780691262598 (ebook)
Subjects: LCSH: France—History, Military—18th century. | Soldiers—Family relationships—France—History—18th century. | Soldiers—Family relationships—France—History—19th century. | Families of military personnel—France—History—19th | Napoleonic Wars, 1800–1815. | Women and war—France—History—18th century. | Marriage—France—History—18th century. | Families—France—History—18th century. | Marriage—France—History—19th century. | Families—France—History—19th century. | BISAC: HISTORY / Europe / France | SOCIAL SCIENCE / Gender Studies
Classification: LCC DC151 .H48 2025 (print) | LCC DC151 (ebook) | DDC 940.2/71—dc23/eng/20240509
LC record available at https://lccn.loc.gov/2024019956
LC ebook record available at https://lccn.loc.gov/2024019957

British Library Cataloging-in-Publication Data is available

Editorial: Priya Nelson and Emma Wagh
Production Editorial: Terri O'Prey
Jacket Design: Drohan DiSanto
Production: Danielle Amatucci
Publicity: William Pagdatoon

Jacket image: Anonymous, *The Despair of the Wooden Leg Turner*, c. 1814.
Courtesy of the Carnavalet-History of Paris Museum

This book has been composed in Miller

Printed in the United States of America

10 9 8 7 6 5 4 3 2 1

Dedicated to Hilary Whetu Heuer

CONTENTS

ILLUSTRATIONS

ACKNOWLEDGMENTS

THIS BOOK HAS been far too long in the making, and has benefited from encouragement, wise words, and inspired suggestions from many people. I have inevitably left out names of some who have supported the project at different points; if this includes yours, please know that it is because I am absent-mindeded, not unappreciative of your help.

My colleagues at the University of Massachusetts Amherst have been marvelously supportive throughout this process; I am also deeply appreciative of the institutional support for both research trips and writing time.

I am grateful to audiences in different forums, both in person and virtual, whose questions and feedback helped me discover new connections and rethink key points. These have included multiple iterations of the conference for the Society for French Historical Studies, as well as the Western Society for French History, the British Society for the Study of French History, the Consortium on the Revolutionary Era, and the Australasian Association for European History. Colleagues graciously invited me to give talks on work in progress, including at the Five College History Seminar in Amherst; the University of Georgia, in Athens, Georgia; Clark University, in Worcester, Massachusetts; the University of Hawaii, in Honolulu; Reid Hall, Paris; the Séminaire sur l'histoire de la famille at the Centre Roland Mousnier, Sorbonne-Université Paris; and the Laboratoire d'histoire de Lyon et Grenoble, in France. A special mention to an attentive audience at Otago University, in Dunedin, New Zealand; little did I know in March 2020 that my talk there would be my last in-person presentation for a very long time.

The many people who have read drafts and helped me edit all or parts of the book at different points have made this a much stronger work. A particular shout-out to Alyssa Sepinwall, who has been a consistently brilliant and responsive editing buddy, and who has read far too many versions of different chapters. Anna Taylor made insightful comments and drew creative pictures (including those of weasels to mark obfuscations) on early drafts. Christy Pichichero provided friendship, encouragement, and intellectual exchange, especially for thinking about eighteenth-century developments. Judith de Groat kindly read the full manuscript as it neared completion, while Nina Kushner offered invaluable comments on the introduction. Elisa Camiscioli has been an incredible friend throughout the process, especially in the book's final stages. Anne Verjus too has supported the project in its long gestation, shared discoveries from her own research, and made numerous suggestions. Christine Haynes, my wonderful coeditor at *French Historical Studies*, has provided vital encouragement on many key occasions, as has Mette Harde, my coeditor of the volume *Life in Revolutionary France*. The anonymous readers for Princeton University Press and Priya Nelson also provided invaluable feedback. I add my thanks to my copyeditor, Kim Hastings, who caught many inconsistencies and infelicities; remaining mistakes are my own—or perhaps, in a few cases, those of French revolutionaries and their sucessors, whose strengths were not necessarily those of consistency.

Earlier versions of parts of this book have been published in different forms. A version of some material for chapter 1 appeared as "Celibacy, Courage, and Hungry Wives: Debating Military Marriage and Citizenship in Prerevolutionary France," in *European History Quarterly*. Portions of chapter 3 were first published in "Citizenship, the French Revolution, and the Limits of Martial Masculinity," in *Gender and Citizenship in Historical and Transnational Perspective*, edited by Rachel Fuchs and Anne Epstein. Material that eventually became part of chapter 7 appeared as "Soldiers as Victims or Villains? Demobilization, Masculinity, and Family in French Royalist Pamphlets, 1814–1815," in the *Journal of Military History*; some material for chapter 8 was published as "No More Fears, No More Tears? Gender, Emotion, and the Aftermath of the Napoleonic Wars in France," in *Gender and History*. Finally, a very early version of material in chapter 9 came out in French as "'Réduit à désirer la mort d'une femme qui peut-être lui a sauvé la vie': La conscription et les liens du mariage sous Napoléon," in the *Annales historiques de la révolution française*. I thank the readers of those articles and chapters for their help in developing parts of this project. Please see the bibliography for full citations for all.

I also want to thank my wonderful, generous, inspiring parents, Earl and Berys Heuer, and my sister, Hilary Whetu Heuer—yes, Hilary, you finally have a book dedicated to you!

Finally, I thank my incredible husband, Brian Ogilvie, who has been my daily source of joy, strength, and utter delight for more years than I will note here. He has consistently supported my research, including adapting his own work to spend more time in French archives and libraries, listening to me think through discoveries and ideas, reading drafts, helping with technical challenges, and generally inspiring me to keep going.

THE SOLDIER'S REWARD

Introduction

IN 1792, A French speechwriter invoked the patriotic duty of those taking up arms to defend the struggling revolutionary nation. He proclaimed that "there is no sacrifice that he is not ready to make for our common mother, the *patrie*." The true citizen "concentrates his most tender affections in his *patrie*. He prefers it to his family, his wife, his children, and even himself."[1]

Soldiers' families, however, were not convinced that they should be sacrificed—or that soldiers' sacrifices should be unlimited. Some sought to keep men out of the hands of the state entirely. Others argued that veterans' returns were as necessary as their departures had been. When peace appeared imminent in 1797, one widow presented her son's homecoming as both a patriotic duty and a reward for his service. She pleaded with the government: "Give my son the reward he seeks so ardently, that of coming to lighten the misery of his mother and feed his sisters by his care and his hard work. After serving the *patrie* with so much loyalty and courage, he will serve humanity and fulfill the duties of filial piety; he will only leave the flags of the Republic to fly to the aid of his mother."[2]

If family members dreamt of the return of absent spouses or sons, popular culture throughout the French Revolution and Napoleonic eras promised returning soldiers domestic joys. When peace was proclaimed in 1797, theaters across France sought to lure their audiences with shows vaunting happy unions, like *Marriage with the Peace*. After war had resumed but a new peace treaty seemed imminent in 1801, stages again sought to entice viewers with offerings like *The Preliminaries of Peace or the Lovers Reunited*.[3] Napoleonic theaters brushed off familiar scripts and celebrated fresh rounds of theatrical nuptials each time

1. Michel, *Discours sur l'amour de la patrie*, 6. All translations are my own unless otherwise indicated.

2. Archives Nationales (henceforward AN) AF / III / 313 / 2, Alavoine.

3. Gamas, *Le mariage à la paix*, unpublished; see Kennedy et al., *Theatre, Opera, and Audiences*, 292; and Courtois, *Les préliminaires de paix ou les amans réunis*.

peace appeared likely. Even after Napoleon's empire was overturned and a new king came to power, theaters promised that wedding bells would ring for returning veterans—and for young conscripts saved from the draft.

The possibility of marriage as a reward for soldiers was not just a theatrical fantasy. It was also a very real practice directly promoted by the state. Revolutionary officials promised to support couples deemed to be especially deserving. Napoleon's government arranged public weddings and state-sponsored dowries for veterans throughout his reign. The practice reached its apogee in 1810, with six thousand such weddings planned to happen simultaneously across France, in conjunction with the emperor's own nuptials.

This book takes as its starting point such visions of homecoming and marriage as a "soldier's reward." The French Revolution established the modern concept of citizen-soldiers, and institutionalized forms of mass conscription unprecedented in modern history. Rewards for military service included promotion, financial support, glory, and patriotic recognition.[4] But contemporaries—citizens and officials alike—also envisioned recompense in other ways, as the right to "fly to the aid" of desperate relatives or to earn the "warrior's reward" of forming a new household. Indeed, from the early years of the French Revolution through the beginnings of the Bourbon Restoration, both popular culture and governments presented compelling messages about the joys of family life that would follow the traumas of battle. Veterans would come home to the embraces of patient sweethearts or win new conquests with tales of derring-do and displays of their scars. The state would recognize their heroism and local communities celebrate their return with wedding bells. Their parents and siblings would be similarly rewarded; men and women who had sacrificed loved ones and endured the absences or deaths of young men would see their sons or brothers again, or at least be compensated for their losses.

At the same time, family bonds and responsibilities actively worked against military service. Young men sought to avoid the draft, or deserted the troops, often asking family members to protect them. Couples arranged paper marriages in hopes that young men seen as heads of households would be less likely to be conscripted. Communities' willingness to celebrate soldier-heroes was undercut by financial woes, political and ideological divisions, revolutionary upheavals, and the toll of seemingly endless war. Veterans could be physically impaired and disconnected from families or childhood sweethearts they had not seen for years. Young women and their parents sometimes calculated that an able-bodied civilian man would be a better mate than a soldier who might never return, or would return only as a disfigured, or economically risky, partner. While contemporaries rarely talked directly about such issues, they

4. On other forms of reward, see Blaufarb, *The French Army;* and Ihl, *Le mérite et la république.*

hinted at concerns that ex-combatants' experiences with trauma and violence and exposure to venereal disease made them ill-suited to domestic life.

Citizens also dreamt repeatedly of peace. As the Napoleonic wars reached their climax in 1814, some called for an end to fighting on the grounds that by saving young men from conscription, peace would restore families and rescue mothers from constant anguish. One royalist sarcastically heralded peace as a misfortune that would somehow be welcomed throughout France: "I would wager that mothers are crazy enough to celebrate. They will no longer curse the day they gave birth or fear having children [who are likely to be killed in battle]. No more conscription? What will we do?" He concluded on a more optimistic note about the world that might follow one centered on rewards for military heroism: "All French share one wish today: less glory, more happiness."[5] In the following years, veterans of the Napoleonic armies came back to a world of defeat, rather than victory, and to a political order that tried to reverse many revolutionary changes. Pamphleteers sometimes contended that happy family life should be a reward not for military service, but for its opposite: abandoning a quest for personal glory to support a postwar order.

War was a recurrent aspect of daily life in France for more than two decades. Yet the story of these wars, from April 1792 until Napoleon's definitive fall from power in 1815, is often treated separately from the story of the French Revolution. The Revolution offers so many compelling narratives—of new ideas of rights and new forms of violence, of dramatic ideological experiments and equally dramatic power struggles—that war can appear peripheral. It impinges only at a few key moments, as historians consider, for example, how required military service sparked civil war in 1793, how war fed the period of state-sponsored violence in 1793–94 often known as the Terror, and how militarization contributed to Napoleon's rise. Yet assuming that war and the concomitant militarization of society were marginal to the full story of the Revolution leaves aside how men and women experienced conflict; related it to social, cultural, and political transformations; or anticipated its end. In short, we cannot understand the revolutionary period without taking a close look at the experiences of the wars that were its armature.

Military specialists have certainly explored many aspects of these wars, including the dramatic sagas of battles, the changing social profile of the army, possible motivations of the troops, and recurrent issues of draft dodging and desertion.[6] But if war is often marginal in accounts of the Revolution, military histories can also appear removed from analyses of social and cultural

5. *Collection de différentes pièces relatives à la déchéance*, 49.

6. Overviews include Chickering and Förster, eds., *War in an Age of Revolution, 1775–1815*; Rapport, *The Napoleonic Wars: A Very Short Introduction*; and Mikaberidze, *The Napoleonic Wars: A Global History*.

change.[7] This division is reinforced by disciplinary divides between gender and family history on one hand and military history on the other. Scholars have creatively blended these approaches for a few topics, including the transgressive stories of women soldiers, the bonds between homesick soldiers and their mothers, and the effects of prolonged warfare on fostering more aggressive heterosexuality or, alternatively, new forms of homosexual intimacy.[8] Yet most work on gender history during the revolutionary era focuses on women's political activism or rights, or more generally, on legal and cultural change. Military history and gender and family history are often very separate endeavors for the period, unlike for scholarship on the world wars.

Experiences of war and peacemaking are also often treated separately. Indeed, it is easy to assume that governments need to work to persuade citizens to support war, but that people will simply welcome peace. Making peace after two decades of war was actually a profound challenge. It required not only drafting treaties, changing governments, and dealing with the logistics of demobilization, but also negotiating the aftermath of entrenched militarism. *The Soldier's Reward* builds on work that explores how these postwar years, like the Revolution and war itself, were crucial moments of social and cultural transition.[9] It draws on research into the experiences of veterans, tracing the challenges these men faced after their homecomings and the ambivalence of the post-Napoleonic French state toward former warriors.[10] But it also moves beyond veterans to uncover the importance of postwar transitions in France for those less directly connected to the military, including combatants' parents, siblings, and spouses, and men who had actively avoided service.

The story begins on the eve of the Revolution and continues through the drama of civil and international war. It moves through the Napoleonic era and ends with the return of a monarchy and the uneasy establishment of a postwar

7. For two recent exceptions, see Tozzi, "Home Fronts and Battlefields"; and Dodman, "Ordinary Radicalization."

8. Work on women soldiers includes Brice, *La femme et les armées de la révolution;* Conner, "Les Femmes Militaires" and "La Vrai Madame Sans-Gêne "; S. Steinberg, *La confusion des sexes*; Godineau, "De la guerrière à la citoyenne"; J.-C. Martin, *La révolte brisée* and "Travestissements"; Ross, "La femme militaire"; Bouhet, "Les femmes et les armées"; Hopkin, "The World Turned Upside Down"; Cardoza, "'Habits Appropriate to Her Sex'"; Mabo,"Genre et armes dans les conflictualités locales"; Füssell, "Between Dissimulation and Sensation"; and Cardoza and Hagemann, "History and Memory of Army Women." On sexuality, emotion, and military service, see B. J. Martin, *Napoleonic Friendship* and "Military Mates"; Hughes, *Forging Napoleon's Grande Armée*; Boudon, *Le sexe sous l'empire*; and Dodman, *What Nostalgia Was.*

9. Haynes, Heuer, and Davidson, "Ending War"; Dudink, "After the Republic"; Hagemann, "'Heroic Virgins' and 'Bellicose Amazons'"; and Aaslestad, "Identifying a Postwar Period."

10. Woloch, "'A Sacred Debt'" and *The French Veteran*; Petiteau, *Lendemains d'empire* and "Survivors of War"; Vidalenc, *Les demi-soldes.*

order. War and its aftermath would touch almost every family in France and its empire. It combined with Revolution to reshape both models of masculinity and femininity and relations between families and the state. We cannot fully understand changing family and gender relationships in the period without considering the dynamics of prolonged warfare. But neither can we fully understand the evolution of war in this era, its relationships to changing political and ideological regimes, and the reasons why it was supported, sustained, or ended, if we do not take into account gender and family life.

Combatants, Civilians, and "Total War"

More than two decades of seemingly endless conflict required constantly bringing new men into the troops. Volunteers first joined in 1791 to defend the fledgling revolutionary nation from its enemies. The National Assembly declared war on Austria in April 1792, then on Spain and England. Civil war began in western France in spring 1793. The *levée en masse* in August 1793 inaugurated the first mass mobilization in history. In 1798, the French Republic formally established conscription, and transformed an emergency response into a permanent institution. While many aspects of the Revolution were challenged by Napoleon's rise to power, conscription became one of its most inescapable legacies. At least two million French men were recruited into the troops between 1798 and 1815. Up to three and a half million fought during the periods of the Revolution and the Empire as a whole. Of the men born in France between 1790 and 1795, two out of five served in Napoleon's armies.[11]

Many of those men never returned. In 1814 and 1815, royalist pamphleteers contended that there had been five, six, or even seven million deaths—more casualties than there had been men fighting.[12] Such dubious statistics reflected both uncertainty about the full costs of war and Restoration propaganda about the evils of Napoleonic rule. The real numbers are staggering enough. About half a million French military personnel died during the Revolution, and up to a million under Napoleon. There may have been close to five million deaths for all European theaters of war, military and civilian.[13]

These numbers approach the horrific losses of World War I, though they took place over a much longer period.[14] Several historians have taken the term

11. Forrest, *Conscripts and Deserters*, 20–21.

12. The figure of five million appeared in pamphlets such as *Discours d'un brave militaire* and *Deux mots de vérité*. Guéau de Reverseaux de Rouvray, *La paix de l'Europe avec la France*, estimated six million. The figure of seven million surfaced later, possibly in 1817; see Petiteau, *Lendemains d'empire*, 75.

13. For estimates of casualties, see Germani, "Dying for Liberty," 97–98.

14. David Bell has argued that the probable total of a million deaths for France during the Napoleonic era may have included a higher portion of young men than those who perished in 1914–18. Bell, *The First Total War*, 7. Natalie Petiteau provides a more cautious estimate,

"total war," coined for the twentieth century, and applied it to the revolutionary era.[15] "Total war" heralds a new kind of warfare that requires mass participation, through either a popular rush to arms or the state's power to force its citizenry to fight. It implies the subordination of the civilian state to military control. Perhaps most importantly, it suggests warfare aimed at total victory and complete destruction of the enemy.

Many of these definitions are controversial with regard to the Revolution. In debating whether the term "total war" applies to a period when slaughter was less industrialized than in the twentieth century, historians have argued about the centrality of technology to the term and how much the revolutionary and Napoleonic periods changed the nature of warfare. Arguments involve quantitative assessments of the scale of battles and the extent of casualties. They also involve qualitative judgments about the relative savagery of the revolutionary wars and the degree to which new ideals led to new forms of brutality.[16]

Another idea associated with "total war" has received far less attention: the possibility that war created new and closer connections between combatants and civilians in an all-out mobilization of society or, conversely, led to unprecedented ruptures as soldiers shared experiences unimaginable to those behind the lines. The revolutionary and Napoleonic eras provide evidence for both developments. New forms of warfare combined with revolutionary and postrevolutionary shifts to bring the "home front" (an expression first popularized by US wartime propaganda in 1918) together with the world of the camps and battlefields.[17] In the late eighteenth century, many people in France had surprisingly little direct experience of warfare or interactions with soldiers. The military revolution of the previous century curtailed earlier practices by which armies lived off the bounty of civilian populations. Young men could be forced into service through the royal militia—but only about

---

calculating that Napoleonic wars destroyed about 2 percent of France's total population, while World War I destroyed about 3 percent. Petiteau, *Lendemains d'empire*, 76. Alan Forrest has argued that French losses from 1792 to 1814 can be realistically compared to those in 1914–18 but emphasizes that they occurred over twenty years rather than four. Forrest, *The Legacy of the French Revolutionary Wars*, 64. Annie Crépin contends that mobilization was less than in World War I (when a fifth of the population was called up), but that the risk of death was greater in 1800–1815. Crépin, *Défendre la France*, 158. In contrast, Owen Connelly observes that the French population grew during the Napoleonic wars, suggesting that casualties, although devastating for those directly involved, did not dramatically impact population numbers as a whole. Connelly, *The French Revolution and Napoleonic Era*, 232–33.

15. Bell, *The First Total War;* and Guiomar, *L'invention de la guerre totale.*

16. These include Chickering, "Total War: The Use and Abuse of a Concept"; Broers, "The Concept of 'Total War'"; and Charters, Rosenhaft, and Smith, *Civilians and War in Europe.* See also Bell et al., "Autour de la guerre totale." For the claim that the Napoleonic wars should be seen as the first modern, if not the first total, wars, see Hagemann, "The Military and Masculinity."

17. Forrest, *Conscripts and Deserters*, 20–21.

one in forty eligible men were enlisted, and officers came almost exclusively from the nobility.[18] The Revolution transformed these dynamics, promoting citizen-soldiers, men who proved their patriotism by taking up arms for their country.[19] The levée en masse of August 1793 sent men between eighteen and twenty-five to fight and sought to mobilize the entire population behind the war effort. In instituting formal conscription in 1798, officials proclaimed that the law erased "the line of demarcation that kings traced between the citizen and the soldier; it organizes a truly national army."[20]

War continued to permeate daily life under Napoleon. It influenced everything from popular entertainment to marriage, business to artwork, and political relationships to literary exchanges.[21] It required civilians to interact repeatedly with the state. Women and civilian men petitioned authorities to secure permanent discharges for soldiers to "fly home" to their aid or debated whether a young woman should offer her hand in marriage to a returning veteran. They also engaged with the state in myriad other ways, provoked both by revolutionary upheavals and by the exigences of war. These included asking for financial help; seeking patronage for patriotic writing or artwork; trying to discover what happened to a loved one who was missing in action; regularizing the status of a prisoner of war who wanted to remain in France; and attempting to dissolve a marriage undertaken only so that a man might avoid conscription. Military service may have indefinitely separated a man from home, but it imbricated his family members in new relationships with the state and shaped their own claims to citizenship.

At the same time, home and war front could appear profoundly different spaces. Observing that the term "civilian" did not exist in French or English until the end of the Old Regime, David Bell has contended that the Revolution inaugurated a new culture in which warfare became seen as separate from normal existence.[22] Others have similarly claimed that the military became an increasingly self-contained world, particularly under Napoleon.[23] Soldiers could be away from their homes for years. Men who volunteered during the early Revolution or who were incorporated into the ranks in 1793 believed that they would fight for a few months. Those who escaped serious injury or disease and did not desert were often still in the troops years later. The 1798 conscription law limited terms of service to five years during peace—but made them

18. Tozzi, "Home Fronts and Battlefields."

19. Forrest, "Citizenship and Military Service."

20. *Bulletin décadaire*, no. 7, 1 Frimaire Year VII (November 21, 1798).

21. Studies of the impact of war on social and cultural life include Bertaud, *Quand les enfants parlaient de gloire;* Favret, *War at a Distance;* Forrest, "The Military Culture of Napoleonic France"; Germani, "Staging Battles"; and Padiyar, Shaw, and Simpson, eds., *Visual Culture and the Revolutionary and Napoleonic Wars.*

22. Bell, *The First Total War.*

23. Forrest, Hagemann, and Rendall, "Introduction: Nations in Arms, People at War," 4.

unlimited during war. Even after soldiers returned home, they faced challenges trying to communicate their experiences of war to a civilian audience.[24] The language of violence permeated recruitment literature, and the mentality of combat could penetrate every level of society as men trained in killing returned to civilian life.[25] Yet contemporaries rarely acknowledged veterans' potential for aggression at home. While men and women diagnosed nostalgia or *mal du pays* as a disease that could cripple soldiers, they did not use modern categories like post-traumatic stress disorder to understand the psychological effects of war.[26] Instead, recurrent depictions of warriors as humane, generous, and embedded in familial networks counterbalanced fears of soldiers' violence and emotional distance.

The Consequences and Limits of "Martial Masculinity"

The revolutionary and Napoleonic periods reshaped gender roles in many ways, including the development of what historians have labeled martial masculinity.[27] This book follows ways revolutionaries and their successors wrestled with the possibility that there was, or should be, a central definition of citizenship and masculinity, focused on fighting for the patrie. It shows how they promoted the virility of soldier-heroes and deemed them worthy of reward, and how ideas of martial masculinity evolved over the course of the Revolution, the Napoleonic era, and the early Restoration. But perhaps more importantly, it uncovers the limits of these models. Virility, military service, and citizenship sat uneasily together. The French Revolution may have created modern models of male citizen-soldiers, but it also fostered powerful alternatives.

Many of these alternatives centered on domestic life. Marriage had a fundamentally contradictory relationship to war. It was the reward par excellence for warriors, offering romance as recognition of valor and a means of reintegrating them into the nation. It was also one of the best ways of avoiding

24. This is especially clear in memoirs. See Thoral, *From Valmy to Waterloo*, 175; and Grieg, *Dead Men Telling Tales*.

25. On the language of recruitment, see Hippler, "Service militaire et intégration nationale." On violence and returned soldiers, see Dwyer, "'It Still Makes Me Shudder,'" "Public Remembering," "Violence and the Revolutionary and Napoleonic Wars," and "War Stories."

26. Dodman, *What Nostalgia Was*.

27. "Martial masculinity" is used primarily in Anglophone literature, including Hughes, *Forging Napoleon's Grande Armée* and "Making Frenchmen into Warriors"; and Forrest, "Citizenship and Masculinity" and "Citizenship, Honour, and Masculinity." See also Brown, Barry, and Begiato, eds., *Martial Masculinities*. The term "virility" may be more common in Francophone work, or work translated from French. See Corbin, Courtine, and Vigarello, eds., *Histoire de la virilité*, vol. 2, especially Bertaud, "L'armée et le brevet de virilité" and "La virilité militaire."

military service, as men who could claim to be heads of households had a reasonable chance of avoiding conscription. Marriage was a joyful means of celebrating peace, linking individual homecomings to a national end of violence. Conversely, it was a means of producing a new generation of warriors and inculcating them with a commitment to continued fighting. It was a deeply private decision, a declaration of love between two individuals. And it was a familial decision—a calculation about what alliance would be most advantageous—and a key matter of public interest.

By considering marriage as a crucial pivot point between civilian and military life, *The Soldier's Reward* explores competing ideas about the masculinity and relative worth of those who took up arms and those who did not, while exploring the degree to which virility was compatible with domestic life. It builds on growing interest in the family as both a social and legal unit and a cultural and political construction in the eighteenth and early nineteenth centuries. It also intervenes in arguments about when and how models of companionate marriage developed and investigates the power of the state in private life.[28]

Potential soldier-husbands were often seriously injured or ill. Popular culture lauded combatants as heroes with wounds that demonstrated their courage and patriotism. Wounds also led to prolonged suffering and limited men's abilities after they were demobilized. Although soldiers claimed triumphant noms de guerre—including Victor, Belle France, and Goes-with-a-Good-Heart—Peg-leg was the most common epithet for veterans. Battlefield treatment often meant amputation. Disease was rampant and killed far more men than battlefield injury; even those who survived were weakened and disfigured.[29] Physical incapacity was the surest, and often the only, way to secure an exemption or release from military service. Innovative work on suffering and martial masculinity in World War I has shown the consequences of similar damage. While mustard gas and machine guns destroyed bodies in distinctly horrifying ways, studies of the twentieth century suggest how much war could both reinforce and challenge martial masculinity.[30] The particular constructions of masculinity and citizenship in the French Revolution—which

28. Desan, *The Family on Trial*; and Verjus et al., "Regards croisés sur le mariage." Work on companionate marriage includes Roberts, *Sentimental Savants;* Reynolds, *Marriage and Revolution*; Davidson, "'Happy' Marriages"; and Goodman, "Marriage Choice and Marital Success." See also Cage, *Unnatural Frenchmen*; and Marsden, "Married Nuns."

29. Woloch, *The French Veteran*; Lemaire, *Les blessés dans les armées napoléoniennes* and "Les blessures de la guerre." See also Lamy and Mounier, "La chair et le canon"; and Howard, *Napoleon's Doctors.*

30. Scholarship on masculinity, injury, and World War I is most developed for Britain and Germany. Works include Cohen, *The War Come Home;* Kienitz, "Body Damage"; Meyer "'Not Septimus Now"; Bourke, *Dismembering the Male* and "Love and Limblessness"; Salvante, "The Wounded Male Body"; and Perry, *Recycling the Disabled.*

emphasized collective sacrifice and the ability to contribute to the nation as a whole—could make the long-term effects of injury profoundly relevant not just for individuals but also for broader social and political developments.

If war had the most direct impact on men and masculinity, it also shaped women's lives. The development of martial masculinity helps to explain why women did not get the full rights of citizenship during the French Revolution. Some historians see the distinction between a male world of citizen-soldiers and a domestic world of women as one of the crucial features of the Revolution and one of its most lasting legacies. Joan Landes has reprised André Rauch's argument that "what had been the *métier* of some—carrying arms—became the characteristic of all, a quality that distinguishes the man from the child, from the woman, but also from the sick and the old."[31] Éliane Viennot has similarly contended that the Revolution dug a deep division between the sexes, reinforced by political struggles and by the 1793 levée en masse and the institution of conscription in 1798.[32] Such statements support general interpretations of the Revolution as disempowering women. Other scholars have drawn very different lessons, seeing women's demands to bear arms and stories of women soldiers as radical and enduring challenges to gendered hierarchy. These approaches often dovetail with broader analyses of women acting as citizens during the Revolution, making immediate claims to rights and inspiring later movements.[33]

Yet while historians have touched on how war combined with revolution to foster or limit women's political rights, we have thought less about ways relationships between the "home front" and the camps and battlefields affected other aspects of women's identities and experiences.[34]

A few women did take up arms, whether under their own names or disguised as men. Their numbers are small—perhaps a hundred in an army that fluctuated between 300,000 and 700,000 during the Revolution—although there were likely more cases than have been identified.[35] In April 1793, legislators expelled "unnecessary women" from the troops, including women soldiers, military spouses, and camp followers, permitting only a small number

31. Landes, "Republican Citizenship," 97.

32. Viennot, *Et la modernité fut masculine.*

33. Offen, "Women's Memory, Women's History"; and S. Steinberg, *La confusion des sexes.*

34. Karen Hagemann's work constitutes an important exception. Among other works, see Hagemann, Rendall, and Mettele, eds., *Gender, War and Politics: Transatlantic Perspectives 1775–1830.*

35. The most common number is eighty, although that includes counterrevolutionary women. There were likely more women soldiers, as totals have come largely from records in the archives of the Service Historique de la Défense (hereafter SHD)—primarily limited to women soldiers who sought pensions or state assistance—and accounts of women whose careers were particularly colorful or who were publicly honored.

of laundresses and *vivandières*, women who provided basic foodstuffs. As we will see, their expulsion reflected concerns about women's citizenship. But it also resulted from a decision to treat soldiers as family men and allow them to marry without formal permission from military superiors, a decision that led to unprecedented numbers of women in the troops. For the women soldiers forced to demobilize in the wake of the law, the "soldier's reward" of homecoming still promised honor and financial support, although many ultimately lived in poverty.

Most women experienced war more indirectly. Apart from the horrors of civil war, battles were largely fought outside France's borders until the last stages of Napoleon's empire, meaning that French civilians were protected from its most direct ravages. But women were still intimately tied to war. They played vital symbolic roles, whether as stoic and sacrificing mothers of soldiers or as girlfriends whose anxiety contrasted with the courage of martial masculinity. They were charged with embodying collective emotions of grief and mourning. They were vulnerable to sexual violence, especially in the 1814–15 invasion.

They also played much more active roles. Many sent off sons, brothers, husbands, or lovers to war. They decided whether to marry conscripts or veterans and confronted the consequences of those choices. They dealt with the prolonged absence or death of loved ones. They confronted the economic ramifications of missing men and took up more, and often different, forms of work in their absence. They turned repeatedly to the government for both news and assistance. Indeed, if martial masculinity and war contributed to reshaping gender roles for women and distancing women from the exercise of political rights, war also shaped their relation to the state and claims to citizenship in ways that reverberated long after the most dramatic struggles of the Revolution.

Rethinking Citizenship

Looking at soldiers and their families also challenges our modern vision of citizenship as synonymous with individual rights, to reveal how contemporaries saw it as a familial enterprise. Anne Verjus has shown that family structures underpinned many aspects of late eighteenth- and early nineteenth-century political rights. Among other things, calculating taxes to establish whether men were eligible to vote included the economic contributions of their wives—even when couples were legally separated.[36] Familial dimensions of citizenship become even clearer when viewed in light of the civic duties imposed by the Revolution. The obligation to take up arms to defend the nation did not just involve individual men, or even the few women who claimed to be

36. Verjus, *Le cens de la famille* and *Le bon mari*.

fulfilling their patriotic duty by fighting. The ability of the state to recruit soldiers and sustain prolonged warfare depended both on a man's willingness to place duty above domestic affections and on his family's acceptance of that duty. Authorities thus appealed to men and women to inspire their sons, husbands, brothers, and romantic interests to fight, while inciting men to take up arms to defend their families and the mother country as a whole.

Men and women responded by adapting revolutionary models to depict civic duties as stages of a man's life, in which he filled his patriotic duty sequentially, as a soldier and then as a civilian. This was the idea behind the widow Alavoine's contention that "after serving the patrie with so much loyalty and courage," her son would "serve humanity and fulfill the duties of filial piety." Families also defined citizenship as something that could be divided among sons or brothers. One son would fight, while another devoted himself to farming or supporting needy relatives. Both women and civilian men insisted on their civic contributions in motivating soldiers, "sacrificing" their sons, husbands, brothers, or lovers to the state or actively consenting to their departure and accepting the emotional and economic costs of their absence. They presented such sacrifices as proof of their own citizenship and claimed that the nation owed them because of that support. Revolutionary governments promised that if men fought for the nation, the state would provide for those left behind, though such promises were often unfulfilled.

Soldiers and their families insisted on their social usefulness and civic generosity. Such dimensions of citizenship were critical for men and women in the late eighteenth and early nineteenth centuries. Revolutionaries, at least from the abbé Sieyès's famous 1788 pamphlet "What Is the Third Estate?" onward, defined citizens as people who were useful to their compatriots. Those excluded from, or opposed to, the nation were selfish parasites, egoists who lived at the expense of others. In this vision, citizen-soldiers, who were prepared to lay down their lives for the nation, epitomized civic altruism. Explicit references to usefulness and generosity have largely disappeared from modern theorizations of citizenship, but the image of soldiers as unselfish heroes has carried through to our modern tributes to the men (and more rarely, women) who make the ultimate sacrifice.

Combining familial models of citizenship and of civic and military generosity led to questions. Could civilians—men or women—ever be more useful than those in the military? Was military service still an act of bravery and civic generosity if individuals were coerced to fight? Was it selfish to want war to end? Should the state emphasize veterans' past sacrifices as soldiers—or the promise that they could become newly productive as civilians? Was the marriage of wounded men as a reward for military service also a reward for their brides—or did it require a new sacrifice on their part? How central did ideals of social usefulness remain as ideas of citizenship changed over the course of revolutionary and postrevolutionary regimes?

Managing and Performing Emotions

The French Revolution has become a key site for scholars seeking to understand the role of emotions in shaping public actions. Historians have looked most closely at famous moments during the Revolution, from the collective euphoria that accompanied the abolition of feudal privilege in 1789 to the drama of the Terror.[37] Farewells to soldiers, expressions of grief, and celebrations of veterans' homecomings were other highly charged moments, but ones that have less often been recognized as connected to contemporary political and social change.[38] Such moments reveal tensions between a quest for emotions viewed as "natural" or authentic and a desire to demonstrate stoic resolve.[39] While soldiers were supposed to refrain from crying, their tears could appear as acceptable if they were shed on behalf of others and did not impede sacrifice. When civilian men and women petitioned the state to alleviate the war's effects on their lives, they struggled with balancing demonstrations of their patriotic silence with accounts of their suffering or compassion. Contemporaries repeatedly weighed the competing values of love and courage, gratitude and pity, honor and glory, sensitivity and stoicism, and filial devotion and patriotic sacrifice.

All of the regimes that governed France between 1789 and 1830 sought to elicit strong public displays of emotions and direct them in appropriate ways. They faced persistent challenges in controlling such displays. The send-off of recruits was supposed to be a joyous display of unity and military might, but it was also a wrenching time of separation. Revolutionaries put bodies—especially wounded bodies—on display in unprecedented ways.[40] Authorities sought to showcase injured men both as figures whose mutilated bodies had to be avenged and as heroes worthy of collective devotion and romantic desire. Yet such spectacles could provoke pity, disgust, and despair. Official recognition of those killed in battle and the anguish of their families had to be handled carefully to express appreciation while avoiding calling attention to military losses or vulnerability.

If problems of using public displays of emotion were recurrent, how people understood and framed emotions changed from the eve of the Revolution through the Restoration. William Reddy has contended that sentimentalism (his word for what those in the eighteenth century called *sensibilité*) gave way to passion between 1794 and 1814 as the dominant force in society. Others have

37. For overviews, see Rosenfeld, "Thinking about Feeling"; Wahnich, *Les émotions, la révolution française et le présent;* and Mazeau, "Émotions politiques."

38. See especially Forrest, "Le départ du conscrit."

39. For similar tensions in other revolutionary contexts, see L. A. H. Parker, "Veiled Emotions."

40. Baecque, *The Body Politic;* and Biard and Maignon, *La souffrance et la gloire.*

contested his formulations but agree that the period marks a turning point in how men and women connected emotions to politics.[41] Those in power thus wrestled with changing understandings of the psychological and social effects of showcasing or silencing emotions.

Both revolutionary and postrevolutionary regimes could find it useful specifically to display *women's* emotional responses to war. Starting about 1770, French men and women began to revive the ideal of a Spartan woman, who overcame her distress to place her country's needs before her own. Revolutionaries would seize upon this image of mothers who repressed tears and sent their sons to war to legitimate the superiority of the mother country and its demands upon its children. All, even those who had the most right to be protected, seemed to accept it. In contrast, Napoleonic culture often portrayed men who triumphed over feminine tears to take up arms. By the early Restoration, royalists promoted a distinctive image of young mothers desperate for peace and grateful to a returned king who saved their sons. While these changes reflect many factors—from evolving gender roles to growing weariness with Napoleon's war machine—they also show that accounts of women's emotional responses to war were not simply documents of individual reactions but were mobilized for political ends.

"Cultural Recycling": Using Old Models in New Orders

Alexis de Tocqueville famously argued that there were important administrative connections between the Old Regime and the French Revolution despite revolutionaries' claims to have broken completely with the past.[42] There were also hidden cultural continuities: even as people sought to invent a new world, they quietly repurposed familiar references and rituals. This process, which I have labeled "cultural recycling," was particularly important when it came to promoting war and heralding peace.

Such adaptations did not simply show the persistence of engrained habits. They provided convenient templates for making sense of the world in periods of rapid change, as well as tools that governments hoped to use to legitimate both mobilization and demobilization. They shaped the ways men and women understood the place of the army, imagined soldiers' homecomings, and constructed gender roles during and after the Revolution and war.

Reuses, however, carried awkward associations. When the government of the late Revolution sought to promote conscription, it drew on emotional repertoires developed during the Jacobin Republic. Officials invoked threats to French families, exhorting would-be soldiers to avenge their fellow citizens. But such references could resonate badly in the aftermath of the Terror, as

41. Reddy, "Sentimentalism and Its Erasure" and *The Navigation of Feeling*.
42. Tocqueville, *The Old Regime and the French Revolution*.

men and women had become uneasy with spectacles of gore, and authorities struggled to control popular reactions.

Conversely, royalists rushing to find ways to celebrate peace in 1814 found revolutionary and Napoleonic plays celebrating veterans' marriages to be expedient. Such plays could be approved and performed quickly; censors and actors were familiar with many aspects of the scripts, and audiences could be enticed with recognizable plots and characters. But royalists marking a peace defined by defeat and legitimated in part by the end of conscription stumbled repeatedly over the plays' celebrations of victorious soldier-heroes.

At the same time, apparent cultural recycling could mask substantive changes. When theaters first promoted plays celebrating peace in the late Revolution and early Napoleonic periods, they heralded the marriages of veterans to loyal young women, and imagined that beneficent authorities would magically provide dowries to deserving couples. State-sponsored marriages under Napoleon would seem to be the realization of these theatrical fantasies. But Napoleon's government actually transformed veterans' marriages from a way of imagining collective celebrations of peace into a tool for promoting continued warfare.

From the Creation of Revolutionary Soldier-Citizens to the Challenges of a Royalist Peace

To understand the "soldier's reward" in its various forms requires bringing together sources rarely considered together. This book thus draws on the records of military history, including troop rosters, battle plans, soldiers' memoirs, and reports of anticonscription riots. It combines these records with materials more often associated with cultural history, including music, from drinking songs to heart-rending laments; artwork, from paintings of patriotic departures to engravings celebrating women warriors; and accounts of official festivals. It draws especially on the most important form of both entertainment and political propaganda in the period: popular theater.[43] Hundreds of *pièces de circonstance*, theatrical works produced for specific occasions, celebrated political events, military victories, and peace treaties.[44] These were subsidized by series of different governments, and tickets made free to eager audiences.[45] Censors scrutinized scripts before they were produced, though could push for shows to be staged quickly; police attended performances and kept a wary eye on audiences' reactions, and critics commented with both

43. R. J. Goldstein, ed., *The Frightful Stage*, 5.

44. For listings, see the Calendrier électronique des spectacles sous l'ancien régime et sous la révolution, https://cesar.huma-num.fr/cesar2/;and Lecomte, *Napoléon et l'empire racontés par le théâtre*. See also Kennedy et al., *Theatre, Opera, and Audiences*.

45. Julian, "Les 'gratis' de Napoléon."

indulgence and indignation. Plays, and popular and official responses, were revelatory of how contemporaries imagined relationships between civilians and combatants, or hoped that those relationships could be remade.

I also turn to records most often associated with social history. Personal papers, especially family letters and journals, offer hints of how individuals experienced and negotiated this tumultuous era. Police reports, meetings of town councils, personal petitions, and court records provide other clues. Indeed, we look most at records of individuals' interactions with the government. The experience of revolution brought many men and women into unprecedented contact with the state. So too did the experience of prolonged war and its aftermath. Their records reveal the drama and complexities of individual lives, as writers combined formulaic expressions with vivid biographical details. They illuminate how individuals hoped to persuade authorities of the justice of their cause, and what they believed the state owed them and their families.

Chapter 1 opens with relations between war and family in the last years of the Old Regime. While arms-bearing was an honorable profession for nobles in the eighteenth century, contemporaries viewed military service for ordinary soldiers as something that young men were forced or tricked into doing, or took up selfishly at the expense of their families and loved ones. In the wake of France's defeats in the Seven Years War (1756–63), reformers proposed new models of citizen-soldiers, who would fight for both family and country. They debated how men could become such citizen-soldiers, and especially whether military men could, or should, marry. These debates provide an important and overlooked site for uncovering competing visions of citizenship, gender, emotion, and state power.

Chapter 2 takes us to the heart of the Revolution, when the abstract question of whether all French citizens were, or should be, soldiers suddenly became urgent to resolve in practice. Arms-bearing became entangled with ideas of citizenship as the Revolution radicalized, and new tensions developed between military mobilization and changes to gender and family life. Citizens were supposed to be good family members; they were also supposed to abandon their families to defend the mother country.

Although new ideals and institutions of citizen-soldiers were primarily associated with men, this chapter also investigates the experiences of women soldiers. It considers why such women enlisted, and what happened when they were officially demobilized in 1793. Their experiences and the stories that surrounded them—from debates over whether women veterans could continue to wear military uniforms to plays lauding armed "amazons"—suggest what honor, gender, and citizenship could mean for those forcibly discharged amid ongoing warfare.

Even while revolutionaries heralded soldier-citizens, they expected war to be short. Combatants anticipated returning home after a campaign or a season, once national emergency was over. Robespierre's fall from power in

1794 seemed to promise an end to that emergency. But war continued long afterward. Chapter 3 draws on a previously unexamined corpus of about 16,000 petitions from veterans seeking to come home in the later 1790s, even as battles raged on. Middle-aged volunteers begged for permission to return to their wives and children; teenage soldiers admitted that they lacked the strength to continue; elderly parents longed for the companionship and labor of absent sons; and a few women professed their desperate love for their missing spouses. The chapter uses these petitions, in combination with other materials on soldiers' families, to investigate evolving definitions of citizenship in the later Revolution, the prolonged effects of war on men and women, strategic emotional appeals to authorities, and alternatives to martial masculinity.

In 1798, a new law on conscription transformed military service from a response to emergency into a permanent institution. It would subsequently become the backbone of Napoleon's war machine. Chapter 4 explores how this law was instituted. One moment proved pivotal: the assassination of two diplomats in front of their families during peace negotiations in Rastadt and the apparently miraculous survival of a third diplomat. The Directorial government sought to use the stories of these "martyrs of peace" to call for vengeance and legitimate conscription. But it struggled with the limits of adapting earlier models for promoting mass mobilization in a changed political world.

Chapter 5 turns from the drummers of war to the playwrights of peace. It concentrates on popular theater celebrating short-lived peace treaties in 1797 and again in 1801. Such plays featured veterans' homecomings. Their happy endings made it possible for playwrights and their audiences to consider openly whether war would actually end. Should women remain loyal to absent sweethearts, especially if they doubted such men would return? Would wounded, violent, or impoverished veterans still make desirable husbands and fathers? The plays also reveal both surprising continuities and subtle shifts in imagining peace before and after Napoleon's ascent to power.

Chapter 6 brings us to the marriages of real veterans, specifically to the state-sponsored weddings under Napoleon. These weddings transformed older models of philanthropy and theatrical fantasies of marriage with peace into tools for celebrating Napoleon and legitimating ongoing war. Looking at local attempts to arrange weddings and individuals' experiences shows both ideological and financial challenges when a militarized state tried to become a marriage broker. It lays bare the tensions between rewarding wounded veterans for their past service and establishing new civilian households. The archives also reveal surprising, if rare, attempts to use such weddings as rewards for women veterans.

The final chapters examine the challenges of peacemaking after 1814. Most historians have treated these years as a postrevolutionary moment; I emphasize how much they were shaped by the aftermath of war. Chapter 7 tracks these dynamics through a contemporary explosion of partisan pamphlets.

Many of these works explicitly or implicitly addressed the relationships between gender, citizenship, family, and military service. Royalist pamphleteers vacillated between depicting conscripts as youthful victims of Napoleon's tyranny and seeing soldiers as men who sought personal glory at the expense of their suffering families. These tracts illuminate the challenges of martial masculinity in a period when the most obvious figures of virility were veterans associated with a defeated regime.

Chapter 8 broadens our scope to return to other cultural sources, including theater, songs, and artwork. These tell a hidden story. Even as royalists decried revolutionary and Napoleonic regimes, they drew on earlier models for envisioning the end of war and negotiating soldiers' homecomings, models that included both familiar theatrical plots and the reuse of state-sponsored marriages. Adapting these models to a new order, however, often worked badly. To bolster a royalist peace, contemporaries thus also turned to new representations, especially those of mothers desperate for the end of war and grateful to the king who brought peace and ended conscription. While these images built on the real activities of women in protesting conscription and protecting draft dodgers, they served powerful political purposes.

A final chapter, "Wishing for the Death of the Woman Who Saved His Life," uncovers the lived experiences of a postwar era. The practical and emotional challenges of ending war were enormous, not just for governments and veterans, but also for families. They ranged from trying to track down the fate of husbands, brothers, and sons who were missing in action to the vexed negotiations over whether individuals who had been paid to fight in the place of conscripts were still owed their contractual dues once peace arrived. I look especially at men and women who had made paper marriages so that a young man might be deemed a head of household and thus escape conscription. With the return of a Catholic monarchy and the abolition of divorce, such couples feared being forced to remain together for life. They desperately tried to use the Restoration government's denunciations of conscription and war for their own purposes.

The conclusion touches on the surprising return of a new form of military recruitment in 1818, which officials were careful not to label as "conscription," and the growing popularity of the image of the soldier-farmer (*soldat laboureur*) in the 1820s, a veteran returned home but ready to resume arms. While these developments suggest the ways that contemporaries sought to move past the immediate experiences of the revolutionary and Napoleonic wars, mass mobilization and peacemaking also had longer-term impacts. If the "soldier's reward" of marriage has largely disappeared as a modern point of reference, we are living in a world marked by fundamental tensions it reveals between the demands of family, war, and citizenship.

CHAPTER ONE

Prelude: War and Family on the Eve of Revolution

THE MOST FAMOUS EIGHTEENTH-CENTURY IMAGE OF enlistment may be Jean-Baptiste Greuze's *The Father's Curse: The Ungrateful Son*, first shown as a sketch in 1765. It depicts the moment in which a young man, the only support of a peasant family, is about to join the army. He raises his arm to symbolize his irreversible decision. The father curses his wayward son, while the mother gestures desperately. A young woman, hands joined together, begs him to stay, and a child hangs onto the soldier's tunic. In a second painting, *The Son Punished*, the son has returned, but too late; his father has died.[1]

For nobles, military service as an officer offered a common career path and the possibility of honor and advancement. Those who joined the ranks as ordinary troops had fewer prospects. Soldiering was considered the career of last resort for younger sons of poor peasants or boys at odds with the law or their parents, like those in Greuze's paintings.[2] Once enlisted, men were separated from their families and much of domestic life. In the wake of the seventeenth-century "military revolution," most troops were no longer billeted with civilians, and armies ceased to take most of their provisions from local populations.[3] Some women accompanied the troops, but their numbers declined significantly after the mid-seventeenth century.[4] At the same time, a series of laws actively separated soldiers from familial life, including

1. Jean-Baptiste Greuze, *La malédiction paternelle: Le fils ingrat*, 1777, and *Le fils puni*, 1778 (Collections du Louvre). See also Barker, *Greuze and the Painting of Sentiment*, 76–80.

2. Forrest, *The French Revolution and the Poor*, 139.

3. Tozzi, "Home Fronts and Battlefields."

4. Lynn, *Women, Armies, and Warfare.*

FIGURE 1.1. Jean-Baptiste Greuze, *The Father's Curse: The Ungrateful Son*, c. 1777. Getty Museum Collection.

repeatedly forbidding both officers and soldiers from marrying without the formal permission of their superiors.[5]

In the later eighteenth century, particularly in the wake of the demoralizing losses of the Seven Years War (1754–63), these dynamics began to change. Reformers advanced new projects for improving the reputation of the army and for rethinking the relationships between combatants and civilians.[6] The title of the most influential of these texts is suggestive: Joseph Servan's *Le soldat citoyen*. Written sometime between 1760 and 1771 and published in 1780, it promoted a new ideal of soldier-citizens.[7]

5. Key measures dated from December 15, 1681; April 6, 1686; September 13, 1713; May 24, 1728; January 28, 1764; and July 1, 1788. Pezzani, *Traité des empêchements du mariage*, 279. These paralleled measures in other European countries.

6. Dziembowski, *Un nouveau patriotisme français*.

7. Servan, *Le soldat citoyen*. On the attention paid to the work, and the author's promotion from relative obscurity to a prestigious position as subgovernor of the royal pages at Versailles, see Smith, *The Culture of Merit*, 200. On reform projects, see Hippler, *Citizens, Soldiers, and National Armies*.

To make sense of this ideal and its relation to changing forms of gender and family, we need to bring together several bodies of scholarship that have developed separately. One is on these military reforms in the later eighteenth century. In an innovative study, Christy Pichichero has argued for a distinctive "military Enlightenment." While the brutality of war may seem antithetical to the cosmopolitanism and humanitarianism promoted by *philosophes*, Pichichero contends that military reformers tried to reconcile apparently competing ideals and implement them in training armed forces.[8] Arnaud Guinier has emphasized new visions of honor, and new forms of control over soldiers' bodies.[9] Julia Osman has similarly argued that French officers and intellectuals sought to forge a new kind of citizen army, inspired in part by the American Revolution and models from ancient Greece and Rome.[10] Such reforms fostered new forms of martial masculinity.[11]

At the same time, Enlightenment thinkers increasingly developed another, very different ideal: the citizen as an affectionate father and virtuous head of household.[12] Here another body of scholarship has uncovered the growing civic and intellectual value placed on family bonds. Leslie Tuttle has shown that between 1760 and 1790 authorities combined populationist concerns with a sentimentalized model of fatherhood as they awarded pensions and tax breaks to fathers of large families.[13] Looking at married *philosophes*, Meghan Roberts has argued that men of letters began celebrating intellectually companionate marriage, presenting their loving families as proof of their sociability and virtue.[14] Claire Cage has similarly demonstrated that reformers increasingly identified clerical celibacy as unnatural and counter to French population interests; they proposed making priests into better citizens by allowing them to marry.[15]

This chapter brings these bodies of historiography together to explore countervailing ideas of citizenship, martial masculinity, gender, and emotion in the late eighteenth century. We focus most on cultural representations, beginning with visions of young men's enlistment as rare, but disastrous for families. In the wake of the Seven Years War, reformers began to promote a new image of a soldier-citizen supported by his family. In artwork and theater, fathers increasingly came to endorse their sons' decision. Women were often depicted as distraught, but some works revived references to Spartan women who stoically sent off their menfolk, and celebrated women warriors.

8. Pichichero, *The Military Enlightenment.*
9. Guinier, *L'honneur du soldat.*
10. Osman, *Citizen Soldiers and the Key to the Bastille.*
11. Corbin, Courtine, and Vigarello, eds., *Histoire de la virilité*, vol. 1.
12. Verjus, *Le bon mari.*
13. Tuttle, "Celebrating the Père de Famille" and *Conceiving the Old Regime.*
14. Roberts, *Sentimental Savants.*
15. Cage, *Unnatural Frenchmen*; and Marsden, "Married Nuns."

We concentrate on the site where models of virility and domestic virtue appeared most at odds: military marriage.[16] Debates over whether soldiers should be allowed to marry became increasingly significant in the 1770s and 1780s. They touched on practical matters, including desertion, the risk of venereal disease, the expense of supporting military families, and the most effective means of increasing France's population. But they also raised ideological questions about what made a good citizen and a good soldier, and whether married men would be braver or more cowardly than their single counterparts. Some contended that soldier-citizens should be invested in both war and domestic life; being a better warrior required being a husband and father. For others, soldiers were inherently set apart from other French men, whether because of their social status or the violence of their profession. They needed to be separated from both the obligations and temptations of domesticity.

Forced, Tricked, or Selfishly Choosing to Leave?

Contemporaries knew that Greuze could have blamed the French state for the consequences of the son's departure. As one commentator on *The Father's Curse* observed in 1769, the artist could have depicted "a poor young man who has just drawn lots for military service, who has drawn the black ticket, and brings the news to his family." Other artists had stirred heartstrings with images of the devastating effects of the *milice*, the royal militia, on families. A 1774 work by Saint-Jean, *The Farewells of a Militiaman*, was not by a great painter or beautifully done, but it drew tears from spectators moved by the scene of a young man being forced to leave his family.[17]

The French government had created militias as a reserve force in 1688, briefly disbanded them, and then reestablished them again in 1719. Their direct impact was limited, especially compared to later forms of recruitment. Only about one of every forty men eligible for service enlisted, and various towns and provinces were exempt entirely from the requirement.[18] But the milice was still enormously unpopular, and the obligations associated with it seemed to become more onerous over the course of the century.

Critics challenged the military efficacy of the institution, but particularly denounced its effects on French families. The 1765 *Encyclopédie* attacked the milice for taking the only son of a poor farmer, forcing the young man to leave home when his labor could have supported his parents.[19] Popular culture

16. Material on soldiers' marriages was first published as Heuer, "Celibacy, Courage, and Hungry Wives."

17. The Saint-Jean painting, *Les adieux d'un milicien*, was displayed at the 1774 Académie de Saint Luc. For a critic's judgment, see Cochin, *Réponse de M. Jérôme*, 23–24. See also Barker, *Greuze and the Painting of Sentiment*, 78.

18. Forrest, *Conscripts and Deserters*, 9; Tozzi, "Home Fronts and Battlefields."

19. Jaucourt, "Milice."

dramatized such scenes, as in the 1772 play *The Two Militiamen,* which portrayed a young man who drew the fatal ticket in the lottery to decide who would be forced to serve. His departure threatened to destroy his girlfriend and widowed mother.[20] In this case, the playwright, himself a lieutenant in the regiment of Touraine, produced a happy ending by having a volunteer take the young man's place. Such resolutions worked well on stage but were impractical for most families.

Perhaps the strongest evidence for entrenched resentment comes from the widespread complaints about the milice in the collections of grievances, the *cahiers de doléance,* sent to the king in 1789.[21] Many focused on the consequences of taking strong young men from their families, like those in Château-Thierry, a commune to the east of Paris, who called for the milice to be replaced with voluntary engagements. Those forcibly enlisted were ill-suited for service, and the obligation to take up arms "falls on the son of a widow, or an infirm father, whose fields are abandoned."[22] Some cahiers described these consequences in dramatic scenes, such as one in which the inhabitants of Villamblain in Loir-et-Cher lamented that "A father sweated blood and tears to raise his family until his children were old enough to be useful to him; just when he is about to reach the realization of his hopes, the milice is published, his son is selected, and this poor father, despair in his heart, is obliged to abandon his profession since he cannot afford to pay for help."[23]

The cahiers also reveal another, perhaps more surprising, set of complaints about the effects of the milice on French families: it encouraged young men to marry prematurely, in hopes that they would escape enlistment if they became husbands and fathers. Wed too young, they produced unhealthy offspring they could not support. The inhabitants of Chalmazel in Forez argued that the milice was "destructive for the country in providing only cowardly soldiers and disastrous for families by the hasty marriages that it necessitates."[24] Those in the department of the Maine similarly complained that the milice "leads young men to marry, even though they do not earn enough even to dress themselves. Impoverished families result [from these alliances]; parents teach their children to beg as soon as they are able to walk."[25] Such complaints appealed to the populationist discourses of the eighteenth century, contending that ending the militia would make the nation stronger through healthier and more economically viable families.

20. Azémar, *Les deux miliciens.*

21. Forrest, *Conscripts and Deserters,* 9–12.

22. *Tableau comparatif des demandes,* 179.

23. Lesueur, ed., *Département de Loir-et-Cher: Cahiers de doléances du bailliage de Blois,* 1:303.

24. Fournial and Gutton, eds., *Cahiers de doléances de la province de Forez,* 1:83.

25. Cited in Forrest, *Conscripts and Deserters,* 11.

Other accounts focused on men tricked into enlisting. Popular plays, tracts, and prints denounced *racoleurs*, recruiting agents, who plied young men with alcohol, made false promises, or faked signatures on enlistment records. The most famous example is the 1756 play *The Recruiters*, by celebrated playwright Jean-Joseph Vadé, in which the protagonist mistakenly enrolls when he believes he is investing in a lottery ticket.[26] Comical images mocked the naivety of young men willing to sell themselves for dreams of financial reward, rapid promotion, or adventure. Reformers sometimes attacked racoleurs in harsher terms. Joseph Servan, the author of the *Le soldat citoyen*, condemned the practice of getting young men drunk and enlisting them without their informed consent. Similarly, in his best-selling 1781 *Tableau de Paris*, Louis-Sébastien Mercier described recruiting agents as "sellers of human flesh."[27] Contemporary reports indicate that agents did engage in coercion and deception to fill their rosters, but accounts of lying racoleurs also reflected and fostered popular distrust of the military.[28]

Even when works did not directly denounce racoleurs, they conveyed similar messages. The 1781 play *The Supposed Enlistment*, for example, depicted a young man who makes his mother believe that he is joining the military so that she will consent to his marriage to the apple-seller he loves. Once she approves the match, he tears up his fake enlistment record. The play embodies popular disdain for the military. It ends happily—not with the young man patriotically taking up arms, but by embracing family life.[29]

Reimagining the Citizen-Soldier

Laments about the milice, mockery of recruitment agents, and complaints about the selfishness of young men who enlisted against their parents' wishes persisted until the eve of the Revolution. But they were countered by an emerging emphasis on patriotism and familial support for military service. When the original sketch of *The Father's Curse* was shown at the salon of 1765, it drew considerable approval. Among others, the philosopher Denis Diderot was moved by what he saw as the consequences of the unnatural act of an elder son leaving his family to follow a recruiting sergeant.[30] But when the finished painting was exhibited in 1779, Diderot may have reversed his attitude, declaring himself revolted by Greuze's choice to portray a father cursing a son who had chosen to become a soldier.[31] Certainly, an anonymous contemporary

26. Vadé, *Les racoleurs*. See also Mainz, *Days of Glory?*

27. Mainz, *Days of Glory?*, 63–64, 49–54.

28. Forrest, *The Soldiers*, 33–34.

29. Guillemain, *L'enrôlement supposé*.

30. Seznec and Adhémar, eds., *Diderot: Salons*, 2:156–60.

31. Seznec and Adhémar, eds., *Diderot: Salons*, 4:333. The original text is somewhat ambiguous. Hopkin sees it as a reversal of Diderot's earlier judgment. Hopkin, *Soldier and*

FIGURE 1.2. Jean-Jacques Avril (engraver), after a painting by P. A. Wille, *A French Nobleman Handing His Son a Sword as the Latter Prepares to Go and Fight for the Americans in the American War of Independence,* 1788. Wellcome Collection.

critic argued that "sensitive and decent souls" should be "revolted by the sight of a father cursing his son because he has become a soldier."[32] Others voiced similar disapproval. One critic claimed that focusing on a recruiting officer was an artistic misjudgment; a father should not be angry to see his son prefer the glorious perils of war to the labors of agriculture.[33]

A painting six years later conveyed a message very different from Greuze's: Pierre Alexandre Wille's 1785 *French Patriotism or the Departure,* subsequently rendered as a 1788 engraving by Jean-Jacques Avril. In this image, a father gives a sword to his son, who is about to volunteer in the American War of Independence, and the young man swears a patriotic oath before the king's bust. The father's clear approval of his son's actions contrasts sharply with Greuze's vision of paternal malediction.[34]

The difference was partly due to social class. Wille portrayed military service as an honorable enterprise for the elite, while for the peasants of Greuze's painting, a son's enlistment was far more likely to threaten a family's survival than bring glory. Wille's decision to paint *French Patriotism* may have been prompted by the success of his 1781 *Double Reward for Merit.* The earlier painting showed a general rewarding an officer of the dragoons with both the military honor of the Cross of St. Louis and his own daughter's hand in marriage. The scene left aside his daughter's view of being treated as a reward, while promising the officer domestic happiness as a recognition for bravery.[35] But the popularity of *French Patriotism* seems to have gone beyond its focus on courageous elites. It suggests that wider images of patriotic military sacrifice—and of familial acceptance of such sacrifice—were becoming more plausible in the later eighteenth century.[36]

Devastated Women, New Spartans, and Armed Heroines

Wille's painting also expressed gendered dynamics very different from Greuze's. No longer is an entire family distraught by a young man's decision to fight; instead, the father's calm contrasts with the anguish of the boy's

---

Peasant, 202, and "Sons and Lovers," 27. Barker claims that Hopkin mistakenly quotes another critic as evidence that Diderot changed his mind. Barker, *Greuze and the Painting of Sentiment,* 262n67; this may have been the anonymous author of *Réflexions joyeuses.*

32. *Réflexions joyeuses d'un garçon de bonne humeur,* 24.

33. *Lettres d'un voyageur à Paris à son ami Sir Charles Lovers,* 33–34. See also Barker, *Greuze and the Painting of Sentiment,* 230–31.

34. Pierre Alexandre Wille, *Le patriotisme français ou le départ,* 1785 (Collection of the Musée National de la Coopération Franco-Américain, Château de Blérancourt), followed by a 1788 engraving by Jean-Jacques Avril. On contemporary reactions, see Clarke, "'Valour Knows Neither Age nor Sex,'" 67.

35. Mainz, *Days of Glory?,* 67.

36. Bell, *The Cult of the Nation,* 63.

mother and siblings. Joseph Clarke has argued that tearful women populated many French patriotic paintings after the American revolutionary wars ended in 1783, even as men accepted military duty.[37] The most famous classically inspired image of the period is likely David's 1784 *Oath of the Horatii,* which depicts three brothers swearing to sacrifice their lives for Rome, while their mothers and sisters weep together. The men are muscular and virile; the women prostrate. The painting's invocation of Roman history partially explains the difference; in the incident the painting relates, one sister is engaged to a man of the Curatii, the Horatii's enemies, while another is herself from the Curatii and married to a Horatius. For the men, war may be a chance to prove themselves. For the women, it will be devastating.[38]

Yet not all images of soldiers, or would-be soldiers, pictured agonized women. The painters Louis and his son François Watteau de Lille (following their better-known relative earlier in the century, Jean-Antoine Watteau) tended to show soldiers' relationships as bucolic dalliances rather than agonized separations or dramatic homecomings.[39] More importantly, some artists and writers offered an alternative repertoire, drawing on classical references to present women's patriotic sacrifice and active support for military service.

This set of references seems to have become more common in the 1770s and 1780s. Educated French readers were likely to have encountered Plutarch's accounts of Spartan women, or at least reworkings of his stories. Two anecdotes were particularly resonant in later eighteenth-century France. One featured a mother with five sons. When a messenger arrived with news of a battle, the woman was concerned not with the deaths of her sons, but rather with whether her country had won. The story made its way through eighteenth-century literature. Perhaps most famously, Rousseau played it up in *Emile* in 1762, claiming that such selfless women were true citizens. His contemporaries used variations to boast of modern courage and patriotism. For example, in 1774, the *Journal des dames* recounted the story of a modern Spartan woman, the Marquise de C***, who had five sons in service; the sixth remained with her, because of his youth and weak health. Her older sons were all killed while fighting gloriously. When she learned the news, she armed her youngest son, telling him to avenge his father and brothers.[40]

A second anecdote may have been even more influential, that of a Spartan mother who told her son to return victorious with his shield or dead upon it.[41] It appeared in military treatises, like Louis de Boussanelle's 1770 *The Good*

37. Clarke, "'Valour Knows Neither Age nor Sex.'"

38. Smart, *Citoyennes.*

39. Maës, *Les Watteau de Lille.*

40. The journal was reviewed in *Mercure de France,* April 1774, 1:122–28, with particular attention to this anecdote.

41. Some versions had a wife giving her husband the same message; Rawson, *The Spartan Tradition in European Thought,* 264; and Pomery, *Spartan Women,* 61.

Soldier, artwork, and literature.[42] In 1771, Lagrenée the Elder seems to have painted the first eighteenth-century version of the theme, showing a mother giving a shield to her son dressed in Roman armor. The painting was captioned with the Spartan motto. Critics praised the artist for having chosen the subject, although Diderot complained that if one removed the shield from the painting, it would appear an ordinary sentimental scene.[43] Others similarly championed the selflessness of women who armed their sons. In his 1782 translation of Plutarch's works, the abbé Ricard commented that the image of "these generous women who put shields in their children's hands at the moment of their departure for the army seems to me to be a deeply touching image. What better way to awaken the spirit of these brave Spartans and inflame their courage than to receive arms in a moment of enthusiasm and be inspired by the voice of tenderness."[44]

There were far fewer representations of women who took up arms themselves, rather than arming men. Joan of Arc featured most, though she often appeared as a satirical instrument for criticizing the church rather than as an unambiguous heroine.[45] But starting in the late 1770s, writers and artists also became interested by Jeanne Laisné, or Jeanne Hachette, the fifteenth-century woman who defended the besieged city of Beauvais. While fighting against a siege was one of the most acceptable arenas for women to take up arms, Hachette's story inspired writers and artists to celebrate her courage more generally. Jean-Antoine Roucher featured Hachette in a 1779–80 epic poem, rewriting historical chronicles to portray her at the head of a band of women inspired to fight after their husbands' cowardly flight from the city.[46] Jean-Jacques-François Le Barbier, who would paint a tribute to the courage of the women of Sparta, was inspired by Roucher's vision of courageous women warriors, and painted Hachette leading the charge; the painting was displayed at the salon of 1781 to mixed reviews, but was installed with fanfare in the town hall of Beauvais in 1788.[47] The Marquis de Sade composed a five-act tragedy to

42. Boussanelle, *Le bon militaire*.

43. Louis-François Lagrenée, *La Lacédémonienne*, 1771 (Private collection, Stourhead, Wiltshire). The original French title was based on the quotation "Rapporte ce bouclier ou que ce bouclier te rapporte." *Mercure de France*, October 1771, 1:186; *L'avant-coureur: Feuille hebdomadaire* (Paris: Lacombe, 1771), 579; *Journal encyclopédique* (1771), 7:254. See Krul, "Painting Plutarch," 178.

44. *Oeuvres morales de Plutarque*, 3:202–3.

45. Heimann, *Joan of Arc*.

46. Nochlin, *Representing Women*, 38–42.

47. Le Barbier, *Jeanne Hachette at the Siege of Beauvais*, 1784. The original painting was destroyed in 1940, but reproductions survive. For reactions when it was exhibited in 1781, see Seznec and Adhémar, eds., *Diderot: Salons*, 4:336–37. Scholars have drawn different conclusions about its display. Nochlin argues that it was well received even if some criticized the design, but Clarke has claimed that hostile reception deterred artists from

Hachette in 1783, which he would try in vain to have performed.[48] A 1784 play, signed by Mlle. M. F. A. G***. Cad, had more immediate success. It celebrated both Hachette's courage and that of her eleven-year-old son.[49]

Writers even occasionally praised women warriors as a group. In the 1753 protofeminist tract *Defense of the Fair Sex,* Philippe Caffiaux contended that women were as capable of waging war as men. He countered myriad objections, arguing, for example, that physical differences were less important than they might seem, as the heart was the most important organ for fighting, and women were as courageous as men. Moreover, differences in strength were partly attributable to training and conditioning. Caffiaux provided a long list of historical women warriors.[50] Similarly, Louis-Félix de Kéralio, a prominent soldier and Enlightenment writer, paid tribute to the Amazons in his 1784 *Military Art.* Kéralio presented both mythical figures and women who had taken up arms in different periods. He claimed that in all countries and times, some women had equaled men in courage and the French should imitate their examples.[51]

Such literary and artistic anecdotes were still limited; there were far fewer accounts of women's heroism than that of men. Even accounts of Spartan wives or mothers could be controversial. While some commentators found inspiration in classical anecdotes, others regarded tales of Spartan women with unease or dismissed their relevance for enlightened France.[52]

Debating Military Marriage

Even as reformers, artists, and writers began to rethink what it meant for young men to leave their families to take up arms, they increasingly debated whether soldiers should be allowed to marry. In 1778, the baron de Bourgoing published a novel, *Correspondence of a Young Soldier, or the Memoirs of the Marquis de Luzigni and Hortense of Saint-Just.* Like many novels of the time, it was composed as a series of letters. In one exchange, the marquise de Luzigni sought advice about her son's marital prospects from Monsieur de Lansal, the captain of a regiment and an old family friend. Specifically, she mused about

---

choosing similar topics. Nochlin, *Representing Women,* 239; Clarke, "Valour Knows Neither Age nor Sex,'" 66.

48. The script is reproduced in *Oeuvres completes de Marquis de Sade* (Paris: Pauvert, 1991), vol. 13.

49. Mayeur de St. Paul, *Jeanne Hachette ou le siège de Beauvais.* The play is signed Mlle. M. F. A. G***. Cad, but the Bibliothèque nationale attributes it to Mayeur de St. Paul. It was performed at the Théâtre des Grands Danseurs du Roi in July 1784.

50. Caffiaux, *Défenses du beau sexe,* 1:175–242.

51. Kéralio, "Amazones: Femmes guerriers," in *Encyclopédie méthodique: Art militaire,* 1:71–79.

52. On competing visions of Sparta, see Krul, "Painting Plutarch."

whether a young soldier should wed. She reported that people had advised her against such alliances:

> I have heard everyone say that military men should only marry very late in life or renounce their service. . . . A colonel told me yesterday that if an officer marries, he sees the man as lost for the military; the colonel counts much less on the bravery of a father of a family than on that of an isolated being, whose death does not affect anyone. What do you think, Monsieur?[53]

Monsieur de Lansal responded that it was a common, but false, prejudice to think that marriage stifled the honest ambition of a gentleman and sapped his courage. On the contrary, a family inspired a man to greater deeds. He spoke from experience: "The perspective of sharing my glory with my adored wife and the tender fruits of our love; is that not a new incentive for glory and courage?" De Lansal considered the possibility that a military man could be prevented from risking death by thinking of his weeping wife and small children dependent on his income. He concluded that this could be a momentary distraction, but a brave man would be spurred to action by the legacy of honor he would leave behind, and the knowledge that a benevolent monarchy would adopt his children and see to their subsistence and their education. If he survived, he would be able to inspire his children with tales of his own derring-do.[54]

The novel seems to have been the baron de Bourgoing's only excursion into fiction. It is typical of many sentimental novels of the time and reflected the aristocratic milieu in which he wrote. Yet it entered a more general debate in the 1770s and 1780s about whether marriage was good for military men. If Bourgoing's characters were nobles and officers, contemporary debate was most intense over the legal bachelorhood of the rank and file. The possibility of changing these laws engaged not only those in the military, but also lawyers, doctors, priests, and self-styled *philosophes*. Writers combined practical concerns about soldiers' ability to fight or provide for their families with moral judgments. They did not simply assess military efficiency or individual spurs to bravery, but also debated the appropriated relationship between the army and the nation, combatants and civilians, and men and women.

Reformers were deeply divided about whether a family would make a soldier more willing to fight bravely. For many, it seemed obvious that marriage would make soldiers less courageous. The anonymous author of the 1781 *Reflections on the Corps of the Maréchaussée* claimed that married soldiers would fear death more than their bachelor compatriots and would be torn between the responsibilities of husband and father and those of their

53. Bourgoing, *Correspondance d'un jeune militaire*, 2:168.
54. Bourgoing, *Correspondance d'un jeune militaire*, 2:171.

profession.[55] Others made similar arguments, like de Laissac, the author of the 1783 *Of the Military Spirit,* who contended that the worst soldiers would be married men. Nature justified their distraction: what man would want to leave his family indigent? Could the government expect zeal from a man worried that his loved ones would starve without him?[56]

Yet the reverse—that, as Monsieur de Lansal proposed, married men would fight more courageously than their bachelor counterparts—seemed equally plausible and appeared in both fiction and concrete proposals for reform. In an argument picked up by French newspaper commentators, the German physician Johann Peter Frank claimed in 1779 that married soldiers were braver and more humane. Similarly, in 1782, the novelist Louis-Sébastien Mercier contended that married soldiers would be the most courageous and the most attached to the patrie.[57]

These arguments were not simply speculations about the mental state of soldiers. They rested on assumptions about what would happen to women without men, and where military families would live. A few claimed that a woman could survive in the advent of her husband's absence or death. The abbé Auguste Hespelle took the position in 1775 that soldiers' wives should be hardworking and able to scrape by. In any case, their plight would be better than that of the prostitutes who served the camps.[58] The more common view was expressed by Kéralio, who in his *Military Art* claimed that even the most industrious woman married to a poor soldier would have difficulty earning enough to feed and clothe herself and her children.

There were solutions to the question of dependents: married soldiers might be paid more than their bachelor counterparts, or the state might provide for their wives and children. The latter possibility corresponded to Monsieur de Lansal's assertion that a benevolent monarchy would provide for officers' children. Several reformers put forth versions of this solution. A 1768 tract on population had presented one such possibility. Relatively little is known about the author, de Cerfvol; his name may have been a pseudonym, and he is more famous, or infamous, for championing divorce than soldiers' nuptials. He proposed that the state should provide two sous a day to support the wife of a soldier and one sou for each of their children; he suggested that the government take property from religious communities to house soldiers and their families.[59] The abbé Hespelle insisted that women should work hard to contribute

55. *Réflexions sur le corps de la maréchaussée,* 30–37.

56. Laissac, *De l'esprit militaire,* 218–25. Editions appeared in 1783, 1785, 1788, 1789, and, under the title *Le parfait guerrier,* in 1792.

57. Review in *L'esprit des journaux françois et étrangers,* Year 9, vol. 3 (March 1780), 423; Mercier, *Tableau de Paris,* 4:43, article on "Filles nubiles."

58. Hespelle, *La seule véritable religion,* 1:451.

59. Cerfvol, *Mémoire sur la population,* 106–7. On theories about Cerfvol's identity, see Blum, *Strength in Numbers,* 69–73.

to their families, but recommended that soldiers' sons should be provided for as children of the state. Raised ethically, they would not be effeminate beings, but would instead become brave and virtuous men. In the widely read 1772 *General Essay on Tactics,* Jacques Guibert offered an outline for another book. Chapter 8 was to address the policy of restrictions on marriage that existed in almost all European militaries, but especially in France, which Guibert labeled a "fatal wound" to population growth. He proposed that the government should encourage soldiers' marriages and raise their sons, thus forming a kind of military nation within the nation.[60]

The French monarchy made tentative steps toward such a solution. It instituted a system of *enfants de troupe.* A few soldiers were allowed to marry vivandières, the women who provided foodstuffs for the troops and traveled with them. A 1766 measure provided army pay and rations for boys born from these marriages; the boys followed the armies in the camps and were trained in practical skills, often as musicians and craftsmen. They could choose at age sixteen if they wanted to remain in the military, though they were generally expected to do so. But this system was limited. There were only a few enfants in each troop. The 1766 decree limited support to one per company; a 1788 measure allowed two boys, with a limit of sixteen per regiment.[61] If many soldiers were to marry, the practical challenges of providing for their children would be far greater.

De Laissac's response to proposals that the state support soldiers' children offers us further insights as to why contemporaries might have dismissed such plans. He challenged them partly on pragmatic grounds: could a government as indebted as that of France in the 1780s afford such an enormous expense? But he also had moral reservations. The government would only have an incentive to support soldiers' offspring if they became soldiers themselves—and such obligations would be a kind of slavery. And what interest would the state have in supporting daughters?

Even if the economic survival of soldiers' families was not at stake, most commentators assumed wives and children would be with the troops, and that their presence in the camps would cause problems. There were logical reasons behind the assumptions that soldiers' families would accompany the troops; there had been women associated with armies throughout the early modern period, although their numbers had declined significantly since the mid-seventeenth century. Some formed "May marriages" for a campaign season; prostitutes made more short-term appearances. Laundresses and vivandières accompanied the troops.[62] But contemporaries argued that the numbers of women would

60. Guibert, *Essai général de tactique,* 1:iii.

61. The system of enfants de troupe would continue through the early nineteenth century. Cardoza, "'These Unfortunate Children'" and "Stepchildren of the State."

62. Cardoza, *Intrepid Women.*

skyrocket if soldiers could marry without needing to seek special permission. Kéralio, for example, contended that if soldiers wed, their wives would accompany them into the army, so that instead of the fifteen or twenty women who followed a corps, there might be two or three hundred. Their presence led to economic and social problems, and threatened military virility.

Defenders of military bachelorhood worried that women would distract and weaken soldiers. Jean-Baptiste Robinet, a French naturalist involved with the *Encyclopédie*, acknowledged in 1782 that there were historical examples of married men who had served bravely. But these were exceptions. In general, he asked: "What purpose do women serve in armies, if not to embarrass and enervate soldiers? . . . A bachelor soldier has married war. A married soldier has two wives. All military men think unanimously that a married soldier is not the equal of a bachelor soldier."[63]

Similarly, de Laissac argued that even if military men had no children, marriage would destroy them. Living outside the eyes of his superiors, a soldier's discipline would flag, as would his zeal. His morals would soften; "in the intimate and permanent society of marriage, a woman always communicates an aspect of weakness to a man. This soldier, living almost as a bourgeois, would take on the spirit and the character of a bourgeois."[64] The word "bourgeois" here had fewer associations with class identity than with civilian domesticity. In de Laissac's view, a married soldier would be a citizen, like other citizens, not separated from them by a special position and a distinctive martial masculinity.

This distinction between soldiers and civilians was not just a question of individual discipline or character. Military marriage affected the efficiency and morality of soldiers and their wives—and the good of society. The consensus was that marriage made both men and women into better citizens and strengthened the populace.[65] But the story could well be different for soldiers.

The doctor Jean Colombier thus maintained in 1775 that marriage made citizens more virtuous, healthier, and more useful to the state, but it was counter to military discipline. A married soldier would be forced to share his modest pay with his wife and family; all would suffer. Conversely, if his wife made money, he would live better than his comrades, and cease to share their esprit de corps. Colombier briefly considered whether married soldiers could become vivandiers, providing food for the army. Steeped in the disdain for rank-and-file soldiers that was widespread in the period, he argued that this would make it too easy for them to become drunk and dissolute.[66] Soldiers' marriages would thus undermine military efficiency, while contributing to wider social degeneration.

63. Robinet, *Dictionnaire universel*, 684.
64. Laissac, *De l'esprit militaire*, 221.
65. Blum, *Strength in Numbers*.
66. Colombier, *Préceptes sur la santé*, 130.

Others contended that soldiers' marriages would benefit both soldiers and civilian society. Most significantly, marriages would reduce prostitution.[67] Doctors were concerned about the effects of venereal disease on soldiers, and fear of spreading disease among the troops had provoked a series of ineffectual laws against prostitution over the course of the eighteenth century.[68] Reformers were also concerned about the moral aspects of prostitution. When the lawyer Landreau de Maine-au-Picq argued in 1787 for an end to the legal celibacy of priests and military men, he contended that legalizing marriage would limit sexual depravity. If soldiers were married and enlisted for only a limited time, there would be many fewer "girls who sacrifice uselessly to love, in a commerce as shameful as it is infamous."[69] Society would gain from making soldiers more virtuous and by limiting the circumstances where women turned to prostitution.

Even if military men did not frequent prostitutes, their reputation for sexual conquest made them suspect. In 1781, one anonymous author argued that "Many regard as a great evil . . . the immense number of bachelor soldiers who compose our armies. They create disorder and scandal everywhere."[70] The future revolutionary Jérôme Pétion claimed in 1785 that soldiers were the most depraved of all bachelors. They made a science of seduction; their uniforms, arrogant tone, risqué manners, and air of self-importance helped them succeed with the fair sex. Once married, they would be more circumspect, more attached to their property (meaning their wives), and less inclined to seduce others.[71] Military marriage would benefit society as a whole by making soldiers more virtuous and less likely to indulge in shameful sexual behavior.

The baron de Bourgoing's novel reinforced such claims, arguing that even if the wives of officers stayed home, marriages could make both men and women into more respectable members of society—if they took their vows seriously. Monsieur de Lansal addressed the possibility that a military man's prolonged absence would undermine a couple's love for one another and increase the dangers of seduction. He contended that absence brought piquancy to a relationship; even the best-matched couple could become bored if they spent too much time together. It was true that soldiers were known for sexual misconduct, but debauchery and licentiousness were not inevitable. A married officer could give a shining example of fidelity. Confident in his loyalty, his wife would feel no need to commit adultery to avenge herself for what she imagined her husband to be doing.

67. This was not a new argument in the late eighteenth century but became increasingly common. Corvisier, *L'armée française*, 961.

68. In 1713, 1724, 1734, 1776, and 1777. Lynn, *Women, Armies, and Warfare*, 72.

69. Landreau de Maine-au-Picq, *Digression sur le célibat*, 3:4–5.

70. *De la nécessité et des moyens de placer utilement des aumôniers militaires dans chaque régiment*, Mem 1781, no. 93, n.d., cited in Corvisier, *L'armée française*, 762n44.

71. Pétion, *Essai sur le mariage*, 136.

Proponents of military marriage offered another argument for the social good of wedlock: married soldiers would be more devoted to their patrie. In 1771, Voltaire argued that the state should "make . . . soldiers into married men; they will not desert. Tied to their families, they will also be tied to their patrie. A bachelor soldier is often only a vagabond, who would be equally ready to serve the King of Naples and the King of Morocco."[72] Yet while the French court was willing to accept marriages of foreign soldiers in its troops, it was more resistant to marriages of French soldiers. The historian Corvisier has noted that starting in 1701, children of soldiers in certain foreign corps serving France received limited financial support. A December 1762 law allotted the wives of Irish and Italian soldiers a daily ration of bread while their husbands were on campaign; they were to remain in the quarters of the regimental assembly. This was subsequently extended to the wives of soldiers in all foreign corps.[73] Such policies promised to make foreign soldiers stay in France's service. But the French crown remained unconvinced that marriage would make native French soldiers into more loyal servants of their own country.

Eighteenth-century popular theater also juxtaposed military service against love and familial responsibility. While plays about desertion were rare before the 1760s, at least twelve appeared in France in the decades preceding the Revolution.[74] One series featured a young man who deserted because he feared that his girlfriend was about to marry. The playwright Michel Sedaine popularized a theatrical version of the story in 1769; Louis-Sébastien Mercier adapted the plot in 1770; and Maximilien Gardel created a ballet, which Louis XVI and Marie Antoinette watched in 1786.[75] The story became an international phenomenon, with versions in English and German.[76]

The title character in all these performances is a young soldier. In Sedaine's play, he is named Alexis and in love with Louise. Louise's father, led by his patron the duchess, persuades the young woman to fake a wedding with Alexis's rival, her cousin Bertrand. (The motives and logistics of this charade vary depending on the work.) Alexis is so dismayed at hearing of Louise's impending nuptials that he decides to desert. In the second act, he has been imprisoned and is awaiting execution. Louise begs a pardon from the king. In the final scenes, Alexis is brought to the firing ground; Louise arrives and promptly

72. Voltaire, *Questions sur l'encyclopédie* (London: Rey, 1771–72), 8:32.

73. Corvisier, *L'armée française*, 757–72.

74. Connors, "Total Theatre for Total War."

75. Sedaine, *Le déserteur;* Mercier, *Le déserteur;* and Gardel, *Le déserteur, ballet d'action*. On Sedaine's popularity, see Feilla, *The Sentimental Theater*.

76. There were at least four translations into English. Most notably, Charles Dibdin translated Sedaine's version and made it a musical farce in 1773; D'Auberval produced a 1784 version in London. In 1779, Alessandro Zuchelli, an Italian dancer at King's Opera House, adapted it as a ballet, *Il disertore*. See Taylor, *The French Revolution and the London Stage*, 24–38.

passes out. Alexis makes his farewells as she lies in his arms. When she awakens to reveal the pardon, all ends with rejoicing.

Not all versions ended so cheerfully. Mercier's 1770 play used the story to denounce capital punishment. While Sedaine's deserter is dramatically pardoned, Mercier's is executed. Worse, the deserter's father has searched for his lost son all his life, only to be required to sentence the young man to death. The play contributed to changing policy, as the government relaxed the severity of punishment for desertion in 1775.[77] Indeed, almost all versions of the plot focused on royal clemency and state power. Such works did not directly engage debates over whether ending military bachelorhood would be good for the army or society. Instead, they questioned the government's insistence on compelling men to remain in the troops, rather than releasing them to happy domesticity.

Marriage as Obligation and Reward

Probably the strongest argument about the effects of soldiers' marriages on the nation had more to do with population than with military efficacy, the effects of wedlock on individuals, or the devotion of the troops. There was a widespread belief that France was losing subjects. This was not technically true (France was simply not gaining population as rapidly as Great Britain and the German states), but officials thought that maintaining national strength required raising the birthrate.[78] Soldiers' marriages promised one means of increasing population.

Here comparisons to other national practices were particularly apropos.[79] Contemporary commentators knew that Prussia allowed soldiers to marry. Some argued that this proved France's superiority. The author of *Reflections on the Corps of the Maréchaussée* claimed that France had a more robust population than Prussia and did not need to resort to questionable measures. Others saw Prussian practices as useful models. Mirabeau, writing in 1788 on the Prussian monarchy under Frederick the Great, contended that the practice of conscription meant that all men in the kingdom could be required to serve. The idea that all men were thus born soldiers could appear shocking, but Mirabeau claimed it did not need to be. Since soldiers in Prussia could easily obtain permission to marry, there were many more married men than in the French army. They were more "orderly, happier, and more attached to service" than their bachelor counterparts. It was true that soldiers had fewer children than those in other parts of society. Mirabeau claimed that this was because their wives could not earn enough to be comfortable, especially when

77. Pichichero, *The Military Enlightenment*, 140–45.

78. Blum, *Strength in Numbers*.

79. On the comparative prevalence of military marriage in Britain despite official restrictions, see Hurl-Eamon, *Marriage and the British Army*.

they had young children, so the level of child mortality was high. But if the state were to invest in those children, the results could be different.[80]

Such populationist concerns shaped the fates of both soldiers and veterans. Contemporaries complained about the negative effects of priestly celibacy on the population, but unlike priests, soldiers could eventually marry, even if they were required to remain single while they served. Some reformers thus depicted the marriage of veterans as a reward for military service and a means to increase population. Servan argued that marriage was useful since wives could do housework around the camps, but that it should also be a recompense and recognition of a man's maturity. No soldier should be able to wed unless he distinguished himself by his morals, bravery, intelligence, and character, and had either served for a sufficient time or reached thirty. In this version, it was not marriage that created virtuous citizens, but rather marriage that rewarded military virtue.[81]

There was a darker side to the idea of marriage for veterans: the possibility that wedlock would be an obligation, rather than a reward; a means of making ex-soldiers contribute to the state by forcing them to marry after they had ceased to fight. Here an article by Jean-François-Henri Collot, then minister of war, is particularly revealing. In a 1765 article in the *Encyclopédie,* Collot contended that marriage should be an obligation for wounded veterans, at least those who were not completely incapacitated.[82] In making this proposal, he anticipated several objections. One was that mutilated men would not be good economic partners. He argued that wounded soldiers received a pension equal to the income of most inhabitants of the countryside; they were the equivalent of lumberjacks, winegrowers, and weavers. No girl would refuse a soldier, however crippled, as she would see that such a husband would not be a burden to her. When a soldier's pension was combined with a woman's own work and her savings, a couple could live comfortably.

Collot acknowledged that most veterans were older, and that young women might hesitate before marrying them. He explained how their hesitations could be overcome. Women might experience a "natural antipathy for physical imperfections." This could be solved by ensuring that soldiers be sent back to their hometowns, where they would be known. Their physical shortcomings would not put off prospective mates familiar with their characters. Men over forty-five could still be vigorous and produce good offspring. He admitted that such men might not want to marry, or, accustomed to a licentious life, might abandon their wives and children. He thus proposed both moral and practical arguments to keep them home: an appeal to men's civism and a pension tied to the number of children they produced, so that veterans would be unlikely to

80. Mirabeau, *De la monarchie prussienne,* 3:60–61.

81. Servan, *Le soldat citoyen,* 489.

82. Collot, "Invalides."

abandon honor and income to become vagabonds. In putting forth these proposals, Collot treated women as economically driven baby machines; while his view was perhaps extreme for the period, it was by no means unique.[83] His goal was to foster French population in general and the population of soldiers in particular. To this end, he proposed that sons born of veterans' marriages be potential soldiers and that the state provide a stipend until their sixteenth birthday.

Collot's optimistic belief that women would be eager, or at least willing, to marry wounded veterans had echoes in eighteenth-century literature. Allan Pasco has argued that prerevolutionary theater and novels regularly presented tests of love, in which men faked injuries to see if their lovers or fiancées would remain faithful. For example, in Jean François Marmontel's 1756 story "Scruples," the protagonist Lindor is an impetuous young warrior. He becomes convinced that he should test his sweetheart Bélise's fidelity, and writes to her, claiming that he has lost an eye. The story ends badly. She decides she cannot love a one-eyed man; Lindor is broken-hearted and breaks with her. Pasco argues that by the 1780s, such fictional love tests had become increasingly central to literary narratives.[84] While these narratives were not always focused on the military, they helped shape how much contemporaries imagined that wounded soldiers would be met with romance and reintegrated into domestic society. The frequency of such accounts—especially the failure of love tests—cast doubt on Collot's proposition that young women would be eager to marry veterans regardless of their physical state.

In a 1784 article on invalid soldiers in the *Encyclopédie*, Kéralio critiqued Collot's position directly. He noted that in order to accommodate potential objections, Collot ultimately reduced the number of wounded veterans who would be obliged to marry. "But he does not tell us who will make the choice of those who are forced to marry, nor what will lead young girls to prefer an old soldier, worn down by military work and too often by wine and debauchery, to a young and agile shepherd or a farmworker full of health and vigor." A king who ordered such alliances would be as barbaric as a tyrant who united a living being to a dead one.[85] We see here parallels to de Laissac's concern that soldiers' children should not be supported by the state only on the condition that they follow their fathers in fighting for France.

Kéralio also responded to Collot's discussion of whether veterans might prefer to remain single, and whether it would be wrong to go against their desires. Collot argued that it was not uncharitable to multiply the number of beings made in the model of the divine. Kéralio called this mere wordplay. Finally, Kéralio noted that when Collot sought to prove that young women

83. Dock, *Women in the Encyclopédie*, 132.

84. Pasco, *Revolutionary Love*, 90–92.

85. Kéralio, "Invalides," in *Encyclopédie méthodique: Art militaire*, 3:120.

would prefer veterans to young farmworkers, he gave plausible reasons. But since peasant women would never read these reasons, it seemed unlikely they would be convinced.

Collot's proposals to entice or force veterans to marry were not instituted during the Old Regime. Indeed, they appear to have been more a thought experiment than a serious plan. Nor was the proposed legalization of soldiers' marriage realized. On the eve of the Revolution, a 1788 measure reiterated the ban on both soldiers' and officers' nuptials without the formal permission of their superiors, and maintained an onerous process for obtaining that permission.[86] The king announced his intention to "encourage soldiers' marriages subsequently by helping to provide for their children's subsistence," but this seems to have been more a continuation of earlier policies in providing for enfants de troupe in some regiments than a desire to encourage new liaisons.[87]

An unpublished 1789 tract sent to the Estates General, however, does suggest changing attitudes.[88] Villeneuve, a former artillery officer, championed soldiers' nuptials as a way to increase the number of soldiers without harming agriculture. Like some of his predecessors, Villeneuve claimed that military celibacy led to desertion, which he labeled as the "shameful vice that dishonored soldiers and made them unworthy of serving their king." Marriage would keep soldiers in the troops. But he also argued that soldiers were particularly deserving of the rewards and pleasures of marriage. Marriage, by its nature, had a direct influence on men's well-being, providing a man with a tender friend whose interests were bound to his. And yet the government refused these benefits to soldiers. Villeneuve argued even further, "soldiers more than any others are capable of being good fathers."[89] In this construction, military service was not incompatible with domesticity; on the contrary, it made men into better husbands and fathers.

Villeneuve contended that marriage was both an appropriate reward for soldiers and in the government's interest. He was less interested in population than in courage. Marriage made soldiers braver. In contrast, bachelorhood degraded them; it was not a virtue, but a sign of cowardice, weakness, and libertinage. Villeneuve argued that French soldiers were inherently brave, but they would find it hard to act with courage when they perceived military service as a chain. Conversely, the braver a man was, the more it was in the interest of the

86. Chauvin-Madeira, "Mœurs et droit des militaires."

87. *Règlement provisoire concernant le service intérieur.* See also Guinier, *L'honneur du soldat*, 311–12.

88. SHD 1 M 1718, Villeneuve, *Mémoire sur les moyens de donner des défenseurs à la patrie sans diminuer le nombre des cultivateurs et d'empêcher la désertion ce vice honteux qui déshonore le soldat en le rendant indigne de servir son roi.* My thanks to Julia Osman for sharing this document.

89. Villeneuve, *Mémoire.*

state that he reproduced; the tenderness of a spouse and the cares of a family would be new bonds that joined him to his patrie.

Eighteenth-century debates over the marital status of soldiers and veterans thus reveal both a desire to equate soldiers with other citizens and unease with doing so. On one hand, military service could appear the apex of patriotic duty and a proof of citizenship. This was the message of Villeneuve's tract, Servan's *Soldat citoyen*, and other works, like Louis de Boussanelle's 1786 *To Soldiers*, which began, "The soldier is a citizen."[90]

On the other hand, debates suggest an embedded wariness toward identifying soldiers with citizens, if citizenship meant domesticity and familial duty. The author of the *Reflections on the Corps of the Maréchaussée* argued that the very idea of making a soldier into a citizen was flawed. "Citizen" and "soldier" were "two contradictory words." Mixing them together would create a monster, neither soldier nor citizen. The profession of arms went against nature; it required that soldiers not be too soft. The urbanity and amiability of a citizen was contrary to the demands of war.[91]

Looking at military marriage thus reveals fundamentally different interpretations of how the army and the nation should relate in the years that preceded the French Revolution. Proponents and critics articulated competing visions of both citizenship and the appropriate relationships between military men and their families, or potential families. While some identified soldiers with citizens—including valorizing their roles as husbands and fathers—others argued for maintaining strict divisions between military men and civilians imbricated in domestic life.

Debates over military bachelorhood show us that the development of a new kind of "virility" or "martial masculinity" both coexisted and conflicted with a model of masculinity focused on domestic virtue. Such debates highlighted contesting views about men's liberty to marry or remain single, the effects of wedlock on both men and women, and the ability and right of the state to intervene in familial relations. They also reveal tensions between ideas of marriage as individual choice, a practical contract, and a social duty. Depending on one's vision, marriage could make—or destroy—the soldier-citizen.

Conclusion

Late eighteenth-century men and women could, and did, depict soldiers in contradictory ways, as drunken seducers or good family men, as debauched egoists or devoted husbands, victims of heartless recruiters and despotic authorities or selfless servants of the state. In the later eighteenth century, perceptions began to shift toward seeing the departure of soldier-sons less as

90. Boussanelle, *Aux soldats*.
91. *Réflexions sur le corps de la maréchaussée*, 36.

a devastation for families and more as a patriotic endeavor that men, and possibly women, should support. But if artists began to celebrate citizen-soldiers, rural families remained hostile to the milice.

In considering relationships between domestic duty, military service, and citizenship, reformers touched on practical and ideological issues they did not fully resolve. They debated whether soldiers could be allowed to marry, whether marriage could allow men to avoid military service, whether veterans could be made to wed (for their own good or that of the French population as a whole), and whether women would find injured men desirable mates. They also mused on the extent to which authorities should intervene in personal relations and weighed the comparative civic worth of civilians and combatants.

The stakes of these debates remained limited in the eighteenth century, in part because there were relatively few men in the ranks. When the French Revolution began—bringing with it the possibility that all citizens were, or should be, soldiers, and all soldiers citizens—such questions would suddenly become far more pressing.

CHAPTER TWO

"To Arms, Citizens!"

IN DECEMBER 1789, a deputy to the new French National Assembly sought to persuade his fellow legislators that France should institute mandatory military service. Dubois-Crancé contended that France needed a "truly national conscription . . . every man should be ready to march. . . . Every citizen must be a soldier and every soldier a citizen."[1] Other deputies attacked him for his lack of military experience, denouncing conscription as slavery.[2] But they did not object to seeing citizenship and military service as intertwined. Instead, they insisted that an army based on volunteers would make men both better soldiers and better citizens.

This chapter explores what happened when the possibility that Dubois-Crancé and other legislators discussed in theory—whether all French citizens should be soldiers—became an urgent question to resolve in practice. The increasing radicalization of the Revolution, combined with the start of foreign war in the spring of 1792 and civil war in 1793, made it imperative to determine who could take up arms and who should be obliged to do so. It also meant repeatedly reassessing relationships between citizenship and arms-bearing for men and women.

Since many works address these tumultuous years in depth, I do not offer here a detailed narrative of events and power struggles. Nor do I examine the myriad other ways that people acted as citizens or debated what rights and obligations should be associated with that status. Instead, I look specifically at what it meant for people to take up arms—or put them down—and how revolutionaries sought to reconcile familial roles with civic duties. Doing so allows us to discover experiments and struggles that are obscured if we concentrate only on legal and political changes. Focusing on mobilization also

1. Cadiot, *Collection des principaux discours*, 2:22.

2. *Archives parlementaires* (hereafter *AP*), 10:579–88, 615–20. See also Blaufarb, *The French Army*.

reveals challenges that would resonate long after the most radical stages of the Revolution.

We begin by exploring how citizenship and military service became increasingly entangled over the course of the Revolution, and how these developments related to family and gender roles. Associations between soldiering and citizenship fostered new forms of martial masculinity, distinguishing between a world of citizen-soldiers and a domestic realm of women and cowardly civilian men. At the same time, such associations inspired a few women to take up arms, like the young Reine Chappuy, who declared that she "sacrificed the alarms common to my sex to the burning desire to avenge my patrie, combat tyrants, and share the glory of striking them down."[3] Revolutionaries also found new ways to appeal to families to support war. Looking at these appeals helps explain how the French Republic instituted mass mobilization amid upheaval. In theory, legislators also resolved prerevolutionary concerns about whether male citizens could be both good soldiers and good husbands, by promising that the state would provide for their dependents. In practice, such promises would prove difficult or impossible to fulfill.

In a second section, we look more closely at how revolutionaries reconciled ideals of martial masculinity with legal and ideological changes to family. A March 1793 law overturned Old Regime measures and allowed serving soldiers to wed. But contemporaries remained divided about whether men should combine roles as husbands and soldiers or if wedlock should serve instead as a reward for service. The latter required addressing the desirability of injured veterans as spouses—and women's roles in choosing partners. Marriage could also appear not as a reward for military service, but as a means to escape it.

We then turn from mobilization to a form of demobilization: that of women soldiers.[4] Records have survived for over eighty women in an army that fluctuated between 300,000 and 700,000; there were likely more.[5] On April 30, 1793, the government banned "useless" women from the troops, including women soldiers, combatants' wives, camp followers, and all but a few laundresses and vivandières. We revisit the motives behind this infamous decision. We also look at its aftermath. Some women protested their forced discharge; others continued to fight, either in disguise or with the support of their comrades and superiors. Most ultimately left service between 1793 and 1795. The National Convention simultaneously attempted to honor women veterans and return them to domestic roles. The conditions of their discharge—from financial support to disputes over whether they could wear military uniforms—reveal the

3. *Gazette nationale ou le Moniteur universel*, no. 318, 18 Thermidor Year III (August 5, 1795), 378.

4. The most substantive sources on revolutionary women soldiers are requests for pensions, and historians have noted veterans' poverty and physical distress. But scholars have rarely considered their discharge as a demobilization.

5. See the introduction for a bibliography of sources on women soldiers.

complexities of their return to civilian life, as do their continuing representations in popular culture.

In a final section, we return to men's mobilization in the context of continued warfare and explore how public displays of emotion legitimated—or threatened—recruitment and support for war. These displays were often strongly gendered, and subject to contradictory imperatives. Revolutionaries contended that citizens should express "natural" emotions. They also exhorted people to "silence nature" in the face of patriotic need, and endure absence, economic hardship, and the prospect of loved ones' death with quiet equanimity.

Connecting Citizenship and Military Service?

Dubois-Crancé's assertion that every citizen should be a soldier and every soldier a citizen was doubly problematic in 1789. Even the most enthusiastic champions of conscription realized that not all adult men were capable of fighting and that the nation needed civilian workers. Conversely, not all combatants were legally French, and revolutionary governments were wary of foreigners in the troops.[6] "Citizen" itself was an ambiguous and controversial word. Legislators initially distinguished between "active" citizens, those capable of voting or holding office, and "passive" citizens, who simply lived under French law. Since only those who were over twenty-five, and who paid the equivalent of at least three days' unskilled labor in taxes, counted as active citizens, this distinction excluded younger and poorer soldiers from political rights.

In considering how much soldiers were, or should be, "citizens" in another sense—people imbricated in both civilian and military life—some deputies connected combatants with families and communities. The liberal deputy the duke of Liancourt claimed that if soldiers domiciled in their home canton were allowed to marry, they would bind themselves to the nation by the same means that united other citizens.[7] The engineer Bureau de Pusy similarly proposed that soldiers return home regularly. Rooting them in domestic life would help their families, while protecting them from the contagion of vice that assailed them in their garrisons. Weak or timid men should declare that they would be more useful in other professions, and the army should not be obliged to employ them.[8]

The National Assembly did not immediately follow Liancourt's proposal to legalize military marriage, but it did declare that all French troops, except those in the milice (the royal reserve force) and National Guard (a new form of militia created in July 1789), would be recruited by voluntary engagement,

6. Tozzi, *Nationalizing France's Army.*

7. In Cadiot, *Collection des principaux discours,* 2:35–79.

8. In Cadiot, *Collection des principaux discours,* 2:80–105.

allowing men who saw themselves as more useful elsewhere to avoid service. In May 1790, the Assembly declared peace to the world. In March 1791, it abolished the milice.[9] If the government rejected civic obligations to take up arms, the French constitution inaugurated in 1791, unlike the contemporaneous American Bill of Rights, did not include a "right to bear arms."[10]

Yet even as the National Assembly separated military service from citizenship in some ways, it connected arms-bearing and political rights in other ways. Laws in the spring and summer of 1790 required citizens who wanted to vote to register for the National Guard and be prepared to serve—although it allowed them to do so either personally or through a substitute, often a son or brother. Conversely, service in the Guard was limited to active citizens.[11] Such associations made being in the National Guard appear both a duty and a civic right. Robespierre famously called for the Guard to be expanded in 1791, declaring that "All men have the right to be armed for their personal defense; all citizens have the right to arm themselves for the defense of the patrie."[12]

The subsequent radicalization of the Revolution, and the declaration of both foreign and civil war dramatically changed relationships between arms-bearing and citizenship. By summer 1791, fear of looming war persuaded many to volunteer—including boys, older heads of family, and a few women. On April 20, 1792, the government declared war on Austria, then Prussia. In July, it proclaimed the patrie to be in danger, and exhorted all citizens to defend the nation. In August 1792, revolutionaries overthrew King Louis XVI and declared a republic. They also eliminated property-based distinctions between active and passive citizens in defining who could vote or hold office.

The new French republic soon became embroiled in further war against England and became increasingly desperate for manpower. On February 24, 1793, a draft called up 300,000 men between the ages of eighteen and forty who were single, or widowed and childless. The government labeled these men volunteers, but they were often compelled to fight. Resistance to the draft in the Vendée region of western France triggered civil war, intensified by anger at Louis XVI's execution and the Republic's religious policies. France's second constitution—drafted in June 1793, although never implemented—responded to the growing sense of crisis by proclaiming, "all Frenchmen are soldiers."

On August 23, 1793, the National Convention issued the decree often seen as the origin of modern conscription: the *levée en masse*.[13] It put "all

9. Hippler, *Citizens, Soldiers, and National Armies*, 56; and Forrest, *Conscripts and Deserters*, 9.

10. Shusterman, "Bearing Arms and Arming Citizens."

11. Clifford, "Can the Uniform Make the Citizen?"

12. Robespierre, "Sur l'organisation des gardes nationales," in Vermorel, ed., *Oeuvres de Robespierre*, 185–94.

13. Forrest, "L'armée de l'an II" and "'La Patrie en Danger"; and Kruse, "Revolutionary France and the Meanings of the Levée en Masse," 2.

Frenchmen in permanent requisition" for armed service. It called on single men between the ages of eighteen and twenty-five to fight and sought to mobilize all of society behind the war effort. Married men were to forge arms and transport provisions, women to make tents and clothing and serve in hospitals, children to turn old linen into bandages, and the elderly to stir up the courage of warriors. Men brought into the army were still referred to as volunteers, but they often had little choice.[14] Localities were given quotas to fill and selected recruits by a lottery. Families with several sons in the age range sometimes sent them all; many who had stayed home when their siblings volunteered were now obliged to enlist.

If the levée en masse officially mobilized soldiers, popular culture reinforced the idea that everyone should be prepared to take up arms. Plays particularly promoted this message as the Revolution entered its most radical stages during the Terror of 1793–94. For example, *The First Requisition or the Oath of the French* premiered on October 30, 1793, and would be performed regularly through spring 1794. It portrayed boys, married men, and widowers rushing to France's aid. Similarly, *The Cry of the Patrie*, first performed on December 30, 1793, featured a father who wanted to volunteer even though he was past the age required to fight.[15] Such works presented military service as a patriotic choice, rather than an obligation, showcasing both young men and heads of household as warriors.

To Arms, Citizens?

Individuals enlisted for many reasons, from ideological commitment to economic need, curiosity to coercion.[16] But recruitment propaganda also sought to motivate potential soldiers by contending that men who did not leave home were effeminate cowards, linking the defense of the "mother country" of the patrie to defense of individual families, and promising that the state would step in for missing men.

One striking engraving depicts a woman spinning and an idle admirer who tries to seduce a lacemaker. The title, *You Would Do Much Better to Go to the Army*, makes it clear that the lacemaker would prefer a virile warrior.[17] It

14. Julia Osman defines citizen-soldiers as individuals who chose to take up arms, rather than those forced to do so; in that sense the de facto conscription of the levée should be seen not as the apogee of citizen-soldiers but as its end. Osman, *Citizen Soldiers and the Key to the Bastille.*

15. Neither play was published, but both were reviewed extensively in the *Journal des spectacles*: see no. 126, 15 Brumaire Year II (November 5, 1793), 999; and no. 181, 10 Nivôse Year II (December 30, 1793), 1437. See also Lecomte, *Histoire des théâtres de Paris*, 35–37.

16. Lynn, *The Bayonets of the Republic.*

17. Jean-Baptiste Turlure (artist) and Loubet (engraver), *Vous feriez bien mieux d'aller à l'armée* (Paris: Chez Delorme, between 1792 and 1797). The engraving was inspired by a now lost painting.

FIGURE 2.1. Jean-Baptiste Turlure (artist) and Loubet (engraver), *You Would Do Much Better to Go to the Army*, between 1792 and 1797. Bibliothèque Nationale de France.

reflects a contrast between martial masculinity and women's domestic labor that appeared with early calls for volunteers. On July 17, 1792, the National Assembly proclaimed that "Weak or elderly fathers of family should remain near their wives and children; all robust young men should leave, unless they prefer to take up the distaff and spindle with our women."[18] In February 1793,

18. *AP*, 47:305, 31 juillet 1792.

the newspaper *La feuille villageoise* considered a proposal that municipal governments, or in their absence, assembled citizens and citizennesses, post spindles in front of the houses of men who refused to fight.[19]

Even when women took up arms themselves, those commenting on their enlistment associated spindles with cowardice. For example, in March 1793, the *Journal de Lyon* reported that a young woman, Clémence Alibert, had donned the uniform of the National Guard when youth were being called up. Her lover had been arrested for avoiding service; she scolded him, promised that he would return to duty, and declared that she would accompany him as a volunteer. Her example inspired other young men to enlist. The municipality announced their marriage and promised her twenty sous a day as long as she fought. The *Journal de Lyon* concluded, "If there are still cowards among the French, they should take up the distaff and spindle; those are the only arms worthy of them."[20] When Marie Morell, the daughter of a municipal official, enlisted in Toulon a few months later, she echoed such declarations, proclaiming, "I leave my distaff and spindles to the man who is cowardly enough to stay at home. I will take his gun and saber to fill his place."[21]

Eighteenth-century reformers had occasionally imagined shaming shirkers by presenting them with distaffs. Writers often ascribed the practice to exotic or historic locales. For example, French newspapers in 1788 described the "degradation of cowards in Turkey," including attaching a distaff to the door of a young man's home to show that he was only worthy of acting as a woman.[22] In the context of the Revolution, associations between cowards and distaffs and spindles became more immediate and important. They simultaneously implied that shirkers were insufficiently virile, and identified domestic labor only with women.

Others accused cowards of hiding behind women, indulging in sexual pleasure rather than defending the patrie. The complaint of a sergeant major in 1793 is typical, as he derided men who, "when the country needs their arms and calls them to its aid, are not ashamed to hide themselves behind the skirts of a woman."[23] By implication, such men were themselves effeminate, a connection made explicit when in June 1794 the revolutionary pageant master Jacques-Louis David denounced "vile courtesans, nourished in the midst of sensual pleasures, effeminate Sybarites . . . who bring to camps their arrogance and cowardliness and flee at the sight of the least danger and rush to

19. "Deuxième leçon aux volontaires," *La feuille villageoise*, no. 20, February 14, 1793, 465–67.

20. *Journal de Lyon, ou Moniteur*, no. 69, March 31, 1793, 268.

21. *AP*, 65:661, 1 juin 1793. She enlisted after women had been officially expelled.

22. "Dégradation des Lâches en Turquie," *L'esprit des journaux françois et étrangers*, Year 17, vol. 12 (December 1788), 244.

23. Quoted in Hippler, *Citizens, Soldiers, and National Armies*, 82.

hide their shame in the arms of debauchery."[24] David's imagery had a strong social dimension—contrasting debauched aristocratic courtesans to virile sans-culottes—but it also demanded that men distinguish themselves from women.

Men proved their patriotism and masculinity both by separating themselves from domestic life and by defending their families. Officials insisted on the urgency for men to take up arms to protect loved ones. In August 1792, for example, the Council of the Hautes-Alpes pleaded with men to "March to combat. The slightest delay will leave your enemies masters of your destinies and those of your wives and children."[25] In April 1793, a deputy in southern France similarly warned that if men hesitated, "our wives, our children, our brothers, will fall under the blows of their [cannibals'] ungodly rage."[26]

Such exhortations reflected a sense of national emergency, but also represented a significant change from Old Regime recruitment. In the eighteenth century, most men enlisted into the ranks had been young and single; appeals to defend their wives and children made little sense. In contrast, while revolutionary regimental lists rarely recorded marital status, *registres de contrôle* in 1792 suggest that up to half of the volunteers were married.[27] While threats to home and patrie were closely linked in frontier areas, much popular culture equated the defense of family with that of the country.[28] The "Marseillaise," composed in April 1792 and later turned into France's national anthem, famously called on French men to fight against "Those raging cutthroat soldiers who come / To slaughter our children, our wives / Whom they wrench from our loving arms!"

Urging heads of households to fight for both the Revolution and their families did not resolve the practical questions raised by prerevolutionary debates about married soldiers: how would their wives and children survive, whether they traveled with the troops or stayed home? Recruitment propaganda promised that if men fought for the nation, the state would provide for their dependents. The minister of war declared in September 1793, "Hardworking citizens [who took up arms when the patrie was endangered], the Nation will come to the aid of your families."[29] In March 1794, officials charged with providing soldiers for the Armies of Brest and the West similarly reassured recruits: "Do not worry about the fate of your families; the Nation will take care of your parents."[30]

24. David, *Rapport sur la fête héroïque*, 5.

25. Cited in Gautier, *La période révolutionnaire*, 18.

26. *AP*, 63:62, 20 avril 1793.

27. Bertaud, *La révolution armée*, 82. See also Clarke, *Commemorating the Dead*, 257.

28. The radical Revolution also depicted warriors as young heroes protecting France's women. Forrest, "Citizenship and Masculinity," 114.

29. Dorfeuille, *Commissaire des représentants du peuple*, September 16, 1793.

30. AN AF / II / 273, cahier 2293 (16 Ventôse Year II/March 29, 1794).

Revolutionary legislatures passed numerous laws promising assistance to the families of men who were fighting, or who had died, for the patrie. Many aimed at married men and fathers who had taken up arms to defend their families and their country. In November 1792, Etienne Christophe Maignet sponsored one of the earliest measures on behalf of the Committee on Public Assistance, observing that, "when danger to the patrie was proclaimed, a multitude of heads of families consecrated themselves to its defense." Men "tore themselves from the arms of all those who had up to then been most dear to them, leaving behind unfortunate children and their mothers."[31]

Subsequent decrees continued to position soldiers as husbands and fathers, as well as sons. A series of measures promised support for men's wives, children, and aged parents, sometimes even for their orphaned siblings or dependent grandparents.[32] The law of February 9, 1794, represented the apogee of such efforts. It expanded earlier promises of aid to families of serving soldiers, and declared that every war widow would receive an income of 300 livres a year and that parents who had a child die in the service of the patrie would receive indemnities.[33]

In theory, promises that the nation would take care of soldiers' families resolved Old Regime concerns about military service by heads of households. In practice, these promises would prove illusory. De Laissac's concerns about the ability of the indebted eighteenth-century state to provide for military families applied even more to the struggling governments of the Revolution. Financial resources were deeply inadequate and uneven; so too were structures for certifying candidates' eligibility and distributing resources.[34] The archives contain endless pleas from those desperate for aid. Promises to help military families were a powerful but ultimately inadequate tool for recruiting soldiers and sustaining support for war.

FAITHFUL HUSBAND, HONEST SOLDIER?

If financial support for soldiers' families often defined them as husbands and fathers, this was not only because married men had volunteered, or because the government wanted to appeal to family sentiments. It was also because of a major change in the laws on military marriage. On March 9, 1793, the Convention overturned prerevolutionary measures forbidding soldiers from marrying without their superiors' permission. After the minister of war Beurnonville

31. Maignet, *Rapport et projet de décret sur les secours*, 1–2.

32. Laws from May 4, June 6, July 18, and September 15, 1793, and 6 Nivôse and 21 Pluviôse Year II (December 26, 1793, and February 9, 1794).

33. The amount a war widow received could be augmented depending on how long her husband had served but did not depend on his rank.

34. Forrest, *The French Revolution and the Poor*, 151–52; Clarke, *Commemorating the Dead*, 256–62; C. Jones, *Charity and Bienfaisance*, 159–83.

reported that he had received numerous petitions from soldiers and officers wanting to marry, the deputy Julien de Toulouse proposed ending the 1788 ban. The legislature accepted his motion with little discussion. The Law of the Amalgam on February 21, 1793, had merged professional armies with volunteer forces, including numerous married men; it seems likely that it had become difficult to justify different policies for both groups. The legislature had also removed other constraints on marriage, lowering the age of majority and curtailing parental "despotism" over their children's choices. It was logical to imagine that military men could—and should—be both citizens and soldiers, free to marry as they chose.

If there was little formal discussion about the changing law, popular culture, especially theater, centrally addressed relationships between romance and patriotism.[35] Playwrights portrayed "husband" and "soldier" as reinforcing roles, even as men were required to leave home. One of the most successful early plays of the Revolution, *The Officer of Fortune,* debuted on September 24, 1792, four days after the decisive battle of Valmy. Its heroine Céleste wants to marry the soldier Duval, but her mother insists that she wed a rich man, Grugeat. Grugeat spreads rumors that Duval is a deserter; the soldier is instead revealed to be a hero who saved an officer's life in Saint Domingue.[36] Conveniently, the officer is Céléste's brother. The couple happily wed, while Grugeat is denounced as a traitor. Celeste's new husband and her brother adopt soldiers' nicknames of LaFrance and Victory, suggesting their imminent return to the battlefields.

One song from the show, "Fidèle époux, franc militaire" ("Faithful Husband, Honest Soldier"), was particularly popular. The protagonist Duval boasts that "husband" and "soldier" are his proud titles, as to "serve love and the patrie is the duty of all good Frenchmen." It would inspire a series of other songs, which borrowed both the tune and its sentiments, such as "Adieux d'Isophe à Sophie," in which a young man declares, "Glory and Sophie / Order me to leave this place / Oh my *pays*, oh my love / I want to be worthy of both of you / as a true Sans-Culotte, Sophie / I will serve both you and France."[37]

In many of these plays and songs, fathers appeared concerned about their daughters' well-being as well as the risk that marriage would keep men from the civic duty of fighting. In Duval and Picard's *True Courage*, first performed on December 3, 1793, the heroine's father tells the lieutenant Firmin: "I consent to giving my daughter to you; marry as soon as possible, but I don't want you to leave armed service. France needs your arms, and before thinking about cultivating your fields, think about chasing our enemies."[38] Similarly,

35. Germani, "Staging Battles."

36. Patrat, *L'officier de fortune*. The colony is mentioned in passing; the play does not discuss slavery.

37. *Chansonnier républicain et le décadaire*, 21–22.

38. Duval and Picard, *La vraie bravoure*, 23.

in Tissot's *All for Liberty*, the father of the bride hesitates to give permission because his potential son-in-law is to leave the following day; the young officer declares, "I will take with me the title of her husband, as well as your son, and I will fight more courageously to be worthy of both titles."[39]

If these works suggested that love as spur to courage would be most effective if men married and then took up arms or returned to fighting, it was still more common to present marriage as a reward for bravery. The *Siege of Lille, or Cécile and Julien*, premiered November 1793 and staged through April 1794, is typical of the genre. It ends with a captain of the National Guard marrying his love as a reward for rescuing her from a blazing house and killing two Austrians in battle.[40] The idea of marriage as a reward for courage—including anticipated courage—was so common that it could be invoked even when protagonists' ages would have made it illegal. In *The Death of Young Barra*, first performed in May 1794, the thirteen-year-old soldier-hero Barra has a fiancée who offers her hand as a reward for his bravery, as does a thirteen-year-old character in another play inspired by Barra's story, *The Heroine of Mithier*.[41]

Some revolutionary playwrights echoed eighteenth-century reformers' vision of women as passively embodying this reward for male valor. But women often played a more active role in consenting to marriage, sending off lovers or husbands, and celebrating their return.[42] The song "The Republican Lover," set to the tune of "Fidèle époux, franc militaire," is typical in portraying women's exhortations to their partners; the heroine acknowledges that civic duty must come first: "I love Valcour tenderly / I only breathe for him / But my love is without weakness / And his glory is dear to me too / He owes everything to his patrie / She has his first loyalty / Before I am his love."[43] She offers her heart to Valcour if he is courageous and faithful to the patrie, and promises other women that if they do the same, their lovers will fight with ardor.

A few plays suggested more radical possibilities, in which marriage was a patriotic engagement for both partners. In *The Death of Young Barra*, Aimée thinks seriously about joining up, noting that more than one woman had fought against the enemies of liberty. Rather than contend that women should not fight, her mother laments that Aimée's brothers have not sent news from the front lines, and she does not want to lose her daughter as well as her sons, a plea based less on gendered difference than the need to limit the ravages of war.[44] The play also questions the consequences for women of aligning

39. C.-L. Tissot, *Tout pour la liberté*, 29.

40. Joigny, *Cécile et Julien*, 13.

41. Briois, *La mort du jeune Barra*; and Vée and Barral, *L'héroïne de Mithier*.

42. Germani, "Staging Battles," 208.

43. "L'amante républicaine," *Chansonnier républicain et le décadaire*, 20–23.

44. Briois, *La mort du jeune Barra*, 9, 27. For discussions of the play, see Clarke, "'Valour Knows Neither Age nor Sex,'" 63; Mannucci, "Le militaire," 392; and Nielsen, *Women Warriors in Romantic Drama*, 61.

their fates with soldiers. The girl's father worries that "if he [Barra] becomes your husband, and the patrie calls him to new dangers . . . will you not be the unhappiest of women, always fearing for him? My daughter, a republican woman has nothing of her own; her property, her children, her husband; all belongs to her country; it's essential that each sacrifice she is obliged to make be done firmly."[45] Aimée—only fourteen herself—fears that Barra's valor will make her a widow. She would prefer to wait until peacetime to marry but is won over by Barra's bravery and her father's desire to see her wed patriotically, despite his concerns for her vulnerability. Only the young hero's premature death prevents their nuptials.

Unlike prerevolutionary debates about military marriage, few of these plays imagined married men as distracted by their family. Even when characters questioned marriages, they worried more about timing than the nature of these bonds. Playwrights assured audiences that love, patriotism, and courage were mutually reinforcing; whether couples on stage waited for peace to wed depended less on the possibility that family would weaken a warrior than on how soon they imagined war would end. But theatrical representations of married warriors would become less common after 1794. There were few major recruitment efforts after the levée en masse until conscription was instituted in 1798; playwrights thus focused more rarely on men's departures. As we will see in the next chapter, authorities also quietly allowed married men to demobilize in the later 1790s. Marriage increasingly appeared not as an accompaniment to military service but as a reward for military service—or as an alternative to it.

HONORABLE SCARS AND SOLDIERS' STALWART GIRLFRIENDS

When playwrights invoked love and marriage as a reward for courage, they rarely dwelled on the costs of that courage, especially the possibility of long-term injury. But other contemporary works promised that women would remain loyal even if their lovers were disfigured. The caption to an image by the watercolorist Lesueur from Year II reads: "A young woman, having promised her lover to marry him after he returned from war, however injured he might be, seems ready to make good her promise." The iconography highlights virtue. The soldier is on crutches, with a bandaged leg, but appears otherwise unharmed, while a dog, a symbol of fidelity, stands next to the couple.[46]

The sight of wounded bodies took on new meanings during the Jacobin Republic.[47] In January 1793, the National Convention decided to display the

45. Briois, *La mort du jeune Barra*, 8–9.

46. Carbonnières, *Lesueur: Gouaches révolutionnaires*, 161.

47. Baecque, *The Body Politic*.

FIGURE 2.2. Jean-Baptiste Lesueur, *A Young Woman, Having Promised Her Lover to Marry Him after He Returned from War, However Injured He Might Be, Seems Ready to Make Good Her Promise*, between 1792 and 1794. Musée Carnavalet, Paris.

corpse of Michel Lepeletier, assassinated by a royalist because he had voted for the king's death. Lepeletier's wounds were left visible, in a dramatic rupture with funeral traditions.[48] David's famous painting of Marat, assassinated by Charlotte Corday in his bath in July 1793, similarly displayed the wounded body of the "martyr of liberty." The government of the Republic also showcased men who were alive, but whose injuries marked their sacrifice. Veterans played prominent roles in public festivals, while wounded combatants appeared before the Convention at least a hundred times between spring 1792 and summer 1794.[49] The *Recueil des actions héroïques et civiques des républicains français* further publicized their heroism. Over 150,000 copies of the series, first published in early 1794, were distributed free to every municipality, popular society, school, and army battalion.[50]

The men deemed worthy of public recognition were often very young (between thirteen and twenty) or very old, and those whose blindness, disfigurement, or amputation testified to their service. Men on display rarely suffered from less visible ravages of war, even though disease was the most serious threat to combatants.[51] Instead, they embodied obvious sacrifice. They also spoke little in public ceremonies. Their bodies spoke for them; descriptions of their anguish might have undermined the messages those bodies were supposed to convey.[52]

These displays also called attention to men's past heroism as soldiers, not their future utility as civilians. Married men or men of marriageable age featured rarely, perhaps because what made a man a symbol of sacrifice did not necessarily make for an attractive groom. But given the numbers of single men in their twenties or thirties in the troops and the difficulty of securing permanent demobilization without injury, considering the physical and economic attractiveness of wounded men as spouses could not be avoided.

Veterans' returns to domestic life provided real-life versions of Old Regime literary love tests: would women remain devoted to men who had been disfigured or crippled? Would men looking for partners find women interested in them? The idea of marriage as a reward for patriotic sacrifice revived the questions that had plagued Collot's prerevolutionary plans to establish veterans as desirable mates: what would make a woman prefer a husband made ugly by war or incapable of providing for his family over his able-bodied counterparts?

48. Hunt, *The Family Romance*, 75.

49. Baecque, *The Body Politic*, 297–303.

50. Biard, "L'omniprésence de la guerre"; and Clarke, "'Valour Knows Neither Age nor Sex'."

51. Howard, *Napoleon's Doctors*.

52. The most famous was seventeen-year-old François Lavigne, who stood before the National Convention on March 30, 1793; he had lost both his arms and an eye. The minister of war Beurnonville proclaimed that his body should inspire tenderness, patriotic love, and hate for France's enemies. Biard and Maignon, *La souffrance et la gloire*, 76.

Picard and Devienne's popular play *Rose and Aurèle*, which debuted in August 1794, was one of the few to tackle such questions directly. It features a young woman awaiting her lover's return from the army. When Aurèle finally appears, he has lost an arm and his face is deeply scarred. In his absence, his rival, Lormeuil, courted Rose. Lormeuil, who had been excused from the requisition because he was a few months too old to be required to serve, is sure of his romantic victory, proclaiming, "It's not possible that a girl would hesitate between a wounded soldier and a handsome man like me." Rose does not hesitate. She chooses the brave Aurèle, telling Lormeuil that as he is not a husband and a father, he should have fought regardless of his age. She reassures Aurèle—and the audience—that "a wound will not make one look ugly, because it proves that one has been brave in combat."[53]

In planning a festival for the boy soldier-martyrs Bara and Viala in July 1794, the pageant master Jacques-Louis David similarly called upon women "to be careful not to despise these illustrious defenders with honorable scars." He insisted that "The scars of heroes of liberty are the richest dowry and the most durable ornament. After having served their country in the most glorious war, may they [veterans] taste with you the sweetness of a peaceful life. . . . May each of you be seen in the middle of a large family, showing you respect and saying with admiration: there is a worthy companion of a virtuous citizen who has lost his arm."[54]

David's speech implicitly acknowledged that women might be put off by disfigurement and assured them of the rewards of marrying a wounded veteran. But a "dowry of scars" was of limited use for couples struggling to survive. Marriage to a veteran could appear as a sacrifice—a woman's lifelong commitment to help, and potentially provide for, a mutilated man. Popular culture occasionally acknowledged this possibility. In *Rose and Aurèle,* the wounded Aurèle asks his love if she is still willing to marry him: "my dear Rose, can you sacrifice yourself?" She of course responds that marrying him is not a hardship but the least she can do.[55] Yet such acknowledgments were rare. Artwork and theater seldom depicted marriage to a wounded soldier as an act of sacrifice or even generosity by a woman; it was to be a reward for both partners.

Men could be also exempted from service on the grounds of their family responsibilities. Recruitment propaganda encouraged all to take up arms on behalf of their families and patrie, but legislators recognized that this was impractical, especially after the initial calls for volunteers in 1791 and 1792.

53. Picard and Devienne, *Rose et Aurèle*, 24, 32. The *Journal de Paris* praised it as inspiring men to imitate such glorious heroes. *Journal de Paris,* no. 589, 25 Thermidor Year II (August 11, 1794), 1374. See also Tissier, *Les spectacles à Paris,* 43.

54. David, *Rapport sur la fête héroïque*, 10.

55. Picard and Devienne, *Rose et Aurèle*, 29.

The August 1793 levée en masse aimed most at single men, and exempted those wed before the decree.

Excusing married men from service, however, quickly ran into practical and ideological challenges. It ran against the sense of national emergency, and the claim that all should take up arms to prove their virility and protect both their patrie and their loved ones. It also ran against changing definitions of what constituted family. Among other changes, the National Assembly made marriage into a secular contract in 1791, instituted divorce in September 1792, and in November 1793, allowed children born outside of wedlock to inherit.[56] In this context, some hoped that family obligations would allow men to avoid military service even if they were not formally wed.

In early January 1794, for example, a contributor to the *Journal de Paris* considered objections to the *réquisition*, including the exemption of young men married before the law went into effect. The author related the complaints of unmarried men with romantic attachments: "If they [exempted men] have wives, do we not have mistresses? Does the state accept distinctions founded on religious ceremonies like marriage?" In response, the author raised several points:

> The state distinguishes citizens who have wives from those who have mistresses.
>
> 1. Because civil formalities, always very different and now very distinct from religious ceremonies, make the first known, whereas nothing makes known the second.
> 2. Not all men who don't have wives have mistresses.
> 3. Given the corruption of our former laws, most of those who have mistresses have other men's wives as mistresses.
> 4. Those who have an honest mistress should not blush to acknowledge her as a wife.[57]

While the writer mocked the claims of men with mistresses to a special status, the archives do reveal cases of unmarried men hoping to be exempted from service because of their common-law marriages. For example, Louis Joachim Aulbeaux, in the Pas de Calais, asked for an exemption to provide for his partner and two children. Authorities observed he had to be considered a bachelor, since the law only recognized those legally married. However, they noted that it might be appropriate to make an exception.[58]

Official sympathies for common-law households appeared in other contexts. The government of the radical Revolution implicitly recognized common-law marriages when the decree of 13 Prairial Year II (June 1, 1794)

56. Desan, *The Family on Trial*; and Heuer, *The Family and the Nation*.

57. *Journal de Paris*, no. 375, 21 Nivôse Year II (January 10, 1794), 1511.

58. AN AF / III / 313 / 1, Aulbeaux.

extended the benefits allotted to military families to mothers of "natural children." Yet this recognition did not apply to soldiers' partners without children. It also focused on the rights of the dependents of men under arms, not those seeking to avoid military service.

If officials considered whether dependents could exempt men who were technically bachelors, there was a more pressing issue: whether men would fake marriage to avoid military service or form bonds that existed only on paper. A study of the Puy-de-Dôme shows young men rushed to marry in reaction to the levée of 300,000 men in February 1793. Marriage did not formally excuse them from service, but they likely hoped to inspire pity or secure their position in case of subsequent exemptions. Similar waves of marriages across France took place throughout 1793 and 1794.[59] Authorities had good reason to doubt the validity of such unions, especially those that had taken place immediately after the August 23 levée or its promulgation on September 7.

Some young men thus tried to prove that their marriages were motivated not by expediency but by long relationships. Oudin, a Parisian maker of billfolds, argued that both his health and his marital status should excuse him. He had difficulties walking, which meant he could not tolerate the long marches of military service. Moreover, he was married. He acknowledged that he had been wed for only fourteen months but argued that it would have been much longer if his father-in-law, who had taken up arms to march against the brigands, had been able to send his consent earlier. It was well known that Oudin and his wife had lived together for six years.[60]

In other cases, men and women invoked a woman's pregnancy to show the history of their relationships. For example, François Blondin, married in May 1794, proclaimed that "he cannot be suspected of having married to avoid the requisition, because at the time of its publication, he was already a father; honor as well as the most tender affection required him to unite legally with the fifteen-year-old woman who gave him that title."[61] Similarly Dorothée Karcher petitioned the government on behalf of her husband Jérémie Bricka, a tanner from the Meurthe. They had been engaged before he was requisitioned by the levée en masse and she had become pregnant; Jérémie was able to get a leave to marry her. She insisted that her pregnancy was "an accident that necessitated her marriage." Authorities should not see it as a "pretext [for her husband] to shirk his duties," but as a real union.[62] Such stories reframed morally questionable behavior into patriotic duty or, at least, the result of circumstances beyond individual control.

59. Ciotti, "Les 'embusqués de Vénus'"; and Houdaille, "Marriage under the French Revolution and the First Empire."

60. AN AF / III / 313 / 60, Oudin.

61. AN AF / III / 313 / 10, François Blondin.

62. AN AF / III / 313 / 9, Jérémie Bricka or Brika; both spellings in the dossier.

We do not know what happened to these individuals, but there was no systematic exemption for those whose relationships fell outside the parameters of the law, even if they sought to prove the validity of their bonds. Experiments with defining families outside marriage would largely disappear after the radical Revolution. Jacobin concern with displaying the mutilated bodies of martyrs and soldiers would also prove challenging to sustain in a changing political order. But the questions of the compatibility of martial masculinity and marriage, the desirability of wounded veterans as husbands, and when family bonds should exempt men from service would all become more pressing after 1794, as war continued even as national emergency receded.

Women Warriors and the First Demobilization

"LEGIONS OF AMAZONS"?

While most soldiers were male, a few women took up arms in the early years of the Revolution. One of the most famous, Anne Quatresous, joined at age fifteen in May 1791. She was originally rejected because of her age, but succeeded in enlisting with the artillery in the Vendée and then the armies of the North and Belgium. She spent three years fighting in disguise in many of the significant battles of the early Republic. At least according to popular lore, she had two horses killed underneath her, while at the bombardment of Valenciennes she was laid low by a cannonball and reduced to eating raw horsemeat for three days. She came to the attention of authorities in June 1793 when a chest wound revealed her sex.[63]

Other women enlisted with their spouses. Rose "Liberté" Barreau volunteered on March 5, 1793, at age nineteen or twenty, alongside her husband and brother. After killing a Spaniard in battle on July 13, 1793, she allegedly recharged her rifle with his cartridges and pursued the enemy. Her husband was shot; she turned to help him only after the Spanish were defeated, and then nursed him back to health.[64] Rose Bouillon similarly joined with her husband in March 1793, leaving behind two children, one a seven-month-old infant. On August 13, her husband was shot next to her in a north German town. Like Barreau, Bouillon continued to fight until the battle ended.[65]

63. Sometimes spelled Quatresault. See *Gazette nationale ou le Moniteur universel*, no. 215, 5 Floréal Year II (April 24, 1794), 871; *Les décades républicaines*, 3:9; and SHD 1 Yi 50.

64. *AP*, 70:63–64, 1 août 1793.

65. *AP*, 73:85, 27 août 1793. General Schauenburg solicited a pension for her, implicitly contrasting her heroic conduct to that of the *chef de brigade*, who had abandoned his battalion during combat. He emphasized that Bouillon continued to fight after her husband had been struck and that she was only asking for her release to take care of her family.

FIGURE 2.3. Jean-Baptiste Lesueur, *Théroigne de Méricourt, Amazon,* [1792]. Musée Carnavalet, Paris.

Others joined with male relatives. Most famously, the Fernig sisters Félicité and Théophile enlisted at ages twenty-two and seventeen, along with their father and a brother. They originally disguised themselves in men's clothing. Although they were soon recognized as women, military authorities lauded their courage. Dumouriez, the general in charge of the Belgian campaign, invited them to enlist in his forces, where they took part in the crucial battle of Valmy on September 20, 1792. In April 1793, Dumouriez committed treason and joined the Austrian army; the sisters followed him. They soon sought to return to the French side, claiming they had not understood what the general was doing, but were considered his accomplices and forced to flee the country.[66]

These examples suggest the diversity of women's experiences and the circumstances that prompted their enlistment.[67] Based on a study of twenty-eight demands for pensions, Maria Goupil-Travert has found that a woman soldier was likely to be between fifteen and thirty-five, from a frontier area, and fighting alongside her husband.[68] But if this was the most common profile, there was also significant variation; Anne Quatresous enlisted at fifteen and Madelaine Petitjean at forty-seven. While the majority fought with spouses or lovers, others joined on their own, or with siblings or parents. Those writing about women soldiers have been tempted to treat them as protofeminists, and to represent them either as virgin warriors à la Joan of Arc or as romantic appendages of male soldiers; the range of their situations defies easy generalizations.

EXPELLING "USELESS" WOMEN: REVISITING THE APRIL 30, 1793, DECREE

Regardless of their motives or status, all women were officially expelled from the troops on April 30, 1793. The National Convention dismissed not only women who had taken up arms, but also military wives, camp followers, prostitutes, and auxiliary workers, permitting only a limited number of vivandières and laundresses.[69] In theory, women were given financial assistance to return home; in practice, many were stranded.[70]

It is likely that increased associations between military service, masculinity, and citizenship helped precipitate the decree. Women did not obtain the right to vote or to hold political office during the Revolution; indeed, the

66. *AP*, 53:428, 15 novembre 1792; 56:591, 7 janvier 1793; and 58:312, 6 février 1793.

67. On their diversity, see Godineau, "De la guerrière à la citoyenne"; Conner, "La Vraie Madame Sans-Gêne"; and J.-C. Martin, *La révolte brisée*.

68. Of the twenty-eight women seeking pensions whose files Goupil-Travert examined, twenty-one (75 percent) were married. *Braves combattantes*, 53.

69. Cardoza, *Intrepid Women*, explores the implementation of the decree in depth.

70. Goupil-Travert, *Braves combattantes*, 114. See also Cardoza, *Intrepid Women*, 50.

National Convention would close all women's political clubs in October 1793. Nor was there an organized feminist movement championing women's rights, despite the writings of a few individuals like the Marquis de Condorcet and Olympe de Gouges.[71] Women, however, acted as citizens, including participating in political demonstrations and movements.[72] A few people also called for women to take up arms, linking arms-bearing to political citizenship. In perhaps the most famous formulation, Anne-Josèphe Théroigne de Méricourt called in April 1793 for "legions of amazons" and asked her fellow French men and women to imagine themselves "in the time when Gallic women and proud Germanic women deliberated in national assemblies and fought alongside their husbands to repel the enemies of liberty."[73]

In at least one case, a woman was granted political rights as a result of her military service. Anne Françoise Pélagie Dulierre enlisted as a gunner along with her older brother and was injured in the battle of Jemappes. General Dumouriez proposed promoting her to the position of sublieutenant; the National Convention confirmed her promotion in March 1793, and she continued to fight until September 1793. In recognition of her service, the Parisian *section* of the Mail (a neighborhood north of the Palais Royal) granted her the same political rights as men.[74] Dulierre, however, exercised those rights only within the *section;* her status seems to have received little publicity, and neither she nor commentators viewed it as a general precedent for women's rights. While women soldiers insisted on their patriotism, few linked their service to wider demands.

Women's arms-bearing, however, was still entangled with questions of citizenship. A few days before the April 30, 1793, law, the deputy Pierre Guyomar insisted that women be allowed to vote in primary assemblies. He posed a stark juxtaposition. Women should be considered citizens or identified as slaves and called wives or daughters of citizens, but not citizens themselves. In a speech to the Convention on April 29, Jean-Denis Lanjuinais responded that women's physical state, destiny, and work precluded most from exercising political rights and duties; in its political sense, the word "citizen" should not encompass women.[75] Lanjuinais's arguments would prevail. While legislators did not refer to this exchange when discussing women in the troops, the timing is striking. This view of women as incapable of political rights likely made them appear unfit to be part of the armed forces defending those rights,

71. Verjus, Heuer, and Orazi, "Introduction: Féminismes en Europe."

72. Heuer, "Rethinking Gender."

73. Lacour, *Trois femmes de la révolution;* and Desan, "Théroigne de Méricourt."

74. Hennet, "Une femme-soldat"; and *Journal des débats et des décrets,* no. 187, March 24, 1793, 292.

75. *AP,* 63:564, 591–95, 29 avril 1793.

an association that would appear again in October 1793 when the legislature voted to close women's political clubs.[76]

There was also another, more immediate factor behind the expulsion of women from the troops: the decision, a month prior, to legalize military marriage. Doing so quickly increased the number of women with the troops, particularly in the Army of the North. Officials complained bitterly about the upsurge.[77] Their complaints were partly practical. In a letter dated March 23, the *commissaire* to the National Convention Jean-François Delacroix protested that women consumed too much and occupied wagons that would otherwise carry baggage and fodder.[78] A month later, he provided numbers, declaring that in an army of 30,000 men, there might be up to 8,000 women, leading to great financial losses.[79]

Moral concerns accompanied economic ones. One military official derided women as "mouths that are infinitely expensive for the Republic," and contended that they sapped men's strength so that "our soldiers will finish by being good for nothing."[80] The future minister of war Lazare Carnot blamed women for undermining the army's health and morality:

> A terrible scourge is destroying our armies: the flocks of women and girls who follow them. There are as many women as soldiers. The barracks and camps are glutted. The dissolution of morals is at its height. Women overexcite the troops and destroy with the illnesses they bring ten times as many people as the fire of our enemies. We do not doubt that they are the principal cause weakening courage.[81]

Such protests implicitly built on concern about venereal disease in the army. French revolutionaries decriminalized prostitution in 1791, but Jacobins viewed prostitutes as a threat both to the health of the troops and to a virtuous citizenry.[82] Accusations like Carnot's blurred the lines between prostitutes and women as a group. He did not want to expel prostitutes or camp followers while tolerating "respectable" military wives. Instead, he complained that it was impossible to distinguish married women from pretenders: "The law says

76. Most notably, in justifying the decision to close women's political clubs, the deputy Philippe Fabre d'Eglantine proclaimed that if women "ask for the cap of liberty . . . they will not rest there, they will soon demand a belt with pistols." *AP*, 78:21, 29 octobre 1793.

77. Cardoza, *Intrepid Women*, 48–51.

78. *AP*, 60:562, 23 mars 1793. *Gazette nationale ou le Moniteur universel*, no. 86, March 27, 1793, 385.

79. *Gazette nationale ou le Moniteur universel*, no. 111, April 21, 1793, 492.

80. Letter from J. Defrenne to Bouchotte, Lille, April 27, 1793, in Charavay, ed., *Correspondance générale de Carnot*, 135.

81. Letter from Carnot to the Convention, Dunkerque, April 16, 1793, in Charavay, ed., *Correspondance générale de Carnot*, 116–17.

82. Plumauzille, *Prostitution et révolution*.

we should provide lodging for the wives of married soldiers; they claim they all are."

Francois Poultier, deputy to the department du Nord, reiterated Carnot's complaints in a report for the War Committee. He denounced the excessive number of women following the troops, blaming them for consuming essential food, slowing down the troops, and weakening men's courage. But he also specifically disparaged Dumouriez, the French general who had defected to the Austrians, for surrounding himself with mistresses, singers, and actresses to the point that his quarters resembled a vizier's harem.[83] In such claims, women in the military were not heroines, inspirations for male courage, or even dependents who had to be supported by their husbands or the state, but rather proof of the weakness of self-indulgent leaders.

The ban thus responded to struggles over women's role in the revolutionary polity, and to the possibility that women could, or should, claim political citizenship. But it also emerged from practical and moral concerns about an influx of women in the troops and from the decision to treat soldiers as husbands. Legalizing military marriages had unexpected consequences. It led not to combining men's military and familial roles, but instead to an intensification of martial masculinity and a reinforced legal separation between military and domestic spaces.

HONORING AND DEMOBILIZING WOMEN SOLDIERS

In theory, the April 30, 1793, decree immediately demobilized women soldiers. The continued outpouring of complaints and regulations reveals how many individuals ignored or circumvented the law.[84] A year after the decree, military authorities observed that some officers were still pretending that their wives were laundresses or vivandières to protect them from the law.[85] In fall 1794, one brigadier general with the armies of the North and of Sambre-et-Meuse complained that administrative units serving the army, including ambulances, transport, and food services, contained many women who believed they were exempted. Other military authorities denounced women who claimed that the decree referred only to camps and billeting, allowing them to stay in nearby towns.[86]

83. *AP*, 63:627, 30 avril 1793; *Gazette nationale ou le Moniteur universel*, no. 86, May 2, 1793, 587. One newspaper picked up on Poultier's rhetoric, describing Dumouriez as an effeminate traitor and contrasting the general's harem to the virtuous quarters of a republican soldier. *Courrier de l'égalité*, no. 256, May 1, 1793, 245.

84. Cardoza, *Intrepid Women*, 50.

85. April 23, 1794 (4 Floréal Year II). Coutanceau, *La campagne de 1794*, 1:69.

86. October 21, 1794 (30 Vendémiaire Year III) and November 24, 1794 (4 Frimaire Year III). *Recueil des proclamations et arrêtés des représentants du peuple français*, 1:416–19, 2:88–91.

Women soldiers also did not immediately disappear from the troops. Dominique Godineau notes that only three of the eighty women soldiers she identified left the army in May or June 1793, and only one explicitly because of the decree. Others were dismissed, but months, even years, later.[87] Some hid under a masculine identity and were only discovered when they were wounded, but comrades in arms tacitly or even openly accepted others. A few took up arms after the decree. Marie Anne Bruet, for example, enlisted in March 1796 and fought until December 1800 alongside her husband, stopping only after he was killed at the battle of Marengo.[88] Most women soldiers, however, did leave the ranks sometime between 1793 and 1795.

Their release can be seen as the first demobilization of the revolutionary wars, although contemporaries did not define it in such terms. Unlike many subsequent demobilizations, it involved a very small number of people, and took place as the Republic desperately sought to mobilize male soldiers. Some women actively contested their exclusion. In July 1793, Marie Savonneau wrote General Custine, demanding to know why women were being kept from fighting when the country needed them: "While the worst of storms everywhere shakes the Republic, while the ship of liberty, in danger of sinking, calls to its aid all its friends . . . will only one part of citizens be allowed the honor of sacrificing their blood to preserve it from the furors of the hurricane, and the other part be unjustly rejected?"[89]

Savonneau had enlisted in March 1793 at age thirty, under her own name and without disguising herself. Her enlistment had been supported by her community. The citizen Livré, a former deputy to the Constituent Assembly, had provided her with a full uniform of the National Guard, and the municipal government of Saint-Calais had applauded her enlistment and certified the purity of her morals. She inspired two other women in her hometown to enlist, Marie Trotté and Magdeleine Manceau.[90] In justifying her own engagement, she invoked other women who had defended the Revolution, including those who had participated in the October Days march on Versailles and the citoyenne Bergognoux, who had defended a tree of liberty.[91]

If Savonneau linked her military service to other women's patriotic actions, another woman soldier protesting her demobilization set herself apart. Reine Chappuy had enlisted at the age of seventeen in February 1793, following the example of her five brothers, who fought with the armies of the North and the Vendée. On January 20, 1794, Chappuy sought to persuade the National Convention that "unlike many women perhaps inspired to follow the troops

87. Godineau, "De la guerrière à la citoyenne."

88. SHD 1 Yi 34; Goupil-Travert, *Braves combattantes*, 105.

89. Cited in Poulet, *Les volontaires de la Meurthe*, 158.

90. Deschamps, "Les femmes soldats dans la Sarthe."

91. Poulet, *Les volontaires de la Meurthe*, 158.

by crazed love," she was motivated by "the love of the patrie." She begged to be allowed to prove that "a woman's arm is worth a man's, when her blows are for honor, the thirst for glory, and the desire to kill enemies."[92]

Neither woman seems to have been allowed to return to military service, although in Savonneau's case, it did not help that she addressed her plea to General Custine, who was guillotined for treason in August 1793, soon after she had written him. Chappuy's entreaty was formulated in terms more likely to appeal to the authorities of the Revolution than Savonneau's. The National and Thermidorian Conventions regularly honored individual women soldiers for their service and the *Recueil des actions héroïques et civiques* celebrated their courage.[93] But authorities usually stressed the exceptionality of these women. For example, the *commissaires* to the Armée des Pyrénées Orientales awarded Liberté Barreau and her husband a *gratification* of 300 livres in July 1793, claiming that the example would "not be dangerous and will not at all diminish our desire to limit the number of women in this army."[94]

Seeing women soldiers as exceptional could mean viewing them as honorary men. The August 1793 commendation for the twice-wounded Jeanne-Marie Barrère declared that she "fought with a valor well above her sex."[95] The legislature similarly reviewed Anne Quatresous's case on February 26, 1794, after briefly considering whether indigent women who had long-term partners but were not legally married should receive financial support if their partners had enlisted. Legislators dismissed Léon Bourdon's proposal to support such women, but decided that Quatresous was a very different case, entitled to recognition in her own right. Collot d'Herbois proclaimed that "I would not include her among women; I declare this girl is a man because she, like the most intrepid warriors, has confronted death and the most perilous circumstances."[96]

Even while praising women's masculine heroism, however, contemporaries insisted on their respectability. So did women soldiers themselves. Their eagerness to prove the esteem of their fellow citizens reflected the general importance of reputation during the Revolution. It also reflected a specific concern with women's sexuality; those promoting women soldiers insisted on their modesty as well as their bravery. When the *commissaires* in the Nord wrote the Legislative Assembly in October 1792, they reported that the Fernig sisters were "as modest as they were courageous," and in the middle of the army, were

92. *Gazette nationale ou le Moniteur universel*, no. 121, 1 Pluviôse Year II (January 20, 1794), 487.

93. For example, it glorified Rose Bouillon and Liberté Barreau on December 30, 1793.

94. *AP*, 70:63–64, 1 août 1793; and SHD 1 Yi 1.

95. Conner, "La Vraie Madame Sans-Gêne"; and J.-C. Martin, *La révolte brisée*, 119.

96. *Gazette nationale ou le Moniteur universel*, no. 162, 12 Ventôse Year II (March 2, 1794), 654. Drawing in part on this passage, Godineau has argued that heroism could only be masculine, even if illustrated by a woman. Godineau, "De la guerrière à la citoyenne," 64.

"respected and honored; it's the reward for virtue."[97] They downplayed the sisters' sexuality by referring to them as "children" (*jeunes enfants*), despite their ages of seventeen and twenty-two. Similarly, if the Convention heralded Barrère's masculine valor, it also lauded her as a "generous woman," who "was beyond reproach," while the Conseil d'administration of the Battalion of Nièvre awarded "a certificate of irreproachable conduct" to the twenty-one-year-old Félicité Duquet.[98] When deputy Roger Duclos, speaking on behalf of the Relief Committee, promoted the case of Marie-Barbe Parent in July 1795, he presented certificates testifying that "her zeal, courage, and the decency of her morals earned her the esteem and goodwill of her superiors and comrades."[99] This emphasis on women's respectability countered speculation about their behavior in close quarters with male soldiers. It specifically countered accusations that women associated with troops were prostitutes, or at best, mistresses. Emphasizing women's respectability may also have made it easier to imagine their return to civilian society.

After forcibly demobilizing women veterans, the National Convention did provide them with some financial support, deemed a "national reward" or "national recompense."[100] For example, Duclos heralded Jeanne Perrin in February 1794; she had enlisted in October 1792 and fought under the "honorable national costume," until her health forced her to reveal her sex. Duclos proposed that the government accord "this new Spartiate" 500 livres not as assistance, but as a reward for "the bellicose ardor deployed by this republican woman."[101] In most cases, however, authorities linked charity and recognition, as for Ursule Aby, who had served as a lieutenant and been wounded; the Convention awarded her 200 livres in December 1794 as both "aid and recompense."[102]

Financial support was sometimes tied to individuals' familial situation. In April 1794, the Convention granted Anne Quatresous a pension of 300 livres,

97. Aulard, *Recueil des actes du comité de salut public,* 1:86.

98. Duquet was the daughter of a schoolteacher; she had enrolled in disguise and fought until April 1794. Cited in Godineau, "De la guerrière à la citoyenne." See also Chassin and Hennet, *Les volontaires nationaux,* 3:167.

99. Parent had left home at a young age (different sources give her age as fifteen or close to twenty when she enlisted); she was obliged to give up arms when her family recognized her at Valenciennes in 1793 but resumed fighting subsequently. *Gazette nationale ou le Moniteur universel,* no. 341, 11 Fructidor Year III (August 28, 1795), 1373.

100. Usually "récompense national" or "reconnaissance nationale." Cases include the July 9, 1794, "Décret qui accorde la somme de 500 livres, à titre de gratification & de récompense nationale, à Catherine-Adélaïde Garnejoux"; the July 18, 1794, declaration that "La Trésorerie nationale paiera . . . Françoise Rouelle une somme de 600 livres, à titre de gratification et de récompense nationale"; and the April 5, 1795, award to Rose Goton Marchand of "la somme de 400 livres à titre de secours et de récompense nationale."

101. *Gazette nationale ou le Moniteur universel,* no. 145, 25 Pluviôse Year II (February 13, 1794), 557.

102. *Collection des lois et décrets,* 6:190.

to be augmented by 200 when she married.[103] The proposition simultaneously positioned Quatresous as the support for her future children—rather than, or as well as, her prospective husband—and assumed that she, like other women, would wed, although she seemed to have no immediate plans to do so. Hers seems to have been the only case where support was directly tied to marriage, perhaps because she was unusually young and single. However, the National Convention did occasionally recognize and call attention to other women's familial situations, in ways that paralleled measures providing for male combatants' families.[104]

Women veterans sometimes appeared before authorities in their uniforms, either because they lacked other clothes or because they wanted to call attention to their service. Marie-Barbe Parent wore a military uniform when she stood before the National Convention in 1795, asking for help that her family, ruined in the bombing of Valenciennes, could not provide her. But while male veterans usually kept their uniforms after their release, women were expected to resume female garb. Indeed, authorities occasionally arrested women for wearing men's clothing. Eighteen-year-old Marie-Marthe Bertin was thus apprehended on August 6, 1794, when she left Parisian barracks wearing a sergeant's uniform; on April 1, 1795, police arrested the former gunner Minard for dressing as a man. Women were often liberated with an admonition to resume appropriate garb; Bertin was released because she had a recommendation from the Sûreté Générale, and Minard was ultimately allowed to regain her post.[105]

Demobilized women soldiers regularly lamented that they could not afford to buy women's clothing. Their complaints expressed both real poverty and strategic appeals to authorities, who appeared more likely to respond to such pleas than to general requests for assistance. Félicité Duquet, who had fought under the name of Va de Bon Cœur (Goes-with-a-Good-Heart), complained in July 1794 that she did "not even have the means to resume, as the law requires, the clothing of her sex." She was given provisional support.[106] The trumpeters Marie Lefebvre and Sophie Julien similarly described themselves as returning "without any financial resources, without any clothing appropriate for their sex, or funds to procure necessary clothing."[107]

103. *Gazette nationale ou le Moniteur universel*, no. 215, 5 Floréal Year II (April 7, 1794), 871.

104. Most notably, on August 27, 1793, it accorded Rose Bouillon a pension of 300 livres, supplemented by 150 for each of her two children.

105. On Minard (also known as the femme Fortier), see J.-C. Martin, "Travestissements" and *La révolte brisée.*

106. Chassin and Hennet, *Les volontaires nationaux,* 3:166–70.

107. Schwab, "Variétés: Les femmes aux armées,"10. Sophie Julien had enlisted as an eighteen-year-old and fought in disguise from March 1792 to May 1793. She was granted

The case of one of the last women to be honored by the Convention, Rose Goton Marchand, shows how appeals for women to return to domestic life could still coincide with honoring their service. The eighteen-year-old declared she had done two campaigns as a volunteer. Like other impoverished woman veterans, she emphasized her financial inability to return to civilian life as a woman: "discharged once her sex was known, she lacks the means to procure women's clothing for herself." In reporting her case in August 1795, the *Moniteur* declared that the Convention had wisely expelled not just her, but all women, from the army, since "almost all were drawn by libertinage, rather than the love of glory or liberty. Women should use the shuttle, the needle, and the spindle, give the country robust defenders, and make crowns to adorn the heads of their sons, husbands, and lovers when they return as victors. It's at the expense of the virtues of their sex that they make themselves men and deliver themselves to work for which nature has not destined them." But the National Convention also acknowledged that there were precedents for rewarding exceptional women soldiers, and that Goton Marchand had shown "the zeal and bravery of a true solider and given proof of the greatest of courage at the siege of Maastricht." She was thus allotted 400 livres not specifically to buy women's clothing, but rather as "a national reward."[108]

HAPPY ENDINGS ON STAGE

If official recognition of women veterans reflected a desire both to recognize their service and to return them to domestic life, popular culture also offered mixed messages. Theatrical depictions of women warriors show popular fascination with women long after their expulsion from the troops and suggest an ongoing ambivalence about whether all women should lay down their arms.

Many plays were based on real women, or at least claimed to be. The exploits of the Fernig sisters likely inspired Olympe de Gouges's *Dumourier's Arrival in Brussels or the Vivandiers*.[109] She wrote the play shortly after Dumouriez's victory over the Austrians in November 1792, though it was not performed until January 1793. Bogez-Villeneuve's *Liberty Barrau or the Republican Heroines* premiered September 1794 and was still running a year later.[110] The citoyenne Desmoulins claimed that her play, the 1794 *The*

200 francs on November 5, 1794, partly as a question of equity; she had received 300 francs earlier, but other women soldiers had been awarded 500. *AP*, 100:420–21.

108. *Gazette nationale ou le Moniteur universel*, no. 318, 18 Thermidor Year III (August 5, 1795), 378.

109. Gouges, *L'entrée du Dumourier à Bruxelles ou les vivandiers*. See Verdier, "From Reform to Revolution," 195.

110. Bogez-Villeneuve, *Liberté Barrau ou les héroïnes républicaines*. Performed at the Lycée des Arts from 9 Vendémiaire Year III (September 30, 1794) through 5 Frimaire Year IV (November 26, 1795). See also Clarke, "'Valour Knows Neither Age nor Sex'."

Republican Heroine, was inspired by a woman recognized for her bravery by the Convention, although she did not name the individual.[111] Other plays were more clearly fictional, including what seems to have been the most popular play featuring a woman warrior, *The Girl Hussard*, which debuted in 1796.[112]

The reception of these plays depended most on the quality of the performance. *Dumourier's Arrival* played only three times; Olympe de Gouges claimed that the theatrical troupe had butchered it. When the most prominent theatrical newspaper, the *Journal des spectacles*, reviewed Bogez-Villeneuve's play, it lauded Barreau's valor as well as her ultimate concern for her children, but it paid most attention to the acting.[113] Playwrights and audiences nonetheless made both direct and implicit judgments about the need for women warriors, and what should happen after their service.

Some works, like *The Enlistment of Cadet Roussel or the Departure of Good Children for the Army*, reinforced the message that women should not take up arms at all. The play debuted September 22, 1793, shortly after the levée en masse, and a month before the closing of women's political clubs. Cadet Roussel's wife and mother want to accompany him in the troops; other women similarly propose following their husbands, sons, or boyfriends to war. A commissaire applauds their enthusiasm but explains that a decree forbids them from joining the armies; they ultimately accept the decree and see off their menfolk.[114]

More commonly, plays reveled in the exploits of women soldiers, while treating those exploits as exceptional A few works imagined such soldiers separately from male connections. Olympe de Gouges did not refer to the Fernig sisters' brother or father; in her script, the sisters create their own destiny apart from familial attachments. She also created a third woman soldier, the daughter of a vivandier, who takes up arms both to please her father and to be her lover's equal in serving the Republic. She succeeds in killing two Austrians. Although she marries the man she loves, nothing indicates that she will abandon her role as a warrior.[115]

More often, however, plays depicted women soldiers in relation to men, both in their enlistment and in their demobilization.[116] Theaters often

111. Citoyenne Desmoulins, *L'héroine républicaine*, reprinted in Harten and Harten, eds., *Femmes, culture, et révolution*.

112. Cuvelier de Trie, *La fille hussard*.

113. *Journal des spectacles*, no. 4, 13 Vendémiaire Year III, 56–61; *Journal des spectacles*, no. 5, 16 Vendémiaire Year III, 74–75.

114. Louis Archambault Dorvigny, *L'enrôlement de Cadet Roussel ou le départ de bons enfants pour l'armée*. See *Journal des spectacles*, no. 83, September 22, 1793, 659–61; and Germani, "Staging Battles," 209. There were only three performances, September 19–22; the script was not published.

115. Ross, "La femme militaire," 56–58.

116. David Hopkin has argued that the dominance of cultural representations meant that female soldiers were always viewed in terms of their relationships to men. Hopkin, "The World Turned Upside Down," 84.

portrayed marriage as ending women's military service. This is the case with François-Georges Desfontaines's *Soldier Girl*, which debuted at the Théâtre du Vaudeville in December 1794 and performed through August 1796.[117] Julie, disguised as Victor, has fought for two years, and meets Julien, her potential partner, in the camps. She reveals herself when Julien reads a letter from her father, claiming that her brother is dead and that her father will die without his daughter. It becomes clear that both her brother and father are alive, but Julie/Victor still resumes feminine garb and returns home to take care of her father. The play ends with a song: "Soldier girl owes the state a nice militia of little kids."[118] Julie becomes a baby machine; Julien fights on.

Some shows, however, contended that love and military courage coincided for both men and women. In the 1794 *The Republican Heroine*, Valcour is in love with Zélime; he is moved by her beauty, courage, and unselfishness in battle. Marriage will be a spur for him; he proclaims, "Love causes courage to grow rather than diminish," and that he will have the pleasure of being "a loyal husband and soldier." It will also be a spur for her. While the plot hinges less on Zélime's military deeds than on persuading Valcour's parents to accept her, her wedding does not end her career. Instead, the general who provides a convenient dowry promises that the couple will win glory, and they sing together, "tender love will aid our triumph."[119]

Conversely, a few plays ended with both partners returning to domestic life. *The Siege or the Republican Heroine, by a Citizen of Ville Affranchie* featured Sophie Montreval, who enlists as André. She is in love with Belfort, the commander of her unit. André saves Belfort's life twice before she ultimately removes her helmet and fake mustache. It transpires that her ambitious father had forced her to wed another man. Liberated by her first husband's death, she came after Belfort, but wanted to prove her love for him and that "the love of serving the patrie belongs to all ages and sexes." The couple is united, the siege ends, all return to domestic life. While the concluding song proclaims, "Don't forget your [female] friend / Awaits the return of a victor," the play also presents men as eager for familial roles. It ends with a soldier carrying two orphaned children in his arms, asking to serve as their father.[120]

Similarly, Cuvelier de Trie's *Festival of the Supreme Being*, performed in June 1794, showed mothers, wives, and sisters saying farewell to their men. Adèle appears armed with a rifle; she claims that patriotism will overcome

117. Desfontaines, *La fille soldat*. Performed 23 Frimaire Year III (December 13, 1794) through 4 Fructidor Year IV (August 21, 1796). Reviewed in *L'esprit des journaux françois et étrangers*, Year 24, vol. 1 (January 1795), 300–302.

118. Hopkin, "The World Turned Upside Down," 86; Verdier, "From Reform to Revolution," 211.

119. Reprinted in Harten and Harten, eds., *Femmes, culture, et révolution*, 338–71. See also J.-C. Martin, *La révolte brisée*, 120; and Desan, *The Family on Trial*, 80.

120. Macors?, *Le siège ou l'héroïne républicaine*.

any weakness of her sex and leaves to fight alongside her beloved Tristan. One dark night the army is attacked, and Adèle hit. Enraged, Tristan redoubles his efforts, and saves a representative of the nation from brigands. Adèle's injury proves light. Both partners are released from service under the condition that they have a son every year.[121]

While the most common ending thus was for a woman soldier to leave service, even if her husband continued to fight, these different possible conclusions—in which both partners continue to fight or are discharged together—suggest that it remained possible to imagine women as warriors. If martial masculinity could be compatible with marriage, so too could martial femininity—even as the legalization of military marriage helped expel women from the troops. As we will see in later chapters, the image of partners fighting or demobilizing together would eventually become harder to envision. A few women would fight in the later 1790s and in Napoleonic troops, despite official bans, but far fewer than during the height of the Revolution. Women warriors would also increasingly disappear from the stage, at least until later in the nineteenth century.[122]

Citizenship, Arms, and Emotions

NATURE KNOWS HOW TO SILENCE ITSELF

If women soldiers were slowly demobilized, men continued to take up arms. Some artists represented soldiers' departures as moments of collective joy. The watercolorist Lesueur created several such scenes. One from 1792 shows a volunteer armed by his father, while his mother and sister prepare his bag; all admire the dashing soldier. Another portrays a soldier enthusiastically accompanied to the town's outskirts by his wife, children, and a female relative.[123] Such images reflected the excitement of the Revolution, while downplaying the cost of separations.

Other artwork hinted at the difficulties of farewells, even as it legitimated the demands of the patrie and celebrated the heroic citizen-soldiers who defended it. Le Barbier's 1792 *Departure of the Citizen* provides one revealing example. Best known for his representation of the Declaration of the Rights of Man and Citizen, Le Barbier had celebrated female military action before the Revolution, painting tributes to Spartan women defending their besieged

121. Cuvelier de Trie, *Fête de l'Être Suprême.*

122. Gil Mihaely has argued that images of women warriors became more common in the late nineteenth century after they had ceased to be a real presence in the troops. Mihaely, "L'effacement de la cantinière."

123. *Le départ pour les frontières* and *Équipement d'un volontaire*, reproduced in Carbonnières, *Lesueur: Gouaches révolutionnaires*, 101, 104.

FIGURE 2.4. Jean-Baptiste Lesueur, *Departure for the Frontier, a Citizen Volunteer Accompanied by His Wife, Children, and a Cousin Who Carries His Sack*, 1792. Musée Carnavalet, Paris.

city and to the medieval heroine Jeanne Hachette.[124] *Departure of the Citizen* concentrates on emotional farewells to a male volunteer. Captions explain: "All burst into tears: the Valet, Father, Mother, Sweetheart. The soldier himself is filled with sadness." The father, however, tells the son to arm himself with courage, declaring that he too served the state in his youth. The last lines reverse the title; if good citizens are soldiers, it is also true that "a good soldier will always be a good citizen."[125]

The young men at the center of these images often appeared resolute.[126] A few representations still suggested men's hesitation; for instance, the son's

124. See chapter 1. He continued to draw on classical imagery and would depict a Spartan mother sending off her son in 1806, *Une lacédémonienne donnant un bouclier à son fils*.

125. Le Barbier, *Départ du citoyen* (Collections of the Musée Carnavalet).

126. Joan Landes stresses that the young man in Pierre Antoine Machy's 1792 *Devotion to the Patrie* is iron-willed. Landes, *Visualizing the Nation*, 160, and "Republican

FIGURE 2.5. C. D. (engraver), after Le Barbier, *Departure of the Citizen*, 1792. Musée Carnavalet, Paris.

contorted position in Moreau le Jeune's 1793 drawing of a volunteer's departure implies that he is leaving reluctantly.[127] Such reluctance, including men's tears at departure, could appear acceptable if it indicated the depth of a man's sacrifice and concern for those who would suffer in his absence. In the play *The Lunch of the Volunteers,* which debuted in March 1794, the comrades of one young man discover him crying.[128] They wonder if his tears are signs of cowardice, but learn he is leaving behind a blind father. The play finishes by allowing Julien to devote his salary to his father, with the confidence that his

Citizenship," 108. The 1792 *Departure of the Volunteer* (sometimes attributed to François Watteau de Lille) and Pierre-Charles Coqueret's 1794–95 *You Owe the Sacrifice of Your Dearest Affections to the Patrie* similarly suggest valiant recruits.

127. Jean-Michel Moreau, *Départ du jeune volontaire de la république, ses adieux à sa famille.*

128. Jardin, *Le déjeuner des volontaires.*

comrades will provide for him. Such fantasy was a complement of the optimistic claim that the state and fellow citizens would provide for dependents left behind.

Paternal tears could also indicate virtue. *The Good Father*, a discourse from the Festival of Reason on December 10, 1793, depicted a father sending off his fifteen-year-old son, and struggling to hide his tears. The boy appreciates his father's steadfastness: "Oh, my father, I feared distressing you, but your resolve reassures me and inspires mine." The narrator proclaims, "Ah! Tender and beloved father, let your tears run; they are not signs of weakness. You do not insult your patrie; you pay a tribute to nature; you would not be a father if you did not give a tear to your son's departure."[129]

Effusive male tears were part of the eighteenth-century culture of sensibility.[130] For both young men and their fathers, they reflected revolutionary emphasis on nature and sincerity, and the increased importance of affection in family bonds. But if contemporary works acknowledged the distress all could experience when young men left home, they particularly represented women's agony. While the caption to *Departure of the Citizen* describes everyone as distraught, the painting focuses on women. The soldier's mother clings to him, while a young woman weeps into her hand. Similarly, in *Departure of a Volunteer*, the whole family embraces the departing man, but the soldier's wife, child, and mother are most visible.

These representations of female anguish were countered by recruitment propaganda, which urged women, especially mothers, to face the departures and deaths of loved ones with stoicism. Appeals accompanied all major calls to arms. As volunteers left in August 1792, for example, the newspaper *La feuille villageoise* called upon French women to hold their tears and to show only courage to sons, brothers, and husbands about to depart.[131] Following the February 1793 call for 300,000 new soldiers, the *Journal des débats et des décrets* paired an exhortation to warriors with one to women: "Tender mothers, young wives, inspire the citizens who are dear to you to fight: new Spartan women, far from keeping these men, strike up the hymn to the patrie and prepare their military clothing."[132] The levée en masse inspired further professions of patriotic stoicism. For example, in the "Farewells of a Mother to Her Only Son Included in the New Draft," printed in the newspaper *La vedette* in October 1793, the author declared, "My son, I love you tenderly, but nature knows to silence itself before the patrie, and I will not have the weakness to cry at your departure."[133]

129. Dulaurent, *Le bon père*, 4.
130. Vincent-Buffault, *The History of Tears*.
131. *La feuille villageoise*, no. 46, August 16, 1792, 469–72.
132. *Journal des débats et des décrets*, no. 42, February 23, 1793, 291.
133. *La vedette ou journal du département du Doubs*, no. 76, October 1, 1793, 630.

Perhaps the most influential formulation appeared in the song by Marie-Joseph Chénier, *Song of Departure or the Hymn of War*. In each verse, a representative individual or group incites young men to fight. In one, mothers proclaim, "Do not fear tears from our maternal eyes / Cowardly grief is far from us / Warriors . . . All your days belong to the patrie / She is your mother before us." The song was first performed at a festival in July 1794; it became an anthem for troops going off to war, repeatedly reminding both civilians and combatants of familial support for their service.[134]

STOIC MOTHERS AND CHILD WARRIORS

If both men and women acknowledged the supremacy of the patrie over personal bonds, women's promises to sacrifice their loved ones promised to be particularly powerful. Revolutionaries emphasized one group of women: the mothers of heroic boy warriors. This image reached its apogee in spring 1794 with celebrations for Joseph Bara (or Barra) and Agricol Viala. Bara was a thirteen-year-old killed fighting against counterrevolutionaries in the Vendée. The National Convention mythologized his death, portraying him as affirming his loyalty to the Republic with his last words. Viala also died at age thirteen; the boy reportedly cut a critical cable to a bridge and thwarted royalist enemies in southern France.

While scholars have analyzed many aspects of these boy heroes, they have paid little attention to their mothers.[135] But writers and artists regularly linked the boys' heroic deaths to their mothers' sacrifices.[136] For example, "Hymn to the Eternal" by the citoyenne Cavaillon, first sung at the Festival of the Supreme Being in June 1794, contains a verse by soldiers' mothers. They invoked "the offering and the sacrifice / that mother love makes to the patrie / we give more than life / we give our children." They identified with Bara's and Viala's mothers, promising that, if necessary, they would "endure our tears for our patrie and cover our sons' tombs with flowers."[137]

The boy martyrs lauded as exemplars were anomalous in several respects. The law of July 4, 1792, permitted adolescents as young as sixteen to sign up; Jean-Paul Bertaud has calculated that up to three-quarters of volunteers in 1792 were under twenty-five, and between 10 and 15 percent younger than

134. It debuted on 16 Messidor Year II (July 4, 1794); 18,000 copies were sent to galvanize armies in 1794. Bouzard, *Anthologie du chant militaire français*, 30; and Domine, "Le chant du départ."

135. Among others, see Foissy-Aufrère and Martin, eds., *La mort de Bara;* and Bianchi, ed., *Héros et héroïnes*.

136. Villiers, *Barra, ou la mère républicaine* ; reproduced in Harten and Harten, eds., *Femmes, culture, et révolution*.

137. Harten and Harten, eds., *Femmes, culture, et révolution*, 278.

eighteen.[138] Both Bara and Viala were thirteen—older than the ten they appear in some accounts, but younger than most of their compatriots.[139] The family situation of most boy soldiers was also different, as neither Bara's nor Viala's father was alive.[140] Some boys did enlist on their own or with brothers or comrades, and undoubtedly, some had widowed mothers. But some men brought teenage sons with them, and patriotic engravings celebrated boys who avenged fathers killed in battle.[141]

Bara's and Viala's unusual youth and fatherless status called attention to their relationships with their mothers. Almost all representations of Bara emphasized that he supported his mother with his military pay while he was alive; engravings and prints proclaimed that he was a hero who "provided for his mother and died for his patrie."[142] This proved his virtue; it also made his mother's sacrifice in accepting his death more momentous. But the idea that a boy could support his family through fighting was deceptive.

The prominence of young hero-martyrs and stoic mothers was tied to political developments. Revolutionaries honored "martyrs of liberty" starting in January 1793 with Michel Lepeletier, assassinated after he voted for Louis XVI's death. Many of these martyrs had led controversial lives, especially the most famous one, Jean-Paul Marat. In the intense political struggles of the spring and early summer of 1794, they became increasingly difficult to celebrate. In contrast, boy martyrs represented a devotion to the patrie that had no obvious political agenda; they incarnated both heroism and innocence. Their prominence did not last. While communities would occasionally continue to celebrate local child heroes, boy martyrs would become less visible after Robespierre's fall from power in July 1794.

138. Bertaud, *La révolution armée*, 82–83.

139. Records from soldiers seeking to come home in 1796 and 1797 contain a few dossiers for boys who had enlisted at thirteen, but more often, at fourteen or fifteen. For two who enrolled at thirteen and were allowed to return home in April 1797—Nicolas Moreau and Minet Antoine—see *Procès-verbaux du directoire exécutif*, 1:196, 268. For a nine-year-old, who had joined as a drummer without his parents' consent or prior knowledge and without socks or a hat, AN AF / III / 313 / 64, Pierre Pichou.

140. Hunt, *The Family Romance*, 78.

141. For teenage sons accompanying Parisian gunners, see AN AF / II / 313, dossiers 2486, 2588, and 2589. Related artwork includes the engravings by Charles-Melchior Desfontaine, *L'action du jeune Darrudder tambour âgé de 14 ans est un trait de bravoure et un élan de piété filiale*, and L. F. Labrousse, *Demormand, jeune enfant âgé de 10 ans, tambour dans le bataillon des chasseurs des Ardennes: Non tu ne t'échapperas pas toi le meurtrier de mon père*.

142. Titles include *Bara couronné par la liberté: Ce jeune héros âgé de 13 ans, nourrissoit sa mère sur le produit de sa paye; Joseph Barra: Il nourrissoit sa mère et mourut pour la patrie;* and *Joseph Barra: Citoyen avant l'âge et soldat à treize ans, secourant de sa paye une mère chérie, ce précoce héros mourut pour la patrie, sa cendre au Panthéon repose . . . et vous tyrans apprenez à juger de nous par nos enfants.*

The image of boys supporting their widowed mothers, however, served purposes that resonated long afterward. It played up the patriotism of the entire populace. In turn, the image of mothers who sent their sons to war legitimated the superiority of the mother country and its demands upon its children. All, even those who had the most right to be protected, accepted it.

Conclusion

Many ways that revolutionaries defined, debated, and fought for citizenship would change after 9 Thermidor. So too would strategies for promoting male mobilization and for defining women's relationship to war. But war itself did not end. Civil war in the Vendée would last until March 1796, and international war until 1814–15, with only temporary peace treaties. Contemporaries would continue to struggle with balancing familial responsibilities and rewards with military duty, determining the relative citizenship claims of combatants and civilians, and managing emotions in the face of seemingly endless conflict.

Many early paintings of soldiers' departures were paired with their triumphant return.[143] Le Barbier's *Departure of the Citizen* was followed by the *Return of the Citizen*, joyously captioned, "Finally, tender parents, the heavens bring back / this much desired son / He comes to relieve your labors, your troubles / He will work each day to nourish the patrie / and satisfy nature and love in peace."[144] Moreau similarly followed his sketch of a young man's departure with *The Pleasures of Rural Life: The Young Volunteer Returned to His Family*. All rejoice in the veteran's homecoming. A loyal dog welcomes him, while his wife holds a cap of liberty above his head.[145] In these visions, homecoming is not, as it had been in Greuze's famous prerevolutionary painting *The Father's Curse,* a return too late to save a devastated family, but rather a moment of bucolic joy and revolutionary triumph. Like soldiers themselves, artists imagined that war would be short and glorious: the young son, for example, in Isabey's *Return* looks barely older than in the *Departure*.[146]

In reality, however, if women soldiers were forced to demobilize in the wake of the April 1793 decree, most men who volunteered in 1791 or 1792 or were effectively enlisted in 1793 were still in the troops years later. We turn in the next chapter to efforts by male veterans to return home in the later 1790s as the revolution shifted, but war continued and reconciling familial and military roles appeared increasingly difficult.

143. Mainz, *Days of Glory?*

144. Le Barbier, *Le retour du citoyen* (Collections of the Musée Carnavalet).

145. Jean-Michel Moreau, *Les délices de la vie champêtre: Le jeune volontaire de retour dans sa famille,* 1794–95 (Collections of the Musée de la Révolution française-Domaine de Vizille).

146. Jean-Baptiste Isabey, *Le départ pour l'armée et le retour du soldat* (Collections of the Musée Lorrain, Nancy).

CHAPTER THREE

Bringing Revolutionary Soldiers Home: The Limits of Martial Masculinity

IN JUNE 1797, Hélène Bonat, a young mother living in the department of the Seine Inférieure, made an emotional plea to the government.[1] She begged for her husband to be released from military service, emphasizing her responsibility to him as well as to the nation: "I am a woman and French. I love both my patrie and my husband. I have already proven my love for my country, in leaving my husband at the front for three years; I must now prove the love I have for my husband, in asking for him from this same patrie that he contributed to liberating." Bonat contended further that since their enemies were being forced to accept peace on French terms, her husband was no longer needed to fight.[2]

Veterans themselves made similar pleas. The young Henri Joseph Chevalier insisted that he had done everything in his power to defend France, proclaiming, "I cannot be accused of cowardice or indifference for the happiness of my fellow citizens." He had volunteered at age sixteen. His feet had frozen during a siege; he then received a serious wound to his knee that often made it impossible to walk. Along with recounting his suffering, he too stressed his responsibility to his family; his blacksmith father desperately needed his help.[3]

Chevalier's much older fellow warrior, the fifty-year-old René Ambroise Perot, declared that he had volunteered at the first cry of the patrie, leaving behind his urgent personal interests for the common good. Five years later,

1. Parts of this chapter first appeared as Heuer, "Citizenship, the French Revolution, and the Limits of Martial Masculinity."

2. AN AF / III / 313 / 8, Hélène Bonat.

3. AN AF / III / 313 / 15, Henri Joseph Chevalier.

FIGURE 3.1. C. Les Vernet (artist) and Godfrey (engraver), *Certificate of Permanent Military Discharge*, 1798. Bibliothèque Nationale de France.

that patrie had triumphed over the tyrants who had wanted to destroy it. He longed to give his wife and children the support they begged for, and feared that if he continued to fight, he would not be able to provide for his family even after his demobilization.[4]

These were only a few of some 16,000 petitions beseeching the government in 1796–97. Unlike the women soldiers whose forced demobilization we examined in the previous chapter, these men actively sought to quit the troops; petitioners hoped to see serving soldiers return to their families and those who had received exemptions remain home. Their accounts reveal a familiar story of men who rushed to defend the endangered patrie, leaving behind loved ones to defend the common good. But if boasts of zealous volunteers confirm our vision of soldier-citizens, their attempts to leave military service reveal a far less well-known story, one that challenges any simple equation of individual citizenship, soldiering, and masculinity.

Their stories come from a distinct moment in the Revolution and the wars associated with it, between the recruitment measures of the radical Revolution and the 1798 Jourdan Law on conscription. They represent a specific group:

4. AN AF / III / 313 / 61, René Ambroise Perot.

soldiers who had accepted the demands of the state but wanted to be released from those obligations. Their records also represent a distinct kind of source, shaped by specific laws, conventions of the petition genre, interventions of public writers, and petitioners' guesses about how to appeal to authorities.

Yet these petitions combine stock phrases with vivid accounts of individual experiences, from dramatic stories of escapes by prisoners of war to touching proclamations of love and heartbreak. Formulaic expressions themselves reveal common assumptions, while ruptures with those expressions show alternatives to dominant views.[5] When considered with other records of combatants and their families, they allow us to see the consequences of revolution and war both for soldiers and for those far from the battlefields. They also reveal how citizenship and arms-bearing changed after the radical Revolution, especially as people confronted the unexpected duration of war. Many volunteers, whether boys like Chevalier or older men like Perot, expected to serve only for a short time. They were still under arms years later.

Looking carefully at their petitions allows us to revisit how revolutionaries envisioned the contract between the state and citizens and the place of military service in that contract. Men seeking to return or remain home logically insisted that their duty to fight was limited. But renouncing arms meant articulating their relationship to the state more explicitly than in most contexts, addressing what it meant to volunteer for the nation, how one could acquit patriotic debt, and what sacrifices should be required of both men and women.

By highlighting obligations, rather than rights associated with citizenship, these accounts reveal new ways citizenship was tied to family. If recruitment propaganda sought familial support for men's military service, people trying to bring or keep soldiers home claimed that the nation owed them because of that support. They presented military and civilian service to the nation as intertwined or sequential aspects of citizenship, and as ones that could be shared within families, with one son bearing arms or dying fighting, while another served at home. Women and civilian men also insisted that they had sacrificed to support a soldier's engagement. In their constructions, military service imbricated those at home in relationships with the state and shaped their own claims to citizenship.

Looking at soldiers' hopes for discharge also reveals limits to martial masculinity. Here we return to challenges we touched on in the last chapter, especially the effects of injury on masculinity. The French state promoted the formation of new households to reward and compensate for veterans' injuries, while confronting the possibility that wounds made men unattractive and dependent. Men seeking release from service to come home to existing families

5. For an influential model of analyzing similar sources, see Davis, *Fiction in the Archives*.

similarly struggled to present themselves as too weakened to fight, but still strong enough to be independent citizens. They also promoted alternatives to bearing arms as the defining characteristic of citizens. But demonstrating the social utility of civilians and linking that utility to citizenship meant proving that apparently ordinary domestic labor was essential and addressing the gendered nature of work.

Finally, these sources touch on the history of emotion. Writers emphasized pragmatic concerns, usually asking for a soldier's return to provide for his family, rather than to comfort them or find solace in their arms. But they sometimes presented a man's return as consolation for other losses and invoked strong emotional connections, as with Hélène Bonat's claim that she had to prove her love for her husband. Looking at writers' self-presentations allows us to turn from the prescriptive rhetoric of patriotic sacrifice and emotional control to ways contemporaries recounted their anguish and fortitude.[6] It highlights gendered expectations for expressing emotions, and the possibility that citizen-soldiers should be recognized for both their courage and their sensitivity to suffering.

Taken together, these sources reveal how much ideas of unity or rupture between the "home front" and the worlds of camps and battlefield depended not only on lived experience, but also on the purposes of those describing those experiences. They reveal the pervasiveness of challenges to models of martial masculinity, and a shared belief that veterans should be rewarded for their military service with domestic happiness. Prolonged service both entitled men to that reward and jeopardized their chances of enjoying it.

The Petitioners and Their Pleas

Many men came, or tried to come, home from war after the height of the Revolution. Jean-Paul Bertaud has reckoned that the number of men in the troops dropped from a theoretical total in 1794 of 1.2 million (in reality, closer to 800,000) to 365,000 by October 1797. Alan Forrest similarly estimates that there were 750,000 serving soldiers in 1794, around 400,000 by July 1796, but only 325,000 by late summer 1798.[7] Diminishing numbers were due in part to the government's decision not to engage in widespread new recruitment after 1793. Many men deserted, although authorities hesitated to call attention to the extent of evasion.[8] But the government also oversaw a legal, or semilegal, demobilization, as veterans came home to nurse wounds or recover from illness, tend crops for ailing parents, or otherwise resume civilian lives. Many had received a temporary discharge and sought to secure a permanent

6. Mazeau, "Émotions politiques."

7. Bertaud, *La révolution armée*, 274; Forrest, *The Soldiers*, 82.

8. Forrest, *Conscripts and Deserters*.

release from service. Veterans had few options in seeking to be demobilized. Unless they had become physically incapable of fighting, their best hope was to petition authorities, or to ask parents, spouses, or more rarely, siblings or well-placed connections to petition for them. In 1796 and 1797, thousands beseeched the government.

In asking for release from military service, men and their families rarely questioned military policy or the legitimacy of war. Their accounts are not the most wretched; the truly miserable deserted rather than try for official discharge. Nor do they represent those who weathered war well. By definition, men willing to remain under arms did not petition the government for release. Finally, they do not reflect the experiences of men who had become disconnected from their families during years of service.

The very extent of the archives—about 16,000 petitions, distributed in seventy-seven cartons—makes it difficult to establish statistical information. Selective sampling is also challenging because of the way documents are organized. Cartons are arranged very loosely alphabetically, and by date.[9] Most mix petitions from different kinds of individuals, places, and situations, but there are unpredictable clusters. One carton may include many petitions from students in music and art; another, a group of saddlers, blacksmiths, and other artisans whose skills supported rural communities. Such petitions also appear scattered in other cartons. Finally, eighteenth-century spelling is inconsistent; petitions are occasionally repeated, and supporting material separated from original records.

However, the overall patterns are clear. Petitions cover early 1796 through the summer of 1797. They are geographically mixed, but most come from the Ile-de-France and northern France, especially Normandy. Geographical proximity to Parisian authorities accounts for part of this. There was also a relatively low level of resistance to military service in these regions; soldiers and their families there may have been more willing to try legal avenues for discharge than in areas prone to desertion.[10]

Reflecting the general state of France's economy, the vast majority of petitioners and their families worked the land, and emphasized their role in producing food for the nation. Workers seen as contributing to the war effort, like tanners or millers, or in subsidiary support for agriculture, also petitioned regularly. Those with more unusual professions, ranging from actors to dye manufacturers, and from mathematicians to gravediggers, similarly argued for their utility as civilians.

9. Records are in AN AF / III / 313 / 1 through AF / III / 313 / 77; cartons contain roughly 200 dossiers each. While generally alphabetical, some contain most material from Year IV (1796) and others from Year V (1797).

10. Forrest, *Conscripts and Deserters*, 2. For recruitment in a department that figures frequently in these records, see Crépin, *Révolution et armée nouvelle en Seine-et-Marne* and *Vers l'armée nationale*.

Both men and their families beseeched the government. Fathers of soldiers composed—or had written—many of these letters; their petitions account for 40 to 50 percent of records. A slightly smaller percent were by or for soldiers themselves, especially men who were married, physically incapacitated, or had received exemptions because their civilian work had been deemed essential. Mothers, almost always widows when petitioning separately, were responsible for about 10 percent of petitions; soldiers' wives account for a smaller portion, roughly 5 percent.[11] Other relatives—including siblings, uncles, or grandparents—composed occasional petitions. Employers sometimes sought exemptions for valuable employees, while communities asked for men whose skills were critical for local economies.

In all cases, it was essential that municipal administrations, military officials, or other authorities certify the validity of petitions. Central authorities dismissed requests that lacked corroboration. Where possible, supplicants added supporting material, including marriage or baptismal records—the latter serving as proof of age—reports from health inspectors about the gravity of a veteran's wounds or illness, and records of previous release from service.

Three kinds of situations typically led people to petition for a soldier's discharge. Most often, men were on a temporary leave, usually to recover from injury or illness, sometimes to help with the harvest or deal with legal matters that required their presence. Once home, many discovered a degree of misery that they had not fully understood from a distance. Soldiers' returns reminded parents, wives, and siblings of the benefits of having a veteran home and gave hope that they might be able to turn short-term leaves into permanent discharge.

In other cases, soldiers sought to return from active duty or families tried to bring absent men back, sometimes asking for one of several sons in service. Their requests were usually triggered by specific circumstances, like a serious injury or death at home. It was harder to convince the government to release men who were actively serving, and transport over long distance was expensive; requests promised more success when troops were stationed within France. In many cases, rumors of a general peace precipitated individual requests and reinforced claims that men were no longer required to fight.

The third major category involved men who had received exemptions from service or who believed their discharge was permanent. A measure from November 25, 1795, annulled limited leaves and special exemptions. In some cases, officials arrested men for not rejoining the troops. The government could nonetheless retain men "indispensable for public utility" in their civilian roles.

Petitioners' arguments reflected the legal frameworks in which they hoped to appeal to authorities. This was especially true for those invoking "public utility" or seeking to convince the government that earlier exemptions should

11. This reflected a tradition of widows seeking state support. Fauré, "Doléances, déclarations, et pétitions."

continue. They also reflect the conventions of the genre.[12] It is impossible to tell how much petitioners believed in the rhetoric they used or how intermediaries influenced their accounts. But the very frequency of certain phrases reveals prevailing understandings of the relationships between citizens and the revolutionary state, the nature of citizenship, and the meanings of masculinity and femininity. It also reveals alternatives to those views.

By far the most common story was misery. Economic and emotional sacrifices that seemed tolerable when families believed that a soldier would be gone for a few months ceased to be endurable after years of hardship. This was especially true when a familial situation had changed with the death of a primary breadwinner, illness or the ravages of age, or the loss of crucial resources. But petitioners did not simply recount their woes. They also explained both what they believed they owed the revolutionary nation and what it owed to its citizens.

The Contract between the Nation and Its Citizens

One woman's request for her husband's return encapsulates a common understanding of the nature and limits of revolutionary military service: "His contract with the nation is more than fulfilled. Now the nation should fulfill its [duty] to him."[13] Petitioners rarely set out to theorize their relationships with the state, but in justifying why men should return or remain home, they confronted revolutionary ideas about patriotic duty and mobilized claims about the nation's duties to its members. Even when men asked to be left alone to support their families, they drew on shared assumptions about the mutual obligations of state and citizens.

Many combatants identified themselves as volunteers. They did so for practical reasons, hoping to expedite their demobilization, but their rhetoric presented a vision of citizenship based on finite acts of civic responsibility. Others emphasized the mutability of citizenship. The state might continue to demand further obligations of its citizens, but the nature of those obligations could, and should, change.

SUPPORTING MILITARY FAMILIES

As we have seen, a series of measures promised support for combatants' relatives. Historians have largely analyzed these in relation to an incipient welfare state.[14] Petitioners' requests appear to be the opposite. They asked to be breadwinners for their dependents, not for the state to provide for them or their

12. Fauré, "Doléances, déclarations, et pétitions"; Desan, "Pétitions des femmes"; and Sautel, "Droit de pétition."

13. AN AF / III / 313 / 77, Vidal Bonnefot.

14. C. Jones, *Charity and Bienfaisance*; DiCaprio, *The Origins of the Welfare State*.

FIGURE 3.2. L. Darcis (engraver), after J. B. Isabey, *A Soldier Returns and Is Greeted with Great Affection by His Wife and Child*, 1797. Wellcome Collection.

parents and children. Writers occasionally acknowledged that earlier support for combatants' families had factored into a soldier's decision to volunteer or a family's willingness to consent to his enlistment. They immediately followed this acknowledgment by emphasizing that any promised resources had long been exhausted.[15] The frustration of petitioners who documented the failure of these

15. Among others, three women in the Seine-et-Oise reported that their husbands had volunteered expecting to serve for three months, while their families received 90 livres a month. The payments had stopped, but their husbands were still under arms.

measures suggests why more families did not ask for financial help: the money simply was not there. Funding was inadequate throughout the Revolution, and administrative difficulties made distributing aid challenging. After Thermidor, both the funds and political will to support military families disappeared.[16]

By 1796–97, hyperinflation had further compounded problems. The legislature was unwilling to provide support until collapsing paper currency could be stabilized.[17] Authorities repeatedly sought to forestall mounting complaints. For example, on December 20, 1796, the minister of the interior explained his motives in suspending aid to all military families until the monetary crisis could be resolved, arguing that giving them worthless *assignats* would only be an illusion of help.[18] Families did not abandon hopes of financial support, insisting to the legislature that their situation should be rectified.[19] But many likely calculated that they had better economic odds if they could secure the strong arms of a young man, rather than wait for governmental support that might never materialize.

Petitioners also did not ask for increased pay while serving or after their demobilization. Some may have sought pensions if they succeeded in obtaining a formal release from service. But a June 1793 law made pensions largely contingent on the nature and severity of a veteran's wounds. Men seeking to return to support their families were weakened, but not grievously injured; they did not fit neatly into existing legal categories.

Soldiers' attempts to return home were nonetheless shaped by the history of state support for military families—even as they asked to be independent citizens who sustained their own families. Such legislation provided models for framing petitions. Petitioners often gave their ages, or in the case of soldiers, those of their parents. Noting that men and women were in their sixties or seventies proved their inability to perform heavy manual labor, but it also corresponded to laws that made aid dependent on age. Writers tended to be less precise about children's ages, but assumed that identifying them as young would establish their need.

In most accounts, petitioners made it clear that they were not hoping to better themselves with supplemental income; this was a question of survival. Such cries reflected real desperation. But they also reflected a belief, based on earlier measures, that if individuals wanted the sympathy of the government,

AN AF / III / 313 / 7, Brisson. A father similarly lamented that the aid that a grateful patrie accorded to the indigent fathers and mothers of *défenseurs* had long ceased. AN AF / III / 313 / 3, François Bertin.

16. Forrest, *The French Revolution and the Poor*, 151–52; Clarke, *Commemorating the Dead*, 259–60; and Weens, "Quand la politique d'assistance."

17. Woloch, "A Sacred Debt.'"

18. AN F / 15 / 2835, Le ministre de l'Intérieur aux administrations départementales.

19. Among others, those in Sauveur-sur-Douve complained to the Council of Five Hundred on 4 Vendémiaire Year V (September 25, 1796) that they had not received support for twenty months.

they had to prove that they had no other recourse. More fundamentally, both aid for military families and soldiers' requests to be allowed to support their own families were based on the same premises: those defending the country should be rewarded for their service. The revolutionary state was indebted not only to soldiers, but also to the families behind them. If the state was unable to provide help directly, it could do so by allowing men to fulfill their civic duties as heads of households.

VOLUNTEERING TO BE CITIZEN-SOLDIERS

Many soldiers and their families stressed that they had chosen to serve, sacrificing their own interests for the patrie. They used the word "volunteer" repeatedly and reinforced it with fervent rhetoric. A petition on behalf of the thirty-three-year-old Jean-Pierre Boyer thus declared, "he is not part of any requisition or recruitment and only his goodwill made him abandon his home." Pierre Baratte, who had survived three years as a prisoner of war in Hungary, similarly proclaimed directly that he had "rushed off, on my own initiative, to join the defenders of the patrie in August 1792," adding that "my zeal was so voluntary, so unselfish, that I armed and equipped myself at my own expense."[20] Some reiterated that they had joined up when the government had asked for volunteers, in 1791, or especially, in 1792. Others insisted that they had been too old or too young to be affected by the August 1793 levée en masse, but had still taken up arms.

The frequency with which petitioners emphasized the nature of their service reflects the substantial presence of volunteers in the troops, as well as the obvious hope that volunteers would not have to remain under the force of laws that had not originally compelled them. In some cases, men had been told that they would serve for only a few months—usually three or six—or for a campaign. Some anticipated fighting until an enemy was pacified, often until the civil war in the Vendée ended. Even volunteers who do not seem to have envisaged a specific time period clearly thought that their service would be limited.[21] Most of those who had enlisted at the beginning of the Revolution were still under arms years later.

Volunteers did not see themselves as bound by military discipline, or at least had not anticipated being bound by that discipline. Thomas Hippler has argued that men who had volunteered in 1791 and 1792 defined themselves as citizens rather than military personnel, sometimes even refusing equipment provided by the army for fear of being labeled soldiers.[22] Serving for several

20. AN AF / III / 313 / 9, Jean-Pierre Boyer; AF / III / 313 / 10, Pierre Baratte.

21. For example, one father reported that his son had enlisted at age seventeen, expecting only one campaign, but had already fought two; Caporal Bouret, married with an infirm wife, had anticipated one campaign but fought four. AN AF / III / 313 / 69, Nicolas Robert; AF / III / 313 / 9, Bouret. For volunteers' expectations in 1791, see Forrest, *The Soldiers,* 62.

22. Hippler, "Service militaire et intégration nationale."

years changed their relationship to the military, but it did not prevent them from claiming, or reclaiming, a specific identity as volunteers.

Yet the term "volunteer" needs to be used with care. The rhetoric of revolutionary patriotism described men who were effectively conscripted in August 1793 as volunteers, and some enrolled by the levée en masse adopted the title for themselves. The term was useful both for the state—eager to show that citizens would do their duty without compulsion—and for individuals seeking to delimit their own responsibilities.

Those who could not claim to have volunteered presented themselves, or their relatives, as virtuously obeying the call of the nation. Asserting respect for the law was a wise move in the wake of the Terror. It was also wise when dealing with officials wary of desertion and fraud. But such rhetoric did more: it turned obedience to the laws from an act of submission into a proof of citizenship.

A few petitioners argued that they had been forced to fight. Jean Baptiste Beauvais had been arrested as a suspect during the Terror; enlisting allowed him to recover his liberty. Similarly, Antoine L'Huillier contended that "the reign of the Terror practically compelled him to sign up" to keep his imprisoned father from being treated as a counterrevolutionary. Petitioners occasionally referred to neighbors who had forced them to enlist, presumably because their exemption shifted the burden onto other young men in the community. Pierre François Petit thus complained that "He was assaulted and threatened by the *jeunes gens de la réquisition* of his commune . . . it was thus that he was forced to leave with them."[23]

Such accounts were relatively rare. Even when petitioners complained that they had been coerced into service, the force that had constrained them was not the patrie, but rather the violence of the Terror or men who abused the law. Even those who described being forced into the ranks testified that they had served with honor; Petit, for example, recounted that despite his unwilling enlistment, defending his patrie was a sacred duty. He would have devoted the rest of his days to it if the "voice of nature" was not calling him home. In these accounts, military service appears as patriotic duty fulfilled honorably and enthusiastically. But it was not an unlimited duty.

DEBT, SACRIFICE, AND THE "REWARD" OF NEW DUTIES

Looking more closely at petitioners' rhetoric helps us understand further how they imagined the mutual responsibilities of citizens and their government. Some used an economic rhetoric of debt. They drew on an Enlightenment model that preceded the Revolution, captured by Montesquieu's declaration in

23. AN AF / III / 313 / 4, Jean Baptiste Beauvais; AF / III / 313 / 52, Antoine Jean Baptiste L'Huillier; AF / III / 313 / 64, Pierre François Petit.

his 1748 *Spirit of the Laws* that in being born, "one contracts an immense debt to our country, which can never be discharged."[24] Revolutionary lawmakers had used similar vocabulary in insisting on a civic duty to take up arms; the draft of February 24, 1793, declared that "military service is the debt of all citizens."[25] Yet if petitioners acknowledged that all citizens could be asked to pay this debt, they insisted that it could be discharged. They listed concrete proofs of their civic payments, documenting long service, multiple campaigns, wounds, and harsh treatment as prisoners of war.

A parallel language of sacrifice runs through these documents. The term was broader and more widely used than "debt," and more explicitly covers the economic and emotional costs that civilians shouldered. It was also more voluntary. A contracted debt was an obligation; a sacrifice, a gift. Such rhetoric provided a way of presenting service as a distinct patriotic contribution rather than a lifetime obligation.

Some petitioners mixed languages of reward and obligation, contending that their civic duty changed. Veterans claimed that the state owed them for their services and drew on promises that the government would support their families.[26] Parents and wives advanced similar claims, usually based on their sons' or spouses' military service, rather than their direct contributions to the patrie.[27] Yet they often did not envision this recompense as an actual reward, in the sense of money, romance, or public honor. Instead, it appeared as the opportunity to fulfill another obligation—the duty to family and nature. Clément Huprelle's wife argued that after having helped the patrie, her husband should be allowed to "fly to the aid of a family," while the citoyenne Beauvais proclaimed: "is it not just that after having rescued his patrie, he [André Beauvais] comes to the rescue of his wife and children?"[28] In these formulations, returning home was not abandoning patriotic duty but fulfilling an obligation to aid those who needed it most.

Women were particularly inclined to seize upon the rhetoric of "flying" to aid families. Men more often stressed what they had left behind in their patriotic fervor: fields that remained uncultivated and family members struggling to survive. Petitioners rarely used the word "desertion," but their accounts paralleled those who "abandoned the flag" (a common phrase for those who left the military) and those who abandoned their homes. Soldiers had not deserted their comrades, but they had effectively deserted their families and civilian obligations.

24. Montesquieu, *The Spirit of the Laws*, 60.

25. Duval, *Regards sur la conscription*, 20.

26. AN AF / III / 313 / 4, Louis Bonnet.

27. For an example of a father, AN AF / III / 313 / 5, Nicolas Borsay; a mother, AF / III / 313 / 3, René Beillard; a wife, AF / III / 313 / 9, Marie-Vincent Berthe.

28. AN AF / III / 313 / 41, Clément Michel Huprelle; AF / III / 313 / 6, André Henry Beauvais.

Many of these petitioners thus felt obliged to justify their abdication. The declaration of the forty-five-year-old Charles Brezillon is typical: "His civism alone led him to rush to the defense of the patrie; he abandoned his wife and children without imagining that they would be at the mercy of, and plagued by, misery."[29] Writers explained that they had not considered the consequences of their departures. They had listened only to the voice of the patrie, without reflecting on other responsibilities or the limits to their physical, economic, and emotional resources.[30] But now they could no longer ignore those responsibilities. The reward for their patriotic devotion to the military should be the chance to fulfill duties as civilians.

Citizenship as a Familial Act

Writers also presented family sacrifice as a key part of the contract between individuals and the state. Military service was both a personal duty and something that had to be endorsed by those at home. By the same token, the state was responsible not only to those who fought, but also to those who supported and depended upon combatants.

Parents with multiple sons in the troops often asked for one to return, presenting this as a just division of duty between the state and family. Marie Carcol, the widowed mother of seven children, living in the Côte d'Or, declared, "My other son will continue the profession of arms, and will be even more zealous in the defense of the patrie knowing that his brother will support our unfortunate family."[31] Similarly, the widow Bezancenot, charged with a mentally disabled daughter and with two sons in the military, argued, "I love my patrie, and the patrie must reciprocate: I am its child." She proposed an exchange: "one son will continue to serve the Republic, while the other cultivates my small heritage."[32] Men made analogous arguments, as did the tanner André Aussi, who proclaimed that his wish "has always been to sacrifice in the service of the Republic, but as the support of his father and mother, and with a brother who fights for all. . . . He can best serve the Republic from within as his brother serves it from without."[33]

Those who had bought replacements argued that a substitute would continue to fight even if a son came home. Mentioning replacements could be a dubious strategy for proving patriotism; the levée en masse had treated substitutes as a means for the wealthy to buy their way out of service. The Directorial government would outlaw replacement, legalizing it again only in

29. AN AF / III / 313 / 9, Charles Brezillon.
30. AN AF / III / 313 / 61, Louis Perinet.
31. AN AF / III / 313 / 3, Guillaume Boussu.
32. AN AF / III / 313 / 7, Bezancenot.
33. AN AF / III / 313 / 1, André Aussi.

1799. Petitioners in 1796–97 could, at least theoretically, use the fact that they had purchased replacements as proof of their patriotism—precisely because the sons they had replaced had been subsequently required to fight. Parents thus had provided two or more men for the troops. In this logic, the fact that they had sought to secure a replacement served not as evidence of their wealth or indifference to national welfare, but rather as proof of their sacrifices and desperate need for the men they had tried to keep home.

A few soldiers in 1796–97 argued that they would provide replacements if they were allowed to return. In some cases, local governments seem to have encouraged this policy. For example, one petitioner referred to the administration of the Haute-Loire's decision to demobilize heads of households engaged in agriculture if they found a replacement. Individuals volunteered to act as substitutes or proposed men willing to serve in their stead, like the nineteen-year-old François Fayant, who sought to replace his older brother. Fayant described himself as having the courage, strength, and goodwill necessary to be a soldier. His brother was married, having wed shortly after the levée en masse; he was in poor health, but as a skilled tailor, better placed to help their aged parents.[34]

The Directorial government categorically stated that replacement was not legal, declaring on March 15, 1796, "no cause can legitimate such a faculty, which until now no law has authorized."[35] Rejection did not preclude sympathy. In the brief summaries of arguments for exempting a man from service, officials sometimes noted that a soldier had brothers who continued to serve or who had died at war. They also occasionally acknowledged that families had sent replacements.[36] These notes did not suffice to release men from service but do suggest recognition of the costs to families.

If individuals argued that soldiers had paid their debt or sacrificed to the nation, civilians claimed to have fulfilled their civic duties by sending their loved ones to war or accepting the economic and emotional costs of their absences. They maintained that the state owed them because their male relatives were serving, or had died, in the cause of the patrie.

Petitioners often combined these claims with evidence that they had devoted themselves to supporting the revolutionary nation. In some cases, they chronicled acts of patriotism. As Alan Forrest has observed, women who sought aid in 1792 and 1793 because their husbands were fighting offered proof of their personal civism, noting, for example, that they had taken in an abandoned child

34. AN AF / III / 313 / 29, Elion; AF / III / 313 / 32, François Fayant.

35. *Recueil des actes du Directoire*, 1:811.

36. For example, Jean Dommelier was exempted from military service on 30 Germinal Year V (April 19, 1797) with a note that his mother was a widow, who had given 600 francs to replace her son. AN AF / III / 444, plaquette 2601.

or been wounded while struggling with rebels in the Vendée.[37] Petitioners in 1796 and 1797 similarly added details to establish that they had supported the Revolution; the widow Alagille, for example, reported that she had sold grain to her fellow citizens at the lowest possible price during a famine.[38]

Their narratives also presented military service as inherently involving family. Parents, especially fathers, claimed that they had satisfied their own patriotic debt through their sons.[39] Pierre Richard thus proclaimed, "the Revolution had barely begun when I sacrificed my only son," while Guillaume Lamarre declared that he had been "eager to be useful to his patrie by giving his son."[40] The widow Callory began her request to have one son come home by stressing that "sacrificing one's dearest affections to the patrie is a duty that I have fulfilled for several years."[41] Parents used similar rhetoric when petitioning jointly, like a couple who proclaimed, "when the *patrie en danger* called all her children, we had only one son, then aged twenty, who by his work and good conduct provided for our needs. We did not hesitate to make this sacrifice to the good of our country."[42]

Even when stressing a man's own eagerness to fight, parents, and especially wives, also used the term "consent" to establish their approval, like Clothilde Berthe, who observed that "She could not refuse the entreaties her husband made so that she would consent to allowing him to rush to aid the *patrie en danger*."[43] In such accounts, the sacrifice of a soldier, that of leaving behind the comforts of home to face death on the battlefield, was not his alone. His family chose to send him, or at least agreed to his departure.

The ultimate sacrifice of a child or spouse was his death. Individuals presented these losses as payments to the patrie that should free them from further obligations; they should not be required to send more children to war or accept other sons' continued absence. Philippe Bourdin, for example, asked: "Cannot the sacrifice of one of my children acquit me of the debt that I owe the patrie as a father?"[44]

37. Forrest, *The French Revolution and the Poor*, 151. He notes a Parisian butcher's wife who had taken in an abandoned baby, and a citoyenne with two sons in the army who emphasized that she had lost her husband and herself been wounded in the Vendée. Archives de Police de Paris, AA 59; and AN F / 15 / 2818.

38. AN AF / III / 313 / 2, Jacques Charles Alagille.

39. For example, Nicolas Delamare declared that he had, "in the person of his children, paid the debt that all good citizens owe to their patrie." See AN AF / III / 313 / 25, Jacques Delamare.

40. AN AF / III / 313 / 69, Pierre Richard; AF / III / 313 / 47, Jacques Lamarre. See also AF / III / 313 / 55, veuve Morian.

41. AN AF / III / 313 / 15, Alexandre Callory.

42. AN AF / III / 313 / 50, Lemale.

43. AN AF / III / 313 / 9, Marie Vincent Berthe.

44. AN AF / III / 313 / 6, Philippe Bourdin.

Families also sacrificed economic resources. Such sacrifices were more hidden, but also more ubiquitous. Parents boasted of their pride in their sons' enlistment.[45] Their avowals mixed patriotic enthusiasm with instrumental claims. Regardless of their initial attitudes toward the war, most faced serious hardships with the prolonged absence of a breadwinner, and described themselves as making "sacrifices of all kinds," "true" and "countless" sacrifices. They also documented specific woes, such as crops they could not harvest.[46] This was especially the case when the hardships associated with absent men had been compounded by other demands of the revolutionary state, like horses requisitioned for the war.

Taken together, these accounts reveal that individual military service, the apparent pinnacle of personal male patriotism, depended not only on a man's willingness to place patriotic duty above personal affections but also on his family's sacrifice. Although men and women could articulate this sacrifice differently, all sought to make the state recognize its value. Citizenship was not simply a masculine right or duty, nor was it limited to the individuals who took up arms.

The Limits of Martial Masculinity

If accounts of soldiers' departures and absences emphasized familial sacrifice, veterans' attempts to leave the troops challenged the idea that masculinity, military service, and citizenship were inherently connected. Men who argued that they could not be asked to serve or should be released from service insisted on both their masculinity and their patriotism.

Some claimed that they could not be asked to serve since they had never been capable of doing so. A few directly challenged the idea that the only true citizens were the physically strong. Honoré Mareilly, president of a municipal administration in a small town in the Marne, worried that he would be forced to take up arms. He contended that if the only people who counted as citizens were those robust enough to take up arms, then France, like Sparta, would have to expose sickly children at birth. While such a policy was generally cruel, it was particularly ill suited when modern education had enervated men.[47]

More commonly, however, men portrayed themselves as having exhausted their physical resources. Some had tried to serve, knowing that their health was weak. They had been unable to tolerate military life, as was the case with Jean-Thomas Parisot, who "realized that his goodwill would not suffice to repel the enemies of the Republic."[48] Others presented themselves as having fought as long as they could, like Antoine Barteau, who claimed that he had paid his

45. Examples include AN AF / III / 313 / 41, Gauchet; AF / III / 313 / 47, Letellier; and AF / III / 313 / 3, Boulanger.

46. For a typical case, see AN AF / III / 313 / 55, veuve Morian.

47. AN AF / III / 313 / 55, Honoré Hilaire Mareilly.

48. AN AF / III / 313 / 25, Jean-Thomas Parisot.

debt to his nation with courage, until illness "forced him to retire against his will."[49] Family members adopted similar rhetoric, like Jean-Louis Aubry's parents, who declared that their son "had not tired of harvesting laurels, but . . . saw himself forced, obliged to go from one military hospital to another."[50]

Accounts of debilitating injury were convenient for those seeking to stay or return home. Establishing that one was physically incapable of fighting was often the only way to secure a release from military service. The government thus viewed claims to incapacity with suspicion. They were particularly wary of men who had cut off an index finger to make it impossible to fire a gun, and considered deafness and epilepsy aliments that could easily be faked. Their wariness was warranted; some communities did a lively business in bribing health inspectors.[51]

If claims to physical incapacity were expedient, they were not simple. Petitioners struggled to reconcile accounts of their limitations with a desire to appear virile and independent. They sought to provide convincing proof of their injuries, while boasting of their courage. Many added assurances that they would fight if only their health permitted. As one put it, if "the purest, the most zealous and ardent patriotism sufficed to characterize a good soldier, the citizen Haumont would not hesitate to rush to the front, but goodwill cannot take the place of the physical force and health that he lacks."[52]

As we have seen, recruitment propaganda labeled those who avoided military service as weak, egotistical, and effeminate. Because petitioners could be seen as choosing to leave the ranks, they were at pains to prove that they were neither selfish nor spineless. Some stated repeatedly that they could not be considered cowards.[53] Others claimed that any apparent weakness was not moral, but physical, and itself the result of hard service. Such accounts emphasized both willingness to serve and lack of choice in leaving the military—they were "forced to retire" or "obliged" to quit. Their narratives reversed the emphasis on the agency of those who went to war or sent their sons and husbands, to insist that those who left service were compelled to do so.

HONORABLE WOUNDS, THE MARKS OF VIRILITY?

Injury could not only keep men from fighting, but also prove honor and patriotic virility. The thirty-one-year-old Urbain Guinaudeau thus called attention to "the services, the sacrifices I made in leaving my family, the wounds

49. AN AF / III / 313 / 5, Antoine Barteau.

50. AN AF / III / 313 / 2, Jean-Louis Aubry.

51. On faked injuries and bribery, see Forrest, *The Soldiers* and *Conscripts and Deserters*.

52. AN AF / III / 313 / 41, Haumont.

53. Among others: AN AF / III / 313 / 64, Ambroise Pallu; AF / III / 313 / 15, Hue Henri Chevalier; and AF / III / 313 / 12, Pierre Armand Burirette.

with which I'm covered," while Bachereau proclaimed, "my long services, the fatigues and dangers that I braved, my numerous but honorable wounds that I received in combat; these are my titles in support of my request."[54] Many others made similar declarations.

Soldiers' invocations of their wounds echoed tributes to injured men. In May 1796, the Directorial government celebrated victories in Italy. Plans for festivals called for acknowledging soldiers and their families, including naming combatants' parents, signaling out families who had given the most men to the troops, and presenting palms to those "who had the honor to be wounded fighting" as a testimony to public "gratitude and *sensibilité*."[55] Speakers duly lauded local veterans, listing their injuries and the battles they had fought in and bestowing laurels.[56] In September, the Council of Ancients declared that injured veterans should receive military honors, and that festivals reserve a prominent place for them. The newspaper *Décade philosophique* reflected enthusiastically that "Such measures will form public morals (*mœurs*), and we have a great need of them."[57]

Even as authorities sought to honor men, veterans complained that contemporaries had become indifferent.[58] For example, the military newspaper *Journal des défenseurs de la patrie* lamented in June 1796 that "the souls of misfortune, the cries of innocence and weakness, the sight of a warrior covered with wounds, no longer move people."[59] Such grievances, however, appear rarely in these records. Petitioners hoped that their injuries would in fact move authorities, rather than protesting that their wounds had not done so. More importantly, petitioners were usually not the men recognized in public ceremonies. They were not the most seriously injured. Those who had lost a limb or been blinded had no need to ask to be released from military duty. Instead, these writers walked a fine line between claiming that they were too incapacitated to fight and insisting that they were sufficiently able-bodied to be useful civilians. Even while asking for recognition for their wounds, they promised that they would be able to continue to serve the nation in the future.

54. AN AF / III / 313 / 36, Urbain Guinaudeau; AF / III / 313 / 5, L. Bachereau.

55. On 20 Floréal Year IV (May 9, 1796).

56. For examples, see *Procès-verbal de la fête de la victoire et la reconnaissance* (for Metz); *Procès-verbal de la fête des victoires et la reconnaissance* (for Brussels); and *Discours prononcé à la fête de la reconnaissance* (for Versailles).

57. *Décade philosophique*, no. 1, 10 Vendémiaire Year V (October 1, 1796), 60–61.

58. Jean-Paul Bertaud argues that veterans in the later 1790s resented the indifference of those at home. He draws primarily on complaints about government neglect and lack of financial support. Bertaud, *La révolution armée*, 309.

59. *Journal des défenseurs de la patrie*, no. 50, 22 Prairial Year IV (June 10, 1796), 379. See also Kruse and Thomas, "La formation du discours militariste," 84.

TOO WEAK TO FIGHT, BUT STRONG ENOUGH TO WORK

Parents sometimes longed for the strong bodies of their sons, as did one man who lamented, "I am old, I have no more strength, but I have much work. My son Louis Augustin Benoit is as vigorous as four, and is very necessary to me.... One man more or less in the armies of the Republic can't matter, but [his return] would ensure my happiness and my tranquility."[60] However, most men and their families emphasized not the strength of veterans, but their physical weakness. This was especially the case not when old men dreamed of the help of distant sons, but in the more common scenario of men who had been sent home to heal.

Family members occasionally alluded to the extent to which veterans' aliments required their care. For example, Félicité Dupuis, the wife of Théodore Lefèvre, argued that her husband, a former rifleman, was too debilitated to work, much less undertake military service. She promised that she would do everything in her power to prolong his life.[61] Yet such acknowledgments of veterans' frailty were relatively rare. Petitioners usually wanted to prove men's continued civic value, not their dependence.

To justify permanent release, veterans and their families thus emphasized both their uselessness as warriors and utility as workers. Men and their families sought to prove that they were simultaneously incapable of fighting and capable of providing for the relatives who depended on them. Guillaume Le Roy, a former prisoner of war in Hungary, acknowledged that "his heart still burns with courage and energy ... but his weakened forces make his efforts impotent." He immediately followed by stressing his family's need: "his wife and children, reduced to a hard necessity, clamor urgently for his income and his presence to restore order to his affairs, which have been totally ruined."[62]

Veterans promised to demonstrate such utility by working. Parents, spouses, and siblings also claimed that although a man was impaired, his labor was crucial to their well-being. For example, the father of one cavalry man proclaimed: "I have the most urgent need of his assistance; although he is not strong enough to tolerate the strains of military service, he can be very useful to me in the peaceful labors of agriculture."[63] Such arguments were easiest to make when a property or business was sufficiently large for a veteran to supervise others rather than engage in physical labor, or when a man brought technical expertise rather than brute strength.[64] But parents insisted on their sons' utility even when work was more demanding.

60. AN AF / III / 313 / 6, Louis Auguste Benoit.

61. AN AF / III / 313 / 50, Théodore Lefèvre. Félicité declared that she could neither read nor write, so the formulation is likely that of an intermediary.

62. AN AF / III / 313 / 47, Guillaume Le Roy.

63. AN AF / III / 313 / 3, Pierre Brard.

64. For example, the widow Blondel argued that her son would be more useful doing agricultural work or overseeing others' labor than in the troops, given his infirmities. AN

This emphasis on the labor of weak or injured men corresponds to an implicit calculation that even an injured man in his prime would provide more than he would consume. Families undoubtedly hoped that ailing men would recover, although petitioners rarely mentioned such possibilities, presumably out of fear that if a man healed too quickly, he would be sent back to the front. Emphasizing men's labor was also a strategic appeal. To get out of service, it would suffice to demonstrate physical incapacity. Invoking veterans' value as workers reinforced the possibility that even if authorities did not see aliments as debilitating, they would accept a man's "indispensable utility" to his family.

Petitions thus reveal both the pervasiveness and the limits of martial masculinity. With a few exceptions, they did not challenge virility. Many were eager to prove that they were not cowards, despite their desire to avoid or leave military service; their injuries forced them to stop fighting and proved their valor. But they also insisted on alternate models. Promising to be essential providers both drew on and reinforced a vision of masculine citizenship tied less to physical strength and military prowess than to work and civic generosity.

"Not All Men Can Go to the Army": Citizenship and Social Utility

Defining social utility meant weighing the relative merits of civilians and combatants—and making a case that specific forms of work were valuable. Defenses for civilian labor had appeared throughout the Revolution. One popular play from 1794, Charles Tissot's *The Republican Salpêtriers*, directly addressed the social utility of civilian men. Julien, employed in a workshop producing saltpeter, worries that he has not gone to fight the Austrians. His employer responds that "Everyone cannot join the army. A good republican, who is useful to his country in any form, has always served the patrie well." Instead of contrasting combatants to civilians, the play compared both Julien and Paulin—the real hero, a soldier on a furlough because of injuries—to Cascadet, an aristocratic weakling who complains about blisters within moments of wielding a pickax.[65]

Petitioners similarly argued that good citizens served others, whether they did so as warriors or civilians. As the father of one veteran declared, "every citizen must make himself useful to society."[66] In some cases, writers even used the word "citizen" to refer to civilians, rather than combatants, like one father who

---

AF / III / 313 / 10, veuve Blondel. Sophie Tirel similarly observed that her son was unable to serve because of his health but could be of great use supervising agricultural workers. AF / III / 313 / 74, Simon Tirel.

65. Tissot, *Les salpêtriers républicains*, 9. Debuted 8 Messidor Year II (June 26, 1794).

66. AN AF / III / 313 / 4, Fresnoy Bouchet.

assured authorities, "I am not asking for a coward's rest for my son; instead, after serving his country as a good soldier, he will serve it as a good citizen."[67]

A November 25, 1795, law abolished individual exemptions for service; future exceptions were only for men "indispensable for public utility."[68] Some supplicants twisted the law, presenting it not as a proclamation that the government would make only limited exceptions, but rather as an assurance that the state would exempt those more useful at home than on the battlefield. As one father asserted, "with this law, the government promised to give agriculture and the arts soldiers who are indispensable for them."[69] The term "indispensable" was widespread, but its use in these petitions likely alluded to the decree even when it was not directly invoked.

Petitioners contended that serving their personal interests served the common welfare.[70] This was a logical argument on behalf of combatants who wanted to provide for their families. But it would have been difficult to make only a few years previously; it had been imperative during the radical Revolution to claim that one was placing public good above private gain. Petitioners in 1796–97 were able to associate private and public interest because they presented both as unselfish; in tending their fields or workshops, they were caring for their families and communities.

A FARMER IS AS USEFUL AS A SOLDIER

Tissot's fictional heroes wanted to go to war; making saltpeter for gunpowder was also clearly patriotic. But it was challenging for many real civilians to prove that their work was as essential as defending the patrie. This was especially true when that work involved unspectacular labor in the fields. Most petitioners came from the countryside. To justify their demobilization, they played on the revolutionary government's professed desire to protect agriculture, describing it as "the branch of industry most useful to the state" and the "soul of national prosperity."[71] Those who worked the land were as essential as those who fought

67. AN AF / III / 313 / 12, Victor Beaufils.

68. *Bulletin des lois*, no. 6, law no. 33, Loi qui proroge le délai de l'amnistie accordée par les lois des 10 et 23 thermidor an III et abolis toutes les réquisitions particulières, du 4 frimaire.

69. AN AF / III / 313 / 60, Daniel Nonains.

70. Examples include AN AF / III / 313 / 50, Jean Baptiste Loyren; and the files for Paul Boucher in AF / III / 313 / 3 and AF / III / 313 / 9.

71. AN AF / III / 313 / 64, Mathurin Pestrot; AF / III / 313 / 74, Pierre Tardieux; and AF / III / 313 / 3, Augustin Bertrand. Revolutionaries repeatedly paid tribute to agriculture, beginning with Sieyès's famous "What Is the Third Estate?," which defined agricultural laborers as the first class of citizens sustaining society. The revolutionary calendar also instituted an annual Festival of Agriculture to be celebrated on 10 Messidor (June 28).

for it. As one writer put it, in a version of a common phrase: "A farmer . . . is as useful as a soldier; one defends the patrie, the other nourishes it."[72]

Petitioners argued that fallow land was bad both for families and for the nation. As the widow Hulot declared, "public good requires that fields are cultivated."[73] Such claims corresponded to revolutionary policies that had sought, often ineffectually, to ensure that farmland remained fertile.[74] They also corresponded to real devastation. In places like the Aisne, invading troops had destroyed crops. Even in areas less directly impacted by fighting, the prolonged absence of farmers threatened economic prosperity. Petitioners insisted that forcing farmers to fight undermined their ability to serve their country. As Jean Joseph Marin proclaimed: "he could not abandon the cultivation of his fields without making himself guilty toward his patrie."[75]

Yet the very centrality of agriculture to the revolutionary nation made it difficult to justify demobilizing individual workers. Petitioners thus reminded officials that farming required specialized knowledge. To rebut claims that sons or husbands could be replaced in the fields, parents (and less often, wives) argued that hired laborers were prohibitively expensive—and impossible to find. Men who worked for wages also did not have the same interest as those who owned the land or depended on it.[76]

People in other professions made similar claims. As one shopkeeper declared, "It's also serving one's country to use all one's ability and energy to support commerce," while a miller defined his trade as an "important object of public utility."[77] Individuals also insisted on the critical nature of their work for immediate communities; saddlers, blacksmiths, and veterinarians were particularly likely to play up local need for their skills.

Farmers could be very specific in describing their holdings, the crops they grew, and the animals they raised. In contrast, they invoked the utility of agriculture in generic terms, downplaying social distinctions. Heads of large farms or businesses argued that they served broad public interests, by employing many people or producing food for the nation.[78] There were practical reasons for exempting such men, and the government sometimes responded favorably

72. AN AF / III / 313 / 2, Edme-Jean Arnaud.

73. AN AF / III / 313 / 41, Geneviève Hulot; and AF / III / 313 / 50, François Lemaire.

74. For example, a September 1793 measure required municipalities to designate individuals to farm land belonging to men under arms. My thanks to Hannah Callaway for pointing out this law.

75. AN AF / III / 313 / 55, Jean Joseph Marin.

76. For an example of claims to specialized knowledge, see AN AF / III / 313 / 50, Nicolas Legroux.

77. AN AF / III / 313 / 1, Jacques François Astier, and Aubert.

78. The government often exempted such men, including Antoine Minel, a glass manufacturer in Alsace who employed 120 citizens, and Charles Adeline, who wanted his twin sons home to maintain a cotton manufacture that employed 150 people. AN AF / III / 313 / 55, Antoine Minel; AF / III / 313 / 2, Marin and François Adeline.

to their arguments. But a policy of exempting the relatively prosperous jarred with the ideals of revolutionary equality and universal military service.

WOMEN, MEN, AND ECONOMIC CITIZENSHIP

Petitions indirectly testify to the importance of women's economic activities. In some cases, women were running significant businesses before the Revolution; like male business owners, they petitioned to retain workers. For example, Marie Paignon, who ran a large cloth factory in northeastern France, sought to bring home a man she trained who could speak Spanish, Italian, and German, and was equipped to handle her operations abroad; his continued absence would mean that she would have to abandon commerce with Spain.[79] In other cases, however, women were thrust into roles they were unprepared for, like a nineteen-year-old girl trying to manage a two-hundred-person transport business in the absence of male relatives.[80]

Petitioners also alluded to the essential economic contributions of women when familial survival was precarious, usually when those contributions had ceased. The parents of Claude Bailliat noted that they had raised fourteen children and had four daughters at home. The only one capable of working in the fields had become terminally ill. François Rousiller similarly relied on his daughter, until she broke her leg; the blacksmith Jean-Louis Bontemps reported that he had counted on his daughter's assistance for big projects, but she had just married.[81] In other cases, petitioners noted that their daughters' labor no longer sufficed to offset their own infirmities; Louis Renou, for example, had a daughter "who shared with him his sorrows and the sweat [of their labors]," but he had become too weak to farm even with her help.[82]

It was a given that women would work. Governments did not want to support soldiers' wives unless they were truly unable to provide for themselves. Revolutionaries also imagined that women would make up for absent men. *The Good Mother*, a discourse pronounced at a Festival of Reason in December 1793, is typical; it depicted a mother with four children: one son and three daughters. Both her husband and her son—aged sixteen—leave to defend the patrie. She frets about what will happen if her husband dies but is assured that her daughters can work: Adèle will paint, Justine sew, and Pauline cultivate the fields. The discourse reflected the view of a Parisian, not a farmer, but it suggests that women could step in for men who had taken up arms.[83] In certain circumstances, women's labor promised to secure them rights; Katie

79. AN AF / III / 313 / 20, Marie Paignon Cavillier.

80. AN AF / III / 313 / 3, Jean Bataille.

81. AN AF / III / 313 / 3, Claude Bailliat and Jean-Louis Bontemps; AN AF / III / 313 / 69, François Rousiller.

82. AN AF / III / 313 / 69, Louis Renou.

83. Dulaurent, *La bonne mère*. He also argued that laws had banned women from political assemblies, but they had honorable functions in inspiring courage.

Jarvis has argued that the Dames des Halles, the women who provided basic foodstuffs for Paris, believed that they had earned citizenship through their economic contributions.[84]

At the same time, petitions downplayed women's economic power. This is partly the nature of the sources; women who were able to run a business successfully or sustain a farm were less likely to want to bring soldiers home. Petitioners had a vested interest in showing that women could not operate independently. Pierre Balde claimed that his widowed mother "could never tolerate the weight of this burden [of running his farm], lacking knowledge of agriculture," while Guy Louis declared that "the profession of blacksmith cannot be exercised by a woman; this profession requires care, labor, and knowledge that only a man who has continually exercised it is capable of."[85] Women themselves pleaded ignorance of key aspects of their husbands' work. Dorothée Karcher, for example, claimed she wanted her husband home because she knew nothing of his profession as a tanner.[86]

Such claims reflect real differences in training, skills, and expectations between men and women. They reveal hidden costs of war, including challenges women faced when they lost intermediaries to handle business transactions and critical tasks. Women were more likely to be illiterate than men, although their very recourse to petitions suggests that they were able to find help with writing.[87] Writers' rhetoric also associated work (especially skilled work), citizenship, and masculinity. The model of a male breadwinner would be reinforced by industrialization, but these records suggest ways it could also emerge as a counter to a model of masculinity defined by military service.

"Suffering in Silence"? Citizenship, Gender, and Emotion

If petitions reveal contemporary attitudes toward work, citizenship, and gender, they also reframe our understanding of the history of emotion. Hélène Bonat was unusual in insisting that she had to prove her love for her husband. Petitioners rarely used the word "love," except to assert their relationship to the patrie, liberty, or the Revolution itself. But they drew on other expressions of sentiment and suffering. They simultaneously insisted on their stoic

84. Jarvis, *Politics in the Marketplace*.

85. AN AF / III / 313 / 4, Pierre Balde; AF / III / 313 / 36, Guy Louis.

86. AN AF / III / 313 / 9, Jérémie Brika. In contrast, a widow in Calvados had been running her husband's tanning business successfully but needed her son's help to continue. AF / III / 313 / 1, Marie Augerville.

87. Some used their illiteracy as an argument for their need. The widow Marchand argued that because she could not read or write, she could not sustain her business as a butcher without her son's help, while a seventy-year-old miller asked for her literate grandson's return; she had trusted a *homme de confiance*, but the man had died. AN AF / III / 313 / 55, Marchand; and AF / III / 313 / 4, Jean Bouvin.

patriotism and used emotional narratives to make claims on the state. Both men and women negotiated a careful line between lamenting their sorrows and showing their acceptance of the demands of the revolutionary state, but petitioners more readily ascribed tears to women, while women were more likely to appeal to officials' humanity.

Petitioners boasted of their stoic silence. François Ory, the father of eleven children, claimed, "I silenced my needs, I silenced nature, during the three years that my son fought, I silenced myself."[88] Similarly, a petition on behalf of the widow Benoist, a farmer in the Seine-et-Marne, reported that "Like these ancient Romans, she will await your decision in silence, hoping that it will conform to her wishes. But if the needs of the patrie order otherwise, she will be quiet and die."[89] Such arguments foregrounded writers' willingness to bear personal hardships for the good of all. Scholars have called attention to stoicism as a model for educated elites during the Revolution.[90] These petitions show how much ideals of patriotic restraint could resonate beyond elites.

Petitioners, however, had to justify why, if patriotism required emotional fortitude, they were describing their woes. A few explained that their circumstances had changed; Ory recounted that his oldest son was convalescing with him and could provide urgently needed assistance. Most emphasized that national circumstances had changed, making their continued silence unnecessary. As the petition of the widowed mother of Quentin Rochard thus declared, "while the patrie was in danger, [she] maintained a profound silence and bemoaned in secret the absence of her son." Imminent victory allowed her to break her silence.[91] Such arguments positioned writers as patriotically stoic, while allowing them to enumerate their hardships.

Individual claims need to be regarded with caution. Intermediaries likely imposed the rhetoric of patient endurance on petitioners. The petitions for Rochard and Benoist, for example, note that the widows could not sign their names, while Benoist's promise to be "quiet or die" appears in a petition for another woman in the same department.[92] Yet the prevalence of such rhetoric suggests that even if individuals did not themselves accept hardship without complaining, they were expected to do so.

The tension between presenting suffering and emphasizing endurance is also suggested in how petitioners related the loss of a son—or more rarely, a brother or husband. They were more likely to note it as a qualification for exemption than to dwell on grief, focusing on the economic consequences that would follow if a surviving male relative could not return home. But the way writers physically

88. AN AF / III / 313 / 60, François Ory.

89. AN AF / III / 313 / 3, Etienne Benoist.

90. Outram, *The Body and the French Revolution*; Mazeau, "Émotions politiques."

91. AN AF / III / 313 / 69, Quentin Rochard.

92. AN AF / III / 313 / 4, François César Boulange.

underlined or capitalized references to their losses suggests hidden emotions.[93] Hints of emotional toil show through elsewhere. For example, Nicolas Espagnol, the father of eight children—four girls and four boys—presented a narrative of desolation. Two of his sons had died in battle. He had no news of his youngest, who had volunteered at age sixteen, since the battle of Quesnoy in September 1793. Espagnol concluded, "doubtless he perished in some skirmish, where his young courage hid danger from him, allowing him only to see glory, as we have had no news of him since that episode." He petitioned for the return of his remaining son with the "anxiousness of a father who only has one son left, as necessary to his affection as to his household."[94]

If fathers sometimes acknowledged their sorrows, both men and women most often attributed grief to women, especially mothers.[95] Pierre Brochet's petition is typical: he related the consequences of his son's death for himself, but focused on his wife's distress: "The memory of this cruel event made my wife weep endlessly; it would dig our grave, if the hope of seeing the one son who remains did not strengthen our exhausted courage."[96] Emotional pain appears as the cause of death of several women. One petition recounted, "The mother of Edme Jacques Bonnard died of the sorrow of seeing herself separated from her son." The citoyenne Bataille similarly related that her mother's "loss of her two sons to whom she was closely attached, combined with her great troubles, led her to succumb."[97] Physical strain compounded emotional anguish, as in the case of Jacques Castels, who reported he had sent four sons to war without complaint. Two died gloriously; the others returned in such bad state that his wife nursed them day and night for six months. She then died of exhaustion and grief.[98]

Such accounts testified to the real costs of the revolutionary wars, but also appealed to the sensitivity of administrators. They beseeched authorities "on behalf of suffering humanity," framing their needs as part of a wider good. While both men and women employed similar pleas, women were especially likely to entreat authorities. As one woman put it, "you are humane and generous; all good republicans are; I am sure that my deplorable situation will interest you, and my tears and laments will reach the delicacy of your spirit and you will be touched by my misfortunes."[99]

93. Including AN AF / III / 313 / 6, Pierre Bataille; AF / III / 313 / 55, Julien Menard; and AF / III / 313 / 64, Jean-Louis Polbot.

94. AN AF / III / 313 / 50, Nicolas Espagnol.

95. "The tears of his mother" and "my tears and the cries and tears of his children," AN AF / III / 313 / 1, Michel Abonnel and François Aubry; "the tears torn from me by the death of my husband," AF / III / 313 / 29, Nicolas Enaux.

96. AN AF / III / 313 / 6, Pierre Brochet.

97. AN AF / III / 313 / 5, Edme Jacques Bonnard; AF / III / 313 / 3, Jean Bataille.

98. AN AF / III / 313 / 20, Jacques Castels.

99. AN AF / III / 313 / 1, Marie François Fournier, femme Aubin.

Associating anguish with women appealed to officials' duty to intervene on behalf of the needy. It may seem at odds with recruitment propaganda, which portrayed women as restraining tears to send men off to war. These petitions show how women themselves, or at least those writing on their behalf, both claimed stoicism and emphasized the depth of their sorrow. If women were supposed to be particularly resolute in sacrificing their sons, they were also particularly deserving of aid.

Being a good citizen could also mean responding to others' trauma. Veterans emphasized their anguish in seeing loved ones suffer. The twenty-three-year-old Jacques David declared, "it is painful for a sensitive child to see himself far from a father and mother who subsist on his labor,"[100] while the volunteer Pierre Audebert identified himself "as good a son and brother as he is a soldier" and described the misery of his widowed mother and younger siblings as a "spectacle that ulcerated his sensitive soul."[101]

The idea that a good citizen had a duty to respond to others' needs reflected both anguish and strategic entreaty. It also reflected the widespread understanding of citizenship as civic generosity. As a character in one 1793 play proclaimed, "A true republican is sensitive to the sufferings of others."[102] These views persisted in the later Revolution, even as political relations shifted. A good citizen—even a good soldier—was not one who was hardened by the battlefield but one who responded to human need.

The idea that a soldier should be capable of compassion is not unique to France or the Revolution. Among other cases, Christy Pichichero has shown the power of *sensibilité* in the eighteenth-century French military, while Holly Fumeaux has argued that writing on the Crimean War depicted British combatants with remarkable capacities for tenderness.[103] Such claims coexisted with strategies for dehumanizing enemies, and fears that soldiers would become soft.[104] But ideals of compassionate soldiers were particularly powerful in the French Revolution. Accounts of devoted family men were both instrumental and propagandistic; they disguised the brutality of war, and linked soldiers to other citizens.

Granting Exemptions

The number of pleas in 1796–97 overwhelmed authorities. In some cases, officials scrawled a note that the soldier was to be exempted or had been given "provisional authorization." More rarely, authorities marked a petition as

100. AN AF / III / 313 / 25, Jacques David.

101. AN AF / III / 313 / 2, Pierre Audebert.

102. Rézicourt, *Les vrais sans-culottes*, 4.

103. Pichichero, *The Military Enlightenment*; Fumeaux, *Military Men of Feeling*.

104. Philip Shaw has emphasized fears in Britain that soldiers would overidentify with suffering, and not fight vigorously; similar fears plagued French officials. Shaw, "Longing for Home."

"refused." They often struggled simply to organize records. Files contain associated tables roughly organized by date, rather than name or category. The brief summaries accompanying a few petitions hint at reasons for denying individual requests—especially the possibility of fraud—but authorities rarely explained rejections. Many petitions contain no records of what happened; we are left to guess individuals' fates.[105]

But responses do reveal patterns. Two categories were likely to be exempted because of their age and familial status: married men and youth. The Directorial government concluded that marriage should not exempt *réquisitionnaires*, but quietly allowed many married men, especially those with children, to remain with their families. It also allowed men who had joined the troops as teenagers to return home. Both groups offered standard arguments for their release—including their status as volunteers, their physically weakened state (boys and older men had less stamina than men in their twenties), and their responsibilities to their families and their communities. They also made specific arguments based on their age and social positions. Their discharge reflects concern with military efficiency. It also suggests an emerging redefinition of a soldier as a young, but fully adult, man, whose family responsibility should come only after his military service.

A HUSBAND AND A SOLDIER?

The question of whether married men, especially volunteers with dependent children, should be allowed to leave the troops had haunted authorities since war began. In a few cases, revolutionary governments had brought home heads of households; most notably, the Thermidorian Convention allowed Parisian gunners to return if their wives and children needed them.[106] Some individuals called for blanket exemptions, like M. Févert in Lille, who asked in May 1796 that all men who had established households be allowed to return, with a new requisition for single eighteen- to twenty-five-year-old men.[107]

The government was wary of exempting married men. On March 15, 1796, the Directoire exécutif considered circumstances that might release citizens

105. AN AF / III* / 270 and 271. The most frequent commentator was Lazare Carnot. A member of the Committee of Public Safety starting in August 1793, he became minister of war and commander in chief of the French armies and was a driving force behind the levée en masse. He was one of the five directors from 1795 until the coup of 18 Fructidor Year V (September 4, 1797), when he was exiled. He subsequently returned to France and was appointed minister of war in 1800.

106. A decree from 25 Brumaire Year III (November 15, 1794) permitted some married gunners in Parisian corps to be discharged. AN AF / II / 312 and 313. Most were artisans and small shopkeepers in their thirties and forties, a different milieu than the predominately rural world that dominated military recruitment.

107. AN AF / III / 144B, dossier 682, pièce 43.

who had been subject to enlistment in 1793, including those who married after August 23, 1793. They concluded that "marriage should not be a cause for an exemption since, even leaving aside the great number of fathers in the ranks of *défenseurs de la patrie*, a law of March 9, 1793, allows all soldiers to marry without the approval of their superiors."[108]

Yet the government quietly, but systematically, released individual married men from serving, often noting if a man had children or had married on the faith of an earlier exemption or discharge. On May 23, 1797, the Directoire wrote to the minister of war, observing that while peace appeared imminent, victory could be ensured only by maintaining the strength of the troops. The minister should thus avoid granting discharges. But it would be possible to "grant provisional leave to the class of married soldiers, whose presence is more necessary than any others to their families."[109]

The "class of married soldiers" actually included two groups: men, often in their thirties and forties, who had volunteered to fight; and those who had wed after the levée en masse in August 1793. In many cases, they had been granted exemptions or discharges that they believed (or at least hoped) to be permanent and had married on the strength of those releases. The government was more willing to exempt older volunteers than recently married recruits. This was partly military efficacy. Older men were less likely to have the strength of their younger counterparts; they were also likely to have more dependent children. It was, too, a question of trust. Authorities doubted the validity of recent unions, especially those that had taken place shortly after the law of August 23 or its promulgation on September 7, 1793; as we have seen, they had reason to be suspicious.

Petitioners sometimes voiced an understanding of these suspicions. Marie Fournier regretted that she and her husband had been married a day after the promulgation of the law, which was published locally on September 8; they wed on the 9th. She understood that she might not be able to get her husband home for good, but longed for a visit: "Not having the satisfaction of seeing her husband for a minute since his departure feels like a century to her, while she observes not with chagrin but with envy other volunteers obtain permission to see their families."[110]

Other families had postponed marriages until they were confident that a man would not be called up or called to serve again. This was particularly true for professions that had been exempt from military service under previous dispositions, like tanners and millers. Women recounted waiting to wed until they had verified that their husbands would not be forced to abandon them. For example, a young woman who had been married for a year and was eight

108. *Recueil des actes du Directoire*, 1:811.
109. AN AF / III / 450, dossier 2660.
110. AN AF / III / 313 / 1, Nicolas Aubin.

months pregnant petitioned for her husband, who ran a mill in the department of the Seine Inférieure. She had consented to their alliance only after local administrators verified that millers would not be required to fight. But François Boucher was now being hassled to leave, and his wife was afraid that the strain of managing without him would harm her unborn child.[111]

Authorities did periodically grant exemptions for the recently married. They did not dismiss the possibility that such marriages were genuine—or that men had shouldered responsibilities as a result—but required extra proof. While increasingly leery of married men within the troops, they were also leery of men whose marriages might exempt them from their military duty as citizens.

BOY SOLDIERS REVISITED

If married men formed one special category in the troops, youth formed another. Between 10 and 15 percent of volunteers in 1792 were younger than eighteen.[112] The law permitted adolescents as young as sixteen to sign up. At least a third of youths seeking military discharge during the Directory had enlisted at a younger age, fifteen or more rarely fourteen or thirteen—and in at least one case, nine.[113]

Boys had been part of the army before the Revolution. Beginning in 1786, French armies adopted a system of *enfants de troupe*. Armies incorporated some soldiers' sons; boys followed in the camps, and were trained in useful skills, particularly as musicians and craftsmen.[114] The boy soldiers Joseph Bara and Agricol Viala celebrated during the radical Revolution were unusually young and received extraordinary attention, but they were not alone. Records of petitions for Parisian gunners seeking to leave military service in late 1794 reveal fathers who had taken their teenage sons with them. Among others, Armant, the father of fifteen children, had taken his fourteen-year-old, while Pierre Lafond, aged forty-six, had brought his thirteen-year-old son "in order to inculcate him with the love of his patrie and liberty."[115] Other boys who enrolled as teenagers left with their brothers or comrades.

111. AN AF / III / 313 / 10, François Boucher.

112. Bertaud, *La révolution armée*, 82–83.

113. I found 10 fifteen-year-olds and 5 fourteen-year-olds out of 44 cases. At least two boys who had enrolled at thirteen received exemptions in April 1797: Nicolas Moreau and Minet Antoine, both of Paris. *Procès-verbaux du directoire exécutif*, 1:196, 268. For a nine-year-old, who had run off without his parents' consent or prior knowledge and without socks or a hat, see AN AF / III / 313 / 64, Pierre Pichou.

114. Cardoza, "'These Unfortunate Children'" and "Stepchildren of the State."

115. AN AF / II / 313, dossiers 2589 (Armant) and 2588 (Lafond). The shoemaker Benoit Heriné had similarly brought his thirteen-year-old son with him, leaving behind his wife and six other children; AF / II / 313, dossier 2486.

Asking for the return of young soldiers required special strategies, as parents sought to establish respect for their sons' bravery while contending that boys were different from adult recruits. Parents emphasized that teenage soldiers, like volunteers generally, had not been required to fight—they were too young to be enlisted—but had chosen to defend their patrie. Yet they also argued that boys had not been sufficiently independent to have made that choice freely. Writers sometimes played on technicalities. Joseph Robert, for example, argued that he had left at sixteen without his widowed mother's knowledge. As a minor, he had needed her permission to enlist. It seems unlikely that he would defer to his mother's authority after having been at war for several years, but he hoped that invoking her lack of consent would allow him to return home.[116]

Others argued that the boys' prospects as useful citizens placed them in a special category. Some parents begged to launch their sons in a good career. Boys who could be spared in their early teens were now at an age where it was important to begin working professionally. These were rarely the agricultural laborers who dominated the army. Instead, writers invoked relatively skilled positions, like those in the postal service, working as weavers (in at least one case, at the prestigious Gobelins factory), or in the cloth trades. Petitioners still argued less for the benefit of specialized training for individuals than for young men's utility to their families and their country. One father thus acknowledged that "I know that my son belongs more to the patrie than to me . . . but [he is] a child who enrolled at sixteen, who has fought for four years . . . it is urgent that a young child born to a poor father take up some profession that will make him still useful to his *pays* but also put him in a position to provide for his family's needs."[117]

A disproportionate number of young veterans—about a quarter of the cases I have identified—seem to have been prisoners of war. Contemporary documents do not explain why, but they were likely less able to escape or more likely to be captured than killed. As with many former prisoners of war, their discharge was motivated less by the fact that they had been imprisoned than the damage that imprisonment had done to their health.[118]

The most common call for releasing youth was their inability to tolerate the "fatigue of war."[119] Boys did not have the stamina to sustain the hardships of military service. Such claims corresponded to the general discharge of those incapable of serving, at least when authorities testified to their

116. AN AF / III / 313 / 69, Joseph Robert.

117. AN AF / III / 313 / 10, Vincent Baget.

118. On the effects of imprisonment on young men, see AN AF / III / 313 / 3, René Beillard; and AF / III / 313 / 64, François Pascal.

119. Petitions for teenagers who had joined up at fifteen and sixteen include AN AF / III / 313 / 36, Gabriel Gros; and AF / III / 313 / 55, Toussaint Maigret.

incapacity. Invoking physical strain also provided a reason for releasing young men without questioning their patriotism.

The number of teenagers in the army diminished substantially in the later 1790s, as the government allowed many to return and made it more difficult for others to volunteer. Boys remained part of the military; the system of enfants de troupe continued into the nineteenth century, and a few young men found their way into the ranks throughout the Napoleonic Empire. These men, however, were anomalies. The Jourdan Law, which instituted conscription, would aim at men from age twenty to twenty-five. It welcomed volunteers but required them to be over eighteen; some boys who tried to volunteer would be conspicuously turned away in 1799.

Exemptions for teenagers thus corresponded both to their unquestionable status as volunteers—too young to have been compelled to fight—and to the damage that war, often accompanied by a stint as prisoners of war, had wreaked on their health. Ideal soldier-citizens were to be virile and young, but adult, men. To the extent to which the armies of the early Revolution had experimented with creating troops that included boys and fathers, those experiments largely ended during the Directory.

This change represents a particular view of the family. Many of the arguments that justified the demobilization of heads of families—including the need for able-bodied men to provide for dependents—could apply to young men with elderly parents. Officials were sympathetic to individual cases. They nonetheless increasingly defined the familial duties of citizens as those of fathers rather than the filial obligations of sons.

Soldiers vs. Civilians?

A few petitioners complained that more was being asked of them than of others. After five years of fighting, the volunteer Vidal-Bonnefot returned on a temporary leave to discover his wife and four children sleeping on straw, exposed to the elements. He complained about their situation, as did his wife, who contended that twenty lazy men in her commune had been discharged under the pretext that they were needed for agriculture or the arts. She begged authorities to ignore their specious pleas and listen instead to the plaintive voice of the poor.[120]

Yet if this couple were resentful of their fate, most writers expressed little bitterness about unequal burdens of service. Such acceptance of the trials of war and separation may appear surprising, given the extent of resistance to recruitment. Because these records insisted on the need for veterans to return, they downplayed tensions between the home front and battlefront. They did not touch on the problems of transforming veterans back into peaceful workers

120. AN AF / III / 313 / 77, Vidal-Bonnefot.

and supportive husbands, fathers, or sons. Petitions also rarely addressed conflicts caused by soldiers' long absences, including disputes over land, business affairs, and marital strife. The same emphasis on civic usefulness that led men and women to acknowledge military service as necessary and define reward as the opportunity to fulfill familial obligations led to a relative absence of complaints about conflicts within families.

Other sources not only revealed such conflicts, but also mobilized them to make political claims. Their complaints reflect a "malaise" that Bertaud and Kruse and Thomas have diagnosed, in which combatants in the later 1790s resented a civilian population they saw as indifferent to their sufferings.[121] Military men sometimes framed that selfishness in familial terms. Two cases illustrate the range of their complaints. In conflicts over inheritance law in late 1795, younger sons protested that their older brothers profited at home while they risked their lives. Legislators seeking to change marriage law in 1797 invoked soldiers whose wives pushed for divorce in their absence. Both argued that civilians were not engaged in a common national struggle but were preoccupied with their own interests.

BROTHERS VS. BROTHERS

Men could return home to find that arrangements were far less satisfying than they had anticipated. The law of January 6, 1794 (17 Nivôse Year II) was especially controversial, as it guaranteed all siblings equal shares of an inheritance and empowered sisters and younger sons at the expense of their older brothers. It also contained a retroactive clause to July 14, 1789. In September 1795, the legislature maintained the law, but debated overturning the clause.

By 1795, there was a strong backlash against women's equal inheritance, including the role of the Nivôse law in establishing their rights.[122] Critics of the law derided women as quintessential civilians who profited at the expense of soldiers; they were lazy, selfish, and indifferent to their brothers' sufferings. As petitioners in La Manche put it, "our brave defenders, after having bought with their blood the most glorious peace, will return to find that the house and the bed they counted on to refresh them after their fatigues, and the field that would have nourished them, has become the share of their sisters . . . who have enriched themselves while their brothers were at the front."[123] In this logic, women were stealing the rewards owed to those who had sacrificed to protect them.

121. Bertaud, *La révolution armée*; Kruse and Thomas, "La formation du discours militariste."

122. Desan, "'War between Brothers and Sisters'" and *The Family on Trial.*

123. *Extrait des réclamations du département de la Manche,* 16–17.

The most common complaint made by soldiers, however, was not against sisters but against their older brothers. Here combatants often sought to defend, rather than overturn, the retroactive clause. Younger sons or *cadets* were less likely to have been married and more likely to have volunteered or been incorporated in the levée en masse than their older siblings. They protested the general inequity of privileging older sons and the specific unfairness of disinheriting men away from home defending the common good.

The belief that young men hesitated to join the troops for fear of losing claims to familial property had been one motive in changing inheritance law. On March 7, 1793, the deputy Pierre Philippeaux declared to the tribune, "There are a hundred thousand *cadets* awaiting this law to rush to arms, but the fear of being reduced to misery by parents who would disinherit them prevents them from leaving."[124] The legislature subsequently voted to make it impossible to disinherit a child.

Soldiers in 1795 worried that this principle would be overturned, at least in its retroactive form. They claimed that older siblings had abused the system, profiting while they risked their lives. Those from Caux (in the Hérault, in southern France) complained that their siblings had rushed to arrange marriages simply to conserve their rights. The *cadets de famille* in Riom (in Auvergne, in central France) claimed that their older brothers, believing that they would dishonor themselves by fighting, had purchased false proofs of injuries. The anonymous authors of *The Great Conspiracy of Older Sons against Younger Ones* portrayed firstborn sons as whining that their hands were too delicate to fight, and hypocritically sending their siblings off to war with touching farewells—and then plotting against them.[125]

Younger siblings also argued that it was only knowing that an inheritance awaited "at the end of their glorious efforts" that gave them a "perspective that compensates in advance for the fatigues of war." Losing the hope of just rewards would destroy them. As a group in Saint-Chély (in Lozère, southern France) demanded to know, "What will become of those who, penniless and possibly maimed, return home after having sacrificed their best years to the public? Do you want to make them regret their sacrifices?"[126]

The legislature ultimately annulled the retroactive clause on September 5, 1795, but did not change the essence of the Convention's inheritance laws.[127] The protests of these aggrieved younger brothers matter less for the change

124. *AP*, 59:681, 7 mars 1793.

125. AN D / III / 338, Les cadets volontaires de la 76eme 1/2 brigade, and Les cadets de famille à la convention nationale (Riom, département du Puy de Dôme); *Grande conspiration des ainés de famille.*

126. AN D / III / 338, Saint-Chély, 8 prairial an 3.

127. They remained largely unchanged until a March 25, 1800, law authorized parents to add a "disposable portion" to a favored child's share of inheritance. The Civil Code later enshrined the principle. P. Jones, *Peasantry in the French Revolution*, 252.

they inspired than for how they positioned themselves. Rather than emphasizing shared sacrifice between soldiers and their suffering relatives, they contrasted the generous bravery and legitimate expectations of those who took up arms to the selfish indifference of their siblings.

WIVES VS. HUSBANDS

A few petitioners in 1796 and 1797 argued that they needed to come home to deal with wayward wives. Joseph Allemand insisted that he had to return to Lyon. He had volunteered in August 1792, at age forty-three, leaving behind five children and entrusting his haberdashery business to his wife. In his absence, a treacherous draft dodger had seduced her and was destroying his family and business. Rather than blaming her, Allemand claimed that she had fallen victim to a false rumor that his battalion had been destroyed. In the "name of suffering humanity," he asked to be allowed to sort out his family affairs.[128]

Allemand's is one of the few petitions in this collection to hint at marital problems. Other kinds of sources suggest more widespread concern that women looked to other partners during soldiers' absences. The revolutionary government had legalized divorce in September 1792. A supplementary law on April 23, 1794, allowed women to divorce absent husbands, but only within limits. Lawmakers worried that "the wives of the défenseurs de la patrie will take advantage of their absence to obtain a divorce, and to claim rights at the expense of their husbands."[129] The law stipulated that women could only seek divorce in their last common residence or their husbands' current residence. Moreover, they could only claim the property they had brought to the marriage, and all settlements would be provisional until their husbands' returns.

Beginning in late 1796, legislators began to challenge divorce more systematically. Several lawmakers focused on soldiers whose greedy wives sought divorces in their absence. They associated women left on their own with immorality, rather than virtuous sacrifice; such women were taking advantage of the law to contest marriages against their husbands' wishes.

The deputy Guillaume Favart thus presented the petition of an angry dragoon captain in the army of Italy to the legislative assembly. The captain's wife, the mother of his four living children, was attempting to divorce him and claim their property. Favart used the case in December 1796 to call for a law that would prevent divorces based on mutual incompatibility or at least suspend proceedings against serving soldiers. He returned to the case in January 1797, describing a woman as "forgetting what she owes herself and the husband who is sacrificing himself in the defense of the country, burning to leave

128. AN AF / III / 313 / 1, Joseph Allemand.

129. *Gazette nationale ou le Moniteur universel*, no. 216, 6 Floréal Year II (April 25, 1794).

him to throw herself into the arms of a seducer whose merit in her eyes is that of having fled danger, and who will live a weak and licentious life with her."[130]

Favart's rhetoric denied any legitimate reason for a woman to seek divorce and identified civilian men with selfish cowardice. He claimed that restrictions on divorce would assure our "brave defenders that if they defend us abroad, their personal interests are always safe in our hands."[131] His arguments build on legislation designed to conserve soldiers' property, especially a law from December 26, 1796, which suspended judgments against serving soldiers until peacetime, or until an individual was permanently discharged. Other legislators voiced similar complaints. At the end of a long attack on divorce for mutual incompatibility, the deputy Antoine-Baptiste Ludot argued that it was particularly inappropriate for soldiers' families. Men's prolonged absence from their wives meant that claims to incompatibility were based only on memory and disguised other motives. Serving soldiers were also deprived of the possibility that relatives and friends could intervene to save a failing marriage.[132]

Accounts of divorce reveal the strains prolonged warfare could place on couples, compounded when, as in Allemand's case, women had had no news of absent men or heard misleading rumors. Such strains were likely more common than we can easily document, especially in the political turmoil of the Revolution. Yet legislators' fears of abusive divorces by soldiers' wives did not correspond to a wave of women seeking separation from their combatant husbands, in part because the number of married men in the troops had already shrunk by 1797. Instead, rhetoric like Favart's challenged the legacy of the radical Revolution while defining men as generous citizens and women as gullible and selfish.

Conclusion

Accounts of families desperate for soldiers' return, complaints about inheritance, and polemics over divorce all reveal how much war impacted households far from the battlefields. This impact was not uniform, even if hardship was widespread. Nor was it unmediated. Taken together, contemporary sources suggest the need to be attentive to contexts when thinking about the relationships between home front and battlefront, and to consider not just individuals' experiences, but also the ways they presented those experiences. Both petitioners'

130. 5 Nivôse Year V (December 25, 1796), in *Procès-verbaux du Conseil des Cinq-Cents*, 71. See Desan, *The Family on Trial*, 268. "Conseil des Cinq Cents. Suite de la séance du 20 nivôse de l'an cinquième," *Journal des débats et des décrets*, no. 443 [January 9, 1797?], 290. See also Naquet, *Le divorce*, 225–26.

131. "Conseil des Cinq Cents. Suite de la séance du 20 nivôse de l'an cinquième," *Journal des débats et des décrets*, no. 443 [January 9, 1797?], 290.

132. "Conseil des Cinq Cents. Suite de la séance du 28 nivôse de l'an cinquième," *Journal des débats et des décrets*, no. 450, January 17, 1797, 406.

insistence on shared sacrifice by soldiers and civilians and combatants' complaints about siblings and wives reflected suffering and strategic pleas. The lessons here are useful for thinking not just about the revolutionary era, but also about relationships between home fronts and warfronts in other periods.

At the same time, even as arguments over inheritance and marriage reveal tensions between soldiers and families, petitions show us how much models of citizenship were entangled with family. Contemporaries envisioned the social contract as one not just between the state and individuals, but also between the state and families, arguing that the government had a responsibility toward the relatives of soldiers and veterans. Family members presented themselves as actively sacrificing or consenting to a man's departure and prolonged absence. They portrayed military service and domestic duty as forms of citizenship that could be shared among family members. In many accounts, service appears as a collective act of citizenship.

Petitioners did not challenge the value of martial masculinity or the need for war. Yet they struggled with physical and ideological limits of virility, walking a fine line to prove themselves too weak to fight but strong enough to provide for families. They sought to show that civilian labor—especially the skilled labor of men—was as valuable as military service, and to insist that sensitivity to others' suffering could be as important as taking up arms.

Veterans hoping to return home in 1796–97 also sought to forestall charges of selfishness or cowardice by emphasizing their obligation to family members—the "reward" of new forms of civic duty. They could link private and public interest because they presented private interest as unselfish. Other combatants accused soldiers' siblings or spouses of selfishness to further their own causes. Such arguments represented both practical strategies and ways of talking about social usefulness and civic generosity that were distinct to the later 1790s.

In the next chapter, we turn to the 1798 Jourdan Law on conscription, which transformed military service from a response to emergency into a regularized institution. Rather than bring veterans home, it would feed Napoleon's war machine. Instituting this law in the late 1790s, however, would force contemporaries to confront anew the effectiveness of revolutionary strategies for mobilization, and the appropriate relationships between combatants and civilians, soldiers, and their families.

CHAPTER FOUR

La Patrie en Danger Again: Gender, Emotion, and Conscription

ON SEPTEMBER 5, 1798, the French legislature instituted conscription. The measure—which would become known as the Jourdan Law—put into place the "blood tax" that would define the Napoleonic Empire. Over the course of the next seventeen years, over two million men would be conscripted into the French military under its auspices.

The government began to enlist conscripts in late 1798 and especially the spring and summer of 1799—a period that has fascinated scholars for other reasons: it encompasses the last gasps of the French revolutionary republic and leads to Napoleon Bonaparte's coup of 18 Brumaire (November 9, 1799). Because the law was integral to Napoleon's ascent to power across Europe, historians have usually assessed it in light of subsequent developments.[1] But conscription was inaugurated in a distinctively revolutionary context. Authorities sought to reuse earlier models for mobilizing the population for war. They also encountered unexpected challenges in using these tools. Looking at these dynamics reveals not just the stakes of "cultural recycling"—ways of repurposing old practices in new political orders—but also changing ideas about citizenship, the political uses of emotion, and gender roles.

1. Annie Crépin has addressed conscription in the period most extensively. See her *La conscription en débat*, 24–30; *L'histoire de la conscription*, 120–36; and *Vers l'armée nationale*. See also Bergès, "A l'origine de la conscription nationale"; and Catros, "Tout français est soldat." On implementation of the law, see Vallée, *La conscription dans le département de la Charente;* and Bèrges, *Résister à la conscription*. A few historians have contended that conscription in 1799 should be treated separately from Napoleonic drafts but focus on administrative aspects. See especially Ciotti, *Du volontaire au conscrit*.

To motivate conscripts, French officials drew on strategies developed during the radical Revolution. Inspired in part by a revival of Jacobinism, authorities retook the rhetoric of threats, sacrifice, and vengeance to encourage would-be soldiers and their families.[2] They reworked accounts of collective joy as young men marched from home, adapted ideas of martial masculinity to humiliate shirkers, and revived tales of "new Spartan women" who could face their husbands' or sons' departures with equanimity. These references promised to make military service acceptable at a point when many might have expected a definitive end to combat.

If such strategies promised popular support, they were difficult to use in new political circumstances. This reflects the demographic and social changes we considered in the previous chapter. The relative disappearance of married men from the troops meant that appeals to defend families resonated differently than during the early years of the Revolution. It also reflects changing visions of the contract between the state and its citizens. The Directorial government of the late 1790s increasingly sought to confine the people to a more passive role within that contract—while still promoting collective action.[3]

Instituting conscription revealed the conflicts between these goals. Legislators wanted universal support for war but not universal mobilization. In making conscription law, deputies resolved contradictory impulses by distinguishing between registration for the draft as a civic duty for all young men, and the limited number of men required to serve.[4] In putting that law into place, however, authorities confronted tensions more broadly. Appeals for mobilizing a broad public behind war, including inciting recruits and their families to respond to renewed national emergency, fit poorly with efforts to control soldiers and to ensure the docility of the populace.

New understandings of emotion compounded these challenges. We have seen in previous chapters that revolutionaries heralded strong emotions, especially those that bound individuals to their families, while calling upon people to display stoic resolve and overcome suffering and natural attachments. In the later 1790s, men and women began to rethink how to connect emotions to politics, especially in the wake of trauma.[5] Several historians have called attention to this transition. William Reddy has claimed that the model of "sentimentalism"—associated with eighteenth-century beliefs that certain stimuli provoked intense responses, and that men and women should display strong emotions publicly—was subsiding in the later years of the Revolution.[6] Guillaume Mazeau has observed that the aftermath of the Terror encouraged

2. Gainot, *1799, un nouveau Jacobinisme?*

3. Jourdan, *Les monuments de la révolution*, 191.

4. Hippler, "The French Army," 420.

5. R. Steinberg, *The Afterlives of the Terror*.

6. Reddy, "Sentimentalism and Its Erasure" and *The Navigation of Feeling*.

a privatization of emotions, while ideologues tried to make the populace less politically passionate.[7] Jan Goldstein has postulated an analogous move away from a sensationalist philosophy, which increasingly appeared as a threat to political order.[8]

Throughout the Revolution, officials sought both to enflame and to control public reactions. In heralding "martyrs of liberty" like Marat in 1793 and 1794, for example, festival organizers had sought to inspire audiences with outrage at their enemies, but risked encouraging feelings of vulnerability and despair, or provoking audiences to ill-directed plans for vengeance. But authorities in 1799 had become particularly leery of effects of emotional displays. They feared "sterile" tears that did not lead to action. They also feared that gory spectacles would backfire.

Looking closely at conscription also allows us to see how military service continued to reshape gender roles for both men and women, long after the formal exclusion of women from the troops. The Jourdan Law can appear as the triumph of martial masculinity. It enshrined connections between virility, citizenship, and arms-bearing that had earlier appeared as responses to crisis and made them permanent. Yet many men sought to avoid conscription, whether legally, by certifying their lack of fitness or paying for replacements to fight in their stead, or illegally, through draft dodging, destroying records, and desertion. In justifying their decisions to avoid warfare, they emphasized responsibilities to family. Conversely, authorities attempting to shame shirkers linked civilian life to feminine realms—and claimed that men should take up arms to defend their families.

In the following pages, we look first at the Jourdan Law itself. Lawmakers viewed it as a recruitment tool and a means of educating patriots that would "erase the lines of demarcation" between citizens and soldiers. Officials were eager to depict broad enthusiasm, but the number of men who avoided service, and their families' complicity in protecting them, quickly undercut images of renewed collective zeal.

We then turn to a dramatic moment in the spring of 1799. Two French diplomats were assassinated during peace negotiations at Rastadt; a third, Jean Debry, barely escaped with his life. Orators swore vengeance for the "ministers of peace" torn from the arms of their wives and massacred in front of their children. Officials used the incident to justify renewed warfare against Austria.[9] Since the assassinations took place shortly after the legislature had decreed a second draft, reports of Austrian brutality promised

7. Mazeau, "Émotions politiques," 107.

8. J. Goldstein, *The Post-Revolutionary Self.*

9. Chappey, "L'assassinat de Rastadt." For doubt about Austrian responsibility, see Frey and Frey, *The History of Diplomatic Immunity*, 132; and Vonau, "Les événements tragiques."

to inspire potential soldiers and their families. Plays devoted to the Rastadt martyrs echoed works from the radical Revolution, depicting men who were not required to leave home but were moved to take up arms. Censors' remarks on proposed scripts, however, show a growing unease with presenting the Republic as vulnerable, stirring dangerous emotions, or insisting on universal mobilization.

In the last sections, we look more closely at constructions of masculinity and femininity in the face of conscription. In 1799, the government reintroduced the practice of paying men to fight in the place of conscripts. But even as authorities uneasily tolerated replacements, they sought to humiliate men who evaded service illegally, from proposing dressing deserters in women's clothing to displaying the names of draft dodgers. Such strategies promised to inspire recruits, but risked losing control of the messages that authorities wanted to convey. Finally, we revisit appeals to feminine stoicism and to romance as a reward for bravery. Even as authorities made conscription obligatory for men—and reiterated that women should not take up arms—publicists insisted on women's roles in inspiring male combatants.

"All Frenchmen Are Soldiers": The Beginnings of Mass Conscription

The Jourdan-Delbrel Law of 19 Fructidor Year VI (September 5, 1798) transformed military service. Few initially imagined the extent to which it would create an international war machine. Legislators discussed projects for the law in early 1798 in a period of relative calm, and debated conscription for close to a year, focusing more on its implications for citizenship than its potential for expanding the French Empire. As Annie Crépin has observed, it was the first time since 1791 that a recruitment measure was not conceived of as mobilization in the face of national crisis.[10]

The law responded to a drastic reduction of the number of men under arms. There were about half as many soldiers in the later 1790s as there had been at the peak of the revolutionary army in 1794. Shrinking numbers were attributable to both desertion and the legal demobilization explored in the previous chapter. There had been no major recruitment measures since the levée en masse in 1793; those who left the ranks were rarely replaced.

If the new law reflected practical concerns, it also introduced a new vision of the relationship between the military and the nation. Its author Jourdan claimed it was a true revolution in military institutions.[11] Revolutionaries had rejected conscription earlier. Even if the 1793 levée en masse sought to

10. Crépin, *Histoire de la conscription*, 120–22.

11. Philippe Catros has argued that while the law drew on military experience, it was fundamentally innovative. Catros, "Tout français est soldat."

rouse the entire populace, it presented calls to arms as a response to emergency. Legislators in 1798 saw conscription instead as a long-term means of shaping citizens. While the decree began by establishing how volunteers could join the army, it laid out a systematic plan for conscripting young men. Lawmakers aimed to turn military service—or at least the obligation to register for the draft—into a regular part of life.

The law was not intended to rouse the entire population. Legislators wanted all men to register, but not to fight. They expected troops to consist of young, single men. Instructions welcomed volunteers between eighteen and thirty (forty in the case of experienced soldiers). Conscripts were divided into five classes by age, from twenty to twenty-five. The youngest would be called on first every year; older classes would be required to enlist only if there was need. Those over twenty-five who had not been called up were exempted from service. This was very different from the levée en masse, which encompassed all men from eighteen to twenty-five and led to brothers fighting together. It was also different from calls for volunteers that inspired both boys and middle-aged fathers to defend the *patrie en danger*.

The law would ultimately provide the basis for Napoleon's army. But in its inception, it was an ambivalently revolutionary measure, seeking simultaneously to create citizens and soldiers, to promote mass support for war and limit mass mobilization. In this context, soldiers' departures appeared as moments of collective patriotism, joining together civilians and soldiers even as conscripts left their families.

DEPARTED WITH JOY

In December 1798, in the immediate wake of the new law, deputies boasted that the conscripts in their departments had departed joyfully. Brémontier, a deputy from the Seine Inférieure, proclaimed, "All the conscripts left with joy and the ardent desire to share the laurels that our invincible armies have already won." Others declared that civilians shared conscripts' enthusiasm and were moved by their patriotism, like Duviquet from Nièvre, who gushed, "We cannot express adequately all the joy that these young citizens inspired."[12] Municipal administrators in Provins similarly heralded "the delicious emotions that the intrepid courage of these young citizens inspired in all our hearts."[13]

Why such repeated references to joy, especially in a population keenly aware of the costs of prolonged warfare? In part, public joy was a powerful

12. Brémontier, *Discours prononcé . . . sur le départ des conscrits de la Seine-Inférieure;* Duviquet, *Discours prononcé . . . sur le départ des conscrits de la Nièvre.* See also Darracq, *Discours prononcé . . . sur le départ des conscrits des Landes.*

13. AN C / 459, Admin. municipales de la commune de Provins et canton rural extramuros, département de Seine-et-Marne, le 27 prairial an 7.

force during the Revolution.[14] Descriptions of collective enthusiasm reprised earlier rhetoric around recruitment. References to eager young men, sent off with the support of their families and communities, retook iconography like Jean-Baptiste Lesueur's 1792 watercolor *Joyous Departure of Volunteers for the Armies*.[15] Conscripts in 1798 and 1799 welcomed—or were told to welcome—the opportunity to rival the accomplishments of their "older brothers."[16]

Declarations of joy served other functions. They proclaimed the loyalty of each department to the Republic, while downplaying the coercive role of the state. An emphasis on cheerful, unforced participation corresponded to the legislators' decision to establish procedures for volunteers before enumerating those for conscription in the Jourdan Law. It was reinforced by reports that individuals who had not been conscripted had volunteered to fight, and that *réquisitionnaires*—soldiers from earlier campaigns who had returned home—had rejoined the troops.

It also portrayed unity between the home front and the military, between men and women, and between soldiers and their families. The description of a December 1798 festival from Nevers, in central France, is exemplary. Local officials reported that more than two thousand men and women witnessed the conscripts' send-off. Ceremonies concluded with a song promising the new warriors that "Mars [the god of war] and Love will guide your steps." Lyrics proclaimed that each soldier was leaving behind a tender lover, but that all sentiment ceded to the vows of the patrie. The lines both acknowledged painful goodbyes and suggested that all soldiers had sweethearts to defend, if not yet wives and children. The song promised that "Your parents, your friends, your sisters, and your lovers / Will soon crown your triumphant weapons."[17] Conscripts and family members appeared bound together in a common enterprise.

THE LIMITS OF RECRUITMENT

An undercurrent in many speeches suggests that legislators understood young men did not leave with unadulterated enthusiasm, and that local communities did not always welcome their departure. In the fall of 1798, legislators tended to blame reluctance on the corrupt agents of royalism and fanaticism. Such rhetoric made it possible to claim that the mass of French citizens were patriots, whatever their momentary hesitations. Once soldiers understood the evils of their enemies, they would fight enthusiastically. Administrators lauded zealous fathers and mothers who brought wavering sons back to the path of

14. Valade, "Public Celebrations"; and Mazeau, "Émotions politiques," 131–37.

15. *Joyeux départ des volontaires aux armées*, in Carbonnières, *Lesueur: Gouaches révolutionnaires*, 145.

16. Doche-Delisle, *Discours par . . . sur le départ des conscrits du département de la Charente.*

17. *Procès-verbal de la fête célébrée à Nevers*, 9.

duty. The official newspaper of the Republic, the *Bulletin décadaire,* recounted numerous anecdotes, alongside stories of brigands and heroic rescues of those about to drown.[18]

Yet when writers heralded brave soldiers, they invoked worried families; in praising resolute parents, they called attention to reluctant recruits. The numbers tell a different story from either eager conscripts or sternly virtuous parents. Despite deputies' boasts that their departments had met or exceeded quotas, this was rarely the case. The government began to recruit a few weeks after the new law. Officials hoped to mobilize 300,000 soldiers from the first class of those aged twenty, supplemented, if need be, with recruits from the second class, aged twenty-one. Only 74,000 men joined up. A new call to arms seven months later, on April 17, 1799, aimed to enlist twenty-year-olds who had not yet joined up, followed by those from the second and third classes. It resulted in only 57,000 new departures. A third draft on June 28, 1799, called on all five classes of conscripts; only about half of those expected to march took up arms.[19]

Some difficulties were logistical. There were few reliable lists of names. Other challenges related to military circumstances. In the spring and early summer of 1799, France faced a renewed threat of invasion. This created a new urgency for recruitment, but it also meant that those conscripted could anticipate immediate active duty. As the drafts were being put into effect in spring 1799, news came that would change the ways that authorities tried to appeal to potential soldiers and their families.

A Story of Murder, "Unprecedented in All Humanity"

On May 20, 1799, Jean Debry recounted a bloody story to the French legislature. He, Claude Roberjot, and Ange Elisabeth Louis-Antoine Bonnier had served as plenipotentiary ministers at the peace conference of Rastadt, intended to work out the boundaries between the French and the Austrian Empires. On the night of April 28, armed men ambushed their carriages. They killed Roberjot and Bonnier. Debry was left for dead but recovered from his wounds. He became the chief witness to what contemporaries, in hyperbolic rhetoric, would deem a crime unparalleled in history, an attack not only on the ministers and the people of France, but on humanity itself.

18. The department of the Eure particularly lauded parental patriotism. See Eude, *Discours . . . sur le départ des conscrits du département de l'Eure.* For a mother who brought her conscript son, who had deserted while drunk, and a father who rounded up his son and two other deserters, see *Bulletin décadaire,* no. 9, Frimaire Year VII, and no. 20, Germinal Year VII. For an artisan father in the Seine Inférieure who took his draft-dodging son to the municipal authorities, see no. 28, Messidor Year VII.

19. Waquet, "Un essai," 182.

FIGURE 4.1. C. Monnet (artist) and Helman (engraver), *Assassination of the French Plenipotentiaries at the Rastadt Congress*, 1799. Bibliothèque Nationale de France.

French authorities immediately denounced the assassinations as Austrian treachery. Their accusations played into a long-standing current of Austrophobia, as well as rhetoric about the savagery of France's enemies.[20] There was a strong emotional reaction when the *Moniteur*, the government's official newspaper, publicized the story on May 4, 1799.[21] Officials demanded vengeance and sought to mobilize the public behind a renewed war effort. François de Neufchâteau, the minister of the interior, planned a state funeral on 20 Prairial (June 2), accompanied by funerary rituals throughout France. He called for an outpouring of art, verse, and prose testifying to the "universal sensibility" shocked by the murders.[22]

FAMILY AND VENGEANCE

In denouncing the attacks, orators dwelled on horror. Debry proclaimed that Roberjot "was killed in the arms of his wife. Sensitive fathers and mothers, what guarantee can you count on now? Was I not struck in front of my pregnant

20. Kaiser, "From the Austrian Committee to the Foreign Plot."

21. Gainot, *1799, un nouveau Jacobinisme?*, 200.

22. The law of 22 Floréal Year VII (May 11, 1799) ordered all cantons in the Republic to hold funeral festivals in memory of Bonnier and Roberjot.

wife and the eyes of my two young daughters? My blood spurted on them."[23] Debry testified to real brutality, and other witnesses, including the daughters and widows of the ministers, corroborated his account.[24] But the narrative of violated innocence did not simply document the attacks; it also stirred up public sentiment. It retook earlier revolutionary rhetoric of threats to families and the mother country and used that rhetoric to justify renewed warfare.

Orators focused on Roberjot's and Debry's families, embroidering on the widow Roberjot's testimony that she had tried in vain to protect her husband.[25] In Strasbourg, Sébastien Bottin lamented that "Roberjot [was] massacred on the breast of his wife, who held him, trying fruitlessly to make a rampart of her body."[26] Chénier, one of the master organizers of ceremonies throughout the Revolution, gave the death a further patriotic gloss, proclaiming that "blood spurted on Roberjot's tender wife; 'my wife,' he cried, 'take courage': in saying these words, he died, his eyes turned toward his patrie."[27] In Besançon, local officials added gory details: Roberjot "was struck before her [his wife] and almost in her arms. He fell on his back, and turning to his side, pronounced these words: *my wife, take courage*. At that instant, his throat was slit. His assassin removed his skull, took his brain, and put it his pocket."[28]

Speakers also played up the shock to Debry's family. There were two slightly different versions. One followed Debry's words, emphasizing his blood on his pregnant wife and children. The other drew on the testimony of his daughter Victoire. Brigands stopped their carriage, asked if her father was Jean Debry, and then seized him. When Victoire begged to know her father's fate, she was told, "You no longer have a father."[29] Orators took up the phrase and made it general, repeating: "there is no more father."[30]

The funerary procession in the Champs de Mars also concentrated on the martyrs' families. Family members appeared at the center of the cortege. The

23. Debry, *Discours prononcé par . . . Séance du 1er prairial an VII*.

24. For eyewitness testimony, including of family members and servants, see *Déclaration individuelle sur l'assassinat*.

25. *Déclaration de la citoyenne veuve de Roberjot (assassiné par les hussards de Szecklers)*, in *Déclaration individuelle sur l'assassinat*. A few works lamented Bonnier's tragic demise, such as *Le cri de l'Europe*. But Bonnier tended to be overshadowed, as his death did not directly involve his family.

26. Bottin, *Éloge funèbre des citoyens Bonnier et Roberjot*, 8.

27. Chénier, *Discours prononcé par M.-J. Chénier, de l'Institut national*, 13.

28. Jarry, *Discours prononcé par le citoyen Jarry*.The desecration of Roberjot's brain appears in the *Déclaration du citoyen Belin, secrétaire du citoyen Jean Debry*, in *Déclaration individuelle sur l'assassinat;* and Deschodt, *Discours prononcé le 20 prairial*, 10.

29. AN AD / 114 / A, *Déclaration des citoyennes Félicité Artaud, épouse du citoyen Jean Debry, Victoire et Eléonore Debry, ses filles, rédigée par Victoire Debry, sur l'assassinat du 9 floréal, à Strasbourg, le 21 floréal an VII.*

30. Chénier, *Discours prononcé par M.-J. Chénier, de l'Institut national*, 14; Bottin, *Éloge funèbre des citoyens Bonnier et Roberjot*, 9; and Cubières-Palmézeaux, *Au peuple français*, 30.

daughters of the dead men were dressed in black, those of the survivor in white. Chénier, as master of ceremonies, appealed to participants to avenge the widows and orphans.[31] Even the absence of key family members could emphasize trauma. The newspaper *Le Rédacteur* reported that the spectators at the funeral, "with troubled eyes dampened with tears, tried vainly to recognize Roberjot's widow. Her limited strength did not allow her to drag herself to the place of the ceremony. She is still followed by the horrible image of her husband's assassination, his throat slit and cut into shreds in her arms, while she tried to cover him with her body and begged the barbarians for the awful grace of letting her share her husband's fate."[32] Such stories made Austrian (or allegedly Austrian) violence appear especially brutal, and French warfare justified.[33]

The Directorial government sought to draw upon the stories of the martyrs to inspire young men.[34] Officials asked conscripts to envision themselves in place of the ministers.[35] In a speech reprinted in the *Moniteur*, General Menard exhorted his troops on June 28, 1799, by claiming that

> This coup aimed at us soldiers; it is up to us to avenge the honor of the murdered nation. . . . The bloody death of our ministers, the cruelties wreaked upon their wives and children, let us know what fate our barbarous enemy prepares for the French, especially for us the soldiers who have so often been humiliated by its haughtiness. What tortures are not reserved for us, for our wives, our children?[36]

Such rhetoric painted the Rastadt attacks as precursors to attacks on soldiers' ow 1 families.

Some conscripts adopted similar logic when interacting with authorities. Jacques Lefèvre, for example, wrote to the Council of Five Hundred that "married last Thermidor, and leaving a wife who is eight months pregnant, these bonds attach me even more strongly to my patrie. If in the presence of the enemy, I could experience some weakness, the memory of the atrocities committed on our ambassadors by these Austrian criminals, the idea of the awful treatment that such monsters prepare for my patrie, my wife, my child, rekindles my courage."[37] Lefèvre appropriated the argument made by prerevolutionary reformers that a family made a military man braver and combined it with revolutionary rhetoric denouncing enemy atrocities.

31. Livesey, *Making Democracy*, 215.

32. Aulard, *Paris pendant la réaction*, 5:555.

33. Chappey, "L'assassinat de Rastadt," 71.

34. Waquet, "Un essai." See also Alzas, *La liberté ou la mort.*

35. As one put it, "generous defenders, you have felt each of the blows against the ministers of peace." *Procès-verbal de la fête funèbre célébrée par l'administration municipale du 12e arrondissement.*

36. *Gazette nationale ou le Moniteur unversel*, no. 288, 18 Messidor Year VII, 1172.

37. AN AF / III / 158, dossier 752.

Lefèvre, however, was probably more inclined to such rhetoric than many conscripted in 1798–99. He was steeped in republican ideology, having volunteered at sixteen and fought in the Vendée. Believing that defending his family and patrie went hand in hand, he pleaded with the government to provide for his loved ones and those of other conscripts. He proposed optimistically that if the public treasury were insufficient, his fellow citizens would accept a light addition to local taxes, knowing that funds would support soldiers' families. His wife also petitioned the authorities, noting that her "husband left again, if not with joy, then with satisfaction," and arguing that as a wife, mother, and sister of soldiers, she deserved recompense.

While such accounts suggest that appeals to soldiers to defend their wives and children still had resonance, they were increasingly difficult to make. As we have seen, fewer soldiers were married in the late 1790s than in the early years of the Revolution, and married men who had volunteered often quietly returned home. Marriage also served as an increasingly important means of avoiding service. The Jourdan Law exempted married men, although it placed constraints on what marriages counted. It excluded only those wed before January 12, 1798, the date when Jourdan proposed the law. In August, the Council of Five Hundred considered extending this exemption to July 19, but legislators worried that young men who had married between January and July had been motivated not by love, familial duty, or social responsibility, but only by a desire to escape conscription.[38]

Officials charged with overseeing conscription were most preoccupied by fraud and cases where priests or local authorities had conspired to antedate marriages but also called attention to obviously mismatched or suspiciously rushed arrangements. Individuals denounced corrupt officials and neighbors who used marriage to cheat their way out of service.[39] Authorities often forced men to leave if their marriages appeared doubtful. Some conscripts strongly protested this policy, using emotionally charged language in hopes of proving the reality of their bonds. For example, on November 8, 1798, one young man proclaimed that his departure would put a knife to his wife's throat, forcing her to beg for a morsel of bread. He concluded, "I cannot write more about my situation because my eyes flood with tears thinking about my dear wife, whom I love more than life itself."[40]

38. Ciotti, "Les 'embusqués de Vénus.'"

39. See complaints from Saint-Maurice in Charente Inférieure (February 5, 1799), in AN F / 9 / 288 and from Gorze, Moselle (March 31, 1799), cited in Forrest, *Conscripts and Deserters*, 47. See also "Leros, Conscrit de Paris, au corps législatif, pour demander que les citoyens mariés avant le 23 nivôse an 5 et censés d'être divorcé sans enfants soient compris dans la conscription," in AN AF / III / 158, dossier 752; and L'accusateur public près le tribunal criminel du dépt des Hautes-Alpes, Gap, 2 germ. an 7, in AN F / 9 / 286.

40. AN C / 568, dossier 370.

Authorities also reiterated concerns that married men were hard to motivate. In January 1799, the minister of the interior warned against allowing both deserters and men who had been demobilized to wed, on the grounds that they might be required to take up arms again, and "a married soldier does not easily abandon his wife and children and scorns the obligation that he has taken to serve his country and his duty towards it."[41]

In an effort to persuade women to support war, officials played up the distress of the ministers' families who had witnessed violence. In Brussels, for example, the orator Vidal asked women to imagine themselves in the position of Roberjot's wife and promised them vengeance: "O tender wives put yourself in her place and imagine the horror of her torture. . . . Who would not have wanted to die with him. . . . I swear by my country, the time is near when she will see her husband avenged."[42] Orators in the festivals of 20 Prairial made similar allusions, sometimes emphasizing the role of women in inspiring vengeance. In Strasbourg, the *secrétaire adjoint* of the central administration of the Bas-Rhin pledged support for the wives of Roberjot and Bonnier. He then called upon all French women to rouse their sons to take revenge:

> Tender and faithful wives, vengeance! It was in the arms of his pregnant wife that Jean Debry was covered with wounds. It was the breast of Roberjot's wife that was covered with the spurting blood of her husband. . . . Nursing mothers, may the first word that your son stammers be vengeance![43]

The stories of the diplomats' gruesome fates and the plight of their families promised to encourage people to support renewed warfare and inspire conscripts. The changing demography of the troops limited the reception of these stories, but so too did the ways authorities chose to manage accounts of the assassinations.

THE SPECTACLE OF THEIR BLOODY BODIES

Officials commemorating the Rastadt murders faced a difficult question: how much could they use earlier strategies to stir up emotion, while controlling displays? Most descriptions used a theatrical mise-en-scène, with a virtual stage set, protagonists, and tragic effects.[44] Yet authors and speakers were

41. AN F / 9 / 288, Lettre du Ministre de l'Intérieur, à M le préfet du Rhône, 17 nivôse an VI (6 janvier 1799). See also Forrest, *Conscripts and Deserters*, 32.

42. C. Vidal, *Discours prononcé au temple de la Loi, à Bruxelles, le 20 prairial an 7, sur l'assassinat des plénipotentiaires français au congrès de Rastadt* (Brussels: Hayez, (1799); repr. in *L'esprit des journaux françois et étrangers*, Year 28, vol. 10 (Messidor Year VII), 93–94.

43. Bottin, *Éloge funèbre des citoyens Bonnier et Roberjot*, 20–21.

44. Chappey, "L'assassinat de Rastadt," 70.

unsure what should go on these stage sets. Legislators particularly debated whether they should display the ministers' bodies, as those of "martyrs of liberty" like Marat had been exhibited during the radical Revolution.

In May 1799, the deputies Moreau de l'Yonne and Garat clashed over whether to follow these precedents. Moreau sought a prominent exhibition of the corpses of the Rastadt martyrs, while Garat opposed the practice. He argued that in Greece and Rome, representatives of the people might have had to display the bloody remains or clothing of assassinated ministers, but that with a sensitive population capable of reacting to oral descriptions, "we don't need these horrible spectacles that prolong suffering without adding anything to the depth and duration of indignation."[45] It would suffice to read a narrative of events at the same hour across the Republic and to read the description to conscripts as they prepared to leave.

The government ultimately decided not to show the bodies of the murdered ministers. Instead, Chénier called upon Debry to "show your torn and bloody clothing, unveil your body pierced with blows . . . let these images inspire in the common thought the horror of tyrants and may the holy love of country be reinvigorated by the sight of your scars."[46] In the funeral ceremony on 20 Prairial, two veterans carried a figure of the Justice of Nations pointing to Debry's coat.[47]

Not all commentators were pleased with this compromise. Several speculated that displaying the bodies would have stirred up more emotion. The commissioner of executive power in the Seine reported on May 16 that while news of the attacks had touched some, it had failed to "excite this sublime enthusiasm that could have electrified spirits." This was largely owing to the absence of the martyrs' corpses:

> It's in the capital of the Republic that we should have transported the remains of the unfortunate victims of the perfidious Austria; it is on their bloody corpses that we should swear war and the death of this murderous court. It is on a public funeral place that we should have exposed the martyrs of liberty. Great spectacles speak to the soul, to the physical sensibility that causes durable and powerful impressions on hearts. Perhaps instead of sterile regrets, this funeral altar would be surrounded by new soldiers and covered with civic offerings.[48]

In their view, the sight of injured bodies was necessary to inspire a powerful collective reaction and motivate soldiers to fight.

45. Garat, *Discours prononcé par Garat, après la lecture du message*, 8; Chappey, "L'assassinat de Rastadt," 79–80.

46. Chénier, *Discours prononce par M. J. Chénier de l'Institut national*. See Wrigley, *The Politics of Appearance*, 20.

47. Wrigley, *The Politics of Appearance*, 20.

48. Tableau analytique de la situation politique du département de la Seine pendant le mois de floréal an VII, in Aulard, *Paris pendant la réaction*, 3:521–22.

Similarly, citizens in Laon in the Aisne complained that Roberjot and Bonnier had been buried at Rastadt. They lamented that "the bloody bodies of these unfortunate ministers were not displayed in funerals in all parts of the Republic, carried in the ranks of all our armies. If, in olden times, the corpse of a tyrant shown to Romans could excite their vengeance, what impression would the spectacle of the mutilated corpses of two friends of liberty not have made on the hearts of our young defenders?"[49] Carrying rotting corpses from camp to camp seems an impracticable proposition, though perhaps less so than a contemporary proposal to create an "aerial sarcophagus," decorated with scenes of the assassinations, that, "pushed by the wind, could reach the peoples in the far north."[50]

Other commentators expressed optimism about the effects of describing horror without showing it. Deschodt, speaking in the northern French town of Hazebrouck, proclaimed that the thought of martyrs' wounds would remind young warriors that they were fighting against monsters. But he did not seek a more vivid spectacle: "the simple account of their [the ministers'] devotion and the circumstances of their death are more than sufficient to preserve their memory and move all who have a human heart."[51]

The question of whether French audiences were too "sensitive" to consider horrific images directly was not simply a debate about how to control reactions to a political incident. Instead, it was part of a larger trend toward rethinking the political uses of emotion and spectacle. The response to the Rastadt murders shows both a continued use of sentimentalism and fear that authorities would not be able to elicit the responses they desired. Municipal assemblies thus repeatedly proclaimed that citizens were not indifferent but shared in collective indignation. Tears would not be sterile, but would lead to action.[52]

Some officials celebrated other displays of strong emotion. They used the rhetoric of joy to herald soldiers' departures, even as they expressed outrage at the assassinations. For example, officials in the Oise proclaimed that "The enthusiasm that reigned in 1789 manifested itself in this canton the day of the departure of the conscripts; they left their homes with all demonstrations of joy, they seem to forget their families to concern themselves only with the patrie; they concealed with courage the regrets of friendship, the tears of tenderness."[53] Even while reviling the misdeeds of the Austrians, Chénier assured his audience that songs of victory would replace those

49. *Un grand nombre de citoyens de la Commune du Laon*, 5.

50. AN F / 1/ c / 1 / 113, Lettre de Garnerin proposant de fournir un sarcophage aérien, 20 floréal an VII.

51. Deschodt, *Discours prononcé le 20 prairial*, 4.

52. Language around sterile tears appears in multiple speeches in AN C / 459 and 568.

53. Département de l'Oise, canton de Liancourt, *Bulletin décadaire*, 2nd décade of Prairial Year VII, 24.

of sorrow. Debry's survival was welcome in this context.[54] If the journal *Le Rédacteur* dwelled on the widow Roberjot's grief, its authors soon turned to Félicité Debry's relief in witnessing her husband's miraculous recovery. Others linked Debry's survival to France's ultimate triumph. This was a variation on a standard theme of moving from tears to joy, from outrage to action. In the context of 1799, it still promised traction.

Contemporaries could be well aware of attempts to manipulate emotion. The anonymous author of *Reflections on the Catastrophe of the Ministers of the Republic at Rastadt* observed that "No invention had been overlooked" to create scenes of horror. He asked if there had been as much grief for the victims of the terrorists Carrier and Robespierre, or "for dead or injured soldiers? Has one shown such apparent distress for the two hundred thousand soldiers that the war has brought down?" The number likely underestimates the number of casualties, but it reflected both a common guess at the costs of war and an unusual denunciation of official indifference to those costs. The author claimed that the members of the Directory laughed at public credulity, congratulating themselves that chance had served them so well.[55]

Chance did not actually serve the Directory well, at least not after initial expressions of outrage. Even by May, the police grumbled that only a few newspapers portrayed the crimes of the Austrians with sufficient indignation; by early June they complained about widespread indifference. There were many reasons for a lack of enthusiasm, from the loss of interest as the news ceased to be fresh to a growing apathy toward official festivals.[56] But the ways in which commemorations for the Rastadt murders echoed the radical Revolution in a changed climate contributed to the reasons why the government hoped they would be powerful and challenges to that power.

Theater, Calls to Arms, and the Limits of Mass Mobilization

The response to the Rastadt murders was not limited to festivals and patriotic addresses. Several theaters also presented versions of the story in May and June 1799.[57] Like contemporary debates, these plays combined dramatic

54. The comparison with the "living martyr" Geffroy, wounded while defending Collot d'Herbois and Robespierre, is instructive. Baecque, *The Body Politic*.

55. *Réflexions sur la catastrophe*.

56. Forrest, *Conscripts and Deserters*, 43, notes that the effects of crisis were short-lived. On waning responses to the assassinations, see Aulard, *Paris pendant la réaction*, 5:509, 547, Rapports du Bureau Central du 24 Floréal and 16 Prairial. On the lack of enthusiasm for festivals during the Directory, see Chappey, "L'assassinat de Rastadt," 90; and Ozouf, *Festivals and the French Revolution*, 185–86.

57. Including *Ministres français à Rastadt*, at the Théâtre de la Gaîté on 29 Floréal (May 18); *Clarice et Valcour ou le cri de vengeance*, at the Théâtre des Arts on 4 Prairial

references with a reluctance to dwell on a gory spectacle of national vulnerability. Their plots also echoed the theater of 1793–94, portraying the patriotic departure of young and old alike to fight against France's enemies. They similarly echoed connections between love and military courage, usually depicting marriage as a reward rather than an accompaniment to service. But they also reveal a new belief that mass volunteering was unnecessary, impracticable, and even dangerous.

Some troupes staged relatively faithful accounts of events. As the newspaper *Courrier des spectacles* noted, the *French Ministers at Rastadt*, first performed at the Théâtre de la Gaîté on May 18, "followed step by step the narrative of events."[58] Most playwrights took more license. They invoked the assassinations but concentrated on domestic responses to the news rather than the attacks themselves.

The Théâtre des Jeunes Artistes presented the *Return from Rastadt or France's Cry* on May 24. The script seems not to have survived, but the censors in the Ministry of Police who read a preliminary version provided a synopsis of the thin plot: "Peasants in a village near Strasbourg prepare to receive our ministers, whose return is eagerly awaited. Arrangements for a marriage mix with these preparations, as our French plays always require a little bit of romance. All at once, one announces the most atrocious of crimes. All cry vengeance, all arm themselves, regardless of age, and prepare to punish an assassin-government."[59] Such images of universal mobilization echoed the enthusiasm (or at least the fantasy of enthusiasm) of early volunteering.

The same theater presented *The Apotheosis of the Martyrs of Rastadt or the Departure of Conscripts* a few weeks later, on June 10. Like the *Return*, it proclaimed that those who could have been excused from service felt compelled to take up arms. It featured Francœur, an old veteran, who sought to inspire conscripts to take revenge for the murders. Looking at the list of names of those who were to leave, Francœur was shocked to see Alexis, who was too young, instead of Maurice, who was legally required to go. He discovered that Alexis had wanted to relieve his mother's misery; to help her, he had accepted a thousand écus to serve as a replacement. Maurice, electrified by this act of filial piety, declared that he would personally "fulfill the duty of a French

(May 23); *Retour de Rastadt ou le cri de la France*, at the Théâtre des Jeunes Artistes on 5 Prairial (May 24); *Cri de vengeance*, at Montansier and Palais Royal on 7 Prairial (May 30); *L'apothéose des martyrs de Rastadt ou le départ des conscrits*, at the Théâtre des Jeunes Artistes on 22 Prairial (June 10); *Nouvelle au camp de l'assassinat des ministres français à Rastadt*, at the Académie Royale de la Musique on 26 Prairial (June 14); and *Crime de Rastadt*, at the Palais des Cités-Variétés on 8 Messidor (June 26).

58. *Courrier des spectacles*, 1 Prairial Year VII (May 20, 1799).

59. AN F / 7 / 3492, dossier 10, no. 103, Retour de Rastadt.

citizen." His father applauded his patriotism and offered his fortune to Alexis's mother.[60]

Structural aspects of performances also promoted mass support for war. In *Clarice and Valcour or the Cry of Vengeance*, debuted on May 23, news of the attacks enflamed the courage of the conscripts "who refuse to draw lots and leave en masse," and of "many citizens exempted by their age from all requisition."[61] The play ended with the "Chant du départ," the 1794 song proclaiming that all supported war. Other plays concluded similarly; *Return from Rastadt*, for example, ended with a related song, with verses sung by conscripts, their fathers, and their girlfriends. The law of January 7, 1796, obliged theaters to play patriotic songs before their performances, and authorities encouraged them to intersperse or end shows with such melodies. In many cases, the music likely served more as a familiar ritual than a conscious reflection about unity in the face of mobilization. The lyrics, and the use of songs played when real conscripts departed, nonetheless reinforced a message of shared sacrifice and eventual reward.

For the most part, the playwrights who addressed the Rastadt murders were not the ones who had composed works promoting military service in 1793–94, but the plots they chose echoed earlier plays. For example, in Landon's *The First Requisition or the Oath of the French*, first performed on October 30, 1793, boys, married men, and widowers rushed to France's aid, although legislators had called up only single young men between the ages of eighteen and twenty-five.[62] Similarly, Parenti's *The Cry of the Patrie*, debuted on December 30, 1793, showcased a husband and father who wanted to volunteer even though he was past the age of being called up.[63] Plays in 1799 also portrayed volunteers whose age or financial status exempted them from military duty, but who were moved to take up arms to defend their homeland.

Censors' comments on proposed scripts, however, reveal limits to these parallels. Their remarks have not survived for all scripts, but several suggest official wariness of universal mobilization for war. The minister of police applauded the patriotic zeal that had inspired the author of *The Apotheosis of the Martyrs of Rastadt* but criticized lines that emphasized threats to France: "Scene one contains the line that 'all are ready to fly to the aid of the patrie in danger.' The last scene has the line 'We will save the Republic.' This exaggerates our misfortunes. . . . False alarms can be very harmful."[64]

Censors also rebuked the author of *The Apotheosis* for depicting a character, the replacement for a conscript, as having signed up only out of greed.

60. Aulard, *Paris pendant la réaction*, 3:561.

61. AN F / 7 / 3492, dossier 3, no. 118.

62. The play was performed regularly in fall 1793 and intermittently in spring 1794. Lecomte, *Histoire des théâtres de Paris*, 35–37.

63. *Journal des spectacles*, no. 181, 10 Nivôse Year II (December 30, 1793), 1437.

64. AN F / 7 / 3491, Apothéose des martyrs de Rastadt.

They insisted that the playwright excise lines chiding the young man for having decided to fight "for gold!" and telling him "that he will never be a good soldier." The censors concluded, "the author has forgotten that the law permits replacements."[65] It is not surprising that the playwright either forgot that replacements were legal or chose to depict them as reprehensible. The initial Jourdan Law excluded the possibility of replacement; the second draft, which permitted it, dated only from April 17, 1799, a month before the censors considered the play. But the censors' response emphasized that it was legally—and implicitly, morally—acceptable for citizens of military age to be excused from conscription or to accept money to take up arms for someone else.

Corresponding to the move toward making the army into one of single young men, plays from 1799 increasingly depicted young soldiers who postponed their weddings until their demobilization. In both *Return from Rastadt* and *Clarice and Valcour*, the protagonists were about to marry when they heard the news of the assassinations; they vowed to delay their weddings until the murders were avenged. Such plots suggest both a growing separation between domestic and military life, and a renewed belief that war would be short.

Martial Masculinity and Those Who Chose Not to Fight

The version of *The Apotheosis* that appeared on stage a month after the censors considered the script had made the desired alterations and depicted a conscript who fights rather than allow someone else to go in his stead. The police reported that in the performance at the Théâtre des Jeunes Artistes: "A *remplaçant* gives the money that he received to a poor family; this act of virtue makes the conscript blush for his weakness; the voice of honor resounds in the depth of his heart, and he covers his shame at the sacrifice his replacement made by joining the flags alongside his replacement, who becomes a generous volunteer." The audience responded enthusiastically.[66]

This theatrical resolution reflected a common strategy of imagining that those who were tempted to avoid military service would ultimately take up arms. It echoed other contemporary propaganda; for example, on May 14, the newspaper *Les amis des lois* recounted an anecdote of a conscript whose family had tried to "deprive him of his right to defend and avenge his patrie" and who ultimately decided to fight alongside his erstwhile substitute.[67] Yet the question of who could, or should, avoid military service raised difficult questions about martial masculinity. The Jourdan Law institutionalized connections between citizenship, masculinity, and military service that had

65. AN F / 7 / 3491, Apothéose des martyrs de Rastadt.

66. Aulard, *Paris pendant la réaction*, 5:561.

67. Aulard, *Paris pendant la réaction*, 5:511.

appeared during the radical Revolution. But it also institutionalized new ways for men to avoid service, including paying for a replacement. Both substitution and draft dodging challenged martial masculinity.

NEITHER GREEDY NOR COWARDLY: BUYING ESCAPE FROM CONSCRIPTION

The practice of replacement was largely new. During the Old Regime, men required to serve in the militia had been able to avail themselves of substitutes. The draft of February 1793 tolerated the practice. But the levée en masse of August 1793 precluded replacement, on the grounds that substitutions allowed the rich to buy their way out of serving their country. The 1798 law continued to ban it; it was only reintroduced in 1799 in hopes of increasing the number of men who enlisted.

The measures that authorized the practice, however, were complicated. The law of April 17, 1799, opened the door. Articles 19 and 20 allowed conscripts in the second and third class (aged twenty-one or twenty-two) to procure replacements. Conscripts and their families had only a few days to find substitutes. On June 28, 1799, the government repealed earlier measures, and required those who had purchased replacements to march if their substitutes had deserted, been declared unfit for service, or been conscripted themselves. A little over a month later, in August 1799, it reauthorized replacement. A law on March 8, 1800, systematized procedures and required notarized contracts.[68]

Replacement touched on recurrent issues in the Revolution, including masculine honor, the obligations of citizenship, and the acceptable role of wealth in social relations. In 1799, discussions reflected the tension between a vision of universal military service, led by patriotic volunteers, and the desire for controlled mobilization. To legitimate replacement, contemporaries both presented those seeking release from service as ultimately joining up and reframed substitution as domestic responsibility.

The idea, presented in *The Apotheosis*, that men were taking money only for their needy families—or better, for other families—was one of the most common strategies for making replacement ideologically acceptable. In portraying a man who ultimately chose honor through fighting, *The Apotheosis* acknowledged replacement while downplaying its extent (as well as expressing hope that such examples might motivate reluctant soldiers to join the ranks).

In describing conscripts' departures, deputies to the legislature claimed that the practice was rare; the French were too virtuous to accept that others serve for them. Officials in the department of the Ardennes reported in

68. Schnapper, *Le remplacement militaire*, 18–23. See also Ciotti, *Du volontaire au conscrit*, 322; Pigeard, "La conscription sous le premier empire"; Crépin, *Vers l'armée nationale*, 83, and *Histoire de la conscription*, 131–36.

May 1799 that almost no one had taken the option of paying for a replacement.[69] Administrators in the Yonne provided multiple examples of men who could have sought replacements or who volunteered freely even when offered money for their services. In June 1799, they heralded a young man supposedly offered a large sum of money to be a replacement, but who turned it down, saying that he gave his services to the patrie, he did not sell them.[70] A month later, they praised men who had used replacements, but only to benefit those in need, like Beaudot D'Avalon, whose health exempted him, but who paid for a replacement to serve for a widow whose only son had been called up. They extolled one young man who presented himself in place of his brother suffering from weak health, and another who substituted for a conscript married with a "wife already a mother."[71]

While there is no comprehensive record, local studies of conscription reports and notarial contracts between conscripts and their substitutes suggest that the ability to purchase surrogates was widely used, at least after 1800.[72] But the frequency of the practice did not preclude anxieties about both those who looked for replacements and those willing to act as substitutes. The censors' proposed revision of *The Apotheosis* reveals these anxieties: men seeking to be replaced were rich and cowardly, while those willing to fight in their stead were motivated only by money.

In much contemporary propaganda, men who initially sought to be replaced realized their cowardice and enlisted. One telling example comes from a *Dialogue between a Conscript and a Royalist in a Café near the Arsenal*, by an otherwise unknown writer, Colasin. The work was composed shortly after the Rastadt murders, as the hero proclaims that the French "cannot make peace with assassins" and promises that those who fight will find "brothers and heroes who are filled with the desire to avenge the Plenipotentiaries massacred in the arms of their wives and children."[73] The emblematic characters are a conscript and a royalist. The royalist is a true coward. He quakes in the presence of the conscript and his friends and tries to escape their company. The treatise then introduces another young man, who initially also seems cowardly: the young Jacques, son of the charcoal burner who has come to the café to discuss terms with a possible replacement. His father is hoping to dissuade Jacques and is delighted to meet a brave conscript. The conscript quickly persuades the youth to enlist. Jacques's would-be replacement sees which way the wind is blowing, and leaves. The exchange ends in a burst of patriotic élan: "Other conscripts who were present and had planned to buy

69. Chauchet Bourgeois, *Discours prononcé . . . en présentant au Conseil.*

70. AN C / 459. On 14 Prairial Year VII (June 2, 1799).

71. Moreau de Vormes, *Discours . . . sur le départ des conscrits du département de l'Yonne.* The text is from 16 Messidor Year VII (July 4, 1799).

72. Crépin, *Histoire de la conscription*, 133, and *Vers l'armée*, 83.

73. Colasin, *Dialogue entre un conscrit et un royaliste,* 2.

replacements annul all their arrangements and plan to leave together; their potential replacements, equally brave, swear to fight with them and to give back the money." Since no one wants to take the money, the father proposes that it go to "the mother of a *défenseur de la patrie* who dies on the battlefield." The tract is typical in both its vision of patriotic fervor and the hope that money destined for replacements would go to needy dependents.

Such tracts echoed the cultural propaganda of 1793–94, particularly invocations of generous volunteers who help others. A typical example is Dorvigny's play *Perfect Equality*, premiered on December 23, 1793. Félix has gone to war in place of Francœur and returned with a broken arm. Francœur informs his daughter and the audience that if he did not leave, it was because replacement had been legal, and his family needed him. He would gladly have fought if he were single to provide an example to those younger. He also expresses his gratitude to his substitute: "Oh my dear Félix, you have shed your blood for me; I must share my fortune with you." The play deals with the unsavory dimensions of replacement by imagining financial exchange as an expression of gratitude, not the greed of the man who took the money or the selfishness of the man who remained home.[74]

Writers in 1799 continued to celebrate volunteers who stepped up for others, most famously Théophile Malo Corret de La Tour d'Auvergne, who, although retired from active duty, took up arms to substitute for the conscripted son of an elderly friend. La Tour d'Auvergne would be heralded as the "First Grenadier of France" for his civic virtues and military exploits.[75] But the relegalization of replacement meant that contemporaries had to confront the financial aspects of substitution more systematically. Presenting the decision to fight or seek a substitute as a question of generosity toward those in need rather than individual cowardliness or selfishness made it easier to reconcile ideals of martial masculinity with domestic virtue.

THE SPINDLES OF SHAME: HONORABLE MEN AND EFFEMINATE COWARDS

Both the limits of martial masculinity and attempts to mobilize public emotion become clearer when we turn from legal substitutes to draft dodgers and deserters. While authorities wanted to motivate conscripts, they also experimented with humiliating those who avoided military service. Officials drew on older ideas for shaming cowards or deserters, but also introduced new aspects of public spectacles.

When François de Neufchâteau, the minister of the interior, decreed that all the cantons of the Republic hold a funeral festival for the Rastadt martyrs,

74. Dorvigny, *La parfaite égalité*.

75. Hughes, *Forging Napoleon's Grande Armée*, 86–99.

he also proclaimed that each canton should set up two columns. A white column, decorated with the attributes of courage and liberty, would honor conscripts and volunteers by publicizing their names. A black column, covered with emblems of cowardliness, would condemn those who refused to fight. Their names would remain in ignominy until they did their duty.[76]

Neufchâteau's program left the design of these emblems to the imagination and resources of each canton. In the most important festival in Paris, the names of those who had joined the army were placed on a white column, adorned with a saber and a crown of laurels. Cowards' names appeared on a black column, painted with two distaffs and a spindle, implicitly returning to earlier associations of spinning with male cowardice.[77] Another Paris neighborhood erected a black column with the inscription "they turned their backs on the *Patrie* and glory." It was topped with a figure representing shame, "who held in one hand the list of names and with the other tried unsuccessfully to draw a veil over the list of the dishonored."[78] Communes with less imagination or financial resources simply posted lists of names in town halls.

Regardless of the emblems that festival organizers chose, their iconography drew on two major themes: public humiliation and an identification of cowardice with women. Neither theme was new in 1799. A year earlier, the minister of general police lamented that a young man had cut off the index finger of his right hand to exempt himself from service. It demanded that

> avenging infamy fall, across the Republic, on this name henceforward covered with opprobrium. Formerly, he would be paraded in public places, a distaff in hand; in the silence of the laws, we can at least execute a moral sentence . . . , and repeat in all the communes of the Republic, that during six years of war, Plantizé was the first Frenchman unworthy to be one, who had the courage to mutilate himself to avoid having the courage to fight.[79]

As everyone must have known, there had been more than one case of self-mutilation to avoid military service. Military records from the 1790s show intense concern with verifying the cause of injuries reported by would-be soldiers or former soldiers. The ministry's exaggerated rhetoric nonetheless revealed both an iconography of cowardice and desire to shame cowards in as public a forum as possible.

76. Neufchâteau, *Ordre de la marche et des cérémonies*, 2.

77. *Gazette nationale ou le Moniteur universel*, no. 262, 22 Prairial Year VII (June 10, 1799), 704.

78. *Procès-verbal de la fête funèbre célébrée par l'administration municipale du 12e arrondissement.*

79. *Gazette nationale ou le Moniteur universel*, no. 136, 16 Pluviôse Year VI (February 4, 1798), 345.

More specifically, the police longed to see Plantizé paraded with a distaff. As we have seen, the association of spinning with women and cowardice, in contrast to a virile world of the military service, appeared early in the Revolution. In shaming apparent cowards, the Directorial government seems to have retaken these contrasts.[80] Administrators also directly considered humiliating draft dodgers by dressing them as women.[81] In October 1798, a *juge de paix* in the department of the Tarn proposed to the minister of the interior that men who had mutilated themselves so that they could not fight be publicly humiliated. He wanted them to wear women's bonnets, be forced to carry a distaff, and marched around the town flanked by four women. (The judge did not seem to have reflected on how women might feel about participating in the procession.) He noted that this would draw crowds otherwise indifferent to republican institutions, but eager to take pleasure in public mockery.[82]

Other administrators proposed similar demonstrations. The central administration of the department of Moselle made an impassioned address on 9 Prairial (May 7, 1799, eleven days before the funerary festivals for the Rastadt martyrs). It sought to shame those who refused to fight by associating them with women:

> Those with pusillanimous and failing souls, who persuade themselves that they lack the necessary courage, should be shown all the contempt and indignation inspired by their cowardliness and their shameful weakness; they should be justly reviled, booed, pointed at by their neighbors and even their parents: they should be rejected as men unworthy of the title, as effeminate beings, in whom nature was mistaken, and whom one should cover with the clothing of the sex they imitate and whose attributes of weakness and indolence they share.

The author of the report further proposed that "he who refuses to march should be exposed to booing and contempt; he should be displayed in public assemblies dressed in the night cap of the woman near whom he wanted to hide, since he could not tear himself from the arms of voluptuous pleasure and spineless leisure."[83] By associating draft dodgers with women, he claimed that they were unnaturally weak; he also labeled them as lazy and inherently selfish.

Authorities did not implement proposals to mock deserters and draft dodgers by dressing them as women. The proposal by the juge de paix from

80. It also retook practices in *sociétés populaires* in Year II. Alzas, *La liberté ou la mort*, 255.

81. There were also some eighteenth-century precedents for considering punishing soldiers by dressing them in women's clothing. See Seriu, "Du féminin dans les discours militaires."

82. AN F / 9 / 218, Tarn; Hufton, *Women and the Limits of Citizenship*, 328.

83. AN F / 9 / 223, dossier 2, L'administration centrale du dept. de la Moselle aux administrations municipales, 9 prairial an 7.

the Tarn hints at why the state would not want to do so: officials sought to control, not excite, popular unruliness.[84] In Neufchâteau's vision, shaming was to come from public authorities. Women were asked to inspire young men to fight, but there does not seem to have been an equivalent to the "white feather" campaign in World War I Britain, in which women shamed apparently able-bodied men not at the front by presenting them with white feathers.[85] In late revolutionary France, cowards were to be accused in front of their compatriots, but the state was to control who was heralded or humiliated.

But even naming draft dodgers was controversial. When the deputy Bailleul proposed doing so, his colleague Andrieux opposed the measure, fearing that it would divide the French when unity was critical. Andrieux was generally opposed to public distinctions between citizens. In a debate shortly before the news of Rastadt, over who should wear the tricolor cockade, he had argued that it symbolized national citizenship, not military service. Unlike most of his colleagues, Andrieux was willing to imagine that women, as French citizens, could wear the national symbol. This inclusive vision fits with his reluctance to call attention to those who avoided military duty.[86] Others were more inclined to make distinction, though they proclaimed optimistically that there would be few names on the list of those who avoided service.[87]

Local administrators followed Bailleul's proposal to publicize names. In Orléans, the list of draft dodgers and deserters was read out loud and attached to a post of infamy, while a musician sang "Hatred and Scorn to the Children Unworthy of the Patrie." Several names were subsequently removed.[88] Cantons in the Lot reported that they had posted two lists: one of those who had left for the army and one of shirkers. The latter would not be erased until individuals did their duty.[89] Like the police minister's denunciation of Plantizé, their rhetoric exaggerated both the rareness of draft dodging and the effects of disgrace; cowards were to be humiliated in the eyes of the universe and posterity.

As far as I know, this was the first time the French government resorted to the public shaming of shirkers, even if officials had sought to punish deserters earlier.[90] It would have been easy to extend the practice of nominative lists

84. On attempts to control popular festivities, see Ozouf, *Festivals and the French Revolution;* and Mazeau, "Émotions politiques."

85. Gullace, *The Blood of Our Sons*, especially chapter 4, "The Order of the White Feather."

86. Heuer, "Hats on for the Nation!"

87. *Gazette nationale*, no. 233, 23 Floréal Year VII, 950; Chappey, "L'assassinat de Rastadt," 82.

88. "Fête funèbre célébrée à Orléans en l'honneur des plénipotentiaires français assassinés à Rastadt," in Lottin, *Recherches historiques sur la ville d'Orléans*, 240–45. Some names were removed on 30 Prairial Year VII (June 18, 1799).

89. AD Lot L225.

90. On earlier penalties for desertion, see Guinier, *L'honneur du soldat.*

from those eligible for conscription to public lists of those who served and those who did not. Certainly, officials had long lambasted deserters as cowardly; they would continue to use related rhetoric throughout the Napoleonic era. But a general condemnation of those who refused to fight was different from the display of individual names.

The dangers of such displays paralleled those accompanying the exhibition of martyrs' bodies. Focusing on martyrs' fatal wounds risked calling attention to their vulnerability and inspiring revulsion or despair rather than outrage. Publicizing the names of those who escaped, or sought to escape military service, similarly risked provoking undesired emotion: sympathy or even admiration rather than scorn. Rather than honoring men who took up arms, it emphasized the numbers of those who avoided conscription, and potentially, both divisions within the French populace and the weakness of the state.

The Return of Sacrificing Mothers?

In 1822, the Bonapartist Pierre Colau produced a retrospective celebration of military heroism: *The Soldier-Worker or Farmer Heroes*. Most of the heroes were men, but Colau opened with a "French Spartan woman." He described conscripts' departure from a village in the Ardennes in 1799. Mothers wept over sons they feared they would never see again. Marie Labbé (the heroine of the account) cried out, "When the patrie needs your children, why are you weeping to diminish their courage? I had five sons; three left as volunteers, one is dead on the field of glory, the fourth leaves today; the fifth, aged eighteen, is with me. But if his strong arms are necessary to defend liberty, he is ready to leave, and the sacrifice made." Colau claimed that no woman in ancient Sparta would have had more courage, and that inspired by Marie Labbé, other mothers dried their tears and conscripts left to shouts of "Vive la République!"[91]

As we will see, Colau's rhetoric responded to royalist propaganda in the early Restoration, which depicted mothers devastated by the loss of their sons and grateful to a returned monarchy that ended conscription. Several collections of anecdotes published after the end of the Napoleonic wars related versions of the story.[92] Alluding to women's support for war invoked feminine patriotism without engaging the politically charged imagery of the Revolution. But it is also striking that to demonstrate maternal selflessness, Colau turned not to the radical Revolution or to later years of the Napoleonic wars, but to this moment: the beginning of conscription.

Colau's account echoed Plutarch's story of a Spartan woman more concerned with national victory than the fate of her sons, a story initially revived

91. Colau, *Le soldat laboureur,* 13–15.

92. Among others, see P. F. Tissot, *Les fastes de la gloire*, 1:22–23; and Arnault, *Biographie nouvelle des contemporains*, 10:189.

in late eighteenth-century France. This version may have corresponded to a real incident, or at least Jean-Baptiste Bara, the deputy from the department of the Ardennes, reported on December 16, 1798, that "Mothers, whose sons have been in the army for years, inspire the fifth, and last son, remaining at home with them to fight, and forget their own needs to think only of the patrie."[93] Other deputies presented similar tales, like the representative from the Eure who praised the "generous mother, who herself took her son to the flags of honor, and watched him incorporated into the troops to cries of 'Vive la République!'"[94]

Speeches, songs, and artwork in 1799 suggest a renewed emphasis on maternal sacrifice. Recruitment propaganda contrasted the militia of the Old Regime with forms of recruitment allegedly accepted by all, including conscripts' mothers. The 1792 song "Comparison of the Old and New Regime" had juxtaposed the despotic prerevolutionary government, when mothers sobbed to see their sons taken for the army, with the new order: "all mothers arm their sons, prepare their bags, and send them to serve in the camps."[95] Orators in 1799 used similar language. Representatives of the department of the Cher thus reported in January 1799 that "Once upon a time, the mere word 'militia' provoked consternation, and one heard only the cries and whimpers of mothers. Today, a thousand men leave; the law orders, and all obey. Mothers, wives, and girlfriends silence themselves, and warriors leave singing."[96]

Officials also promised families that their sons were defending them—and exhorted them to send off their children. In Gand, in modern Belgium, the professor of literature Pierre Botte assured parents that warriors would protect their homes:

> Fathers of families, tender mothers! You fret that a necessary law will separate you temporarily from your children and calls them to the field of honor. Reassure yourselves: vengeance will be as prompt and glorious as it is legitimate. You will rejoice in their courage; if you are attacked by an assassin, you will see them ardent and ready to defend you . . . you will not refuse the country the arms it calls to its defense.[97]

Botte's theme reflected an optimistic hope of a speedy victory. It also reflected a very real worry that parents would keep their sons at home.

In Beauvais, the songwriter Boinvilliers presented a hymn on 16 Prairial (June 4). Like the "Chant du départ," it featured figures bidding farewell to

93. J.-B. Bara, *Discours prononcé par . . . sur le départ des conscrits*, 3.

94. Eude, *Discours . . . sur le départ des conscrits du département de l'Eure*, 3.

95. Boussemart, *Le républicain moustache*, 8. The song appeared in November 1792.

96. *Bulletin décadaire*, no. 13, 1st décade of Pluviôse Year VII.

97. Botte, *Discours prononcé par le citoyen*, 10.

new warriors. The singers included a magistrate, a mother, and a young warrior. The mother proclaims: "My husband serves the state / he has his share of glory / My sons ease the hardships of a long widowhood / They remind me of his virtues / But because the patrie calls upon the virile and sublime courage of a Brutus / Go, my sons, I will no longer hold you back."[98] Her declaration implied that she had hesitated, but ultimately acknowledged the legitimacy of the patrie's demands.

Such feminine sacrifice did not, however, mean taking up arms themselves, as the minister of war Bernadotte made explicit when one woman, the citoyenne Laville, wrote him in August 1799, asking to be allowed to fight for the nation. He replied that he was moved by "the generous sentiments that inspire your love of the country and lift you beyond your sex." But it was a question not of his personal opinion, but of law: the April 30, 1793, law forbade women in the troops. Women could promote "the courage of male soldiers; they must not provide the example in combat."[99]

Two moments from September and October 1799 are particularly revealing of the ways that the Directorial government sought to use women to demonstrate their sacrifice of men: the funeral for General Barthélemy Joubert and the exhibition of a painting by Guillaume Guillon-Lethière, *The Patrie en Danger or the Enrollment of Volunteers*.[100] Joubert's funeral retook aspects of the ceremonies for the Rastadt martyrs, but it also highlighted feminine sacrifice in face of war. Guillon-Lethière's painting similarly reworked earlier iconography. Historians have taken it as exemplary of prescriptive masculine and feminine wartime patriotism at the end of the 1790s. Considering it closely shows both its endorsement of republican sacrifice and changing reactions to that vision.

THE FUNERAL OF GENERAL JOUBERT

General Barthélemy Joubert died on August 15, 1799, at the battle of Novi, a significant defeat for France against the joint Russian and Austrian army. Funeral ceremonies took place a month later, on September 18, and blended with contemporaneous festivals celebrating the Foundation of the Republic.[101] Unlike the ceremonies for the Rastadt martyrs, the funeral involved an empty cenotaph. Orators also assured their audiences that they would not dwell on gore. For example, the captain Herbin promised that he

98. Boinvilliers, *Le cri de l'humanité*.

99. SHD 1 Yi 33, cited in Goupil-Travert, *Braves combattantes*, 43.

100. Guillaume Guillon-Lethière, *La patrie en danger ou l'enrôlement des volontaires*, 1799 (Musée de la Révolution française, Vizille).

101. Bernard Gainot has argued that while the festivals tried to present civic appeasement, they were subverted by calls to vengeance. See Gainot, "Le dernier voyage" and "Rites et contexte."

would not depict a tragic scene, uncovering a bloody corpse and invoking the patrie in tears. Simply hearing Joubert's story would touch their hearts. At the same time, Herbin and other speakers promised that emotions would provoke action. Tears—for both men and women—would not be sterile but lead to vengeance.[102]

In planning the ceremony, the minister of the interior Quinette imagined wives and girls throwing flowers on the cenotaph of a young warrior "taken from victory and love. They will think of his unfortunate widow and shed tears; they will see the patrie in mourning, with the death of one man, and will excite their husbands, brothers, and lovers, to avenge him or to die like him."[103] While this was standard revolutionary rhetoric, Quinette also linked feminine patriotism directly to the continuation of war.

Accounts of Joubert's death played up his wife's role in inspiring his heroism and women's own heroism in accepting the deaths of their husbands and sons. Joubert had married shortly before leaving for Italy. In bidding farewell to his wife, he reportedly promised that "You'll see me return either victorious or dead." On the day of his death, he showed a portrait of his wife to his aides de camp, declaring, "I'll be victorious today, I've sworn it to her and to the Republic."[104] Funerary speeches depicted her as supporting his resolve and inspiring others. The legislator Mathieu-Augustin Cornet proclaimed that the funeral was "a spectacle for the sweetheart and the wife! The women of Sparta said to their husbands and sons, in giving them their shields, return with this or on it; Joubert returned on his."[105]

A day before the funeral, the *Journal de Paris* printed an article by Auguste Hus, a commissioner in Turin. Hus assumed the voice of French women speaking to new conscripts. His imaginary patriots invoked the heroines of antiquity and resolved that "As mothers of families, we will make the greatest effort that nature can require, silencing a mother's heart; we will say to . . . our young children . . . if you prefer slavery to liberty, your cradle should become a tomb; we are no longer your mothers. As wives, the image of Joubert's widow is under our eyes. We will sacrifice our husbands to Bellone [the goddess of war]."[106] Such speeches asserted that women should not only accept conscription law, and with it, the ongoing hardships of war. They should also play an active role in sacrificing their loved ones.

102. Herbin, *Éloge funèbre du citoyen Joubert*, 12–13.

103. AN F / 1 / c / 1 / 113 and F / 1 / a / 23.

104. *Bulletin officiel du Directoire helvétique et des autorités du Canton de Léman*, no. 2, September 3, 1799, 12.

105. *Procès-verbal du Conseil des Anciens*, 25 Fructidor Year VII, 520.

106. *Journal de Paris*, no. 361, 1 Complémentaire Year VII (September 17, 1799), 1581. Hus's exhortation is discussed briefly in Bordes, "La patrie en danger."

GUILLON-LETHIÈRE AND THE "PATRIE EN DANGER"

Prominent works of art also depicted familial and communal sacrifice with soldiers' departures. One of the most striking is Guillon-Lethière's *The Patrie en Danger or the Enrollment of Volunteers*.[107] The painting was displayed to acclaim in the salon of late September and October 1799; it was subsequently made available as a print. In the center, a group of recruits raise swords to salute a seated statue of liberty, while another gives a passionate farewell kiss to his sweetheart. To the left, a woman holds up a baby as an apparent offering; on the right, another woman brings an armload of weapons.

The painting celebrated both men's and women's patriotic sacrifice. It recalled older iconography, like Machy's 1792 *Devotion to the Patrie*, which depicts a woman offering her son to the nation. Darcy Grimaldo Grigsby has argued that the painting also revised *The Oath of the Horatii*, exhibited fourteen years earlier. The fatherland is menaced, and brothers rally with arms held high; but in this version, women are actively supporting, rather than lamenting, war.[108]

Critics applauded its depiction of patriotic femininity. Writing on the salon exhibition, J. P. Chaussard remarked,

> Enflamed and beautiful with virtue and the passion for liberty, the women love these heroes. The young men receive their kisses and embraces; they will be victorious. . . . How the arms and soul of this woman are wrapped around this young warrior, how he is full of love and courage! The action that these women bring to arms is energetic and true. How I am grateful to the painter to have represented women in this way. It serves to remind them of their most beautiful titles to love and glory, these two truly French passions.[109]

The speech highlighted both women's actions and their imagined effects on men.

The title of the painting echoed the July 11, 1792, declaration of the patrie en danger, which had been promoted by Jean Debry himself. The term was controversial in 1799. In September, General Jourdan proposed that the legislature proclaim that the patrie was again in danger. The Council of Five Hundred, led by Lucien Bonaparte, rejected the proposal; legislators feared that neo-Jacobins wanted to use it to seize control from the Directory.[110]

107. Bordes and Chevalier, *Catalogue des peintures*, 90–93; and Bordes, "La patrie en danger." See also L'histoire par l'image, http://www.histoire-image.org/site/oeuvre/analyse.php?i=251.

108. Grigsby, "Revolutionary Sons."

109. J. B. P. Chaussard, *La décade philosophique, littéraire, et politique*, 10 Vendémiaire Year VIII (October 2, 1799), 41–42. The text is reproduced in Bordes and Chevalier, *Catalogue des peintures*, 93.

110. Gildea, *Children of the Revolution*, 26.

Indeed, while the painting celebrated volunteers, it stepped back from universal mobilization. Alan Forrest has called attention to a second focal group, centered on a clerk who records the names of those called up. A young boy carries weapons, while a magistrate in the uniform of a Director restrains two older men wearing laurels from earlier victories and offering their services anew. The figures of the older men suggest that what is desired is not a new universal levée en masse, but rather the departure of one group: virile, young, single men.

While the painting showed patriotic devotion, it heralded romance rather than sacrifice. The language of love and reward echoes through Chaussard's tribute. He emphasized less maternal sacrifice than the passionate kiss farewell. His rapture about a woman's arms around a young warrior is similar to the postcard imagery of World War I, which represented soldiers inspired by the love of women at home.[111]

The idea that the brave man gets the girl while the coward is condemned to a loveless life appeared throughout the Revolution. But the theme of romance as a reward for military service became increasingly resonant in the late 1790s. Officials presented Joubert as "taken from victory and love" and his funeral as "a spectacle for the sweetheart and the wife!" Hus's article in the *Journal de Paris* began by exhorting women to overcome nature to send off their sons but switched gears to claim: "The coward cannot experience love. Condemned to vulgar pleasures, the coward, the slave, will never know the real enthusiasm of love, this sublime sentiment."[112]

Conclusion

Guillon-Lethière had intended to follow up his work with a larger painting. The art historian Philippe Bordes provides compelling explanations for why this did not happen. An official command was unlikely, given that the competition had ended. The military situation improved in late 1799, making the patrie en danger less relevant. Perhaps most importantly, the emerging cult of personality around Bonaparte provided a rival iconography.

Guillon-Lethière had particularly close connections to the first consul—he went to Spain in 1800 with Bonaparte's brother Lucien—but his loss of interest was not simply individual.[113] Instead, it corresponds to a shift away from republican imagery, both a long-term transition and an immediate response to the challenges of using radical iconography to legitimate war in 1799. The very aspects of the Rastadt commemorations that seemed most powerful as military propaganda ultimately limited them. Accounts of threats to French

111. For examples, see Huss, *Histoires de famille*.

112. *Journal de Paris*, no. 361, 1 Complémentaire Year VII (September 17, 1799), 1581.

113. Bordes, "La patrie en danger," 306.

families, the display of bloodstained clothing, and cries of vengeance reworked earlier strategies for stirring popular emotion and directed it to military ends. But by 1799, the image of blood spurting on shocked wives and children was less effective in promoting continued warfare. Instead, contemporaries turned more to promising glory and romantic reward, while the Napoleonic state would also quietly become more effective in exercising police and administrative control.

Decrying attacks on the Rastadt martyrs as ministers of peace was convenient, but also hints at real hopes of peace, even if those hopes seemed to be dashed. In the next chapter, we turn from calls for renewed war to the ways people imagined peace, both before and soon after the Jourdan Law.

CHAPTER FIVE

The Theater of Peace: Imagining Soldiers' Homecomings

IN FEBRUARY 1801, the actors of the popular Parisian theater Montansier performed a new play to celebrate peace between France and Austria: *The Guinguette, or Celebrations for the Peace.* The heroine, Georgette, wants to marry a soldier; her mother wants her to wed a wealthy children's toymaker named Frivolous. The mother admits that Frivolous is a coward, but dismisses his lack of courage as irrelevant since war is ending. Even if war continues, a fainthearted husband means that Georgette would not need to worry about the risks of prolonged absence and infidelity associated with soldiers. Despite her mother's prodding, Georgette remains loyal to the sergeant Courchamps (Braves-the-Fields). Her rich uncle saves the day by offering the young couple 600 gold francs, making the sergeant more than equal to the wealthy Frivolous. When thanked, the uncle regrets that he cannot provide more, claiming, "I would like to be rich enough to offer the same thing to all the brave men of the army."[1]

Another theater, l'Ambigu Comique, offered a similar celebration: *The French Artemisia, or the Happy Effects of Peace.*[2] It featured a colonel's wife, Madame Vermancourt. After hearing that her husband and her daughter's fiancé have died in the battle of Arcole, Madame Vermancourt makes a wax image of her husband and visits it faithfully. Once peace is declared, the colonel returns. Learning of his wife's devotion, he decides to surprise her. When Madame Vermancourt makes her daily pilgrimage to the memorial and

1. Villiers and Bonel, *La guinguette, ou réjouissances pour la paix*, 24.
2. Belfort, *L'Artémise française ou les heureux effets de la paix.*

FIGURE 5.1. *Detail of a Fan Celebrating the Benefits of the Peace of Campo-Formio, 1797.* Bibliothèque Nationale de France.

caresses the wax statue, she finds it replaced by her living husband. After she recovers from fainting, she rejoices. Her daughter's fiancé also returns, and the young couple weds happily.

A few months later, in October 1801, as Napoleon prepared a triumphant festival of peace, the Théâtre Louvois offered its own take on the end of war: *Café in a Small Town.*[3] It presented a café owner, Froment, who wants his daughter, Lise, to postpone marriage until peace arrives. Two men court the young woman. One, Durand, is a rich but gullible grocer. He is outwitted when Dalbain—a patriotic soldier and Lise's true love—fakes a letter from a supposed business acquaintance of the grocer. According to the letter, Persia,

3. Aude, *Le café d'une petite ville.* He was adapting works he had composed earlier, first with Tissot, *Les bruits de la paix,* and then as *La paix.* He also reprised the play in 1809.

China, and Goa are opposed to peace; England will not sign a treaty without the consent of the emperor of Morocco, and the whole world will soon be on fire, making cinnamon outrageously expensive and sugar worth its weight in gold. Durand is convinced by these predictions and seeks to profit from continued warfare. Instead, peace is declared. Lise weds her Dalbain, while the shocked grocer finds that his stocks of sugar and spices are worth little.

The playwrights behind each of these works were quite different from one another. Pierre-Antoine Villiers, one of the authors of the *Guinguette,* was a veteran who had been a captain in the third regiment of dragoons. Madame Belfort composed *The French Artemisia.* Women playwrights were relatively rare; she was a member of an acting family and may have authored at least one other play. Joseph Aude, the author of *Café in a Small Town,* was a prolific and well-known dramatist, old enough when war started not to be compelled to fight.[4]

Yet if the playwrights differed, their offerings were all typical of topical theater produced to celebrate peace. In February and March of 1801, theaters rushed to commemorate the Treaty of Lunéville between France and Austria. They offered new celebrations in October and November for the preliminaries of the Treaty of Amiens with England, timed to commemorate the anniversary of Napoleon's ascent to power on 18 Brumaire (November 9, 1799). While producing new shows, they also adapted plays that been produced three years prior in the autumn of 1797 to celebrate an earlier peace with Austria, the Treaty of Campo Formio.

Most of these plays were formulaic, although more talented writers added colorful details and actors could make stock characters memorable. Performances featured happy endings. The wounded and the supposed dead proved to be alive and well, and recognized for their valor. Cowardly men, or greedy figures hoping to profit from ongoing warfare, met with appropriate comeuppances, while well-intentioned but misguided parents came to appreciate their daughters' devotion to soldiers and rejoiced in their nuptials.

Indeed, whatever the specifics of the plot, almost every play ended with a wedding. Contemporaries remarked that this was almost obligatory in French comedy.[5] Modern surveys of revolutionary theater confirm the ubiquity of the theme.[6] The depiction of marriage as an end to uncertainty and distress was particularly prominent in works celebrating peace; shows included *Peace or*

4. Finch, *Women's Writing in Nineteenth-Century France*, 279n29. Belfort's other surviving work is *Ne jugez pas sur l'apparence* (Paris: Fages, 1804).

5. Mercier, *Le Nouveau Paris*, 5:211. When assessing *Retour de Rastadt* in May 1799, censors noted that French plays required romance. AN F / 7 / 3492.

6. Kennedy, "The Most Performed Plays," 21–22.

the Lovers Reunited, *Marriage with the Peace*, and *Peace and Marriage or the Warrior Rewarded*.[7]

These plays offer a rare window onto the effects of war and peacemaking on gender relations and family life. In the previous chapter, we looked at how conscription was instituted in 1799 shortly after the Jourdan Law. Here we turn to visions of peace both before and after that law. Popular theater dedicated to treaties in 1797 and in 1801 celebrated the moment that peace had arrived, but before men were demobilized. It imagined veterans' homecomings and portrayed the creation of new households that went beyond their return to existing families.

The joyous resolutions of theatrical performances allowed contemporaries to address anxieties that were otherwise difficult to discuss. If petitioners seeking to come home presented soldiers' demobilization as a desirable—even desperately wanted—outcome, theater raised doubts. Could rumors of peace be trusted or was it better to assume that war would continue indefinitely? Would absent lovers or husbands ever return? If one never saw a body, could one be sure that a man really was dead? How long should one wait to wed a soldier, especially if there had been no news of him for months or even years? Would young women find disfigured veterans attractive mates? Would returning soldiers be loyal to their sweethearts, or had they learned too much debauchery and violence on the battlefields? Were soldiers sensible economic choices as partners or would women be better off with other husbands? Was marriage in fact an appropriate reward for veterans?

This chapter begins by looking more closely at the overlapping roles of theater as propaganda, entertainment, and means of making sense of the world. Then we turn to works specifically devoted to peace, exploring both the doubts such works reveal about the reality of treaties and the explanations they provided for why soldiers had often disappeared from contact. In the third section we explore how plays both celebrated martial masculinity and confronted its limits. Playwrights sought to defuse concerns that men would return too injured and weakened to be useful citizens or desirable spouses; they also addressed the opposite possibility: that combatants would have become too aggressive, trained to conquer both on the battlefield and in the bedroom. The subsequent section moves from worries about men to models of feminine behavior. Plays insisted on young women's loyalty, despite doubts about men's survival and physical, moral, and economic attractiveness. They added a critical generational aspect: young women were expected to be loyal to soldiers even when their parents sought alternative grooms. In the last section, we return to the dynamics of cultural recycling, the practice

7. Mittié, *La paix ou les amans réunis*; and Cambronne, *La paix et l'hymen ou le guerrier récompensé*. Gamas's 1797 *Le mariage à la paix* was unpublished but described in Lecomte, *Napoléon et l'empire racontés par le théâtre*, 18.

of reusing familiar references in a new political order. While recruitment practices shifted significantly after the institution of conscription in 1798, the theater of peace looks remarkably similar both before and shortly after Napoleon's ascent to power.

Vaudevilles

Companies produced hundreds of pièces de circonstance. Performances marked current events, from anniversaries of revolutionary *journées* to military triumphs and the birth of Napoleon's son. Many were bellicose, trumpeting the brave deeds of French troops and the marvels of Napoleon. But a surprisingly large number celebrated peace. Jean-Paul Bertaud has claimed that of 143 plays performed between 1799 and 1815 that treated war or military life, at least 70 were devoted to peace.[8] There were at least 100 works from the Treaty of Campo Formio in 1797 through 1815, or slightly fewer than half of the 236 plays connected to war I have documented. At least 70 date from either 1797 or 1801–2. A few playwrights also celebrated peace with Austria in 1806, the Peace of Tilsit in 1807, and armistices in 1809; the early Restoration would bring a new set of performances.

While these works reprised older traditions, most plays used to celebrate peace were part of a relatively new genre, vaudeville. This is not the burlesque associated with the American stage, but rather a mixture of songs and spoken dialogue. It had its roots in prerevolutionary comic opera and was linked to the Théâtre du Vaudeville, opened in January 1792. The term "vaudeville" to identify a style seems to date from 1794. The genre was less clearly defined than another contemporary innovation, melodrama, and troupes adopted various labels, including vaudeville, folie, parade, bagatelle, and bluette.[9] Vaudevilles were particularly useful for celebrating peace. Unlike melodramas, they were short, one, or at most two, acts. They could be written and rehearsed quickly. Audiences were promised laughter and a happy ending; they were sent home with catchy, upbeat melodies. As the *Moniteur* reported, "The Vaudeville is well positioned to interpret public joy; its language is loved and can be easily repeated."[10]

Analyzing this corpus is difficult, in part because shows ceased to be topical after a few days, weeks, or at most, months, and works rarely became standard parts of theatrical repertoires. Many scripts were never published;

8. Bertaud, "Le théâtre et la guerre,"188. Bertaud bases his numbers on Lecomte, *Napoléon et l'empire racontés par le théâtre*. Lecomte's interest, however, was Napoleon; he catalogued plays related to war and peace as a secondary concern, so records are incomplete.

9. Fournier, "Le vaudeville ou l'art de s'adapter."

10. *Gazette nationale ou le Moniteur universel*, no. 151, 1 Ventôse Year IX (February 20, 1801), 630.

others are preserved only in rare copies, and there is no systematic finding guide.[11] Newspapers, censorship records, and police reports, however, provide clues to the plots of missing works, and information on reception. Press coverage is more extensive for the 1790s, before Bonaparte slashed the number of papers in Paris from sixty to thirteen in January 1800. Several newspapers were dedicated solely to theatrical reviews, most notably, the *Courrier des spectacles ou journal des théâtres,* published from 1797 to 1807.[12] Others appeared briefly, like the 1797 *Censeur dramatique, ou journal des principaux théâtres de Paris et des départements* or Fabien Pillet's *Année théâtrale pour l'an X*. General newspapers, like the *Journal des débats et des décrets* and the *Journal de Paris,* also reported on popular or controversial performances.

Censors' comments also reveal both what authorities expected to resonate with audiences and what they feared.[13] Beginning in January 1791, revolutionaries tried to eliminate controls over the stage. Like many optimistic innovations of the early Revolution, this freedom did not last. From 1793 onward, multiple groups, including local councils, the Committee of Public Safety, and the Commission of Public Instruction, sought to repress works judged dangerous or unpatriotic.[14] While some forms of surveillance relaxed after the Terror, the minister of police was charged with oversight of theaters in January 1796. Authorities kept a keen eye on audiences, noting what characters or lines provoked most reactions.[15] Censorship would become even more intense after 1806 when Napoleon's government slashed the number of officially approved venues.[16]

11. Kennedy et al., *Theatre, Opera, and Audiences,* lists performances, but little information on most plays. The Calendrier électronique des spectacles sous l'ancien régime et sous la révolution also lists performances (https://cesar.huma-num.fr/cesar2/), but does not go beyond 1800 or describe plots. Summaries of many, but far from all, later works appear in Lecomte, *Napoléon et l'empire racontés par le théâtre.*

12. *Le courrier des spectacles ou journal des théâtres* (Paris: Migneret, 1797–1807), 21 vols.

13. Krakovitch, *Les pièces de théâtre soumises à la censure,* "Le théâtre de la république et la censure," and "La censure théâtrale"; and Roy and Emaljanow, *Romantic and Revolutionary Theatre.*

14. An August 1793 decree gave local councils the right to suspend performances, but the Committee of Public Safety also intervened, while a decree of 2 Floréal Year II (May 14, 1794) charged the Commission de l'instruction publique with overseeing the stage.

15. For police reports on theater, see Aulard, *Paris pendant la réaction* and *Paris sous le consulat.* Some reports on censorship during the Directory are in AN F/7/3491 and F/7/3492.

16. On June 6, 1806, Napoleon's government limited the number of officially approved theaters in Paris to twelve, so that the remaining theaters could be more effectively policed. The decree of July 29, 1807, reduced these further, to eight, a major diminution from the fifty Parisian theaters in 1791 and even the twenty-five or twenty-six (depending on how one classified performance spaces) at the beginning of the Napoleonic era. These included four "great theaters" (the Théâtre-Français, the Opéra, the Opéra-Comique, and

Information about the playwrights, actors, and the audiences of shows is uneven. Some writers were obscure; a few, like Joseph Aude, were extraordinarily prolific.[17] In theory, playwrights became known only if a show was successful, as audiences called for the author to reveal himself (or rarely, herself) at the curtain. In practice, critics sometimes noted playwrights' identities even if the audience did not ask for them. Published scripts usually included authors' names, but the scripts for many shows were not printed.

Audiences included people from a broad reach of society, from artisans to former aristocrats.[18] Shows provided cheap amusements, and star actors drew crowds.[19] Those who could not attend a performance or who wanted a record could purchase scripts or associated music and lyrics.[20] Theater marking major events was even more affordable. Revolutionary and Napoleonic governments paid theaters to perform on major holidays.[21] Companies offered free tickets to celebrate the Treaty of Lunéville on March 21, 1801, and police reported that theaters were full.[22] Similarly, theaters opened free on November 8, 1801, in celebration of the peace.

This followed an older tradition; as the cultural critic Louis-Sébastien Mercier had noted, troupes in the 1780s gave free performances on historic occasions such as the declaration of peace or the birth of a prince.[23] But in 1798 and 1801 there were far more theatrical venues than there had been in the Old Regime. Not all subsidized performances were pièces de circonstance; theaters trotted out other plays likely to be popular and possible to present on short notice. But even such shows often began by acknowledging the nature of the occasion.

In general, critics, censors, and audiences were all accepting of plays produced for major events, especially celebrations of peace. They acknowledged

---

the Opéra-Buffa) and four secondary ones (the Théâtres du Vaudeville, des Variétés, de la Gaîté, and de l'Ambigu Comique). There were thus far fewer performances of any sort after 1806, but the procès-verbaux of censors are richer after 1807. Krakovitch, "La censure théâtrale," 102; and Welschinger, *La censure sous le premier empire.*

17. Loubinoux, "Les figures du théâtre de Joseph Aude" and "Ambitions mal placées."

18. On audiences, see Davidson, "Making Society 'Legible'" and *France after Revolution.*

19. For ticket prices and affordability, see AN F/7/3491.The most celebrated actor was François-Joseph Talma, who appeared primarily at the Comédie Français. Works like the 1797 *Critique des acteurs et actrices des différents théâtres de Paris* commented with a mixture of admiration and acidity on performers' careers.

20. The price hovered around a franc; scripts were advertised for 90 pence in 1797, a franc or 1 franc 20 pence in 1801, and perhaps surprisingly, often the same price in 1810. Prices are listed on scripts and in the *Journal général de la littérature de la France.* Songs from vaudevilles were available individually, or in collections, like *Chansonnier de la paix pour l'an X*, or Winckler, *Le répertoire du vaudeville.*

21. For a list of free performances in Paris during the Consulate and Empire, see Lecomte, *Napoléon et le monde dramatique*; and Julian, "Les 'gratis' de Napoléon."

22. Aulard, *Paris sous le consulat*, 2:215.

23. Mercier, *Tableau de Paris*, 3:18.

implausible plots, repetition, and hastily written or clumsy verses, but forgave them. As the critic Aubin Louis Millin put it, "it is impossible to judge rigorously a play whose goal is to celebrate peace. One is disposed in advance to indulgence."[24]

Such "indulgence" could serve propagandistic goals.[25] Napoleon's government sought to disguise propaganda as free expression. Officials planted items in newspapers as if they were reports by objective observers and protested if contemporaries acknowledged censorship. Theater similarly served governmental aims; shows praised Napoleon, starting in 1797 (well before he was in power, but when the cult of the Petit Caporal was spreading with the Italian campaigns) and intensifying during the Consulate and especially the Empire. Because plays ended happily, worries expressed on stage could add realism, while legitimating both state power and war.

But theater also provided a more indirect means of conveying political and social messages than art or newspapers, as characters could function as mouthpieces for different views. While certain shows were subsidized, playwrights and actors also relied on the pocketbooks of audiences. If the characters, plots, and messages did not resonate with popular preoccupations, theatrical troupes could risk financial loss or even bankruptcy.

Doubts, Bets, and Dreams: Visions of Peace

On April 17, 1797, France and Austria negotiated the preliminary treaty of Leoben; on October 18, they signed that of Campo Formio. Although France remained at war with England, these treaties effectively ended hostilities on the European continent. When the news reached Paris, theatrical troupes read the announcements to their audiences and added lines to their performances to celebrate impending peace. In April, actors performing *Anacreon* at the Théâtre de l'Émulation proclaimed, "Leave in peace the god of combats," to great applause; and the audience at the Théâtre Feydeau warmly welcomed spontaneous verses from the actor playing the lead in the *Barber of Seville*.[26] On the day peace was announced in October, the Théâtre du Vaudeville changed *The Balloon of Mousseaux*, so that the protagonist—a parachutist—declared, "I descend from the sky to bring heavenly news."[27]

Companies soon rushed to produce shows specifically devoted to peace. The *Courrier des spectacles* observed on November 3, 1797, that "All the

24. *Magasin encyclopédique*, 6th year [1801], 5:550.

25. Holtman, *Napoleonic Propaganda*; and Forrest, "Propaganda and the Legitimation of Power."

26. Aulard, *Paris pendant la réaction*, 4:80.

27. *Journal de Paris*, no. 37, 7 Brumaire Year VI (October 28, 1797), 152. See also *Décade philosophique, littéraire et politique*, no. 5, 20 Brumaire Year VI (November 10, 1797), 299.

theaters of the capital are racing to celebrate the peace. . . . Five different comedies, all under the title *The Peace,* were presented yesterday in this city."[28] Provincial theaters similarly marked the occasion, presenting versions of plays that had appeared in the capital and staging original works.[29]

The 1797 peace did not last, as France became embroiled in renewed war against a Second Coalition that united Russia, Great Britain, and, eventually, Austria. On February 9, 1801, France and Austria signed a new agreement, the Treaty of Lunéville. Contemporaries celebrated with topical plays, operas, and vaudevilles in February and March of 1801. They did so again after the preliminaries of peace between England and France on October 1, 1801, and the Treaty of Amiens, signed on March 25, 1802. Subsequent treaties and rumors of peace would inspire further, if less intense, bursts of theatrical celebration. Most notably, theaters celebrated hopes for peace in January 1806, after Austria's defeat in the Battle of Austerlitz. Although the battle of Eylau against Russia in February 1807 was too indecisive and bloody for easy commemoration, playwrights welcomed the Peace of Tilsit, signed with Russia in July 1807. A few plays in 1809 marked French victory over Austria and the subsequent treaty.[30] Works could be crafted to cover a variety of political contingencies. Commenting on one proposed play in October 1809, censors noted that "the details are so vague that they could apply to any kind of peace, whatever its nature or conditions."[31]

Throughout both the late Revolution and the Napoleonic era, plays produced to celebrate peace often began with a basic concern: could one really believe that war would end? Could news of a treaty or alliance be trusted? If so, would it last? While French governments tried to control news about the war, popular speculation was heated. Parisian police regularly reported on *bruits de paix* (rumors of peace) and *bruits de guerre* (rumors about the war). Titles of plays alluded to such speculations, as did Aude's *Rumors of Peace* (first performed July 1796, again in April and November 1797) and Magol's *New Rumors of Peace* (February 1801).

28. Aulard, *Paris pendant la réaction*, 4:434.

29. On April 11, 1800, the minister of the interior told all theater directors that only plays authorized for performance in Paris could be staged in the rest of France; the written order was to be shown to the prefect of police in Paris or to the departmental prefect in provinces before a play was announced. See Roy and Emaljanow, *Romantic and Revolutionary Theatre*, 86; and Holtman, *Napoleonic Propaganda*, 150. But a number of plays were staged in provincial towns in 1801 that had not appeared first in Paris.

30. Plays celebrating peace in 1806 included Aude's *La paix*, Barré's *Les deux n'en font qu'un*, and Seville's *Le dernier bulletin de la paix*. At least fifteen works celebrated peace in 1807 and six in 1809.

31. AN F / 21 / 987, "Ils reviennent." The censors were commenting on a script subsequently published as Balisson de Rougemont, *La paix*.

While rumors fed hopes of peace, men and women fretted about whether war would actually end. Much news was unreliable, at least until treaties were promulgated. In April 1797, the Central Bureau of Police reported that "The most sensitive individuals and women already applaud the preliminaries of peace, hoping that they will lead to the end of fighting and stop the outpouring of blood. Others appear uncertain, and do not dare believe the news, objecting that it is not official."[32] Even official news was not seen as trustworthy. A survey of French newspapers in 1800 (shortly before censorship reduced the number of papers) typifies wariness: it lambasted the *Journal des défenseurs de la patrie* for its misleading claims that the enemy purportedly lost 400 or 500 men, while not even an officer was wounded on the French side.[33]

By 1801, hopes for peace had been repeatedly disappointed. Playwrights sometimes incorporated references to the vagaries of peace negotiations into their works. *Finally, We're Here*, first produced at the Vaudeville in February 1801, featured Germain, who hesitates to marry his daughter during wartime—but rushes to propose a husband for her every time a peace treaty appears possible.[34] Germain's judgment, however, is flawed; the grooms he favors include a hack writer, a war profiteer, and a pastry-maker. Such characters provide comic relief, but also call attention to the comparative dignity of soldiers. Germain's plans flounder in ways that follow the twists and turns of French fortunes. He thinks the peace will last with "Leoben, then Campo Formio, but these two imperfect treaties did not advance affairs." Here the playwrights (in the mouth of the eager father) used the occasion for a punning reference to stalled arrangements for the young woman's nuptials; matchmakers, "like the peace, had stopped with the preliminaries."[35] They also reminded their audiences of failed negotiations for a peace treaty with Austria in 1797. While the celebrations for peace in 1801 promised to be more durable—and the authors were savvy enough to proclaim that Napoleon had brought lasting peace—the play's less obvious message was that peace treaties could fail.

Various other works portrayed characters' disbelief in the reality of peace, especially in the spring of 1801. In Bardel's *Rosine's Marriage,* performed in Grenoble on March 26, the heroine's father does not want her to marry until peace arrives. When her lover, Duval, frets that war could last another ten years, Rosine's father, Deschamps, reassures him that the wait will be much shorter. In this version of a common plot, Duval has not yet been called up to fight, though he is likely to be enlisted. Deschamps tells him that it would be better to be free if he were called up than to "leave an adored wife in

32. Aulard, *Paris pendant la réaction,* 4:81.

33. *Petites vérités au grand jour,* 107–8.

34. Radet, Desfontaines, and Barré, *Enfin nous y voilà.*

35. Radet, Desfontaines, and Barré, *Enfin nous y voilà*, 7.

desolation," but also predicts that "peace will come at the moment you least expect it." Duval admits, "It has been so long that peace has been promised that I no longer believe in it." Deschamps insists that he should not lose faith in the ability of valorous soldiers to bring an honorable peace to France.[36]

In *The Coward*, performed in April 1801, it is the father's turn to worry that peace would never come: "It has been promised for so long that I do not dare count on its return."[37] In Maurin's *Peace or the Triumph of Mars*, the allegory of Peace herself is uncertain whether she will be able to return.[38] A year later, in a play celebrating the Treaty of Amiens, one character sighs after "peace! But it has been so long that it has been promised," while another acknowledges that he had begun to believe that it would never arrive.[39]

As we saw in chapter 3, veterans seeking to come or remain home in 1796 and 1797 invoked the imminent arrival of peace, expressing their confidence that the French government would be victorious. Their claims echoed official propaganda but were particularly useful for men seeking to prove that they were no longer needed as soldiers. Popular theater hints at the converse: the persistence of doubts about the reality of peace treaties, even as characters reassured each other that they had been wrong to question the government's ability to end war or the sincerity of its desire to do so. While skepticism appeared throughout the period, it seems to have surfaced most in 1801 and 1802, after earlier peace agreements had proved to be short-lived.

Playwrights alluded not only to individual doubts, but also to bets about whether war would end. Plots acknowledged the widespread social practice of gambling. Wagers about the outcome of a battle or diplomatic negotiations were common, even in the charged political atmosphere of the Terror, and continued during the Directory and Consulate.[40] For playwrights, bets provided a useful literary device; they heightened dramatic tension and necessarily entailed a winner and a loser.

These theatrical losers were almost always selfish, men who had mercenary reasons for wanting war to continue. They were the opposite of the useful and generous citizens revolutionaries celebrated, and inevitably met just comeuppances. The 1797 *The Bet*, by five of the playwrights associated with the Théâtre du Vaudeville, thus featured Dubreil, a young doctor who owes

36. Bardel, *La paix ou le mariage de Rosine*, 18–20.

37. Noël, *Poltronet*, 42.

38. Maurin, *La paix ou le triomphe de Mars*.

39. P. G., *Que d'heureux tu vas faire*, 5, 19.

40. Caron, *Paris pendant la terreur*. See the rapport de Dugas on 29 Nivôse Year II (January 18, 1794), 3:24, the rapports de Le Breton on 30 Nivôse Year II (January 19, 1794), 43, and on 5 Pluviôse Year II (January 24, 1794), 131. For later examples, see Aulard, *Paris pendant la réaction*, 4:179 (June 16, 1797), and *Paris sous le consulat*, 3:380 (June 30, 1801). Definitions of *gager* (to bet) in late eighteenth-century dictionaries regularly used the example of wagering on whether or when war would end.

a thousand écus to Jobin, the father of his beloved Caroline. Jobin wants to marry his daughter to the rich war profiteer, Boursier (Stockbroker). To pay his debt, Dubreil bets Jobin that peace will come within a month. As the time is about to expire, Boursier gleefully announces that war will continue, which means that Dubreil loses both his money and his chances of winning Caroline. But real news of peace arrives, Dubreil wins his bet after all, the war profiteer is ruined, and Dubreil and Caroline marry happily. *It's Done or the Wagers*, performed in October 1801 at the Théâtre de la Gaîté, similarly featured an old egotist who bets a thousand écus that peace will not arrive. When the news of the end of hostilities is published, he bets that the brave soldier Victor has died in the army. Unbeknownst to him, he bet against Victor himself.[41]

Many lives were at least partially on hold until peace. Maintaining a family farm or business often depended on the presence of an able-bodied man. Even in more prosperous households, projects for the future could depend on the return of young men trained in their chosen fields or able to take over work from aging parents. In popular theater, this state of limbo was represented not in terms of sustaining existing families, but in creating new ones. Theater showcased fathers reluctant to marry their daughters and establish new households until peace was assured.[42] In other cases, young women's loyalty to absent soldiers kept them from accepting more readily available partners. Theater promised that combatants would return sooner rather than later. It explained the lack of news from those fighting and assured audiences that men would come home virile, capable, and eager to return to civilian life.

Welcoming the Missing and the Supposed Dead

Plays depicted the joyous reunions of parents and children, brothers and sisters, and especially soldiers and their faithful lovers. This was not simply the imagined happy meeting of long-separated loved ones. It was also the fantasy of an end to uncertainty. Families often did not know the fate of a soldier. The absence of news for months or even years suggested that a man had died but did not prove it. Record-keeping and control over troops were far from perfect, and some rosters just noted men as *rayés pour longue absence* (removed because of a long absence)—a designation that encompassed hospitalization, capture as a prisoner of war, desertion, and death.[43]

It was not unusual to wait for news from someone who had left home in search of work, adventure, or better prospects. Old Regime laws required

41. Defontaines et al., *Le Pari*; Lecomte, *Napoléon et l'empire racontés par le théâtre*, 76.

42. This was most common in 1797; see Aude and Tissot, *Les bruits de la paix* (April 1797); Gamas, *Le mariage à la paix* (November 1797); Jouy, *La paix et l'amour* (December 1797); and Patrat, *La petite ruse* (November 1797). But it reoccurred in 1801; see Bardel, *La paix ou le mariage de Rosine*; and Radet, Desfontaines, and Barré, *Enfin nous y voila.*

43. Petiteau, *Lendemains d'empire*, 15.

a missing man to have been gone ten years without news before heirs could claim his property, while some revolutionary laws made five years the minimum period to establish that a person was legally absent.[44] Article 115 of the Civil Code (in a section promulgated in March 1803) decreed that relatives could go to court to establish legal absence if they had received no news from a missing person for at least four years. The names of those seeking news and the people they sought were printed regularly in the official newspaper, the *Moniteur*.

The number and range of cases indicate just how many people disappeared from view; approximately seven hundred were reported each year.[45] They also suggest how long family members could wait before pursuing formal inquiries. Some of those absent had been gone since the 1770s or 1780s; others had vanished during the early Revolution. A substantial number had disappeared en route to the new world or in its distant expanses. Soldiers formed an even larger group. Their ranks included men who had left home to fight in the Old Regime, but most had become part of revolutionary and Napoleonic armies. Family members guessed at their fates, but often had little idea. They turned to the courts when resolving questions of inheritance, contracts, or property arrangements became imperative.

If legal cases show the practical implications of absence, artwork conveys contemporary longing for information. The title of a painting exhibited in the 1799 salon captures this well: Louis Benjamin Devouges's *A French Woman Consulting an Oracle about the Fate of Her Husband*.[46] A gloss on a similar painting, Mme Azouz's 1802 *Love Overcoming Alarm*, noted that it depicted Thélaire, "a woman distressed by a dream that her absent warrior love was unfaithful. She ran to the Temple of Love and sacrificed two doves she had raised herself; the god, touched by her distress and sacrifice, showed her lover looking tenderly at the portrait she had given him. In her rapture, she cried 'He lives! And he loves me!'"[47]

44. As in most matters, Old Regime law was complicated. However long an absence, a woman could not remarry unless she could prove her husband's death. Ferrière, *Nouvelle introduction à la pratique*, 1:9. After ten years of absence, heirs could divide up property, with the provision that they would return the goods if the missing person returned. In 1792, revolutionary law allowed divorce for absence after a spouse had been missing without news for five years.

45. Usually under the rubric *ministère du grand juge*. Reports mixed investigations (*enquêtes*) and formal declarations of absences after investigations were completed, so the same person could show up multiple times.

46. Louis Benjamin Marie Devouges, *Une française consultant un augure sur le sort de son époux*. The painting does not seem to have survived. See *Collections des livrets des anciennes expositions*, 24.

47. *L'Amour dissipant les alarmes*. See *Explication des ouvrages de peinture et dessins*, 2. The work sometimes appears under her maiden name, Jeanne Marie Catherine Demarquets.

Plays for peace treaties offered more definitive answers than soothsayers: they provided comforting explanations why those at home had not heard from soldiers and reassured audiences that men would return—even if they had been assumed to be dead. Theater also gave answers that could be more easily related to individual fates than unreliable newspaper reports or rumors about the fate of armies. These works hint at the challenges of living without knowing what might have happened to a loved one, as well as the range of explanations offered to make sense of their absences.

Plays regularly noted both how long men had been gone and how long since they had provided news. Five years—the legal requirement for establishing absence in several measures in the late 1790s and early 1800s—was the most common number. But the length of imagined silence varied dramatically, and there was no systematic relation to political events. In Cambronne's 1801 *Peace and Marriage*, a soldier has been absent for five years and gone three without news, while in the 1806 *Policy by Default*, Paul has been in the army for three months and it has been "a long month" since those at home have heard from him. What mattered for theater—rather than law—was the experience of a prolonged period of uncertainty, rather than the specific interval of silence.

To explain the lack of news, some works blamed deceitful enemies. In the 1797 *Thumbing Your Nose*, the royalist rival for the heroine's hand claims falsely that the French army has been taken prisoner and her beloved killed.[48] Similarly, a script submitted to censors in October 1798, *Old Bachelors, or the Ghosts*, featured three disreputable suitors—a former marquis, a former Benedictine monk, and a war profiteer. The villains intercept letters from soldiers, circulate a rumor that the men had been killed, and even produce false death certificates. The play was not performed, but it was suppressed only because the censors judged several scenes too risqué.[49]

Blaming villains for soldiers' silences combined revolutionary belief in scheming enemies with literary conventions of trickery.[50] It became less common as revolutionary belief in conspiracies subsided, but the idea that personal enemies were to blame was too convenient a device to abandon completely. In 1809, for example, the short-story writer Lombard de Langres retook the theme of a deceitful intermediary. In this case, a magister hides a soldier's letter from his illiterate father and lover, concealing news of the man's promotion to colonel and his concern for his loved ones.[51]

48. Lecomte, *Napoléon et l'empire racontés par le théâtre*, 18.

49. AN F / 7 / 3491, Les vieux garçons ou les revenants.

50. For example, in the 1793 *Charles et Victoire*, a speculator lies to Victoire and tells her that her love, a valorous lieutenant, is dead, while in the 1794 *Rose et Aurèle*, the soldier's rival spreads false news of his death.

51. Lombard de Langres, *Contes militaires*. Ferrand, *La diligence du Havre à Rouen*, also portrays a traitor who circulates the false rumor that a farmer's son died at the hands of the Austrians.

Other explanations were more benign. Plays depicted warriors as too busy dealing with enemies (*Charles and Victoire*, 1793), or simply as having no time to write (*The Bet*, 1797). Some suggested that soldiers were men of action, not of words. In the 1794 *The Badly Kept Secret*, the hero proclaims, "it is with the sound of canon that the French soldier writes his correspondence." In the April 1801 *The Coward*, Lavaillance apologizes for his long silence by saying, "I prefer to campaign than to write a letter."[52]

Mail could also easily go astray.[53] Even when the state succeeded in delivering letters, there were limitations. Many soldiers were at best semiliterate; even in 1830, the earliest point for which there is reliable data, only 52 percent of conscripts were able to sign.[54] Moreover, literacy rates were uneven across France; those in the north and east of a line from Saint-Malo to Geneva were more likely to be literate than those in the south and west. Urban populations were more literate than those from rural backgrounds. Even if soldiers could write, those at home, especially women, were often unable to read their letters or respond to them directly. In the camps, officers served as intermediaries; in towns and villages, priests, innkeepers, and blacksmiths read and drafted letters for their illiterate compatriots.[55] But intermediaries were not always available or willing to write, and contemporaries hesitated to use them.

In *Rose and Aurèle* (first performed in August 1794), for example, there has been no news from Aurèle for eighteen months. The soldier-hero is unable to write; his waiting lover Rose similarly cannot read. While acknowledging that they could get a letter deciphered, Rose and her friend Alix admit discomfort with having others know the secrets of their hearts. Similarly, Radet's 1801 popular *Finally, We're Here* emphasized the inability of women to communicate directly with absent soldiers. It opens with a crowd of girls and women dictating letters to the magister to send to their lovers in the army; the magister is so overwhelmed that he does not know where to begin. The play also hinted at other problems; the heroine, Joséphine, has had no news of her lover for four months and has no idea where to send a letter to him.

Yet illiteracy was actually a rare theme on stage. It was mentioned in *Rose and Aurèle* to praise the Revolution's role in educating all citizens, not just the rich. The few works that acknowledge the challenges of written communication often emphasized women's illiteracy rather than that of soldiers. Illiterate figures could appear as easily tricked buffoons, and officials during the Revolution, and especially the Napoleonic period, were deeply concerned that soldiers on stage seem dignified.[56]

52. Philipon de La Madelaine and Léger, *Le dédit mal gardé*, 16; Noël, *Poltronet*, 27.

53. Forrest, *Napoleon's Men*, 165.

54. Forrest, *Napoleon's Men*, 36.

55. Forrest, *Napoleon's Men*, 38.

56. Krakovitch, "La censure théâtrale," 85–88. See also complaints in AN F/7/3491 and F/7/3492 about performances that ridiculed soldiers.

The most common explanation for the lack of news was that soldiers had been prisoners of war. A few works specified where a soldier had been held. For example, in Desfontaines's *The Bet*, the hero escaped from prison in Franconia, while in Cambronne's *Peace and Marriage*, Firmin had been a prisoner in Egypt. In many cases, however, audiences knew that a central character had been imprisoned but were unclear where; theatrical geography tended to be hazy.

The belief that prisoners could not easily return home during wartime was accurate. While there were wartime exchanges during the Revolution, prisoners (particularly below the rank of officers) could spend two or three years in captivity before being exchanged. Letters were the main way that families and prisoners of war exchanged news, but those frequently went astray. In theory, for example, the Sick and Wounded administration in Britain conveyed correspondence to prisoners, but men were often moved from one depot to another before letters reached them. Sending mail back to France from prisoners was also not a priority.[57]

Interest in prisoners of war likely intensified in response to the campaign for the invasion of England. Speeches and tracts from late 1797 and 1798 portrayed the cruel treatment of the English toward French prisoners as a reason for the French to crush heartless barbarians.[58] By 1801, however, the theatrical image of prisoners of war softened. For example, Boutard's 1801 *The Prisoner in London or the Preliminaries of Peace* transposed a familiar plot to England. The merchant Mr. Happy and his family host a French officer and prisoner of war; the officer is in love with the Happy daughter, whom Mrs. Happy wants to wed to a rich speculator. Peace makes possible the union between the soldier and the daughter, an indirect symbol of union between England and France.

The idea that families and friends had not heard from soldiers because they were imprisoned was both plausible and useful. It promised that men would return; there was no reason for states to retain prisoners of war after hostilities ended. It absolved individuals of responsibility for long silences, implying that they wanted to write but had been prevented from doing so. It also absolved the French state of responsibility; the nation's enemies rather than government had been responsible for failing to maintain contact between home and battlefield. Reassurances that those missing and reported dead were alive were especially common in 1801. In Cambronne's *Peace and Marriage*, a veteran assures the audience that "we have often seen during war that soldiers, believed to be dead, return after seven or eight years of absence."[59] *The French Artemisia* took these fantasies of return further, to audiences' delight.

57. Private correspondence with Renaud Morieux, August 26, 2011.

58. Morieux, "Patriotisme humanitaire et prisonniers de guerre."

59. Cambronne, *La paix et l'hymen*, 18.

The *Courrier des spectacles* judged it to be a great success, and the theater where it was staged profited from its reception.[60]

Aspects of *The French Artemisia* were unusual. It was written by a woman, unlike most contemporary works. It also focused on a husband, rather than a lover—although the return of a daughter's fiancé permitted the requisite celebratory wedding to close the piece.[61] In other ways, the play was typical of the period, including its use of historical conceits. The figure of Artemisia would have been familiar to many. The historical Artemisia, the wife of Mausolus, king of Caria, was said to be inconsolable at her husband's death; she built him a magnificent tomb—the Mausoleum—ranked as one of the marvels of the universe. In early nineteenth-century France, *Artémise* served as a common reference for distraught widows.[62]

Madame Belfort's message also expressed a more general hope. She addressed the audience through the character of Colonel Vermancourt, the officer who returns to his devoted wife. Belfort promised that "many women who believe themselves to be widows, will rediscover their husbands . . . fathers will embrace their sons, sisters see again their brothers." She was realistic enough to acknowledge that "many are dead defending their country." For those who were not reunited with loved ones, she offered a standard refrain: "Our tears water their tombs, but will soon dry up, realizing that these men sacrificed themselves for such a beautiful cause."[63]

Declarations like Belfort's corresponded to the hope that those rumored to be dead would return, and an implicit recognition of widows' grief. Public ceremonies sometimes singled out such women. In July 1800, officials in Lyon organized a parade through the city of the "mothers, sisters, widows, and daughters of défenseurs de la patrie who had died on the field of battle."[64] In a November 1801 festival at Montauban, administrators sought to celebrate the Festival of Peace "by relieving the poverty of the mothers and widows of soldiers and sailors who died defending the country and liberty. They [such women] suspended their regrets for a moment to participate in public joy."[65]

Public acknowledgment of grief would become less common as the Napoleonic period progressed. There were proportionately fewer grieving widows; the number of widows' pensions actually decreased as causalities grew.[66] There were also proportionately far fewer married men in the Napoleonic

60. *Courrier des spectacles*, 1 Germinal Year IX (March 22, 1801), 1483. Lecomte, *Napoléon et l'empire racontés par le théâtre*, 68.

61. The 1797 *La petite ruse* also depicts a father who has gone to war but has children of marriageable age.

62. *Courrier des spectacles*, 1 Germinal Year IX (March 22, 1801), 1483.

63. Belfort, *L'Artémise française*, 28.

64. Archives Municipales Lyon, I 1 155.

65. AN F / 1 / c / III / Lot 8.

66. Woloch, "War Widows Pensions and Social Policy."

army, as it increasingly became one of young men conscripted through the Jourdan Law of 1798, rather than one with a substantial number of volunteers.

Perhaps more importantly, authorities became increasingly reluctant to focus public attention on mourning, loss, and sacrifice; however patriotic sacrifice was alleged to be. But sacrifice did not only imply death; it also included injury and physical strain. Would the wounded men who did make it home be desirable husbands and citizens?

"Wounded, Mutilated, What Does It Matter to Love?"

In October 1797, the playwright Jean Mittié depicted a soldier, Valence, who worried that the loss of his leg would mean he had to renounce his plans for marriage. Valence's fiancée reassured him that "wounded, mutilated, what does it matter to love? It only makes you dearer to me, how could you doubt the heart of your Lise?" Mittié drove home the point by having a servant ask Lise if she really wanted to marry a lame man. When she insisted that she did, the servant proclaimed that hers was a rare example of love.[67]

Mittié claimed that journalists had asked the directors of spectacles in the provinces to perform his play, *Peace or the Lovers Reunited*, to shape public opinion.[68] The directors did not refer directly to his treatment of a wounded hero as a tool for cultivating patriotism, but it fit with contemporary tributes to injured men. Mittié's wording still suggests that the playwright doubted how readily women would follow Lise's fictional example of fidelity to a crippled man. Patriotic declarations—and undercurrents of worry—run through Mittié's work, as well as many of these plays. They ultimately promised not only that soldiers would return home but also that they would be welcomed, whatever condition they were in.

Such reassurances were not unique to the theater of the late Revolution; Old Regime literary works had imagined fictional injuries.[69] But revolutionaries were confronted with very real wounds. There is no reliable data for Year VI, when Mittié's play was performed, but the following year, there were 11,600 veterans drawing pensions and 5,000 new pensions. By Year IX (1801), the number was 46,000, a statistic that indicates less a sudden jump in injuries than the government's processing of a backlog of requests.

Men could request veterans' benefits for retirement, serious wounds, or infirmities. The latter category came to include hernias, deteriorating eyesight or hearing, pulmonary aliments, and wounds that were not severe enough to cause the loss of a limb. By 1802, the majority (52 percent) of those who received pensions were grievously wounded. The proportion would increase

67. Mittié, *La paix ou les amans réunis*, 17–18.

68. He referred to *L'ami des lois* of 15 Brumaire Year VI (November 6, 1797).

69. See chapter 1.

dramatically during the Empire.[70] Battlefield treatment often meant amputation, because of both limited resources and medical theories about how to reduce the risk of infection. "Peg leg" (Jambe de bois) was a standard epithet for a veteran.

Given these numbers, literary depictions of women repulsed by disfigurement were unlikely to be popular. Old plots still circulated, but revolutionaries gave them happy endings. Commentators recognized Joseph-Alexandre Ségur's *Two Widows*, produced at the Théâtre du Vaudeville in December 1796, as a version of a fable by Marmontel.[71] But while the play featured similar characters, including an officer who faked a disfiguring injury, the moral of the work was very different from Marmontel's version. *Two Widows* provided for both suitable chastisement of selfish citizens and the happy ending of a wedding. The central character had to decide between two sisters, both young widows. One, Laure, was "light and gay"; the other, Constance, "sensible and tender."[72] To discover which one was worthy, the officer limped and covered his eye with a bandage. Laure was put off, whereas the loyal Constance consoled him; the officer's choice became clear, while Laure came to regret her distaste for a wounded hero.

In many ways, the focus on a faithful lover welcoming home an injured hero was remarkably consistent from the outbreak of war in 1792 through the end of the century. Plays like Picard and Devienne's popular 1794 *Rose and Aurèle* presented patriotic women embracing disfigured veterans.[73] The 1801 vaudeville *Peace or the Return of the Good Son* described the momentary chagrin of a woman seeing her returned soldier-lover: "Alexis was no longer the same, one arm less, no more youthful freshness." The veteran proclaims that if "combat has disfigured me, it has done nothing to change my sentiments for you . . . I love you tenderly." The young woman reaffirms her loyalty: "She will not betray her vows. Wounded, you are only dearer to her. From lovers, let us become spouses."[74]

Continued public attention to injury may seem at odds with changing attitudes toward displaying those hurt because of their service to the patrie. As we have seen, the radical Revolution obsessed over the wounds of martyrs and war heroes. But by the late 1790s, contemporary cultural works increasingly shied away from acknowledging the risk involved in warfare or publicly displaying martyrs' bodies. Depicting wounded men on stage recognized social reality, while allowing an escape from that reality. It presented injured veterans as embodying martial masculinity and promised that even those disfigured by

70. Woloch, *The French Veteran*.

71. Clément, *Journal littéraire*, 2:191; and *Almanach des muses*, 292.

72. The characterizations are from Clément, *Journal littéraire*, 2:191.

73. Picard and Devienne, *Rose et Aurèle*.

74. Confusing pronouns in the original. Dupont-de-Lille, *La paix ou le retour du bon fils*, 15.

war would still experience marriage and happy civilian lives. Injured men on stage were rarely seriously incapacitated; they were heroes, not martyrs, able to start new lives after their return.

Loyalty, Ridiculed Rivals, and Foolish Contracts

SEXUAL CONQUESTS AND MASCULINE VIRTUE

Popular imagery and music depicted military men as lusty and vigorous. As Michael Hughes has noted, the French soldier in Napoleonic songs—especially ditties for soldiers on the march—was known for his drinking and sexual conquests almost as much as for his military valor.[75] Military memoirs regularly recount sexual adventures, although many stories are likely invented or exaggerated. Caricatures could reinforce images of attractive swashbucklers; Prussian engravings from March 1801 depicted women fighting for the trousers of a French soldier.[76] Such images concealed the brutality of conquest, including frequent violence against women.

Other sources similarly suggest the promiscuity of military men. Internal military regulations regularly addressed the issue of prostitutes in encampments.[77] Scientific treatises openly discussed sexually transmitted disease. Some three hundred scientific works on venereal disease were published during the Directory and Consulate, and concerns about gonorrhea and syphilis would lead to the Napoleonic system of medical inspections of brothels.[78]

In contrast, scripts for popular theater had to pass censors concerned about morality; direct references to sex, and especially to sexual misconduct, were deemed inappropriate.[79] The civilian nature of this theater meant that it often focused on men's relationships to family life. Playwrights implicitly acknowledged a tension between men's roles as virile warriors and good husbands, but also sought to defuse or erase that tension.

Some works thus alluded to the reputation of soldiers as conquering warriors and lovers. In *The Outposts or the Armistice* (first performed at Vaudeville on August 20, 1800), for example, Charlotte, the fiancée of a German miller, observes admiringly: "French soldiers are always gallant / And notable for their bravery / If I was a man, truly / I would have much to fear from their presence / But one says that even when fighting / a Frenchman thinks about

75. Hughes, *Forging Napoleon's Grande Armée*, "Making Frenchmen into Warriors," and "Military Values."

76. For a series from March 1801, see Duplessis, *Inventaire de la collection d'estampes*, 4:234–35, inventory 12715–12721.

77. Plumauzille, *Prostitution et révolution*.

78. J.-C. Martin, *La révolte brisée*, 217.

79. Drawing on literary works, Patricia Mainardi argues that France lost its sense of humor over adultery between 1789 and 1815. See Mainardi, *Husbands, Wives, and Lovers*.

women / Sending cannonballs to husbands / And kisses to their wives."[80] But if playwrights praised French swashbucklers, they also reassured audiences that soldiers were good marital choices who would be loyal to their waiting sweethearts.

Reassurances about soldiers' fidelity punctuated many plays. In Roujoux's 1797 *The Peace* the heroine Columbine asks, "Are you bringing me back a faithful heart?" Arlequin responds that he closed his eyes to women from Milan, Genoa, and Boulogne, and "when a pretty vivandière poured me a glass to drink, I held out my hand but turned my head to avoid temptation."[81] In Jouy's contemporaneous *Peace and Love*, those at home speculated about whether the hero Victor had a liaison in Italy.[82] As we have seen, in the 1801 *The Guignette*, Madame La Treille told her husband that if their daughter married the toymaker Frivolous, she would not need to fear infidelity. The story would be different with a military man: "Can soldiers remain faithful? Don't we see them make new conquests every day? They swear to us to be constant, but can we believe their promises? We know that they have left everything for glory." Her husband responded that a warrior knows how to love better than a Frivolous: "The heart of a soldier is shared / between his mistress and his honor."[83]

The promise of marriage after military service in these works worked in tandem with the increasingly dominant image of soldiers as single young men. It also functioned to separate wartime experience from domestic life. Soldiers would, in theory, settle down after their return and transform from boastful seducers into responsible husbands and fathers. Much theater actually expressed a different and even stronger hope: that absent soldiers would not need to be transformed but would be continuously faithful to lovers waiting at home.

LOYAL DAUGHTERS, MISGUIDED MOTHERS, AND INDEBTED FATHERS

Playwrights rarely played up the risk of young women succumbing to temptation or portrayed their sexual irresistibility. When the Théâtre Feydeau attempted in 1802 to perform Aristophanes's *Lysistrata*, in which women refuse sexual favors to their husbands until men make peace, the play was banned. The issue does not seem to have been its call for peace, but rather its portrayal of women's sexuality. The playwright, François-Benoît Hoffman, responded with indignation, and published the script with elaborate footnotes explaining why apparently licentious phrases were moral and even patriotic.[84]

80. Audras, Tournay, and Vial, *Les avant-postes, ou l'armistice*, 15.
81. Roujoux, *La paix, divertissement*, 19.
82. Jouy, *La paix et l'amour*, 17.
83. Villiers and Bonel, *La guinguette*, 8.
84. Hoffman, *Lisistrata ou les athéniennes.*

Not all contemporaries were offended by the work, and the *Journal de Paris* suggested that the scandalized "belle dames" who denounced it had to "bite their lips" to keep from laughing.[85] But the play was not staged again.

Indeed, plots often sidestepped young women's sexuality to focus on whether girls would be pushed by their parents to choose a seemingly more suitable rival over a brave but absent soldier. The risk was not that they would fall in love with—or seduce—other men, but that parents would force their daughters to marry for security or social advancement rather than love. The theme of fathers trying to marry their daughters against their "inclinations" was a staple of late eighteenth-century and revolutionary theater. But pièces de circonstance used this theme to comment on the status of rivals for the heroine's hand, appropriate forms of masculinity and femininity, and the limits of parental authority.

Several historians have argued for a significant cultural and legal shift during the late Revolution in how people understood familial authority.[86] In her influential *The Family Romance*, Lynn Hunt has argued that a new emphasis on good parents, particularly fathers, was typical of the late 1790s.[87] Pièces de circonstance do depict well-intentioned parents. But such parents are also often foolish or imprudent. Their limits become clear when they are confronted with the figure of the revolutionary citizen-soldier.

Two stories of parental misjudgment were most common. One version featured ambitious mothers, championing candidates for their daughters' hands who seemed to offer financial security and social prestige, but who were actually selfish or cowardly. The other common plot depicted fathers reluctant to exercise their authority over their daughters, but led to do so by their own indebtedness to their daughters' greedy suitors.

Misguided maternal ambition was a common theme both in 1797 and 1801. One of the most popular plays from 1797, *Peace or the Lovers Reunited*, by Mittié, depicted a young girl in love with a soldier named Valence, but courted by an aristocratic fool and military shirker.[88] Her mother had been swayed by the fool's wealth, but the father remained convinced of Valence's virtue. A similar theme appears in *The Peace*, first performed at the Théâtre des Délassements-Comiques, on November 3, 1797 (the same day as Mittié's show). Madame Mathieu wants to marry their daughter Lucette to Brigandeau, a *fournisseur* who has become incredibly wealthy since the Revolution; her husband wants Lucette to wed the impoverished Belmont.[89] Similarly, in the *Festival of Peace,*

85. *Journal de Paris*, no. 127, 27 Nivôse Year X (January 17, 1802), 700–701.

86. See Desan, *The Family on Trial*; and Verjus, *Le bon mari.*

87. Hunt, *The Family Romance.*

88. Mittié, *La paix ou les amans réunis.*

89. Aulard, *Paris pendant la réaction*, 4:438. The play does not seem to have been printed.

first performed a few days later, on November 7, 1797, the heroine's mother initially refuses to let her daughter marry a soldier, and is persuaded to do so only when a local official offers 50 *louis* for the girl's dowry.[90]

Four years later, matchmaking mothers on stage still championed dubious candidates over soldiers. As we have seen, the mother in *The Guinguette* placed her hopes on Frivolous. In the April 1801 *Coward*, the mother wanted her daughter to marry the coward of the title. A similar theme appears in *The Happy Day*, composed by the military commander Palasne de Champeaux and performed in March 1801. The heroine's mother seeks to marry her daughter Julie to Fatentout (Fatuous-in-Everything), but the girl is in love with a soldier, Firmin. It becomes clear that Fatentout wants to marry Julie for her money, but he seems to offer social prestige. Before proceeding to the nuptials, the mother seeks approval from her brother, General Darvaux, from whom she expects an inheritance. Fatentout attempts to win the general over by promising him an introduction into brilliant social circles. The general is appropriately disdainful of Fatentout and admiring of Firmin's valor; he intervenes for his niece's choice over his sister's, and bestows riches on the young soldier.[91]

Mothers were deeply involved with the practical negotiations of marrying off their children, especially their daughters; they vetted suitors and championed favorite candidates.[92] The image of mothers eager to match their daughters with suitors whose names of Brigand, Frivolous, or Fatuous should have sounded warning bells reflects both specific literary tropes and widespread cultural concerns.

As with many other themes, ill-advised matchmaking was partly theatrical convention, a convenient reprise of a well-known plot. It echoed the revolutionary trope of women as easily influenced by bad advisors, especially corrupt priests, and who become hostile to returning veterans. In *The Soldier's Return from the Army of Italy*, first performed in autumn 1797, Madame Martin has been misled by bad newspapers given to her by a priest; she hates the Republic and initially refuses to welcome her son home from the army. Similarly, in the 1798 *The French Officer in Milan*, written by a retired captain, the mother supports the elderly man championed by her confessor over her daughter's youthful warrior love.[93]

Although the theme of priests meddling in family life would be recurrent in nineteenth-century literature, it largely disappeared from the Napoleonic stage after the Concordat. However, theater still portrayed women who did not fully understand war or the relationship between heroism and military service.

90. Apparently not printed. See Lecomte, *Napoléon et l'empire racontés par le théâtre*, 17; and Aulard, *Paris pendant la réaction*, 4:442.

91. Palasne de Champeaux, *L'heureuse journée*.

92. Verjus and Davidson, *Le roman conjugal*.

93. Legal-Lalande, *Le retour du soldat de l'armée d'Italie*; and Soulié, *L'officier français à Milan*.

Or more precisely, it portrayed mothers who did not understand this connection; their daughters—the stalwart fiancées of returning soldiers—know well that military men are better citizens.

In many of these cases, fathers support a worthier candidate. In *The Guinguette*, the mother champions Frivolet; the father, Courchamp. In *Poltronet*, Sans-Quartier appears to support his wife's ambition. But he denies any intention of sacrificing his daughter to financial interest; he claims that he is simply postponing fighting with his wife.[94] In other cases, however, fathers pushed unwelcome husbands on their daughters. In the 1797 *The Happy News*, the young Adèle bewails her father's strictness, lamenting, "Must a father tyrannize his child?"; the father eventually relents, peace is declared, and Adèle marries the volunteer Firmin rather than the war profiteer Rapacious.[95]

Even paternal "tyranny" could be accompanied by genuine concern for daughters' futures. In *The Happy News*, the father is worried about the financial prospects of a simple volunteer. In Olivier Ferrand's *The General Peace*, produced in Rouen in 1801, the heroine Rosalie has twenty-four hours to choose between a stupid and naïve man named Mondor or an officer. Rosalie observes that her own father married for love against his parents' wishes; he acknowledges this, but claims that fortune is all that mattered in the new order. He also admits a real worry that Rosalie's sweetheart courted all the girls of the village before he left to fight; such fickleness does not bode well for a future son-in-law. Fortunately, the officer in question proves to be the young woman's lover, who has been promoted over the course of the war, unbeknownst to the ambitious father; the officer is now devoted to his Rosalie.

Plays from 1801 and 1802 increasingly used another plot device to explain why fathers might seek to marry daughters against their will: debt. Rich but otherwise ill-matched suitors promised to forgive a father's loan in exchange for the hand of a young woman. Like many themes, versions of this appeared occasionally in the Revolution. *The Badly Kept Secret*, performed in June 1794, featured the patriot Roger who owes 600 livres to the "greedy, ridiculous, and idiotic" Simonet; the latter seeks to use the debt as leverage to force a marriage with Lucette. The young woman of course loves a brave volunteer, who has just returned from war after being imprisoned; the couple tricks Simonet into using the IOU to plug a hole in a wine barrel and thus destroy the record of the debt.[96]

If versions of the plot of promising daughters' marriages to pay off debts emerged occasionally in the 1790s, they became widespread in the early nineteenth century. One particularly clear example comes from *The Preliminaries*

94. Palasne de Champeaux, *L'heureuse journée*, 18.
95. Godard d'Aucourt de Saint-Just, *L'heureuse nouvelle*.
96. Philipon de La Madelaine and Léger, *Le dédit mal gardé*.

of Peace or the Lovers Reunited, performed in Douai in March 1801.[97] The play focuses on an orphan girl, Nicette, being raised by her grandfather. Nicette is in love with a soldier, Félix, but has had no news from him in six months, and assumes that he is dead. Cadichon, a hapless peasant, is pressuring Nicette's family so that he can wed her. As he explains in an aside, he is motivated primarily by a desire to avoid military service: "To save myself from conscription / by a legal means / I'll make my declaration to you / and I'll marry you for show / But once the danger's passed / I'll get divorced."[98] Nicette's great-aunt had been imprudent enough to give Cadichon's uncle a document stipulating that if the marriage did not take place, they would pay him 3,000 livres. Nicette and her supporters trick Cadichon into believing that war is over and that he will not need to fight; he tears up the fatal note. Mercifully, all soon discover that war is truly over, and Nicette's soldier-lover returns.

In these cases, the danger of an unwanted marriage is averted by clever deception, with the greedy fool himself destroying the record of debt. In other plays, a rich benefactor helps deserving couples to marry. This is the case, for example, in *The Leave or the Festival of the Old Soldier*.[99] The play was performed in Paris in March 1802, shortly after the Peace of Amiens was declared between France and England. It features Goodman, a British innkeeper in Cologne. Goodman's daughter, Georgette, is in love with Honest Heart (Francœur), a French soldier. But the innkeeper owes money to a German drummer, Tunderton, who seeks to claim Georgette in lieu of her father's money. Goodman anguishes about whether he should accept Tunderton as his son-in-law if his daughter does not want the marriage, and acknowledges that the German drummer is old for her. (The drummer's age is not specified in the script, but he is described as a "caricature.") Tunderton instructs him to tell his daughter that one must obey one's father before one's heart.[100] Goodman hesitates, and fortunately, the father of the French soldier arrives; he initially intends to take his son away, but ultimately becomes Francœur's advocate with Georgette's father, and pays off the family's debt to Tunderton.

Paternal debt to the conniving suitors for daughters' hands remained a common theme throughout the Napoleonic era. Like the theme of ambitious mothers, it was both a reflection of social reality—especially during hyperinflation—and a plot device, which allowed playwrights to depict fathers who wanted the best for their children but still opposed their plans for marriage. The theatrical fantasy of a benefactor who recognizes a soldier's courage and provides him with a reward corresponded to a more general vision of marriage and money as a reward for military service.

97. Courtois, *Les préliminaires de paix ou les amans réunis*.

98. Courtois, *Les préliminaires de paix ou les amans réunis*, 38.

99. Tournay, *Le congé ou la fête du vieux soldat*.

100. Tournay, *Le congé ou la fête du vieux soldat*, 19.

War Profiteers, Cowardly Idiots, and Cultural Shifts

In November 1797, the *Censeur dramatique* newspaper noted that two plays had nearly identical plots. In both *The Happy News* by Godard d'Aucourt de Saint-Just and *The Bet* by five playwrights from the Théâtre du Vaudeville, "it's a thwarted marriage, a war profiteer in place of a lover, etc." The editors pardoned the similarities, given the good intention of the playwrights:

> In pièces de circonstance, one is, and must be, indulgent about the plot. These sorts of works are children of the moment, in a way, only needing to appear and then disappear. They should not be judged with severity. It suffices that a piece works a little, that the details are agreeable, the characters natural or amusing, and one overlooks the rest.[101]

Many plays did present similar plots and characters. They often ridiculed *fournisseurs*, a term that referred to contractors, but was associated with war profiteering. Vaudeville names for fournisseurs, like Rapacious, Devourer, Brigand, Speculator, and Plunderer, made their characters clear.[102] In case the audience missed the message, some playwrights went a step further. For example, the December 1797 play *Peace and Love* begins with a servant describing the characters the audience is about to meet. He is not exactly complimentary about the fournisseur: "Omnivorous. By Jove, he is well named! They say that his name means eat-everything. If we leave him a little time, I believe, God pardon me, that he will swallow all of France. He calls himself supplier of the Republic, but I bet that he supplies himself much better than it." As the show continued, the playwright revealed that Omnivorous had shorted the army in order to enrich himself.[103] Victor, of course, ultimately bests Omnivorous in his quest for the heroine's hand.

Such characters reflected a general distrust of those who had enriched themselves at the expense of the public. Theatrical performances during the Directory regularly mocked greedy speculators. The most popular of these was the fishwife and social climber Madame Angot, who appeared in at least

101. Review of *L'heureuse nouvelle*, in *Censeur dramatique*, 1:492.

102. Some characters are simply identified as "Fournisseur," as in Gouffe's *La nouvelle cacophonie*, first performed at the Theatre de la Cité, on May 4, 1797. But more colorful names were common. Dévorant appears in Martainville's *La paix*, premiered at the Théâtre des Jeunes Artistes on May 3, 1797; Boursier in Desfontaines's *Le pari*, first performed at Vaudeville on October 28, 1797; Brigandeau in *La paix* performed at Délassements-Comiques, on November 3, 1797; and Rapace in *L'heureuse nouvelle*, first performed at Feydeau on November 7, 1797. (Duroc is just an *intriguant* in Aude and Tissot's May 1797 *Les bruits de la paix* but has become a fournisseur in Aude's revised version of the play, *La paix*, debuted at the Théâtre de la République on November 3, 1797.) La Rapinière (Plunderer) appears in *Le dix-huit Brumaire, ou paix au dehors, paix au dedans*, performed in Macon on November 9, 1801.

103. Jouy, *La paix et l'amour*, 3, 21.

a dozen plays in the late 1790s.[104] Angot was a quintessentially comic figure and a caricature of nouveaux riches who made their fortunes in speculating.[105] Depictions of fournisseurs could be similarly entertaining and socially pointed, as critics observed. For example, in the *Censeur dramatique*, Grimod de la Reynière noted the audience's relish in the downfall of a fournisseur: "The public always enjoys the spectacle of vengeance on these scandalous and sudden fortunes made at popular expense."[106]

Attacks on fournisseurs corresponded to a widespread association of the Directorial government with corruption, and a conviction that officials were neglecting the army while enriching war profiteers.[107] The profession was so badly regarded that in his 1798 description of "New Paris," Louis-Sébastien Mercier proposed substituting a new term *fourniturier* for *fournisseur* in order to separate "crooks and thieves" from reputable businessmen.[108]

But if depictions of fournisseurs as selfish men who would meet their just rewards corresponded to theatrical conventions and to general suspicions of war profiteers, they were particularly effective in plays devoted to peace. Their greed contrasted with the honesty and bravery of soldiers. Some works made these comparisons explicit. In the 1797 *The Happy News*, the soldier hero Firmin mocks his opponent Rapacious in a monologue, proclaiming, "What a rival! Interest is his idol, as honor is that of a soldier."[109] In other plays, the contrast was implicit, but likely obvious to audiences surrounded by cultural icons of heroic warriors.

Such juxtapositions also responded to a gap between the home front and the battlefields. If soldiers seeking to return home and their families emphasized common sacrifice, combatants could also portray civilians as selfish and ignorant. Most notably, soldiers seeking pensions in the late 1790s opposed their virtuous service to the greed of bourgeois men who had never fought.[110] Such language corresponds both to a general tendency of soldiers to regard civilians as coddled and to specific denunciations of greed in the late Revolution. Performances that celebrated the marriages of returned soldiers and their waiting lovers—to the detriment of fournisseurs—finessed these connections.

104. The character seems to have first appeared in 1796, with *Madame Angot ou la poissarde parvenue* by Antoine-François Eve; other playwrights quickly appropriated her.

105. Netter, "Great Successes," in Kennedy et al., *Theatre, Opera, and Audiences*, 49.

106. *Censeur dramatique*, 1:302.

107. On the fournisseur in pamphlets and caricatures, see Schröer, "La représentation du Nouveau Régime." On war profiteers during the Directory, see G. Parker, *The Cambridge History of Warfare*, 199; and Forray-Carlier and Bruson, *Au temps des merveilleuses*, 58. On general challenges of supplying the military, Brown, *War, Revolution, and the Bureaucratic State*.

108. Mercier, *Le Nouveau Paris*, 5:161–63.

109. Godard d'Aucourt de Saint-Just, *L'heureuse nouvelle*, 10.

110. Kruse and Thomas, "La formation du discours militariste."

They associated greed with a particular kind of profiteer, not with civilians more generally. Selfishness was ultimately shown to be good for neither warriors nor civilians.

There was another implication: those responsible for perpetuating war were fournisseurs, not soldiers. Military men fought only to achieve a victorious peace, not out of innate brutality or a quest for glory at the expense of common good. Propaganda around Napoleon Bonaparte played up this idea; speeches, medals, and imagery lauded the general as the "great peacemaker."[111] Ordinary soldiers were also portrayed as fighting for peace; in the playwright Joseph Aude's term, they were peacemaking warriors.[112]

The depiction of military men as peacemakers would continue throughout the Consulate and Empire. But by the Peace of Lunéville in February 1801, theatrical rivals to soldiers for the heroine's hand were increasingly men with names like Simpleton (Nigaud), Coward (Poltronet), Frivolous, or Fatuous-in-Everything (Fatentout).[113] Fools had pranced or shuffled across the stage during the Old Regime and the Revolution, but they were now more common, and often more explicitly cowardly as well as comically naïve. Conversely, although the fournisseur still appeared in 1801, he was a less frequent character.[114]

Comic idiots provided ready entertainment. They provoked amusement through their misuse of French language and their obvious misunderstandings of events. For example, the character Nicolet, in Cambronne's 1801 *Peace and Marriage*, revealed his unworthiness of the heroine's hand by confusing the words "ambassador" and "courier"; he was equally unable to grasp an army the size of 4,000 or 5,000 men, beyond the double of his village.

The increasing prominence of such characters was a theatrical development; the naif became a stock character in the early Consulate. Melodramas often contained a character to offer comic relief; vaudevilles made such figures central. Not all audience members were enchanted with their prominence. As one dyspeptic commentator observed in an 1801 review of a play celebrating a treaty between France and England: "I have noted for a while that simpletons have come to play a major role in Vaudeville; it seems that

111. This is especially common in addresses to the first consul in Years IX and X. See AN AF IV / 1449, where Napoleon appears as the "pacificateur du monde," peacemaker of the world.

112. Aude, *Le présent du gouvernement*.

113. Nicaise appears in Bardel, *La paix ou le mariage de Rosine;* Poltronet in Noël, *Poltronet ou Marions nos filles;* Frivolet in *La guingette;* and Fatentout in Palasne de Champeaux, *L'heureuse journée*. Characters with less blatant names were described in terms to make their identities clear. Simonet, the pastry-maker's son, is called *nigaud* (simpleton) in *Enfin nous y voila*, 6, while Nicolet is described as an imbecile in Cambronne's *La paix et l'hymen*, 22.

114. The 1800 *Dix-huit Brumaire* features a fournisseur, as does *Les préliminaires et la ratification*, performed in Toulouse in April 1801. The 1801 *Enfin nous y voila* has both a fournisseur and a nigaud.

these authors involuntarily put enough inanities in their works, without adding a character whose role it is to add more."[115]

When juxtaposed to iconic soldier-heroes, however, a naïve figure also reinforced a message. Men who stayed home rather than fighting were not mature enough to become heads of households. They were makers of pastries and toys, not swords; they were weaklings incapable of understanding the world beyond their doorstep.

The increasing depiction of romantic losers as cowards, rather than greedy war profiteers, reveals an important cultural shift and a concomitant transformation in ideas about manliness. During the radical Revolution, the most serious crime was parasitic selfishness, the betrayal of the revolutionary community for individual gain. The reaction against aestheticism after the Terror tempered this rhetoric, as *incroyables* and *merveilleuses* indulged in conspicuous consumption.[116] But contemporaries continued to link self-interest with antipatriotic and dangerous behavior in the mid-1790s, while veterans hoping to return home in 1796 and 1797 sought to forestall accusations of selfishness by emphasizing their duty to family members.

The rhetoric of common interest increasingly lost traction at the end of the century.[117] Contemporaries continued to connect social usefulness and citizenship, but by 1801, the more serious flaw was cowardice. Certainly, revolutionaries had regularly derided their enemies as cowards. But the institutionalization of conscription in 1798–99 led to an intensified campaign to portray deserters and draft dodgers as effeminate weaklings. While Napoleonic officials abandoned specific strategies republicans had considered using to humiliate shirkers, the contrast between cowards and brave military men became even more central.

Conclusion: The Promise of Reward

In most of these plays, a deus ex machina appears, often a superior officer or local doyen eager to reward a soldier's courage with a bountiful dowry. This plot device was not unique to the theater of the period. But it was a useful means of allaying the fears of the financial risk of marriage to a soldier. As we have seen, the 1801 *The Guinguette, or Celebrations for the Peace* ends when Georgette's uncle offers his niece and her love, a sergeant, a purse of 600 francs in gold. His proclamation when he is thanked—"I would like to be rich enough to offer the same thing to all the brave men of the army"—makes it clear that

115. Review of *La paix dans la Manche* in M. Peletier, *Paris pendant l'année 1801* (London: Cox, Fils, et Baylis, 1801), 368.

116. Spang, "The Frivolous French"; and Forray-Carlier and Bruson, *Au temps des merveilleuses*.

117. Germer, "In Search of a Beholder."

this is not simply a personal reward, but one aimed at all soldiers.[118] Similarly, in the contemporaneous *Peace and Marriage*, by Cambronne, a wealthy man plans to hold an impressive festival for returning soldiers. His hope is that several men from the local village would act as heroes, and he proclaims that "I will give a thousand écus to whoever among these men who has earned a national reward (*récompense nationale*) by his courage, on the condition that he marry the daughter or the sister of a soldier of this canton on the day of the Festival of Peace."[119] The rich man's friend, Rémond, a retired soldier himself, proposes the captain Firmin. Firmin appears the perfect candidate, as he is the son of a close friend and fellow officer, and more importantly, engaged to Rémond's daughter. However, there has long been no news of him, and he is assumed to be dead. The captain of course returns with the peace. He has performed his assigned role of hero and performed multiple acts of bravery. These include having entirely destroyed a corps of 1,500 Arab Bedouins, who were about to surprise Firmin's camp in Egypt, and victory over 6,000 Mamelukes. The wealthy man applauds such great deeds and showers money on Firmin and his fiancée, who wed amid great rejoicing.

Such well-timed rewards were fantasy. In reality, benefactors were short on the ground, and the resumption of hostilities often made soldiers' marriages impossible. Yet fantasies served a purpose. Works produced to celebrate peace provided a means for imagining the return of all soldiers as living and loyal figures, wounded but fundamentally unharmed and inherently heroic. The idea of a marriage as both a financial and moral reward took this a step further. It provided the means to picture the easy reintegration of veterans into civilian society. It suggested that the virility and courage of a soldier would overcome the financial risk of marrying a military man and that authorities would expedite the creation of new families and new citizens.

Nor were such fantasies without consequences. As we will see in the next chapter, Napoleon himself would adapt the theater's dreams of marriage and money as a reward for soldiers—turning them from a celebration of peace to a tool for legitimating ongoing war. His government would organize weddings between young girls and select veterans and publicize their marriages in public festivals held across France. The state would also promise such couples government-paid dowries as recognition of both military valor and domestic virtue.

118. Villiers and Bonel, *La guinguette*, 24.

119. Cambronne, *La paix et l'hymen*, 16.

CHAPTER SIX

Napoleonic State-Sponsored Marriages of Veterans

IN 1803, THE British writer Anne Plumptre took advantage of the recent Peace of Amiens to explore France. She was interested in how the country had changed during the Revolution, commenting on an aspect of Napoleonic festivities she deemed "most novel": state-sponsored weddings. To celebrate the Feast of the Assumption on August 15, twelve soldiers wed twelve young women. The government provided couples with dowries and defrayed the cost of their weddings. Plumptre attended one event, and observed, "We were much pleased and interested by the ceremony. The bride had been a servant to Madame [wife of] the Prefect of the department, who had given her a white gown, and cap and a handkerchief trimmed with lace, as her wedding suit. . . . The bridegroom was a genteel-looking young man, with a very open and ingenious countenance; and the bride a decent, modest, and pretty young woman."[1]

Foreign travelers are not always the most informed observers; Plumptre missed the fact that the bridegrooms were likely veterans, not serving combatants. But she was right to see these weddings as novel. The ceremonies she witnessed were the beginnings of an extensive use of new form of state-sponsored marriages. The hopes of a lasting peace would fade as the Napoleonic Empire replaced the Consulate, and Napoleon Bonaparte became embroiled in a continent-wide struggle for military dominance. Yet public marriages involving veterans actually became more important as war resumed. Bonaparte's government began to promote the weddings of veterans and young women in 1802, and expanded the practice when Napoleon became emperor in 1804. By 1810, authorities aimed to marry six thousand soldiers simultaneously across the French Empire as part of the festivities for Napoleon's own wedding with Marie-Louise.

1. Plumptre, *A Narrative of Three Years Residence in France*, 1:183.

Intrigued by the phenomenon, scholars have unearthed numerous stories of couples whose weddings were promoted by the state, but usually present these discoveries as local curiosities.[2] A few historians have placed them in broader contexts. Most notably, Isser Woloch and Natalie Petiteau have argued that the 1810 wave of marriages served to reintegrate veterans into civilian society.[3] Denise Davidson has compared weddings in Rouen, Lyon, and Nantes to show that while Napoleonic laws restricted the role of women as citizens, festivals repeatedly brought them into politicized public spaces.[4]

Thinking about these weddings within the framework of revolution, war, and peacemaking, however, uncovers other dynamics. On first glance, state-sponsored weddings present an unsurprising story of men heralded for their military service and women for their virtue as hardworking daughters and future mothers. But looking more closely reveals hidden challenges to dominant gender roles and state power; among other things, these marriages placed physically incapacitated men as heads of household, called attention to the controversial role of the government in private life, and juxtaposed the dictates of love against those of pity, gratitude, and financial calculation.

To make sense of these marriages and to see what insights they might offer us, this chapter brings together very different kinds of sources. Municipal councils reported on their choices of candidates, and local officials boasted to central authorities of the success of their festivals or complained about costs; their correspondence reveals both official visions and the challenges administrators faced.[5] In some cases, they even confronted soap-opera-like denouements, as when a woman a soldier had married and abandoned in Prussia showed up just as he was about to wed again in southern France.[6] Individuals asked to be selected, contested the choice of a rival, defended their choice of partners, or complained that a dowry had not been paid; their petitions suggest what marriages could mean for the people most intimately involved. Weddings were accompanied by speeches and festivals—for which programs often survive—and by plays that authorities paid theaters

2. Most studies date from the late nineteenth and early twentieth centuries, including La Sicotière, "Les rosières en Basse Normandie"; Rouvière, "Les rosières du premier arrondissement du Gard"; Nancey, "Fêtes à l'occasion du mariage de l'empereur"; Haize, "Saint-Servan sous le premier empire"; Baraud, "Les rosières de la Roche-Sur-Yon"; Vovard, "Les rosières de l'empereur"; and Claeys, "Dotations et mariages de rosières." For somewhat more recent studies, see Becquert, "Les 'mariages de l'empereur'"; Tintou, "En Haute Vienne"; and Lévêque, "Les mariages impériaux."

3. Woloch, *The French Veteran*; Petiteau, "Les mariés de l'an 1810" and *Lendemains d'empire*.

4. Davidson, "Women at Napoleonic Festivals" and *France after Revolution*.

5. Most of these materials are in AN subseries F / 1c / III, series M in departmental archives (henceforward AD), and in the Archives de Paris, in VD / 4 / 8.

6. AN F / 9 / 54 Bis, Aveiron.

to perform so audiences could attend for free.[7] Local dignitaries escorted couples to performances; plays also presented characters given public dowries as counterparts to real couples being honored.[8] Such productions hint at the cultural imagination that legitimated—and sometimes challenged—these ceremonies.

We begin by exploring how Napoleon's government came to use weddings as a tool of state power and what authorities may have hoped to accomplish with them. We then look more closely at what made these marriages distinctive. State-sponsored weddings drew on a variety of French traditions, including royal philanthropy, Old Regime celebrations of "rose queens," and revolutionary festivals. Tracing how Napoleonic celebrations adapted such precedents allows us to reconsider the processes of "cultural recycling" (the practice of reusing tools developed in one political order in a very different regime) analyzed in previous chapters, this time in a postrevolutionary empire. Napoleonic ceremonies shared many features with their predecessors. But they transformed these precedents in fundamental ways, turning philanthropy and celebrations of peace into a means of promoting long-term war.

Such innovations required new forms of legitimation—and created new sites of uncertainty and contestation. In the rest of this chapter, we explore the state's role as matchmaker and give voice to the couples themselves. Historians of marriage have debated the origins of companionate marriage and weighed the influence parents have had over their children's choice of partners.[9] We saw in the last chapter how plays celebrating peace in 1797 and 1801 depicted parents, especially fathers, who championed rich but cowardly civilian grooms, while their daughters remained loyal to distant combatants. All ended well when peace came and young women wed soldier-heroes. These marriages highlight instead ways the Napoleonic state itself intervened in selecting partners and trying to ensure that young women would wed veterans, while trying to deny or disguise coercive aspects of its involvement.

Looking at such weddings also allows us to test what happened to ideals of martial masculinity in the wake of the Revolution and in a context not of imminent peace but of seemingly endless war. They show how much these ideals went beyond the military to affect even small-town courtship. But the very conditions that entitled ex-combatants to reward—including fighting multiple campaigns and being injured—challenged hopes that veterans could become independent men, productive husbands, or civilian workers. Men seeking to

7. Julian, "Les 'gratis' de Napoléon."

8. One prefect reported in 1807 that he had placed the new bride in his loge in the theater. AN F / 1 / c / III Eure 11. Similarly, ten honored couples sat in the front rows of a performance in Rouen in 1810. Bouteiller, *Histoire complète et méthodique des théâtres de Rouen*, 3:186.

9. Among many other works, see Davidson, "'Happy' Marriages"; Goodman, "Marriage Choice and Marital Success"; and Gougelmann and Verjus, eds., *Écrire le mariage.*

be discharged from troops in the late Revolution had walked a fine line in trying to present themselves as too weakened to continue as soldiers but still fit enough to be capable of providing for needy family members.[10] Arranging state-sponsored marriages required Napoleonic authorities to confront similar tensions, while presenting ex-combatants as men to be rewarded for their heroism with the chance to start new households.

Terms for marriages also prescribed desirable forms of femininity; they rewarded women's morality and hard work, and defined women in terms of their familial relationships. Yet arrangements for weddings reveal limits to women's willingness to accept veterans as partners and repeated questions about who—men or women—were really being honored, and why. In a few exceptional cases, state-sponsored marriages even raised the possibility that women should be given dowries and official recognition for their own martial courage.

Instituting State-Sponsored Weddings

Napoleon first proposed state-sponsored weddings in late June 1802. France was at peace with Europe, following the Treaty of Lunéville, which ended war on the continent in February 1801, and the Treaty of Amiens, which ended war with Britain in March 1802. Such marriages appeared to be a real-life counterpart to theatrical fantasies celebrating peace, in which soldiers returned home from war to wed loyal sweethearts.

The plan was to reward one couple from each major district within Paris. A prospective groom was to be "a young man of good conduct and morals, who had served for at least three campaigns and exercises a profession that assures his livelihood." The bride was "to be from a poor but honest family; a dowry of a thousand francs should allow her to help the business of the man she marries."[11] While Napoleon's government viewed such dowries as charity, they were different from other philanthropic acts that accompanied festivals, such as the distribution of food. Both the men and women who received imperial munificence as dowries were judged on their capacity to provide for themselves after they wed. State support for marriage was a one-time spectacle but also a long-term investment.

There was little time to organize these marriages, and local officials were hard-pressed to find candidates.[12] Police reported that crowds nonetheless seemed more pleased with the weddings than with the fireworks and games

10. See chapter 3.

11. Archives de Paris VD / 4 / 8, 7 messidor an X, CPS Dotation des jeunes filles à l'occasion de la fête du 14 juillet.

12. Archives de Paris VD / 4 / 8, 7 messidor an X, CPS Dotation des jeunes filles à l'occasion de la fête du 14 juillet.

that had marked previous celebrations, though those entertainments continued.[13] Officials almost immediately sought to use marriages to celebrate other occasions. Parisian authorities considered promoting weddings as part of the Feast of the Assumption on August 15, 1802, a holiday renamed Saint Napoleon's Day in 1806. They decided, however, that the interval was too short to find couples who wanted to unite, choosing instead to arrange a new round of marriages on September 23, 1802, the anniversary of the founding of the Republic.[14]

Napoleon dramatically expanded the uses of such marriages when he became emperor. On May 20, 1804, he decreed that Paris, Bordeaux, Lyon, and Marseille should honor a "poor but well-behaved *(sage)*" girl from each major district of their respective cities. He also proclaimed that the communal arrondissements of the Empire should reward deserving young women. The arrondissements corresponded to divisions (usually three to five) within each of the 108 departments in France in the period; ceremonies thus promised to encompass several hundred couples. This time Napoleon was planning well ahead. The weddings were to take place six months later, during his coronation, on December 2, 1804. Two years later, the decree of February 19, 1806, established that to celebrate the anniversary of the coronation, each district in France with more than 10,000 francs in tax revenues should provide a dowry to a "well-behaved girl" so that she could marry "a man who has gone to war"; similar weddings were to be held every subsequent December.[15]

The use of state-sponsored marriages of veterans reached a peak in 1810 when, to commemorate his own marriage to Marie-Louise, Napoleon decreed that "six thousand retired soldiers, who have served for at least one campaign, will be married on April 22, to young women from their commune. They will be accorded a dowry of 1,200 francs for Paris and 600 francs in the rest of the Empire."[16] Arranging six thousand marriages for the same day was no easy task, particularly given that weddings were again planned on short notice. The March 25 decree called for marriages less than a month later, on April 22; in many cases, the interval was even shorter because the decree did not reach remote localities until late March or early April. While numbers are uncertain, it seems likely that about five thousand marriages took place.[17]

When Napoleon's son was born in March 1811, authorities planned for yet another series of weddings, intended to coincide with the child's baptism on

13. Aulard, *Paris sous le consulat*, 3:152.

14. Archives de Paris VD / 4 / 8.

15. Archives de Paris VD / 4 / 8.

16. *23 mars 1810, Décret contenant les actes de bienfaisance et d'indulgence à l'occasion du mariage de sa majesté l'Empereur et Roi*, titre IV, article 5.

17. For example, it did not reach Dunkerque until March 31. The committee met on April 4 and called for nominations by the 7th, giving couples three days to decide whether to marry. Nancey, "Fêtes à l'occasion du mariage de l'empereur," 16.

June 9. The goal remained similar: "to provide a dowry for a poor orphan girl so that she can marry a former soldier."[18] Perhaps because of challenges with earlier arrangements, Napoleon did not call for a specific number of weddings, but only for marriages (usually ten to fifteen) in each of the major cities of the Empire; smaller cities and communes celebrated when municipal budgets permitted.[19] This time, there were probably only several hundred, rather than several thousand, weddings.[20]

The government continued to promote state-sponsored weddings on the anniversary of Napoleon's coronation through 1812. A few major cities, like Paris and Lyon, still celebrated such weddings in December 1813.[21] In much of France, however, municipal governments faced more urgent needs as the Empire collapsed, deciding that money for festivals and dowries would be far better allotted elsewhere.[22]

Initially instituted during peacetime, such marriages became a tool for celebrating the emperor and the war machine that underpinned his rule. They faltered alongside that machine. Indeed, the administrative continuity of the practice from 1802 onward masks a fundamental change starting in 1804: weddings came not to celebrate an end of war, but to reward those who fought and encourage others to take up arms. To understand better what was involved in the new role of the state and the challenges with using marriage to persuade both men and women to support war, we need to return to the precedents for these celebrations.

Royal Philanthropy, Local Beauty Queens, and Revolutionary Patriots

As the prefect of the Seine described it, the first consul's "intention [in 1802] was to reestablish an ancient institution whose goal was to associate charity with festivals for a great event. This institution consists of marrying girls distinguished by their virtue and deprived by poverty of the means to find an establishment."[23] However, the prefect immediately introduced innovations in

18. "Doter une fille pauvre et orpheline pour la marier à un ancien militaire."

19. Letter from Napoleon to the minister of the interior, April 13, 1811, in *Correspondance de Napoléon Ier,* 22:59.

20. A sampling of about half the cartons in the Archives Nationales documenting weddings in individual departments indicates almost two hundred marriages.

21. Archives de Paris VD / 4 / 8. On Lyon, see Davidson, "Women at Napoleonic Festivals," 320.

22. For example, the council of Wazemmes decided in 1813 that the Bureau de Bienfaisance would make better use of the money. Alfred Salembrier, *Annales de la Société d'études de la province de Cambrai* (Seclin: Huet-Thuet, 1912), 298.

23. Archives de Paris VD / 4 / 8, 7 messidor an X, CPS Dotation des jeunes filles à l'occasion de la fête du 14 juillet.

this ancient institution: criteria not just for selecting brides, but also grooms, as reputable men who had fought multiple campaigns and had viable civilian professions.

In promoting state-sponsored marriages, the Napoleonic government actually adapted not one "ancient institution" but rather several traditions. The first was royal philanthropy. In 1751, Louis XV's court dowered six hundred Parisian women to celebrate the birth of the son of the royal dauphin; officials were encouraged to dower young women elsewhere in the kingdom.[24] Madame de Pompadour, the king's mistress, claimed that she provided the inspiration for these weddings, and gave fifteen young women dowries from her own estates; the number was chosen to honor the king.[25] Contemporary sources provide very different accounts about who really paid for such charity, and the extent to which her actions inspired imitators.[26]

Louis XVI similarly dowered a hundred couples in February 1779 to celebrate the birth of his daughter, after eight years of worrisome childlessness. The archbishop initially proposed marrying all one hundred couples in one ceremony in Notre Dame cathedral, but realized that the proceedings would be too time-consuming for the king and queen to witness. The honorees were married separately in the morning, and newlyweds lined up in the cathedral in the afternoon—the women in orange, the men in puce—to honor their sovereign. A hundred birds released into the cathedral completed the spectacle.[27]

Napoleonic weddings involved similar, if smaller scale, pageantry. They sought, however, to duplicate it across the country. Such pomp not only displayed imperial munificence; it also honored veterans within local communities. Comparing the financial aspects of these arrangements reveals other shifts involved with featuring soldiers. Both Old Regime and Napoleonic officials wanted to ensure that couples would be able to support themselves after an initial act of state philanthropy, but eighteenth-century authorities were more controlling of their beneficence. Priests, charged in 1751 with distributing 300 livres for each marriage, were not to "give it the husband who could squander it; it is reserved to their [the curés'] discretion to use it in all or in part, in furniture for those who have none, for tools, merchandise, *mâitrisés* [the qualification to work as a master artisan], and other things necessary and useful to establish a household."[28] In contrast, Napoleonic officials usually gave couples money directly, without stipulations on how it was to be used. This reflected the

24. Barbier, *Chronique de la régence et du règne de Louis XV*, 119.

25. Pompadour, *Mémoires*, 2:8; Lacretelle, *Histoire de France*, 3:163.

26. For a critical assessment, see Soulavie, *Mémoires historiques et anecdotes*, 281.

27. Berthre de Bourniseaux, *Histoire de Louis XVI*, 1:249.

28. Barbier, *Chronique de la régence et du règne de Louis XV*, 119. The *Journal de Paris* similarly reported in 1779 that the queen had given 500 livres to curés for each girl's dowry; this money was only to provide subsistence or to purchase the right to work in certain fields; *Journal de Paris*, no. 38, February 7, 1779, 150.

changing position of priests, no longer as powerful as before the Revolution. It also reflected the legacies of revolutionary celebrations of soldier-citizens and the new uses of state-sponsored marriages as a reward for military service.

I have found no concrete evidence that Napoleon was aware that marriages had been used to mark royal events, but it seems likely. It is indisputable, however, that Napoleonic officials were aware of another model: eighteenth-century rose festivals, especially those in the village of Salency in northern France. In 1800, the minister of the interior wrote to officials in the department of the Oise asking about the festivals as he began to plan new programs; locals responded in detail about their history.[29] Eighteenth-century villagers had selected three young women for their virtue and beauty every year. The local seigneur then chose among these women and bestowed a dowry of 25 livres on the winner. The Contesse de Genlis "discovered" the festival in 1766 and her accounts inspired several plays, light operas, and engravings. The Salency *rosière* might still have remained a local affair of short-term interest if it had not been for a scandal. In 1773, the seigneur Danré sought to choose the woman himself rather than wait for the villagers' recommendations, and tried to avoid paying for ceremonial gifts. The villagers brought suit to the local *bailliage* court and won; Danré appealed and took the case to the Parlement of Paris, where he ultimately lost again. The affair became a cause célèbre for discussing aristocratic greed and rural virtue; it also inspired other localities to create their own festivals, some of which persisted into the nineteenth century.[30]

Not only did Napoleonic administrators actively research the history of the rosières de Salency, but theatrical troupes also revived plays celebrating them to mark events in Napoleon's life. Among other cases, theaters performed the 1771 *Rosière of Salency* in Liège to celebrate Napoleon's coronation in 1804 and in Arles for the birth of Napoleon's son in 1811.[31] The work had the advantage of being readily available; troupes did not have to wait for playwrights to produce a new work or get permission to use a recent composition. Performances could also remind audiences that such rituals had long connections to French rural communities.

29. AN F / 1c / III Oise 9.

30. Maza, "The Rose Girl of Salency" and *Private Lives and Public Affairs*.

31. Masson de Pezay, *La rosière de Salency*. The Théâtre de l'Opéra-Comique also performed the play in 1796. On the 1804 performance in Liège, see Jules Martiny, *Histoire du théâtre de Liège depuis son origine jusqu'à nos jours* (Liège: Vallant-Carmanne, 1887), 91. For an 1811 performance in Arles, see *Procès-verbal des fêtes célébrées à Arles département des Bouches du Rhône à l'occasion de la naissance et du baptême de sa majesté le roy du Rome le 10 11 12 et 13 juin 1811*, in AN F / 1c / III Bouches du Rhône 10. Editions of the play were published in Paris in 1808, and under the title *La rosière de Salenci*, in 1811 and 1812. *La rosière de Stockholm, ou la fête de la rose, imitée de celle de Salency*, was published in 1808 in Sweden.

Some Napoleonic officials lauded prerevolutionary rose festivals as inspiration for their own practices. Bougault, the mayor of Suresnes, wrote the minister of the interior in 1802 describing an eighteenth-century tradition of rosières in his commune. He referred to the program the minister had sent describing state-sponsored weddings in Paris, and claimed that rural districts had as much, if not more, to offer.[32] The minister was interested, but unwilling to provide money. Instead, the tradition was initially carried on by local elites, like Madame Desbassayns, a rich woman who revived it as a memorial to her daughter, Camille, in August 1805. The four-year-old girl had been in a carriage when it slid over a ravine; she initially appeared unharmed but died a few weeks later. To preserve her memory, Madame Desbassayns asked that villagers elect the "most virtuous girl" every year among those born in Suresnes or who had lived there since at least the age of twelve. She would then pay for the young woman's marriage, on condition that her firstborn daughter be named Camille.

Napoleonic administrators called attention to such local traditions to explain how the state had come to play a more central role and to honor both women and men. In 1810, the mayor of Auxonne, near Dijon, claimed that the Salency model for honoring rosières had been combined with a practice in a nearby village. The village gave a "silver medal to a young man whom an assembly of fathers of family judged each year to be the wisest and most hardworking of the village."[33] The mayor contended that Napoleon, alert to all that was great and useful, had melded the two traditions to create a new institution that was extended to the entire Empire. His explanation seems more likely to reflect local pride than a definitive origin of Napoleon's use of public marriage.

Indeed, Napoleonic marriages differed from *fêtes de rose* and local celebrations in several critical ways. New representatives of the state played a more central role. In prerevolutionary Salency, villagers selected candidates. The selection committee for the eighteenth-century rosière de Suresnes consisted of the mayor, the curé, and "twelve of the most reputable citizens" of the village. In the mayor of Auxonne's account of prerevolutionary celebrations in Neuilly, an "assembly of fathers" chose the hardworking youth.[34] In contrast, the deciding figures in Napoleonic state-sponsored weddings were local officials. The March 25, 1810, imperial decree established that in cities, municipal councils would choose couples, subject to the prefect's approval in departmental capitals, or the subprefect's in other cities. Special commissions served

32. Bertaux, *Notice sur la rosière de Suresnes*, 25.

33. Amanton, *Discours prononcé par le maire . . . le 2 décembre 1810*.

34. Amanton, *Discours prononcé par le maire . . . le 2 décembre 1810*, 5.

rural areas, usually comprising two village mayors, two priests chosen by the subprefect, and a local justice of the peace.[35]

The most important difference between Old Regime and Napoleonic festivals, however, were the honorees. Eighteenth-century festivals did not even identify potential husbands; Napoleonic ceremonies honored both men and women. Unlike earlier rituals, Napoleonic festivals did not just reward hardworking youths, but aimed specifically at veterans. As one Aveyronese administrator put it in 1810: "We honor at the same time military courage and the virtues of modesty, we reward simultaneously the love of glory and the practice of good morals."[36]

This practice drew on revolutionary precedents, including promises that patriotic warriors would be rewarded with women's love. Some revolutionaries specifically championed marriages for military valor. The October 1793 play *Marriage Paid for by the Nation* exemplifies this logic. Its heroine, Agathe, is the most virtuous girl in her village. A sign over her door proclaims her to be a "national dowry, to be given to the most courageous [man]."[37] Agathe is courted by two men: Paulin, a young volunteer whose poverty has kept him from marrying; and the unnamed chief of the Spanish forces. Agathe of course marries Paulin, after he demonstrates his bravery.

The most immediate precedents for Napoleonic state-sponsored marriages of veterans were the popular plays celebrating peace, especially in 1797 and 1801. As we have seen, such works configured marriage as a moral and financial reward for military service. Plays also featured a range of benefactors who helped make marriages possible. A few works portrayed collective generosity, like the 1799 *Turenne's Tomb, or the Army of the Rhine at Saspach,* which celebrated a young man injured in fighting who was eager to wed. Hermann's companions in arms donated three days of their pay as a dowry for the wounded man.[38] More frequently, however, theaters treated audiences to fantasies in which wealthy local elites, well-placed relatives, or high-ranking military officials rewarded courageous but impoverished soldiers. This reflected both pragmatism—rank-and-file soldiers were not usually well positioned to enrich their comrades—and a cultural shift away from Jacobin egalitarianism to renewed social hierarchy.

Napoleonic celebrations thus drew on aspects of all of these precedents, and reworked them for a new political regime. Like earlier authorities, officials

35. Titre IV, Du Mariage de six mille militaires, Décret contenant les actes de bienfaisance et d'indulgence à l'occasion du mariage de Sa Majesté l'Empereur. See also Woloch, *The French Veteran*, 247–48.

36. AN F / 1c / III Aveyron 9, *Extrait des registres des procès-verbaux de la mairie de Villefranche, département de l'Aveiron,* séance du 22 avril 1810.

37. *Mariage aux frais de la nation,* unprinted, but reviewed in *Journal des spectacles,* no. 123, 12 Brumaire Year II (November 2, 1793); Germani, "Staging Battles," 208.

38. Bouilly, Cuvelier, and Chaussier, *Le tombeau de Turenne, ou l'armée du Rhin à Saspach.*

sought to honor couples who would be moral and hardworking, and who would not threaten social order. Like eighteenth-century royal philanthropy, Napoleonic rituals used state-sponsored dowries to mark events in a monarch's life and to promote national strength through population growth—although they focused less on increasing the total numbers of subjects than on the numbers of future soldiers.[39] Like fêtes de rose, they celebrated local beauty and virtue. And like revolutionary festivals, they rewarded military courage.

But they also introduced critical innovations, including the increased role of the state in selecting couples, the choice to recognize both men and women, the prominence of wounded veterans, and the use of public weddings to legitimate war rather than to celebrate peace. These innovations reflected both administrative transformations and the militarization of society, and worked to legitimate Napoleonic order. But they also brought unexpected questions. Could a postrevolutionary government interfere directly in family life and decide weddings across the country—while still insisting that love united couples? What would make both men and women want to wed? What did such weddings actually reward—and were marriages really an effective tool for promoting military masculinity—or of domesticating former veterans?

The State as Matchmaker

THE LOCAL AND THE NATIONAL

Napoleonic celebrations were simultaneously local and national. The intersection of these levels emerges most clearly in the attempt to marry six thousand couples in 1810. Couples were chosen across France. Cities were allotted quotas depending on their size: ten each from the largest cities, five from the next largest group of 54 cities, and two from 555 smaller cities. Each rural canton was to have one couple; about two-thirds of the total were to come from such hamlets.[40] Plays, speeches, and poems stressed the scale of the weddings that accompanied Napoleon's nuptials. The play *The Festival of Meudon* provides one acknowledgment of such numbers. In a thinly disguised tribute to Napoleon, Marguerite, the sister of François I, tells a virtuous young bride: "your marriage will not be the only one. The King wants six thousand to celebrate his." The young women of the village repeat the number in awe: "What? Six thousand!"[41]

Such national celebrations were also supremely local. The decree awarded dowries for couples within specific localities, not for couples whose

39. On claims that eighteenth-century state marriages would strengthen population, see, among other works, Lévy, *Journal historique*, 77; and Berthre de Bourniseaux, *Histoire de Louis XVI*, 1:24.

40. Woloch, *The French Veteran*, 270.

41. Dupaty, *La fête de Meudon*, 69.

relationships transcended municipal or communal boundaries. This was a pragmatic choice; local authorities were best placed to distinguish among candidates, and most willing to bestow largesse on those within their bailiwick. The central government was eager to profit from a display of philanthropic concern but not to become enmeshed in the details. Delegating the task of finding couples to local authorities was critical given the limited time for organizing marriages.[42]

There are, however, broader implications to this mixture of local marriages and national celebration. Historians have noted the extent to which French revolutionaries sought to destroy local allegiances in favor of a common national identity. Festivals—held simultaneously across the country—offered one means of fostering such connections.[43] Napoleonic authorities continued to promote national celebrations, while limiting popular dimensions of festivities.[44] Yet the requirement that couples marry only within their town or commune anchored people within deeply local communities and reinforced the boundaries of those communities, even as it promoted national unity.

In practice, these restrictions posed challenges. Men and women did not limit their search for romantic and economic partners to their immediate localities.[45] Veterans in particular looked farther afield. The complaint of the mayor of Boissy-Saint-Leger in 1811 is typical; it was difficult to arrange a marriage because "there are many girls and few soldiers, and the latter have inclinations outside of their communes."[46] Even within Paris, administrators who insisted on local roots encountered the complexities of immigration. They repeatedly chided municipal authorities who sought to reward women who had not been born in the city, as well as those who were considered too old.[47]

Focusing on local communities did not resolve the question of what legitimated authorities' ability to act in loco parentis. The state's ability to designate appropriate couples had been an issue for Old Regime marriages. But eighteenth-century priests exercised a certain authority, while local elites could claim bonds of traditional patronage. The relatively new municipal figures of Napoleonic France lacked such connections. Promoting state-sponsored marriages thus entailed persuading French men and women that this was an appropriate role for government, particularly in the context of backlash against revolutionary experiments in transforming family law.

42. Officials began planning in late June 1802 for July 14 weddings. The March 25, 1810, decree similarly gave less than a month to organize weddings.

43. The most significant work remains Ozouf, *Festivals and the French Revolution.*

44. Davidson, "Women at Napoleonic Festivals," 305.

45. Bonneuil, "Démographie de la nuptialité."

46. AD Yvelines 4M 17, Boissy St Leger, 22 mai 1811.

47. Archives de Paris VD / 4 / 8. Complaints appeared most in 1812 and 1813.

"YOUR CHOICES PRECEDED OURS"

One of the most important strategies in legitimating the state's matchmaking activities was to downplay authorities' involvement. Officials were at pains to convince their audiences that men and women had chosen their marriage bonds freely. In a speech in April 1810, the mayor of Villefranche in the Aveyron thus proclaimed: "Young husbands, you know well that neither the Municipal Council nor the Commission of the Canton forced your choice; they did not mandate your preference for the wives you are about to marry. Your choices have in fact preceded ours; you have distinguished your future companions; you have given them your hearts and your faith; we have been satisfied simply to confirm the choices that you have made."[48]

In a few cases, authorities' desire to make sure that both parties consented could backfire. In a town near Bayonne, François Gaillardon beseeched authorities to reconsider his fiancée Catherine's apparent refusal. When the wife of the justice of the peace came to fetch his intended, she adopted a tone that made the poor dayworker think that it was an April Fool's joke. When she was summoned again, Catherine, overcome with modesty, was so intimidated by the prospect of appearing before local elites that she hesitated too long to confirm her desire to marry François and receive a state-sponsored dowry. The couple thus lost their chance; local authorities choose a different couple instead.[49]

It seems that most administrators wanted couples to be genuinely compatible. As the prefect of the Ariège observed, "I do not think one should make illusory the favor accorded by his Majesty by forcing the inclination of a soldier." In that case, the prefect was concerned about a local justice of the peace who was overly interested in finding a husband for his servant and wanted to rig the selection process.[50] In general, officials overturned individuals' choices only when the morality of a partner was called into question, municipal funding was too limited to support marriages, or a potential bride or groom clearly did not fit the qualifications of the decree. But they also wanted to *appear* as honoring preexisting arrangements rather than forcing new ones.

THE PATERNAL STATE?

Parental metaphors further legitimized state involvement in private life. The language of the *Mercure de France* is typical; the newspaper reported on March 1810 that the "mayors and the justices of the peace, fathers and tutors of the communal family, will elect the couples who are worthy of his

48. AN F / 1c / III Aveyron 9, *Extrait des registres des procès-verbaux de la mairie de Villefranche, département de l'Aveiron.*

49. AN F / 9 / 54 Bis, dossier Pyrénées Inférieures.

50. AN F / 9 / 54 Bis, dossier Arriège. Woloch, *The French Veteran*, 250–51.

Majesty's blessings."[51] Popular theater often presented the paternal solicitude of municipal officials literally, depicting mayors as having a familial connection to the couples they united. The 1810 play *The Happy Day*, performed free in Versailles for Napoleon's wedding, featured a mayor who wanted to add two young women to the three who had been chosen for dowries in his town. He selected his own niece Clémence, engaged to a colonel, and Thérèse, the fiancée of his soldier son; not coincidentally, Thérèse was also the granddaughter of a former soldier. The mayor received a cross of honor for his generosity.[52]

In practice, municipal officials rarely honored couples with whom they had real family relations.[53] Too blatant a connection smacked of favoritism. The portrayal of mayors as wise fathers jarred with the attitudes of many central administrators. They viewed the forty thousand unpaid mayors in France with suspicion, a view that reflected both the lack of experience of many local administrators and the scorn of Parisian elites for provincial subordinates.[54] Theatrical fantasies could ignore these social relations to herald familial and state unity.

Artistic conventions also encouraged playwrights to imagine familial connections; fathers made for more compelling characters than did officials. Such conventions may explain why other figures involved in choosing real couples seldom appeared on stage. Priests, designated by the subprefect in rural communities to select couples, usually presided over church ceremonies for the weddings of actual rosières. But they rarely showed up in theater. This was in part because Napoleonic productions sought to avoid religious characters who might stir up controversy.[55] The status of priests as single men also limited their usefulness as theatrical matchmakers. Revolutionaries had sought to make priests marry and have children, but by the Empire, that policy had changed.[56] It was no longer possible to portray priests as having direct familial bonds with their flock.

If popular theater suggested the paternal role of mayors, another fatherly figure was far more prominent: Napoleon Bonaparte himself. Both theatrical characters and municipal officials emphasized Napoleon's role as "father of the country" and couples' responsibility to raise children who would be loyal to him. Commentators made this connection explicit, like the Lyonnais mayor who proclaimed in 1811 that "it's the Emperor who weds you; you will owe him your children." The honored couples dutifully responded, "We owe him our children."[57] Some veterans seem to have taken this vision a step further. One groom, overcome with emotion in 1804, had his brother read a statement he had prepared expressing his thanks. He praised the "hero of France, who has

51. *Mercure de France*, vol. 41, March 1810, 317–18.

52. Baillot, *L'heureux jour*.

53. I have found no examples. If they exist, they were not publicized.

54. Dunne, "Napoleon's 'Mayoral Problem.'"

55. See Krakovitch, "La censure théâtrale."

56. Cage, *Unnatural Frenchmen*.

57. Cited in Davidson, "Women at Napoleonic Festivals," 320.

become our father" and promised that "our grandchildren will undoubtedly say, we hope, that he who sits on the throne of France is our protector and our father; his generosity endowed our ancestors."[58]

Some commentators also depicted the emperor as an exemplar for soldiers who would themselves become fathers. For example, when exhorting the crowds in 1810, the mayor of Lorgues in the Var claimed that "this conqueror, so terrible in combat, who leads you always to victory, is in the breast of the great family a father whose authority can serve as a model for yours."[59] Yet presenting Napoleon as a model was challenging—precisely because he continued as a military leader after his marriage, while the men who received state support for their weddings had left the battlefield. Certainly, officials promised that military triumphs would bring peace, and that general prosperity would follow Napoleon's marriage. But war remained the defining feature of the Empire. It was not surprising that orators downplayed the contradictions involved in heralding a paternal warrior emperor while celebrating veterans who were to take on a new role as civilian fathers.

Imperial Rosières and Wounded Heroes?

If public marriages required justifying the role of the state in private lives, they also required resolving tensions over who or what was actually being rewarded. Here it is useful to look more closely at the couples themselves. Authorities sometimes acknowledged uncertainty about whether to prioritize men or women, as in the case of one honoree, Pierre Créchet, married on March 25, 1810, and separated from his wife soon after receiving the dowry. Créchet falsely accused her of epileptic fits. The local mayor attributed the separation instead to "the weakness of Créchet's character and to his sisters, who could not get along with his new wife, and feared that she would persuade her husband to leave them"; if he left, he would take his money with him. The mayor proposed paying the dowry to the wife; doing otherwise would "slander the rosière." A marginal note called this into question, wondering if "His Majesty wanted to favor soldiers rather than women." In that case, "the sum should belong as much to the man as to his wife." Unfortunately, surviving records are unclear about who ultimately received the funds.[60]

Créchet's case reflected a fundamental ambiguity. Some measures clearly aimed at women. The 1804 marriages heralded women, the *rosières impériales;* the term recurred during the anniversaries of Napoleon's coronation.

58. AD Yvelines 4M 17, Extrait du procès-verbal de ce qui s'est passé à Corbeil le mardy 13 frimaire an 13 à la célébration du mariage ordonné par le décret impérial du 13 prairial an 12.

59. AN F / 1 / c / III Var 10, Discours prononcé par M. Allaman, Maire de la ville de Lorgues, dans le conseil municipal, à l'occasion de la fête du 22 avril 1810.

60. AN F / 9 / 54 Bis, dossier Indre.

Similarly, the 1811 decree in honor of the King of Rome provided dowries for "poor orphan girls," although it specified that they marry soldiers. But other decrees configured marriage as a reward for men. The 1810 decree directly addressed veterans, arranging for the marriages of "six thousand retired soldiers." That contemporaries perceived the decree as focusing on men is clear from the newspaper *Mercure de France*, which observed that "faithful soldiers, retired in their homes, will receive a mark of imperial munificence worthy of their services: six thousand of whom will receive a wife and a dowry."[61]

Popular culture also called attention to the question of whether the state was really awarding men or women. This was the case with the 1804 play *The Camp in Boulogne*. Napoleon Bonaparte himself saw the play when he visited the camp, and lauded the playwright, Charles-Guillaume Etienne.[62] The hero of the piece expresses his certainty that the heroine will be chosen, but doubts that he is worthy of the same recognition. Marguerite, the daughter of a fisherman, is known for her dedication: "she works day and night for her poor and infirm parents. Her patience and resignation are admired by all, and the votes of the commune will award her in advance the prize of virtue."[63] She, meanwhile, is convinced that Théodore will be awarded the dowry because of his glorious service, but that officials will not be interested in her. This is a variation on an old plot, in which lovers praise each other's virtues while disparaging their own qualities, but it expressed real questions. Whose qualifications were most important? Would officials reward men and women who wanted to be together?

Choosing men was, at least in theory, more straightforward than choosing women, as veterans' service records established the campaigns in which they had fought. Other criteria played important secondary roles. For example, in the department of Yvelines, the mayor of Houdan reported that there were only two unmarried veterans in his town in May 1811. Neither was acceptable. One had impregnated a girl (albeit the one whom he now sought to marry) and was thus immoral; the other, a Breton native and apprentice locksmith, could not be trusted to stay in the town.[64]

While decrees specified that men should have served in the military, a few civilians sought state-sponsored dowries, like Jean Legrand, a schoolteacher in the department of the Meuse, who sought to play upon the happy coincidence of his name to the epithet of Napoleon the Great (Napoleon Le Grand) and promised to name a future son Napoleon if he received a dowry. Although a civilian, he did not lack connections to the military. His two brothers had joined the army; one had perished after sixteen years of fighting, and the other

61. *Mercure de France*, vol. 41, March 1810, 317–18.

62. Wicks, *Charles Guillaume Etienne*, 15.

63. Etienne, *Le camp de Boulogne* (1804), bound in *Théâtre de C. G. Etienne* (Paris: Cabinet d'un amateur, 1919), 516–17. Bibliothèque de l'Arsenal GD-1469 (20).

64. AD Yvelines 4M 17, 1811 Houdan.

had disappeared without news. A recent widower, Legrand had six children. He was eager not only for a dowry for his own second marriage, but also for Napoleon's patronage for his oldest son, who served as a quartermaster: "the young man has a good hand for writing, good spelling, and is instructed in decimal calculation, but what is that worth without protection?"[65]

Legrand does not seem to have received a response, to either his desire for a dowry or his attempt to intervene for his son. Yet if his query went unanswered, other men who had not seen battle were sometimes honored if their prospective brides had close relatives who were at war. Weddings marking Napoleon's coronation in 1804 focused on women's relationships to soldiers, echoing the promise in an 1801 peace play that a bridegroom receive a dowry on the condition that he "marry the daughter or the sister of a soldier of this canton."[66] It was not essential for a rosière to have a relative who was fighting in French armies or who had been killed while doing so. However, it was a common qualification, as it proved both the family's patriotism and their need in the absence of able-bodied young men.[67]

The practice of prioritizing women whose family members were in the military was particularly clear in Lyon. The prefect of the Rhône told his subordinates in 1804 that "if other things are equal, decide in favor of those whose brothers or close relations died in the service of the country or are currently serving in the army."[68] In 1810, the mayor of Lyon sought to award "twelve girls who have brothers or close relations in the armies of the Emperor, and whose behavior is irreproachable." He specified that eight of the women—as well as their grooms—were to be employed in the city's silk works.[69]

Authorities selected women by their relationship to soldiers, and their reputation, age, and financial need. Moral criteria were more central for women than for men, though they could be difficult to judge; as Denise Davidson has noted, poverty was easier to recognize than virtue.[70] The short time for arranging marriages meant that officials could be taken by surprise when they rushed to find candidates. Administrators in one small town, for example, reported their dismay in early 1805 in discovering that a prospective bride had given birth just before her scheduled wedding; they hastily chose an alternate.[71]

65. AN F / 9 / 54 Bis, dossier Meuse.

66. Cambronne, *La paix et l'hymen*, 16.

67. See Rouvière, "Les rosières du premier arrondissement du Gard," on rosières in 1804 in the department of the Gard; for Bordeaux and Lyon, AD Gironde 1M 698 and AD Rhône 1 M 111.

68. AD Rhône 1 M 111.

69. Archives Municipales Lyon III 156; Davidson, "Women at Napoleonic Festivals," 316, 317.

70. Davidson, "Women at Napoleonic Festivals," 316.

71. AD Gironde 1M 698, 1 ventôse an 13 (February 20, 1805).

Personal accounts suggest that some women circumvented official requirements or definitions of morality. This may have been the case with Marguerite, a young woman in Brittany who married a gardener on August 15, 1805. She seems to have qualified as a rosière since she was poor and her father had died in battle when she was eleven. In a later memoir, the lieutenant colonel Parquin boasted that Marguerite had an affair with him when she worked as a laundress in the hospital where he recovered from his wounds. Parquin returned to service, and Marguerite's boss, the mother superior, used the possibility of a state dowry to persuade her to marry the gardener who had long been courting her.[72] It is unclear how much the retrospective boasts of her alleged lover should be trusted, but Marguerite's story suggests that young women and those around them could sometimes use state-sponsored marriages to their own ends.

While judging women's morality could be challenging, there was an advantage to focusing on them: it was easier to present a dowry as a philanthropic act while indirectly supporting war. Rewarding men for their military service with marriage raised serious questions about how to balance compensation for service and charity for the suffering. It also raised the question of how to promote martial masculinity while ensuring that honored veterans had a civilian livelihood. The men who had proved their courage by fighting were often those most in need of governmental help and least able to provide for families. Their wounds proved their heroism—while limiting their independence and future productivity.

"YOU JUSTIFY OUR CHOICES SIMPLY BY UNCOVERING YOUR CHESTS"

The question of wounding was in fact central both to many of these marriages and to the ceremonies that surrounded them. In the 1804 play *The Camp in Boulogne*, the hero Théodore worries that he will not be chosen for a state-sponsored wedding because he has no evidence of his valorous deeds. His comrades respond that his wounds speak for themselves: "What? You worry about papers? / What good are such scribblings? . . . . / if you need indisputable evidence . . . / Expose your chest and show your wounds."[73]

Théodore's story was fictional, but Napoleonic officials often invoked the injuries of real veterans to justify their selection. The speech of a Bordelais mayor in 1811 is typical of such rhetoric: "brave soldiers . . . you justify our choices simply by uncovering your chests. We will see your wounds, incontestable witnesses to the blood that you shed for the glory of the Sovereign,

72. Parquin, *Souvenirs de gloire et d'amour*, 32.
73. Etienne, *Le camp de Boulogne*, 517.

for the defense of the patrie."[74] Individuals also sometimes insisted on their wounds as evidence that they deserved dowries; Pierre Gaillard, for example, protested that he had been overlooked in favor of an alternate candidate, because his injuries were supposedly light and hinted at cowardice. He retorted that "The company that he had been part of [in the battle of Wagram] was almost entirely destroyed . . . if he returned home, it was only because of his wounds . . . and not because of cowardliness." Unfortunately for Gaillard, authorities were not convinced of his merits. He had served for only fourteen months and injury to his hand did not prevent him from working in his profession; his rival had suffered more.[75]

Because there was no formal mention of injury in the decrees on state-sponsored marriage, there were no clear guidelines as to what forms of injury were serious enough to merit recompense while still leaving men able to act as productive husbands. Pensions did provide one point of reference. Starting in 1791, laws established that soldiers who left service because of injury would receive a pension, the amount of which depended on the nature and length of their service, the nature of their wounds, and the degree of their infirmity. Laws were revised several times, most notably in 1803. Earlier decrees had assimilated the loss of the use of a limb and other debilitating injuries to amputation; Napoleonic law emphasized the unambiguous loss of a limb over other injuries and compensated soldiers accordingly.[76]

Pension law served as compensation for injury and military service—not as a guideline for what was necessary for starting a new household. Wounds proved soldiers' devotion to the state. But prospective husbands could not be so wounded that they would require hospitalization, be likely to die in the near future, or be completely dependent on the state. Nor were the seriously injured likely to be interested in marital arrangements. As Natalie Petiteau has observed, veterans whose wounds were still oozing were often more focused on recovering their health than on planning their weddings.[77]

As we have seen, Napoleonic arrangements, like Old Regime royal philanthropy, favored men who could clearly provide for their families. The 1802 decree thus required that a potential groom had "a profession (*métier*) that assures his existence." Subsequent decrees also imagined new households that would enrich France's population without draining state coffers. The problem was precisely that many veterans could not exercise a métier that assured their existence—and as in the case of Gaillard's rival, their very inability to return to their professions proved the seriousness of their sacrifice. It is

74. AN F / 1 / c / III Gironde 7, *L'Indicateur: Journal du département de la Gironde*, no. 2433, 10 juin 1811.

75. AN F / 9 / 54 Bis, dossier Ardennes. See also Woloch, *The French Veteran*, 250.

76. Bertaud, *Quand les enfants parlaient de gloire*, 143; Woloch, *The French Veteran*, 100–108.

77. Petiteau, *Lendemains d'empire*, 191.

hard to know how many lacked a viable profession, in part because records emphasized men's military qualifications rather than their civilian occupations. There are indications that many did not have regular employment. For example, in the municipality of Nontron, in the Dordogne, almost all of the sixteen men chosen in 1810 lived on their pensions; only a few had a recorded profession, like shoemaker, baker, or farmer.[78] The question was whether a man's pension, along with his wife's labor, sufficed to provide for a family—and whether men who lacked pensions were still eligible for state recognition.

The 1810 decree honored retired soldiers, but "retired" was an ambiguous term that referred both generally to war veterans and specifically to those who received a pension. There were an increasing number of veterans, known as *réformés*, who were honorably discharged but who did not merit a pension. In some areas, officials chose réformés because they believed it was more equitable to support veterans otherwise uncompensated for their services; in other cases, réformés were excluded.[79]

Such debates reflected not only different understandings of the law and ideas of equity, but also different ideas of masculinity: how much did a husband need to be able to provide for his family? How could that ability be proven? Was marriage primarily a reward for past service or suffering—or was it a future obligation to act as a productive head of a household? There was a related question: were disfigured men actually attractive, even if they had been courageous or might be economically stable? Given that local authorities were compelled to report on the success of their celebrations to central administrations, they could not easily describe revulsion toward the injured. But there are hints that women did not flock to wounded men. For example, the subprefect of the department of Allier noted on May 5, 1810, that "The city of Montluçon has chosen a soldier who wants to marry but the girls he likes don't want him because of his infirmities."[80] In that case, the honored veteran, a baker, finally found a bride on his third marriage proposal.[81] The archives are silent on the cases of men who did not succeed in finding partners.

WHEN LOVE AND GRATITUDE COLLIDE

As we have seen, theatrical works celebrating peace treaties in 1797 and again in 1801 alluded to injury, but usually portrayed men who were not seriously incapacitated. By the Napoleonic Empire, popular theater increasingly depicted injuries themselves as a way of winning affection; men were attractive not in spite of their wounds, but because of them. In one typical

78. Becquert, "Les 'mariages de l'empereur.'"
79. Woloch, *The French Veteran*; see also AN F / 9 / 54 Bis.
80. AN F / 9 / 54 Bis, dossier Allier.
81. Janin, *Histoire de Montluçon*, 246.

1805 play, a woman welcomes her injured lover and proclaims that "Far from damaging him in my eyes / This wound is dear to me. . . . / More than one before me has thought / That it's a sure-fire means of charming. / It takes a wounded lover / To wound one's heart."[82]

If playwrights depicted war-related injuries as attractive to women, they also presented marriage as both a compensation and a duty for wounded men. In 1810, the Bordelais Joseph Ernest depicted a would-be bride musing on her duties to her fiancé: "you have told me to love him, to console him, to make him forget by my care, this wound that stopped him in the middle of his success. He can no longer be a soldier. But he must be a husband, and it is me you have charged with his happiness."[83]

Such attentions could appear as a sacrifice on the part of a woman, an unselfish decision to put the well-being of her husband and country above personal happiness. Here it is useful to look comparatively, especially at a 1915 British proposal for a "League for the Marrying of Wounded Heroes."[84] The Swedish feminist Ellen Key called attention to the initiative, noting that it appealed "to woman's self-sacrifice and patriotism to make the lives of these men bearable and to propagate children who will inherit their fathers' qualities of heroism."[85] Key saw such arrangements as dangerous. Others were more enthusiastic; one historian writing about Napoleonic state-sponsored marriages in 1914 even suggested that they might serve as inspirations for his contemporaries.[86] Napoleonic writers themselves, however, seldom acknowledged the possibility that caring for wounded men could entail hardship for their wives, even if taking on that hardship could itself be seen as patriotic. At least in the official view, public marriages rewarded virtuous women—even while charging them with the happiness of their husbands—rather than asking such women to sacrifice themselves.

A few Napoleonic works did, however, acknowledge tensions between gratitude and love, and between a woman's desire to help a wounded man and the dictates of her heart. One of the most interesting is Jean-Baptiste Dubois's *Rose Laurels or the Village Tribute*, first performed on June 10, 1810. The play features Coup de Feu (Gunshot), an orphan and veteran with a wooden leg, chosen as the beneficiary of the state-sponsored dowry. He wants to marry Edmonde, the daughter of a gardener. Edmonde, however, loves Edouard, a young man who has been raised by her father's patron. Edouard fears that his

82. Bié, *L'épousera-t-il?*, 4. Similarly, a character in an 1806 play observes of the hero-soldier that "this wound, of which he is proud, only makes him more attractive in the eyes of his lover, and will earn him a double victory." Seville, *Le dernier bulletin ou la paix*, 13.

83. Ernest, *Une fête de village*, in AN F / 1 / c / III Gironde 7.

84. The rector of St. Stephen's, Bristol, placed an advertisement in the *London Times*. See *The Independent*, December 27, 1915, 506.

85. Key, *War, Peace, and the Future*, 171.

86. Vovard, "Les rosières de l'empereur."

sweetheart will yield to the soldier's entreaties, and that "touched by Coup de Feu's infirmity, all the village will be concerned with his fate and applaud his choice."[87] Edmonde is indeed moved by the veteran's situation, telling him, "when you talked to me of your misfortunes, when you told me you were an orphan, when you asked for support that your wound made necessary, I was touched, and this emotion dispelled the majority of my sorrows."[88]

But despite her sympathy for Coup de Feu, Edmonde remains loyal to her Edouard. The former soldier eventually cedes to his rival, acknowledging that the couple is in love. Coup de Feu even gives the couple his dowry, on the condition that Edouard use the money to honor the emperor. They consider dressing villagers in the costumes of the national guard, and arranging them around the busts of Napoleon and Marie-Louise and a lavish display of roses. Unfortunately, the imperial couple does not end up visiting their hamlet to witness this display.

Charles-Augustin Sewrin's 1811 *The New Celebrations or the Impromptu of Nanterre* played on a similar theme. It features a rich colonel who wants to celebrate the baptism of Napoleon's son by offering a dowry to the orphaned Rose. He has only one condition: she must marry a soldier from the area. There are only two veterans to be found, both wounded. Rose's heart lies with neither, but rather with the gardener Bruno. One of the soldiers, Labrèche (the Breach) insists on the rights conferred by his wooden leg. Bruno, desperate, laments, "if I had known that to marry Rose / it was necessary to be part of the military / I would long ago, as a soldier / have left for the war." He announces his intention to be killed in order to be worthy of marrying his love. The wounded veteran "as generous as brave" eventually cedes his rights to Rose as well as to the dowry, on the condition that Rose and Bruno have a dozen beautiful children.[89]

In some ways, such plays were typical of works celebrating Napoleon's wedding, which featured contests to produce poetry, music, or art to herald the imperial couple. Censors saw *Rose Laurels* as an unremarkable if admirable tribute to the emperor.[90] They also responded enthusiastically to *The New Celebrations,* describing its praise for Napoleon and Marie-Louise as "fulfilling well its goal" of celebrating the imperial birth. There was also a literary tradition of elderly suitors displaced by virile youth, which the play echoed in its depiction of the old veteran LaBrèche, to the amusement of the censors.[91]

But in other ways, these works were unusual. When revolutionary plays featured women who rejected injured military suitors, characters regretted their choices. For example, in the 1799 play *Marcel or the Young French Man,*

87. Dubois, *Les lauriers rose,* 12.

88. Dubois, *Les lauriers rose,* 22.

89. Sewrin, *Les nouvelles réjouissances ou l'impromptu de Nanterre.*

90. AN F / 21 / 976, Le Laurier Rose ou le tribut de village.

91. AN F / 21 / 987, Nouvelles réjouissances ou l'impromptu de Nanterre.

Suzette is repulsed by the soldier Marcel's loss of a hand and rejects him, only to learn that he is extremely rich.[92] In *The Rose Laurels*, Edmonde is not repulsed by Coup de Feu; she clearly admires him. But her heart lies elsewhere. In *The New Celebrations*, Rose chooses a gardener over a hero, even while hoping for a dowry the colonel had promised if she wed a veteran. Such works suggested that the calculation of whether to accept an officially sponsored marriage could be far more complicated than authorities acknowledged.

Both Dubois and Sewrin were popular playwrights; it is doubtful that they intended to subvert the idea of love and marriage as a prize for valorous soldiers. While challenging the idea that women should wed combatants, they also portrayed returned warriors as inherently generous, as well as loyal to Napoleon. In both plays, the soldiers magnanimously redirect attention away from their own love interests toward the community. In neither case does the soldier ask for another bride; instead, they seek to celebrate the emperor, and in Breach's case, to convey his potency—twelve children!—to the able-bodied nonsoldier.

REWARDING FEMININE COURAGE AND DOMESTICATING WOMEN WARRIORS?

While Napoleonic weddings honored men's military service and women's domestic dedication, contemporaries occasionally considered using state-sponsored marriages to reward for women's military valor. An anonymous 1805 novel, *Our Misfortunes Are Over, or Two Lovers Married during the Coronation Festivals*, provides a striking example. Its heroine, Augustine, accompanies her lover to war disguised as his younger brother. After a series of misadventures, the couple weds during the celebrations for Napoleon's coronation. The mayor of their new hometown presents them with a state-sponsored dowry and gifts of his own.[93]

In many ways, the novel was a riff on a common theme, in which a woman follows a man—usually a lover, husband, or brother—into battle. As we have seen in chapter 2, an April 1793 law banned women from the troops, apart from a few laundresses and vivandières who provided basic foodstuffs. The law appeared to end the activities of women warriors, even as the government continued to honor exceptional figures whose heroic deeds were safely over. Yet a few women still took up arms into the Napoleonic era, often in disguise.

92. Pierre Blanchard, *Marcel ou le jeune français*. The script was not printed, but the play was performed at the Théâtre des Jeunes Artistes in March 1799. See AN F / 7 / 3491 and the *Courrier des spectacles*, 1 Germinal Year VII (March 21, 1799), 3.

93. *Nos malheurs sont finis ou histoire de deux amants mariés pendant les fêtes du couronnement.*

Popular literature also returned repeatedly to the spectacle of women warriors, whether as titillating transgression, heroic inspiration, or comic relief.

Descriptions of Augustine resonated with other portrayals of female warriors: she is a lioness who inspires her fellow soldiers with her courage, a tender nurse as well as a brave fighter. The conclusion of the novel with the couple's nuptials echoed some earlier works of fiction, such as the 1794 play *Festival of the Supreme Being*, which portrayed a man and woman jointly released from service on the condition that they marry and have a son every year.[94] The novel also echoed contemporary flattery for Napoleon. The mayor tells them it is in the emperor's name "and under his orders that I marry you, and it is to him you owe the end of your misfortune."[95] But other parts of the novel were far removed with the realities of state-sponsored weddings. Most notably, Augustine has a child out of wedlock. She is concerned with disguising the pregnancy from fellow soldiers and her experience of motherhood ends in tragedy when disease takes the child. Illegitimacy as such, however, seems irrelevant to the ultimate happy conclusion of the novel.

A few actual women warriors sought state-sponsored dowries as a reward for their military service. In 1810, the *Mercure de France* presented a letter from a petitioner who claimed to be young, but to have participated in six campaigns, and received five wounds. The writer had not decided on a spouse and asked the appropriate authorities to choose one.[96] After the petition was received favorably, it was revealed that the writer was a woman. The press claimed that this was a true story; it is difficult to verify, in part because the paper announced that it was using a pseudonym.

It is definite that Jeanne Jacqueline Saeger (or Saegher) received a dowry in 1812. She was the daughter of Marie-Jeanne Schellinck, who had fought as a sublieutenant during the Revolution. In one popular account, Napoleon Bonaparte lauded her in 1808, saying: "Madam, I give you 700 francs as a pension and make you a chevalier of the Legion of Honor. Accept from my hand the star of the braves which you have so nobly won." Then, addressing his officers, he continued: "Gentlemen, salute with respect this courageous woman. She is one of the glories of the Empire."[97] The story appears apocryphal, if widespread. It is unclear if she received a cross; if so, it was a symbolic honor, later conflated with the Legion of Honor.[98]

Schellinck had, however, asked for a pension in 1802; her letter noted that she was illiterate, so it is unclear what arguments were hers, rather than

94. Cuvelier de Trie, *Fête de l'Être Suprême*.

95. *Nos malheurs sont finis*, 152.

96. *Mercure de France*, vol. 41, April 1810, 563.

97. Alès, *Les femmes décorées*.

98. SHD 1 Yi 24 contains early twentieth-century correspondence disputing this story. See also Grabilier, "Jeanne Schellinck"; and Déon-Bessière, *Les femmes et la légion d'honneur*, 21.

those of an intermediary, but they echoed those of many veterans. Her request emphasized her poverty and the suffering her wounds caused; she also complained about administrative challenges. She wrote to Bonaparte, then consul for life, to obtain a pension in 1803, and was granted a pension of 607 francs in 1807. It is possible that her requests drew the emperor's direct attention.[99]

When her daughter was awarded a state-sponsored dowry in 1812, newspapers dutifully noted that the rosière embodied virtue, and the husband she had chosen was a brave warrior, "covered with honorable scars." Saeger seems to have been a thirty-year-old lacemaker at the time of her marriage, and had likely lived with relatives in the town as a child while her parents fought. Her groom was a twenty-five-year-old weaver who had been discharged because of his wounds.[100] Saeger was unusually old for a rosière; the choice to honor her reflected her mother's status more than her own. Indeed, newspapers said little about her, focusing instead on Schellinck. They claimed the former warrior was "no less estimable in her private life by her conduct than she was in the camps by her bravery and good behavior," and rehashed versions of her story. They reported that she had entered service in 1792 with her husband; after receiving thirteen wounds at Jemappes, she was promoted to lieutenant on the field of battle—appropriately enough, by a general named Rosières. Seemingly unaffected by the ban on women in the troops in 1793, she continued to fight six campaigns in Italy and was made a prisoner of war in Rome. She then returned to the troops after two months, and fought several more campaigns in Dalmatia.[101] Honoring Jeanne Jacqueline Saeger was clearly honoring Schellinck's own service.

At the same time, awarding a dowry to Schellinck's daughter reveals a mixture of respect for her military prowess and a desire to domesticate her. While Bonaparte praised her courage, he and his government sought to transform her into an unthreatening feminine figure. When the empress Marie-Louise visited Gand in 1811, she allegedly gave Schellinck a silk dress, a brooch, and a pair of earrings—honoring her status while giving her traditional feminine adornments, indirectly echoing the aid that the Revolutionary National Convention had provided women veterans to resume female garb.[102] Providing a dowry for Schellinck's daughter appears to be in the same vein: recognition of courage but also of domestication.

More generally, state-sponsored marriages promoted a view of women as industrious and dedicated to their families. This made it likely that they would

99. SHD 1 Yi 24.

100. "Marie Jeanne Shellynck," in *Biographie nationale*, ed. H. Thiry-Van Buggenhoudt (Académie royale des sciences, des lettres, et des beaux-arts de la Belgique, 1906), 21:667–72.

101. *Journal du département de L'Escault*, no. 101, November 27, 1812. See also *Journal de l'empire*, December 1, 1812, 2; and *Allgemeine Zeitung*, no. 344, December 9, 1812, 1374.

102. Claeys, "Dotations et mariages de rosières," 3:107.

be part of an economically viable household even if a veteran husband was impaired, and promised that a couple would not strain government coffers after an initial display of state generosity. This insistence on women's work corresponded to the long history of requiring that combatants' relatives support themselves whenever possible, but it also contrasts with claims made by men seeking discharge earlier in the Revolution about the distinctive connections between masculinity, citizenship, and work.

Conclusion: The Limits of Marriage as Military Propaganda

Official speeches portrayed Napoleon as a wise father and recipients of his munificence as grateful children. Reality was often otherwise. The dowry should have been attractive; 600 francs was a substantial sum of money when the average annual pension of a private was between 150 and 178 francs. Yet between 15 and 20 percent of marriages authorized in 1810 did not take place.[103]

There were many reasons why marriages did not happen, including the limited time for arranging weddings, the inability or unwillingness of a commune to provide funding, questions about the eligibility of candidates, and couples' own hesitations or preference for alternate partners. Sometimes there was simply general suspicion. The prefect of the Corrèze, for example, reported in 1809 that "at Tulle, there is a prejudice against such dowries; the municipal council allotted 600 francs for a marriage, but despite the mayor's efforts to publicize such munificence, no one presented themselves to profit it from it."[104] In some cases there were no eligible single veterans—or the few who fit the criteria were not interested in marriage. This was especially the case in central and southern France, where resistance to conscription was strong and enthusiasm for Napoleon weak. For example, the sous-prefect of Limoux noted in 1811 that "men who have gone to war are rare here in the canton; there are at most two or three in the city. Although the mayor and the curé identified two deserving orphan girls and several more were presented to them, no marriage took place."[105] It was more unusual for there to be a shortage of interested women, but it could happen.[106]

103. Woloch, *The French Veteran*, 248. Woloch bases his estimates on records in AN F / 9 / 54 Bis, which contains reports from across France. His numbers confirm my impressions, but it is difficult to compile definitive statistics.

104. AN F / 1 / c / III Corrèze 1, Lettre du préfet du Corrèze au Ministre de l'Intérieur, 18 décembre 1809.

105. AN F / 1 / c / III Aude 7, Sous-préfet de Limoux, 20 juin 1811.

106. The mayor of Le Havre, for example, claimed that it was only in the countryside where one could find young women who wanted to be chosen, and merited being so. Borély, *Histoire de la ville du Havre*, 2:493.

Authorities not infrequently congratulated themselves on the wisdom of their choices. The mayor of Lorgues, in the Var, told the Municipal Council that "the same qualities that determined your choice in favor of these couples are precisely those that determine the happiness of conjugal society."[107] Yet official assurances contain hints of unease, as when the mayor in the Aveyron tried to dismiss the possibility that husbands, especially returned warriors, would be brutal toward their wives.[108] Similarly the mayor of Auxonne exhorted a new couple in 1809, "take care that you do not become an ordinary, vulgar couple. Do not disappoint the hopes of those who have undertaken to prepare your happiness. . . . But no, let us chase away such an idea; it would darken the beautiful day for you."[109] Many did in fact become ordinary couples. Looking at veterans in the department of the Vaucluse, Natalie Petiteau has argued their marriages rarely led to dramatic social advancement.[110]

Perhaps even more importantly, the government's promise of a dowry often proved to be as illusory as the theatrical fantasy of a peacetime benefactor had been. The archives are full of increasingly desperate petitions across France from couples who had counted on promised dowries in 1810 to set up their households and had not received them.[111] Not surprisingly, when officials tried to perform new public marriages in 1811, they were undercut by earlier failures to deliver on their promises. Yet the limits of such marriages should not blind us to the fact that many couples found it worth the gamble to rush to the altar when offered public recognition and a dowry. The state also found the practice of state-sponsored marriages sufficiently useful to promote it repeatedly.

Both the uses and limits of these weddings reveal that the Napoleonic era was neither a simple continuation of revolutionary practices nor a straightforward return to the Old Regime. While officials drew on older examples, they created a distinctive amalgam, and transformed a practice associated with celebrating peace into a tool for promoting war. State-sponsored marriages prioritized national interests, even as they rewarded individuals for their service and virtue. At the same time, marriages show authorities' unease with overriding individual or familial preferences by seeming to dictate marriage partners.

Public weddings fundamentally celebrated martial masculinity. They heralded veterans as heroes whose service and injuries not only merited public recognition, but also made them desirable marital partners—and who indeed

107. AN F / 1 / c / III Var 10, Discours prononcé par M. Allaman, Maire de la ville de Lorgues, dans le conseil municipal, à l'occasion de la fête du 22 avril 1810.

108. AN F / 1 / c / III Aveyron 9, Extrait des registres des procès-verbaux de la mairie de Villefrance, dept. de l'Aveiron.

109. AN F / 1 / c / III Côte d'Or, Claude-Nicolas Amaton, Discours prononcé par le maire d'Auxonne, le 3 décembre 1809.

110. Petiteau, *Lendemains d'empire*.

111. For complaints about nonpayment, see especially AN F / 9 / 54 Bis.

could, and should, be turned into civilian grooms; as the fictional Bordelais woman said of her veteran partner, "he must be a husband." The process of selecting and honoring couples shows the limits of this strategy. It called attention to the questionable attractiveness of physically impaired or disfigured men. It also revealed the challenges of balancing reward for veterans' past service with the need for future productivity. Weddings simultaneously validated and undermined the idea that the reward for fighting for the nation as a whole should be the chance for men to provide for their own families. They juxtaposed the relative virtues of domestic virtue and military valor, even as veterans were exhorted to produce sons who would fight after them.

Festivals also reinforced a vision of women as dutiful daughters, wives, and mothers. Yet arranging weddings challenged any notion of women passively accepting partners. Such public ceremonies also raised the question of whether or when women might reject soldier-heroes, whether love could outweigh gratitude for military service, and whether women as well as men could be honored for military courage and service with state-sponsored marriages.

Finally, festivals and public weddings suggest that the promise of marriage and money could help legitimate the militarization of society, at least in the very particular world of the Napoleonic era. But looking closely reveals the anxieties that surrounded such liaisons, and the ultimate limits of trying to link military propaganda to marriage.

CHAPTER SEVEN

Conscription, Demobilization, and Family

AS LOUIS XVIII AND HIS supporters waited to return to power in France in April 1814, they bewailed the horrors of war and the emperor responsible for them.[1] The Provisional Government proclaimed that "every year, [Napoleon] decimated your families through conscription. Who has not lost a son, a brother, relatives, friends? For whom are all these brave men dead? For him alone and not for our country . . . for the most appalling oppressor who ever afflicted the human race." It lamented not only the deaths of brave men, but also the effects of war on French households. The Corsican was responsible for "the tears of our families, the forced celibacy of our daughters, the ruins of all fortunes, the premature widowhood of our women, and the despair of fathers and mothers, who, despite creating large families, often have not a single child left."[2] On April 4, 1814, three days after this proclamation, the Provisional Government ended conscription. Article 12 of the Charter, the founding document of the Restoration, definitively outlawed it on June 4, 1814.

Peace in 1814 was fundamentally different from previous attempts to end hostilities. It was defined by defeat and a dramatic change of government, rather than by victory. Although the Hundred Days of Napoleon's return (from March to July 1815) would bring renewed violence and uncertainty, peace would ultimately prove lasting, unlike earlier treaties. It also entailed the end of conscription and led to unprecedented mass demobilization. Calculations vary, but well over 200,000 men left service in 1814 and 1815; and up to a million French soldiers may have ultimately returned to civilian life.[3] Their

1. Material related to this chapter was first published as Heuer, "Soldiers as Victims or Villains?"

2. *Proclamation du Conseil général du département de la Seine.*

3. Jérôme Louis has calculated that more that 118,000 men were officially liberated from service, and another 100,000 came back as deserters, while Isser Woloch estimates

FIGURE 7.1. *Yesterday, March 31, War Tore Young Peasants from the Land*, 1814. Bibliothèque Nationale de France.

return was accompanied by redrawing the map of Europe. A second peace treaty in 1815 after Napoleon's definitive defeat returned France to the boundaries of 1789, imposed a heavy indemnity, and led to the occupation of parts of the country until 1818, with over a million foreign soldiers in France by September 1815.[4]

We begin this chapter by exploring why the Bourbon government of the Restoration heralded peace by denouncing the familial costs of conscription, and why royalists continued to do so even as they downplayed other aspects of the Napoleonic wars. While military historians have analyzed conscription in the late Napoleonic Empire and subsequent demobilization, they have usually focused on state power, gauging how effectively the state instituted conscription in different parts of the Empire, tracking growing resistance to forced enlistment, and calculating the human costs of seemingly endless drafts, especially in

that about 300,000 of 500,000 demobilized men or deserters returned home. Louis, "La dissolution de l'armée impériale," 30; Woloch, *The French Veteran*, 295. For the figure of a million returnees, see Petiteau, *Lendemains d'empire*, 88.

4. Haynes, "Making Peace" and *Our Friends, the Enemies*.

FIGURE 7.2. *Today, April 1, Peace Brings Them Back to Their Old Fathers*, 1814. Bibliothèque Nationale de France.

1813–14.[5] But declaring the end of conscription served goals that have received less attention. It associated Napoleon's regime with tyranny and destruction and the Bourbon government with peace and liberation. It turned attention from ongoing problems to royalist accomplishments in preserving families. It also turned attention from the agency of men in fighting for the Revolution and Napoleon to the collective victimhood of the French people.

The bulk of this chapter focuses on depictions of conscription and demobilization in a particular kind of source: the explosion of pamphlets in 1814 and 1815. Most were written by supporters of the returned Bourbon government. They discussed myriad issues, from freedom of the press to a new constitution, as well as general legacies of the Revolution. The few historians to have analyzed these texts have focused on what they reveal about political ideologies and contemporary power struggles. But pamphlets also provide an exceptional lens onto tensions within the fabric of the royalist order, and changing ideas of gender, family, war, and citizenship. They addressed both conscription

5. Among other works, see Daly, "Conscription and Corruption"; Stoker, ed., *Conscription in Napoleonic Europe;* and Mikaberidze, *The Napoleonic Wars: A Global History.*

and demobilization repeatedly. Writers tried to persuade French soldiers to return to civilian life, and to convince both combatants and civilians to support an uneasy peace. They dwelled on the domestic costs of war and on relationships between veterans and civilians—especially their families.

After briefly assessing the authors and audiences of these works, we concentrate on the arguments embedded in them. After two decades of war, men and women did not trust the return of peace. Royalists blamed military men for supporting the deposed emperor and perpetuating war; their suspicion became more intense after Napoleon's return. They also viewed the former emperor as a heartless "foreigner" who imposed the draft on a subjected population, where young men were torn from the arms of their families and sent to die on distant battlefields. They struggled with reconciling competing visions of soldiers as both the agents and the victims par excellence of Napoleonic rule.

In depicting soldiers' demobilization, pamphleteers also reversed earlier views of relationships between civilians and combatants. They portrayed soldiers, rather than families, as ignorant about the fate of their loved ones, and suggested that war could be harder on those at home than those on the battlefields. Pamphlet writers particularly called attention to women's sacrifices, not as proof of feminine citizenship, but as evidence of the disorder caused by constant war.

Such disorder risked permanent consequences. Contemporaries were generally torn between dwelling on the lasting destruction of war—seen as both perverting men and ruining their families—and heralding a return to prosperity under a peace-loving monarchy. How they saw soldiers' homecomings and the possibility of rebuilding the nation depended in part on how they viewed both martial masculinity and the recent past. Restoration authorities were generally divided between seeking vengeance for the "crimes" of the Revolution and promoting "union and forgetting."[6] Coming to terms with the legacies of war as well as of the Revolution was especially challenging, given how fresh memories of war were in 1814 and 1815, and how much men and women were still living with its consequences.

Restoration writers also linked their views of soldiers and their return to competing representations of Napoleon and Louis XVIII as fathers. Royalists inverted Napoleonic claims to be a good father, depicting him instead as a tyrannical foreigner, a coward who deserted his troops, and a hypocrite who butchered his children. They sought to depict Louis XVIII instead as a true father—although what fatherhood now meant for a peacetime king was far from clear.

Finally, looking at these pamphlets and associated materials helps us understand the stakes of citizenship after war ended. Because political rights

6. Kroen, *Politics and Theater*; Frederking, "'Il ne faut pas être le roi de deux peoples'"; Scholz, "Past and Pathos"; Petiteau, "La mémoire royaliste de 1814–1815"; Lok, "La culture du silence" and "Un oubli total du passé?"

were deeply restricted under the Bourbon Restoration—limited to a small number of rich property owners—historians have tended to overlook other aspects of citizenship in the period, except inasmuch as underground radical ideas contributed to later revolutionary uprisings. Veterans were rarely able to exercise political rights, and indeed, were forbidden from forming political associations of former combatants. But these debates suggest the continuing importance of civic usefulness and social generosity to ideas of citizenship even for those excluded from the formal exercise of civic rights.

Denouncing Conscription and Demobilizing Men

The human costs of war soared in the last years of the Empire. Napoleon's government instituted a series of extraordinary drafts in quick succession. Between January and June 1813, Napoleon took 960,000 men—more than half of the men from all the drafts from 1800 to 1813. Some were called up four times in a row; even if they escaped one draft, they could easily fall victim to the next. The class of 1815 was called up a year in advance.[7]

Parts of the country had responded very differently to conscription law. Some regions, like the Northeast and the Ile-de-France, were relatively compliant; in others, notably the Massif Central, the Aquitaine Basin, northern France, and to a lesser extent, the West, young men often deserted or avoided the draft.[8] But by 1813, resistance to conscription became widespread across France. Men refused to leave or even to show up at the mayor's office or the recruitment office to draw lots to determine if they would be required to serve. The draft of November 12, 1813, sought to mobilize 300,000 men across France; only 63,000 had enrolled by January 1814. In some departments, like Loire, Loiret, and L'Indre-et-Loire, only a quarter of men subject to the conscription lottery presented themselves.[9] Many men tried to buy replacements to fight in their stead, though the cost of substitutes soared in 1813.[10] Others sought to secure exemptions—including through self-mutilation or hurried marriages—that might keep them safe.

Some actively revolted. As Annie Crépin has pointed out, they did not necessarily do so for political reasons. But if they joined bands protesting the law, their actions quickly acquired a political edge. By the late fall 1813, a growing number of organized protests took place across France, often with royalist

7. Waresquiel and Yvert, *Histoire de la restauration*, 17.

8. Crépin, *Histoire de la conscription*, 150–56.

9. Fahmy, *La France en 1814*, 8. In February 1814, there were 1,028 draft dodgers and deserters among 1,060 men called up in the Tarn. Of 1,800,000 national guards called up across France in January and April 1813, only 20,000 responded. Waresquiel and Yvert, *Histoire de la restauration*, 17.

10. Heuer, "Neither Cowardly nor Greedy?"

sympathies.[11] Desire for peace could outweigh hopes for victory; the police reported in Nantes in September 1813 that "the armies' retreat has even caused satisfaction, as people believe it will be followed by peace. They could care less whether such peace will be glorious."[12]

In seeking to gain power, Louis XVIII and his supporters repeatedly condemned conscription. In a February 1813 speech that would become known as the Declaration of Hartwell, Louis XVIII reasserted the principle of royal sovereignty. He promised that those who had served the Republic or Napoleon would not face repercussions for their acts. He also promised to bring peace and end mandatory military service: "The King renews his commitment to end this disastrous conscription that destroys the happiness of families and the hope of the patrie."[13] Royalists made similar promises a year later. When the emperor abdicated in April 1814, the comte d'Artois (Louis XVIII's brother and the future king Charles X) swore to end both conscription and the indirect taxes that had helped fund war. Two months later, the Charter ended conscription definitively.

Royalists also decried conscription in other media, including sermons, artwork, music, popular theater, and songs. Denouncing conscription was almost always accompanied by praise for Louis XVIII, who had saved families by stopping it. A cleric in Marseille, for example, proclaimed in July 1814, "Desperate mothers, tender fathers, crying wives, console yourselves! Stop your tears. Conscription, this hungry monster, this monster thirsty for blood, this monster with a hundred sharp swords, conscription no longer exists, our good king has forbidden it forever."[14] The anonymous author of *The Truth Is Always the Truth* echoed such sentiments, rejoicing, "By conscription, Napoleon took from families their support and their hope for their old age. Louis XVIII abolished conscription, released the conscripts of year 1815, and brought children back to their fathers."[15]

Royalist denunciations of conscription corresponded to the intense burdens of war and to real resistance to service. They also strategically associated Napoleon's regime with tyranny and the wanton destruction of men and their families, and the Bourbon government with the pleasures of peace. Such rhetoric was a response to the very real ravages of war, especially the horrific years of 1813–14. It was also a particular form of appeal, linking political, military, and domestic realms. If Napoleon had destroyed families, Louis XVIII would restore them. As an orator at one festival celebrating monarchy proclaimed, "Fortunate parents . . . your hearts bled; nature wrenched tears from you at the

11. Crépin, *Histoire de la conscription*, 153. In November 1813, Louis Fruchart led a peasants' war against conscription near Lille, with the slogan "Je combats pour Louis XVII." Mansel, *Louis XVIII*, 160. For further examples, see AN F / 7 / 3732.

12. AN F / 7 / 3781, Bulletin de police, 23 nov. 1813.

13. Reprinted in Norvins, *Portefeuille de mil huit cent treize*, 1:360–62.

14. *Discours prononcé dans la Chapelle du Lazaert*, 9.

15. *La vérité est toujours vérité*, 62–63.

departure of your sons; console yourselves; the thunder of war is extinguished, your beloved children will be returned to you like a new gift from heaven."[16]

Accounts of the horrors of conscription portrayed soldiers as young men—"beloved children"—torn from their homes, rather than as adult citizens invested in fighting. They left aside specifics of battles and the nature of warfare. They also left aside the Bourbons' reliance on the Allies, foreign powers that had until recently been France's enemies. Instead, they appealed to French women and civilian men who had experienced war largely through the departure and absence of young men.

Lamenting the evils of conscription also distracted from the challenges of demobilization. The return of former combatants was a logistical nightmare. The decree of April 4, 1814, stopped conscription, meaning that those who faced the draft but had not left home were free.[17] It did not release those on active duty. Many soldiers and their families understood it to do so, blurring the lines between demobilization and desertion. On April 23, the government declared an amnesty for those accused of crimes related to conscription. Yet while the amnesty was straightforward in theory, deciding the parameters of excusable crimes would prove complicated in practice.[18] On May 12, the government reorganized the troops. It suppressed almost a hundred infantry and thirty cavalry regiments and ordered similar levels of reductions throughout the armed services.[19] This released both men who wanted to come home and those who might have preferred to remain in the troops; the oldest and most disabled were asked to take compulsory retirement.

After Napoleon's hasty reconstitution of the army during the Hundred Days, a royal edict from March 13, 1815, retroactively dismissed all officers and soldiers loyal to Napoleon. The decree was republished in the official *Moniteur* newspaper on August 9, 1815, shortly after the Second Restoration; it required that men return home immediately. An edict from August 1 dictated the retirement of junior officers who had served for twenty-five years, were over fifty, or whose physical state precluded further service; on August 3, the government laid out terms of the release of men serving in the artillery. While military authorities applied the measure broadly to allow impatient men to return home, some remained under arms.[20]

16. AN F / 1c / III Jura 10, *Procès-verbal de la fête célébrée à Lons-le-Saunier, chef-lieu du département de Jura pour l'inauguration du Drapeau-blanc, à l'occasion des événemens arrivés à Paris à la fin de mars et dans les premiers jours d'avril 1814*.

17. Desenne, *Code général français*, 17:310.

18. For the decree, see *Journal militaire contenant tout ce qui est relative à la composition et à l'administration de tout ce qui concerne la guerre et la marine* (Paris: Gratiot, 1814), 2:16. For a sense of the challenges in applying it, see AN BB / 18 / 32, Hérault.

19. Forrest, *The Legacy of the French Revolutionary Wars*, 65.

20. Forrest, *The Legacy of the French Revolutionary Wars*, 66; Petiteau, *Lendemains d'empire*, 85–86.

Many of those discharged were young. Over 71 percent of privates were under twenty-six, and most had served for fewer than twenty-eight months. Older men had been incorporated into the ranks with the retroactive calls to arms between September 1813 and January 1814, but soldiers with over six years of experience were in the minority. Fewer than 3 percent had been involved in fighting since the Revolution.[21] The relative youth of surviving conscripts may have made it easier for some to return to civilian life. But it meant that most soldiers still alive in 1814–15 had been drafted after 1810 and had not served long enough to qualify for pensions. Even for those entitled to government support, pensions were supposed to be extra revenue, not sufficient income to allow a soldier to live decently.[22] Many veterans not only lacked the opportunities for advancement they had experienced in the military but were unable to support themselves and their families. While officers were older than enlisted men, on average thirty-five, many were *demi-soldes*, on half pay, ostensibly awaiting a call to return to active duty. They were obliged to reside in their department of origin and legally prevented from taking other jobs, despite their reduced pay.[23]

Other factors complicated demobilization further. Soldiers in distant parts of the Empire only slowly made their way home. The government officially repatriated about 300,000 prisoners of war on May 25, 1814.[24] Jacques-Oliver Boudon argues that 110,000 to 120,000 foreign prisoners of war left France, while about 150,000 prisoners returned.[25] Social conflicts erupted repeatedly as soldiers, veterans, deserters, and prisoners moved through a country in disarray.[26] In the wake of the Hundred Days, violence broke out between soldiers and civilians, particularly in southern France, while military revolts were common. Veterans were also often victims of the White Terror in late 1815.[27]

Men and women thus negotiated both the dramatic political upheavals of the time and the practical and ideological challenges of ending war and dealing with its aftermath. While those trumpeting the end of conscription presented peace as a universal and immediate good, contemporaries had to confront the continued presence of the military, the difficulties of reincorporating demobilized men into civilian society, and the lingering effects of militarized culture.

21. Calvet, *Les officiers charentais* and "The Painful Demobilization." Chief officers and generals were usually over forty-five; lieutenants, thirty-two.

22. Captains were left with 73 francs a month, sublieutenants 41, privates far less.

23. Woloch, *The French Veteran*, 297; Vidalenc, *Les demi-soldes*.

24. Petiteau, *Lendemains d'empire*, 85; Houdecek, "Le gouvernement de Louis XVIII et le retour des prisonniers de guerre français."

25. Boudon, "Le retour des prisonniers de guerre."

26. For police reports, see AN F / 7 / 3733.

27. Notably, a military revolt in Strasbourg in September 1815. On the White Terror, see Louis, "La dissolution de l'armée impériale"; Petiteau, "Survivors of War," 50; Forrest, *The Legacy of the French Revolutionary Wars*, 65–67; and Triomphe, *1815, la Terreur blanche*.

They addressed these challenges both directly and obliquely, in forums ranging from private letters to partisan songs, and from courtroom proceedings to banners dramatically hoisted or removed from town halls.[28] We turn next to one of the most contested of these forums: political pamphlets.

An Explosion of Pamphlets

On March 30, 1814, François-René Chateaubriand published *On Buonaparte and the Bourbons*, one of the first forays in what would become a vast pamphlet war.[29] The tract appeared in thousands of copies and multiple editions; it was quickly translated into English and German. Chateaubriand launched a scathing attack on the emperor and introduced a new vocabulary for his inhumanity. He lamented that under Napoleon, the government had reached such a "degree of contempt for men's lives and for France to call conscripts *raw material* and *cannon fodder*." The term "cannon fodder" (*chair à canon*) had rarely been used before 1814; it would become common in royalist tracts, poems, and songs in the early Restoration.[30]

At least three hundred pamphlets appeared in April and May of 1814, the peak of this production; hundreds more flooded the market in later 1814 and 1815.[31] They became particularly widespread as the mechanisms of censorship crumbled in the last days of Napoleon's empire, especially after Bourbon monarchy established freedom of the press in June 1814. New censorship laws—established provisionally in October 1814 and then extended until 1819—required prepublication approval of all newspapers and pamphlets under twenty pages; longer works were seen as having a smaller and less subversive readership. Such measures slowed the tide of pamphlets but did not quell it. The Hundred Days brought a wave of pro-Bonapartist tracts. The supporters of the Second Restoration riposted in turn. A November 1815 law outlawed seditious speech or writing, including the publication of news "tending to alarm citizens in their support of legitimate authority and to shake their fidelity." The measure aimed at both explicitly Bonapartist and

28. Fureix, "L'iconoclasme politique" and "Police des signes."

29. Chateaubriand, *De Buonaparte, des Bourbons*, 28.

30. The term was used in pamphlets such as Rougemaître, *L'ogre du Corse*, and Rocheplate, *La conscription: Ode*; and in songs like "Les bienfaits du retour de Napoléon," in *Chansonnier des amis du roi et des Bourbons* (Paris), 61; and "La nouvelle Marseillaise," in *Chansonnier des amis du roi et des Bourbons* (Lille), 17.

31. Fahmy, *La France en 1814*, xiii; and Germond de Lavigne, *Les pamphlets de la fin de l'empire*. The *Bibliographie de l'empire français ou le Journal de l'Imprimerie* (subsequently *Bibliographie de la France)* was published weekly and provides approximate publication dates for most tracts. There was a hiatus between March 25 and May 1, 1814; issues in May and early June combined records of the previous week's publications with those published in April, without distinguishing between them.

republican writing, and tracts that undermined aspects of the monarchical regime.[32]

The titles of many pamphlets suggest the extent of contemporary concern with the aftermath of war and the demobilization of the army. Some were framed as dialogues, whether between two veterans, a soldier and a civilian interlocutor, or veterans and their concerned parents.[33] Others addressed the army as a whole.[34] Many, at least ostensibly, were by members of the military, whether ordinary soldiers or officers.[35] Even when their titles did not directly invoke the military, many pamphlets confronted the consequences of demobilization as they judged France's recent past and proposed directions for the future.

If some authors, like Chateaubriand, were famous, most pamphlets were published anonymously, or signed with initials; sequels were often identified as "by the author of" a popular work. Such anonymity means that it is difficult to know who wrote or promoted specific pamphlets. This is especially true of tracts attributed to former soldiers; it can be unclear when they expressed sentiments of veterans themselves, and when they presented viewpoints that civilians or administrators wanted to imagine in the mouths of returning military men.

It is also difficult to determine the reception of these works. Most had initial print runs of 500 to 1,500 copies. While limited, such numbers were not insignificant. A "best-selling" book in the period often ran only a few thousand copies.[36] Multiple factors amplified their influence. Editions were relatively

32. Welschinger, *La censure sous le premier empire*; R. J. Goldstein, "France"; and Atkins, "Restoration Policies towards Books and Pamphlets."

33. Including the *Conversation de Va de Bon Cœur et de Lavaleur;* the five pamphlets by Fortia de Piles, beginning with *Conversation entre le Gobe-Mouche Tant Pis et le Gobe-Mouche Tant Mieux*; and *Jacques B . . . dit le Boiteux, cultivateur, à son fils, Henry B . . . Capitaine dans le . . . de Ligne.*

See *Lettres du grenadier Lafranchise au grenadier Lavaleur*, during the Hundred Days; and for the early Second Restoration, M. C. A., *Entretiens d'un père de famille*; L. D. M. Y., *Lettre d'un général à son fils*; and *Dialogue entre un paysan, un ancien soldat de Bonaparte et un bourgeois.*

34. Larue de Mareilles, *Aux armées;* R . . . , *Épitre aux armées françaises*; and Ledrut, *Honneur aux militaires.* For the Hundred Days, see A. de B***, *Aux armées (12 mars)*; and for the Second Restoration, *Aux armées françaises par M. D.*

35. Titles include *Discours d'un brave militaire*; *Réflexions d'un soldat à ses camarades sur la chute*; *Lettre d'un ancien capitaine d'infanterie*; and Lestrade, *Opinion d'un ancien militaire.*

Military men were more likely to claim authorship during the Hundred Days; works include *Profession de foi d'un militaire français*; *Réflexions d'un officier supérieur; Liberté, patrie, Napoléon, l'Honneur*; and Arnaud, *Réponse d'un parisien.* Royalist authors also sometimes identified as military men during the Hundred Days and in the early Second Restoration; see especially *Protestation d'un vrai soldat français.*

36. Printers' declarations of print runs appear in the Archives Nationales, series F18. These records are incomplete, especially for works produced outside of Paris, but indicate likely publication. For publication numbers and reading practices, see Lyons, *Reading*

affordable, sometimes only a franc. Readers shared copies, and publications were available in reading rooms, libraries, and bookstores. The periodical press both discussed specific tracts and commented on the general proliferation and influence of pamphlets. Writers engaged one another regularly. Some responded to popular works in their titles (often trying to discredit rival publications); others discussed brochures and their arguments en masse.[37]

The eagerness of the Bourbons to establish their legitimacy meant that there were far more royalist pamphlets than openly republican or Bonapartist ones, except during the Hundred Days. Demobilization also figured most prominently in royalist works, as Louis XVIII's government oversaw both the disbandment of the troops and the postwar reformation of the military. One of their first concerns was ensuring that war was truly over, and that former combatants would not seek to continue or revive it.

The Aftermath of Eternal War

The experience of war had marked a full generation by 1814. As Alan Forrest has noted, men conscripted in 1812 or 1813 could have fathers who had volunteered in 1791 or been caught up in the levée en masse in 1793.[38] Many royalist pamphleteers contended that Napoleon Bonaparte deliberately fostered unending conflict.[39] The author of *Epistle to the French Armies* proclaimed that Napoleon's promises of peace had been lies long before he became emperor; "The Consul swore to make war eternal."[40] Charles de Cheppe, the author of *Exhortation on Tyranny,* similarly asserted that even when war was going disastrously, Napoleon refused to consider an end: "Buonaparte said to his Conseil d'Etat on November 11, 1813, 'One speaks of peace! . . . peace! Peace! I only hear this word of peace . . . while the cry of war should be everywhere.'"[41]

While royalists were convinced of Napoleon's bellicosity, they were divided about whether soldiers would seek a return to combat once peace had arrived. It was plausible that veterans would want hostilities to continue, given that their chances for advancement came largely through military service. Some writers thus countered insistently that soldiers themselves hoped for peace. An

---

Culture and Writing Practices. Lyons shows that while works like La Fontaine's *Fables* ran 35,000 copies, the twelfth most popular work in 1811–15, Buffon's *Le Petit Buffon*, only ran 3,500.

37. For example, Lesbroussart-Dawaele, *Réponse à l'ouvrage de M. de Châteaubriand;* and Barrey, *Le cri de l'indignation.* Examples of more general works include *Des pamphlets, de leur nature, et de leur danger* and Dubroca, *Réponse aux faiseurs de pamphlets.*

38. Forrest, *The Legacy of the French Revolutionary Wars*, 64.

39. *De la fausse gloire de Buonaparte.*

40. R . . . , *Épitre aux armées françaises*, 7.

41. Cheppe, *Harangue sur la tyrannie*, 38. See also *Bibliothèque des souvenirs*, 92.

anonymous article, "Endless Wars and Their Effects on Morals" in the *Gazette de France* in July 1814, told readers to

> Ask the thousands of veterans brought back among us by peace . . . what vow they made in the most dramatic days of their careers, and in the very intoxication of their glory. None of them will say they wanted to make war the habitual state of their existence and the focus of their entire lives; they will instead all say that they only wanted to survive peril, their labors, hardships, and wounds, to return to France to enjoy the honors and recompenses due to their courage and services.[42]

The author claimed that soldiers were entitled to expect a reward for their service, although he did not dwell on the financial, social, or familial aspects of that reward. But he insisted on their fundamental desire to return home.

Others made similar arguments. The 1814 *What Do Soldiers Who Seem to Miss War Want?* admitted that a few military men might think wistfully of the general who took them into battle.[43] But they had faced such horrific conditions and seen such suffering that few could really want to return to the battlefields. Similarly, while acknowledging that rapid promotions were only possible during war, the chevalier de Barrey contended that any superior officer who reflected briefly would realize that his country's interests came before his own career.[44]

Concern about soldiers whose chances for glory would end with peace was not new in 1814. There was an inherent tension between equating masculine achievement with military glory and defining the ultimate goal for the nation as peace, a tension that surfaced throughout the Revolution and Napoleonic era.[45] A few earlier works had explicitly recognized this tension, like the 1797 play *Victory and Peace*. One of the principal characters, a captain, acknowledged that he had been raised in the camps and aspired to glory; war was his element and his means of existence. But he reiterated that he did not want to base his personal fortune on the misfortune of his country. Peace was necessary for humanity, and particularly for the youth of France, who had been torn from the tenderness of their parents and the love of French girls.[46]

Such regrets for the lost opportunities of war, however, were relatively rare in political and cultural discourse during both the Revolution and Napoleonic era. Contemporaries associated peace with victory, imagining that returned soldiers would be welcomed as heroes and find ways of serving the country as civilians. War also did not really end. Peace treaties were short-lived; men who

42. *Gazette de France*, no. 191, July 10, 1814, 759–60.
43. *Que vouloient ceux de nos braves qui ont paru regretter la guerre?*
44. Barrey, *Cri de l'indignation.*
45. Blaufarb, *The French Army*, 12.
46. Ducolombier, *La victoire et la paix*, 39.

wanted to continue careers in the military could do so, at least if their health permitted.

The situation was very different in 1814. Soldiers had come home in defeat. If some were eager to return to their families, others were more reluctant or had become detached from their homelands. Pamphleteers depicted military men as clinging to glory at the expense of their friends, loved ones, and the French nation as a whole. This accusation appeared in the First Restoration but became more common in the aftermath of the Hundred Days, when many veterans had rallied to their former emperor. The dramatist Népomucène Lemercier claimed in August 1815 that, "excited by the desire for promotion, soldiers no longer fight to achieve peace, but rather to better perpetuate war."[47] Similarly, in Fortia de Piles's tract from December 1815, a character denounced "the crazy and ferocious wishes of those who call upon their country a war without end, indifferent to the destruction of two generations."[48]

Even in 1815, however, some royalists contended that soldiers and ex-soldiers could be persuaded to sacrifice glory for the good of humanity. Pamphleteers also personalized the stakes of struggles, claiming that soldiers' individual advancement had come at the cost of both their comrades in arms and their families, particularly their sisters and mothers. For the sake of their loved ones, they should now support peace.

AMBITIOUS SOLDIERS, IGNORANT OF THEIR SUFFERING FAMILIES

One 1814 pamphlet recounted an imaginary conversation between two grenadiers. One, La Valeur (The Valorous), laments that he has had no news of his family for four years while he was hospitalized in Spain. He wants to get a letter to them, and asks Va de Bon Cœur (Goes-with-a Good-Heart) for help. The latter is disillusioned: he claims that there are almost as many broken limbs among veterans as laurels, and that it is time to end the Napoleonic wars. La Valeur is more attached to military glory; he does not want to "vegetate like a bourgeois." But he rethinks his position when his friend informs him of the tragedies that had befallen La Valeur's family in his absence. His two brothers—eighteen-year-old Charles and twenty-one-year-old Auguste—froze to death in the wastelands of Russia, victims of "this hideous conscription." Charles's age is mentioned in passing, but readers would have known that he was under the legal age of conscription, a further indictment of Napoleon's brutality. News of Charles's and Auguste's fate was a deathblow to their father; after his death, their widowed mother had no means of subsistence. She survived only with the help of a few retired military men in the village. Va de Bon

47. Lemercier, *Réflexions d'un français*, 12.

48. Fortia de Piles, *Quatrième conversation*, 13–14.

Cœur tells his fellow veteran that devastated families are everywhere in France, the cost of the grand exploits and drunken glory of ambitious men. La Valeur then proclaims that learning of his family's fate "affects me more than all your beautiful rhetoric."[49]

To appeal to soldiers and their families, writers like the author of *Conversation between Va de Bon Cœur and La Valeur* reversed common ways of thinking about communication between military men and civilians. Revolutionary and Napoleonic popular literature depicted families who had not received news for months or even years from men. In such works—especially in plays celebrating peace treaties—men returned with plausible accounts for their long silences. While those at home feared that veterans might be physically or psychologically maimed even if they survived, playwrights still portrayed them as heroically virile and easily reintegrated into civilian society. In contrast, in Restoration pamphlet literature, combatants, not civilians, are ignorant. Rather than alleviating their families' fears with their homecomings, veterans find that those families have been devastated.

Accounts of soldiers' ignorance about their families' hardships first appeared regularly in tracts from June 1814. In another such work, *Jacques B . . . Called the Lame, Farmer, to His Son, Henry B, Capitan in the . . . of the Line,* a father rebukes his son for his ambition and fear that peace will prevent his career from advancing.[50] The pamphlet presents an implicit contrast between those at home, including ex-soldiers, whose suffering has made them compassionate, and military men who, personally unscathed, have not realized the true costs of war. The son has managed to escape without a single wound. In contrast, the father notes that he himself had been a soldier; lamed when fighting, he could not take a step afterward without being reminded of his service. Returning to his village, he preferred to nourish men than to destroy them.

Jacques B. relates the full story of the devastation war wreaked on his family. His ten children should have provided for him. Instead, like Henry, two more of his sons were swept away by the desire to advance in the military. They paid with their lives for this dangerous desire. With considerable effort and expense, Jacques B. saved three other sons by paying for substitutes to fight in their place, only to be forced to repurchase their freedom a second time. They were ultimately torn from his arms and "perished with no utility to their country." In total, five of Henry's brothers were dead, and without the peace, the captain would likely have met the same fate.[51] Jacques B. here touches on a common theme in anticonscription rhetoric: purchasing replacements bankrupted families without saving their sons. Like much propaganda,

49. *Conversation de Va de Bon Cœur et de Lavaleur*, 2, 7.

50. *Jacques B.*

51. *Jacques B.*, 5.

this had some truth; those who had arranged for replacements could still be conscripted by exceptional drafts, particularly in 1813.[52]

Jacques B. also tells his son that any apparent advances for soldiers would mean new calamity for everyone else. He disparages the idea that his son, or any other soldier, progressed in the military solely on their own merits. Here, like many pamphleteers, Jacques B. invokes the Russian campaign, telling Henry: "You saw Moscow; you were almost naked at your return, exhausted by illness." If his father had not come to the young man's aid, he would have perished; his chief (i.e., Napoleon) did not care about conserving his life. Although the tract does not make the connection explicit, it suggests a clear parallel between Jacques B.'s paternal solicitude and the father-king's support for his people.

"THEY DEPRIVED THEMSELVES OF EVERYTHING": WOMEN'S SACRIFICES

The pamphlet dwelled on the extent to which women had borne the brunt of the war effort. Jacques B.'s daughters have suffered at least as much as his sons: "For at least five years, they could have become good mothers of families, earned an honest living, and been the happiness of their spouses." Instead, he had been unable to find them suitable marriages. Their sacrifices for their warrior brother went further than remaining single; they had worked themselves to exhaustion. "They sacrificed the fruit of their economy to provide for your expenditures. They deprived themselves of everything, so that their brother would lack for nothing."[53]

Descriptions of women forced to work themselves to exhaustion did partially reflect reality. We have seen that the conditions of war led women to take on unaccustomed tasks or wait to wed until they could be relatively sure that a prospective groom would remain or return home. But emphasizing women's labor and suffering in the last years of the Empire and the beginning of the Restoration was not a straightforward description of their hardships. Nor did it serve the same purposes as earlier accounts of the sufferings of soldiers' relations. These sacrifices were not the patriotic choices that men and women presented themselves as making during the Revolution. They did not directly entitle women to recognition or recompense. Instead, they served as evidence of the general hardships of living under Napoleon, and the oblivious selfishness of soldiers.

52. For other laments about men or their families paying for replacements and then being forced to fight, see *Épitre au roi par un garde national*; *Le petit voyage du grand homme*; and *Essai sur les sentiments qu'on doit au Buonaparte.*

53. *Jacques B.*, 4–5, 8–9.

Focusing on women's exhausting and unnatural labor also called attention to the social and economic costs of Napoleon's rule. The writer Charles de Cheppe, for example asked his readers to reflect on "this sad countryside formerly entrusted to [healthy] youth; today, that youth has disappeared and the hardest labors are the task of the weakest sex."[54] Looking back on the Napoleonic era in December 1814, the journalist Lehodey de Saultchevreuil similarly recounted: "the countryside was deserted; in our fields and hamlets, one saw only women, children, and old men bent with the weight of years, painfully dragging along a furrow, seeding and harvesting as they can."[55]

Tales of women's forced celibacy or widowhood suggested general devastation. The anonymous author of the poem *Epistle to the French Armies* praised the "invincible warriors" of the French armies but lamented the consequences of war: "We lose our brothers and friends in combat / Our weeping sisters age near to us / The death of their lovers has deprived them of [future] husbands."[56] Some pamphleteers went further, reproaching soldiers for not recognizing women's grief or the extent of their hardships. Jacques B. rebuked Henry for not appreciating his sisters' sacrifices. The June 1814 tract *Honor to Soldiers,* by the prolific pamphleteer August Louis Ledrut, scolded soldiers for their indifference to the costs of their advancement: "you see in these perpetual and disastrous wars a sure means of promotion. . . . But the object of your ambition comes at the expense of the death of your brothers, your best friends, often even your fathers." In short, "your ephemeral glory [is] too dearly bought by the bitter tears of your tender parents, your abandoned sweethearts, your desolated sisters, whom you left behind as you went off singing to search for glory."[57] Napoleon's selfish ambition had destroyed France as a whole; individuals' quests for glory destroyed their families.

CONVERSATIONS WITH A FATHER

The idea that veterans would be truly unaware of their families' sufferings was most plausible in the initial demobilization. It became harder to sustain as more men returned home. But even in late 1815, many families remained ignorant of soldiers' whereabouts, especially those men returning from distant battlefields or prisons. Veterans themselves could lack news or have received only partial updates about their families. Some works from the early Second Restoration thus continued to appeal to soldiers who had misguidedly (at least

54. Cheppe, *Harangue sur la tyrannie,* 12. See also *Épitre au roi par un garde national,* 7.
55. Lehodey de Saultchevreuil, *Histoire de la régence de l'impératrice Marie-Louise,* 221.
56. R . . . *Épitre aux armées françaises.*
57. Ledrut, *Honneur aux militaires,* 25.

in this construction) followed Napoleon, but who might be won over if they realized the costs of their selfishness to their families.

One of the best examples appeared in early August 1815, *Interviews with a Father about the Events of 1814 and 1815.*[58] The narrator is again a father, in conversation with his children. The book is divided into four parts; the first is implicitly set in early 1814. The narrator describes the death of his son Victor, "innocent victim of reckless ambition"; his worries for a second son, also taken from him by conscription; and his hope of preserving a third son and providing virtuous husbands for his daughters. A dialogue follows between the father, his daughters, and Armand, the son who has remained at home. The family celebrates the end of conscription and vaunts the paternal nature of the Bourbon government. The father nonetheless fears that the conscripted Félix, who has become an officer, will be obliged to follow his corps, and will have contracted a taste for military life. He denounces the Revolution, and laments that soldiers were enticed with stories of rapid advancement, masking the enormous losses Bonaparte inflicted on France. To drive home the cost of war, the father reports that his wife died of grief after Victor's death and Félix's departure.

In a second conversation, Félix has returned. Despite his strong desire to see his family, his transition from a very active life to a sedentary one has been difficult. "Honorable wounds" and favorable circumstances led to his promotion, but his career has now stopped. His father reminds him that his brother Victor did not have the same fortune but was one of the thousands of soldiers whose deaths allowed a few to advance. Félix admits that he was tormented by the fear of a similar fate, and by worries that his brother Armand would be conscripted. While acknowledging that peace is desirable, he laments that returning military men were reduced to the status of demi-solde and lacked employment, seeing their hopes evaporate. The father responds that they are still men, who should put the happiness of their fellow citizens before the fanaticism of glory. Such arguments made the disjuncture between military men and civilians personal, the relationship between individuals and their families.

Revolutionary soldiers seeking to come home during wartime had also stressed their families' suffering. They presented themselves as weakened, but still able to support elderly parents, wives, and young children or siblings. Martial masculinity was to be followed by civic masculinity, as veterans became productive workers, heads of households, and useful civilians. In contrast, while pamphleteers in 1814 or 1815 depicted familial suffering in the absence of men, they rarely emphasized how productively demobilized veterans could work. This is partly a question of authorship and audience; petitioners in 1796 or 1797 sought to persuade authorities to allow them to return to nurse their wounds and provide for their families while others continued to fight.

58. M. C. A., *Entretiens d'un père de famille sur les événements de 1814 et 1815.*

Pamphlet writers in 1814 and 1815 were instead seeking to convince men who had come home that they wanted to stay there.

A few postwar tracts, however, depicted veterans not as oblivious to their family's struggles, but themselves as destroyed men. In December 1815, for example, the Belgian writer Charles D'Auvin described an eighteen-year-old who had provided for his elderly father and five younger siblings; he was conscripted and sent off to war. When he returned, he found his home in ruins, and his family dispersed because they had been unable to pay the rent. D'Auvin added an extra element of pathos: the soldier, still suffering from a serious leg wound, could no longer be useful to his father; it was not even clear that he could procure bread for himself.[59]

Reintegrating Veterans into Civilian Society

Accounts like D'Auvin's sought to portray the destructiveness of Napoleon's empire, rather than to provide an accurate report of the financial or physical prospects of returned military men. Mass demobilization meant that there were proportionately fewer wounded men returning home in 1814–15 than earlier, although absolute numbers were far higher. Men and women reflecting on their return were torn between depicting the lasting and disastrous effects of war on French soldiers and households and claiming that a returned monarchy would bring prosperity for all. One work from July 1815 contended that soldiers were too permanently tainted by their military experience to be able to become happy civilians. Théodore Viel-Castel (the subprefect of Sceaux, in the southern outskirts of Paris) contended that it was hard for soldiers to return to being farm laborers. Veterans could not reaccustom themselves to the drudgery, routine, and limited horizons of civilian life. Viel-Castel also proclaimed that war was a bad training ground for civic virtues. While he did not elaborate on his vision of virtue, he implied that former soldiers were too restless, violent, and focused on their own advancement to be productive members of society. This was rarely a problem when armies were small in proportion to the population as a whole, since a limited number of men would spend their lives fighting and die in uniform. But it was more serious when an entire population was obliged to become soldiers. Those who returned were damaged by the corruption and barbarism of the camps, unable to adapt fully to civilian life. Violent wars, like those that had just occurred, made men particularly incapable of serving their patrie after a military career.[60]

Viel-Castel was less interested in passing judgment on veterans than in denouncing a system that made every man a potential soldier. More virulent royalists claimed that those who had been in Napoleon's armies were

59. Auvin, *Mélanges de littérature et de politique*, 7, 37–39.
60. Viel-Castel, *Réflexions politiques en juillet 1815*, 9–10.

dangerously destructive both to themselves and to others. They were untrustworthy members of the state, undesirable husbands and fathers, as well as bad sons and brothers. The royalist and naturalist Mouton-Fontenille de Laclotte thus lamented the fate of a woman married to a man perverted by his experience of war: "a husband who lives only for war and battle, who passed his life in the armies, accustomed to the tumult of the camps, to the dangers of an idle life, inclined toward evil, immoral by habit, cruel by his state, vicious by nature."[61] Such a man was unredeemable. Marriage and domestic life would not transform him into a good citizen but rather hurt his wife.

There were few means of discussing the difficulties of reintegrating men who had dedicated their lives to violence; terms like "shellshock" or "post-traumatic stress disorder" did not exist to make sense of the social and emotional challenges that faced veterans.[62] Comments like Viel-Castel's and Mouton-Fontenille de Laclotte's hinted at the long-term psychological costs of combat. But political pamphlets like these tended to conflate the trauma of war with the willful depravity of men who had followed Napoleon.

If war had corrupted men who fought, pamphleteers in 1814 and 1815 argued that conscription had also destroyed domestic life. Conscription affected families long before boys reached the age when they could be drafted. The prospect of military service haunted families from birth. An anonymous 1814 pamphlet comparing the "tyrannies of Robespierre and Bonaparte" lamented that the emperor "made families know in advance the moment when their sufferings would start and children know the moment their torments would begin."[63] Or, as a tract supposedly written by the horses in Napoleon's troops wailed: "We, like men, are subject to conscription, and by this barbarous law, made soldiers from our birth."[64]

Royalist writers argued that such perpetual conscription thus led to unhappy unions, or kept couples from marrying or having children. The economist Francis d'Ivernois claimed that good bourgeois girls had been forced to wed unsuitable partners. These included men who had escaped military service because of their deformities or returned mutilated from it; young women also gave their hearts to young men who would never return. While there was hope of peace, people were patient, but once war in Spain made it clear that conscription was a machine "destined to make war eternal," families despaired. Single men and women hesitated to wed; couples, to have children.[65] Songwriters, as well as

61. Mouton-Fontenille de Laclotte, *La France en délire*, 60.

62. Dodman, *What Nostalgia Was*.

63. *Robespierre et Bonaparte*, 12.

64. *Les hommes se plaignent! Que dirons-nous donc?*

65. Ivernois, *Napoléon administrateur et financier*, 149–50. He cited the conclusions of the prefect of the Gers (in southwestern France) on popular reluctance to marry or have children.

pamphleteers, echoed such claims about women's reluctance to have children or their hopes for unhealthy sons who could not be conscripted.[66]

The threat of conscription destroyed families in other ways. Chateaubriand claimed that knowing that military service awaited them made children insubordinate and parents uncaring: "Accustomed from their cradles to view themselves as victims condemned to death, children no longer obey their parents; they become lazy, restless, and debauched, awaiting the day they will go plunder and destroy the world."[67] Fathers and mothers withheld their affections and did little to raise children who were only a source of sorrow and a burden to them. The bourgeois interlocutor of an early 1816 pamphlet accused a peasant of being a far worse father than his own father had been, because he gave up after trying to buy his son's release from conscription once, and saw him off dry-eyed, his heart hardened by the relentlessness of war.[68]

Some writers took this further, to argue that even the possibility for young men to volunteer for war had challenged family unity and paternal authority. Mouton-Fontenille de Laclotte contended that the Napoleonic wars had inspired headstrong youth to disobey their parents:

> The great majority of young men shudder at the very name of conscription, but a few perverse beings ardently desire it, as the moment when they can escape paternal authority. Anticipating by voluntary enlistment the moment that would affect them, they enlist without the knowledge of their parents, against their expressed desire, and breathe only for the tumultuous life of the camps. Neither the example nor the sad fate of their comrades, struck down by the thousands, can turn them away from their hideous resolutions.[69]

Such arguments reconciled the tension between seeing soldiers as victims and instruments of war by presenting most conscripts as victims, while holding a few perverse men responsible for the horrors of war. They contended that a conservative social order, which combined paternal and political authority, would keep selfish youth from the path of destruction—although they hinted that the truly willful might still escape guidance.

66. *Le diable prophète*, 38. Songs include "Le chant du bonheur, dédié à tous les français, couplets chantes sur le Théâtre des Variétés par M. Bosquier-Gavaudan, le 9 juillet 1815," in *La paix est faite! Chantons*, 17; and "Ronde. Sur l'air: La boulangerie a des écus," in *Le chansonnier royal*, 29–30. The last changed tone to focus on mothers welcoming healthy sons in the new regime.

67. Chateaubriand, *De Buonaparte, des Bourbons*, 30–31.

68. *Dialogue entre un paysan, un ancien soldat de Bonaparte et un bourgeois*, 8–9.

69. Mouton-Fontenille de Laclotte, *La France en délire*, 63.

Paternal Rulers?

Pamphlets, songs, artwork, and speeches all heralded Louis XVIII's ascent as the return of a father-king capable of reinforcing the power of individual fathers. The title "father of the French family" was a traditional epithet for a monarch. But as Matthias Lok and Nathalie Scholz have pointed out, there was no longer a clear notion of what a king should be in 1814, nor what characteristics marked both a good father and a good ruler.[70] Much propaganda around Louis XVIII portrayed him as a very particular kind of father, known for his sympathy, tenderness, capacity to forgive, and ability to care for his people.[71] Royalists contrasted this magnanimity to Napoleon's destructive ambition and abuse of his subject-children. Elisabeth Fraser has summed up the stakes of the struggle: "If Napoleon's reign could also be understood as a state patriarchy, he could be portrayed as the bad father to Louis XVIII's benevolent patriarchy."[72]

As we saw in chapter 6, paternal imagery had been central to Napoleon's regime, particularly after his marriage to Marie-Louise and the birth of his son. Royalist tracts thus sought to show that the deposed emperor was not worthy of the title of father. One pamphleteer, allegedly the Duke of Frioul, chided the deposed emperor in May 1814 for his claims to have been a paternal sovereign: "I find it very inappropriate that you are named monarch and father, as if you had received from nature the least spark of this paternal love which men feel."[73] The same theme appears in *Reflections of a Soldier to His Comrades*, an 1814 pamphlet allegedly by an officer of the 58th regiment. The author claimed of Bonaparte: "The duties of a husband, a father, so sweet to fulfill for a man, were nothing to him." The ex-emperor was instead a monster who sacrificed his soldiers for his own vainglory.[74] *Litany of the Dying* described him as taking the name "Father of the French" and then making his children into Isaacs—but with no angel to stop his sword and, implicitly, no deity asking for a sacrifice.[75]

Other epithets for Napoleon reinforced the image of a leader who claimed to be a good father while destroying his flock. Royalists compared the ex-emperor to Saturn, the Greek god who devoured his own children. The theme appeared regularly in both restorations. From a May 1814 tract: "Like Saturn, this father of the people devoured his children; he took them from their most

70. Lok and Scholz, "The Return of the Loving Father," 27.

71. Scholz, *Die imaginierte Restauration*, 84; Wrede, "Le portrait du roi restauré."

72. Legoy, *L'enthousiasme désenchanté;* Fraser, *Delacroix*, 55.

73. *Épitre du Diable à Bonaparte*, 7.

74. *Réflexions d'un soldat à ses camarades sur la chute*, 13.

75. The tract, *Litanie des agonisants*, appears without further publication information in the collection *Le petit homme rouge*, 18.

tender youth and soon all their movements were regulated by the sound of the drum."[76] From an August 1815 pamphlet by Philippe Nettement, the former secretary of the legation to London: "For fifteen years . . . this father of a family, like a new Saturn, devoured three hundred thousand of his children every year."[77]

Royalists also denounced Napoleon as a "new Minotaur," as the July 1814 *The Tombs of the Grand Army*, put it—one "far hungrier than that of Athens."[78] References to the Minotaur, demanding an annual sacrifice of young men and women, paralleled those to Saturn, and emphasized the innocence of those sacrificed.[79] The author of the November 1815 *Essay on the Sentiments Owed to Buonaparte* offered a particularly developed analogy, arguing that Minos was known as one of the most barbarous kings in history for sending twenty young men and twenty young women each year to be devoured by the Minotaur. "But what would one call someone who, while claiming to be a father, took 300,000 men each year, the flower of our youth and the hope and support of families, and sent them to the ends of the earth to perish?"[80]

Such references simultaneously called attention to Napoleon's voracious ambition and to the youth of those conscripted—and thus their status as victims. Pamphleteers regularly described conscripts as boys. In the 1814 *The Tyrant, the Allies, and the King,* Coriolis d'Espinouse claimed that if Draco's laws were written in blood, "the law of conscription was written in the blood of children, mixed with the tears of their mothers."[81] The 1815 *France in Delirium* portrayed soldiers as boys crying for their mothers as they were killed.[82] Louis XVIII's return would allow those boys to stay home; as one description of the Second Restoration promised in August 1815, fathers and mothers could finally trust "that their children will not be taken from them as adolescents."[83]

Pamphleteers challenged not only general depictions of Napoleon as a benevolent father, but also the particular title of "père des soldats" or "father of soldiers." The 1814 *Dictionnaire de l'Académie française* defined the term as "a general who takes great care of the well-being of his soldiers, and only exposes them [to danger] when necessary."[84] Contemporaries used it to praise leaders

76. *Des causes des malheurs*, 23.

77. Nettement, *Le second retour des Bourbons*, 151.

78. Hapdé, *Les sépulcres de la grande armée*, 41. The passage is cited at length in Mouton-Fontenille de Laclotte, *La France en délire.*

79. One chronicler observed that both terms were common in 1814. Beauchamp, *An Authentic Narrative of the Invasion of France*, 16.

80. *Essai sur les sentiments qu'on doit au Buonaparte*, 14.

81. Coriolis d'Espinouse, *Le tyran, les alliés, et le roi*, 19.

82. Mouton-Fontenille de Laclotte, *La France en délire,* 151.

83. *Précis de ce qui s'est passé*, 44.

84. This retook earlier definitions. See *Dictionnaire de l'Académie française,* 5th ed., 4 vols. (Paris: Smits, 1798), 5:266.

like the seventeenth-century marshal Turenne (revived as a hero in 1800) or the revolutionary general Moreau. Colonels supporting Louis XVIII welcomed him as the "father of the army" in May 1814.[85] In contrast, many who applied it to Napoleon during the Restoration did so ironically, insisting that the supposed "father of soldiers" or "father of his troops" should better be called their executioner.[86]

Napoleon and his supporters riposted by using other paternal terms. On March 5, 1815, shortly after his return to France, Napoleon addressed inhabitants of the departments of the Hautes and Basses Alpes. He declared, "The cause of the Nation will triumph again. You were right to call me your father; I only live for the honor and happiness of France."[87] Former soldiers sometimes embraced this image. One song from the Hundred Days thus began, "French! We are all brothers. Our father is Napoleon," while "Vive Napoleon!" proclaimed, "He is a good father and a good husband."[88] Such rhetoric suggested Bonaparte's concern both for his own family and for the nation as a whole.

Yet the republican overtones of the Hundred Days seem to have limited Napoleon's use of paternal imagery. In contrast, Louis XVIII and his supporters seized upon such rhetoric during the Hundred Days and especially the Second Restoration. On April 10, 1815, the king issued a declaration to his followers, asking: "Did I cover the fields of Europe with the bones of your companions? Did I abandon you in the sands of Egypt or the snows of Russia? No, soldiers, whether I am on my throne or in exile, I see in you only my children."[89] Declarations like these emphasized Napoleon's selfish heartlessness, while claiming royal benevolence. They conveniently portrayed the monarch's own hurried flight to the Belgian town of Gand as exile rather than desertion.

Familial metaphors have legitimated or critiqued state power in many circumstances. But such metaphors had particular power in the wake of both revolution and war. Pamphlet literature, like other forms of royalist popular culture in the period, used paternal imagery to present a corpulent, childless, and potentially unpopular monarch as a caring leader. Royalists also inverted this imagery to paint Napoleon as a false father and destroyer of the young, who had tricked or forced his supposed children into marching to their deaths.

85. *Bulletin de Paris, ou relation historique des évènements qui sont arrivés en France*, 86.

86. *Jacques B.*, 8; *Protestation d'un vrai soldat français*, 2.

87. The royalist author who presented the speech in a later collection of ephemera claimed that the cause of the nation triumphed only on July 8, 1815, with the return of the king, the true father of the French. Reproduced in *Correspondance de Napoléon Ier*, 18:7.

88. Pradel, *Le bouquet de violettes*, 39. *Bulletin de Paris, ou relation historique des événements qui sont arrivés en France*, 106.

89. *Bulletin de Paris, ou relation historique des événements qui sont arrivés en France*, 344.

Soldiers or Citizens, Soldiers and *Citizens?*

Whether soldiers were portrayed as adults or children—of a good or bad father—was intimately connected to how much contemporaries viewed combatants as citizens. For royalists, the idea that soldiers were passive was useful. It excused their support for Bonaparte, even as it denied soldiers' political will. As one anonymous pamphleteer—a royalist writing during the Hundred Days—proclaimed in Marseille in 1815, "No, a soldier is not guilty. He obeyed his superiors, a sad necessity, that results from the principle as ancient as civilization that the army is essentially obedient."[90]

Conversely, Napoleon's supporters emphasized their ability to act independently and linked that ability to citizenship. Louis François Lestrade, the author of the June 1814 *Opinion of a Former Soldier*, described himself as "a brave and obedient soldier, without ceasing to be a loyal and free citizen; I knew how to combine the passive obedience of the camps with the useful independence of the forum, and conserve, under military garb, the right to have an opinion and to express it." He argued that courage, wounds, and laurels provided a kind of suffrage to soldiers, entitling them to speak on political issues.[91]

Bonapartists particularly seized upon the term "independence" during the Hundred Days. It invoked national independence from foreign intervention, but also the independence of the army and the agency of individual soldiers. Bonapartist pamphlets repeatedly argued against the idea that the army was, or should be, subservient. The May 1815 *Profession of Faith of a Soldier* proclaimed: "The French army is essentially national, composed of officers and soldier-citizens, who do not regard themselves as the property, the patrimony, the servile flock belonging to the prince, but as the defenders and conservers of the independence, glory, and prosperity of France. French soldiers are not passive and blind instruments."[92] The contemporaneous *Letters of the Grenadier Lafranchise to the Grenadier Lavaleur* similarly contended, "The French soldier is not a robot who fights because he is told to fight."[93]

Some writers used familial metaphors to describe soldiers' relative autonomy or subservience. A pamphlet from July 1814, *Conversation between Foolish Pessimist and Foolish Optimist,* developed the argument that soldiers, at least while they were serving, were not part of the nation. Foolish Optimist proclaimed succinctly: "soldiers are not citizens." His interlocutor, Foolish Pessimist, suggested that French soldiers were still French. The response: a "soldier, sworn to a passive and absolute obedience, has renounced his *qualité de citoyen*." The dialogue continued: Was such a man not a citizen before being a

90. *Appel aux français*. The tract is royalist but published during the Hundred Days.
91. Lestrade, *Opinion d'un ancien militaire*, 3–4.
92. *Profession de foi d'un militaire français*, 3–4.
93. *Lettres du grenadier Lafranchise au grenadier Lavaleur*, 3.

soldier? The response: does the fact that a woman belonged to herself before her marriage allow her to do anything she pleases?[94]

The same pamphleteer retook this reasoning in September 1814. Fortia de Piles contended that in 1790, soldiers had acted as citizens; they argued, went to political clubs, and debated politics. But the disastrous results of this "impracticable amalgam of citizen and soldier" were obvious. Fortia de Piles declared that a soldier's identity as citizen was, and should be, suspended as long as he was in service. He offered a lengthier version of his parallel between marriage and military service, arguing that the liberty of a single woman or a widow was constrained when she married, like that of a serving soldier. Once her husband died or a soldier's term of duty was over, they both retook their liberty.[95] Such comparisons were not new in 1814.[96] But the equation of soldiers with married women had a particularly damning connotation in the aftermath of the Napoleonic wars. It identified the men who had been associated with the pinnacle of virility and independence with women legally subjected to another's authority.

While demi-soldes remained in limbo, veterans were officially liberated from the authority of their military superiors. But the relative poverty of many ex-combatants meant that they were excluded from formal political rights in a system with a very narrow property-based franchise. Writers still debated whether ex-soldiers were, or could become, an integral part of the nation, or whether they remained a separate group. In the *Protestation of a True Soldier*, dated March 18, 1815, and written by, or at least in the voice of, a veteran, the royalist author claims that his contemporaries had treated military men as a class apart, with interests different from the rest of the nation. He reminds his fellow veterans that "we were citizens before we were soldiers." They had worked hard for glory, but glory was only real when it had a useful goal; otherwise it was just bragging and selfishness. The tract concludes, "Citizens and warriors, we should have only one will."[97]

Royalists in the early Second Restoration both denounced the army as disconnected from the civilian populace and called for veterans to abandon a separate identity. The *Overview of the Revolution of 1815*, from August 1815,

94. Fortia de Piles, *Conversation entre le Gobe-Mouche Tant Pis et le Gobe-Mouche Tant Mieux*, 22.

95. Fortia de Piles, *Seconde conversation*, 32–33.

96. For example, in his 1793 *Cours d'organisation sociale*, the political philosopher Pierre-Louis Roederer argued that women, servants, and soldiers were all incapable of exercising political rights because of their positions as dependents. Roederer, "Cours d'organisation sociale," in *Œuvres du comte P.-L. Roederer, . . . , publiées par son fils* (Paris, 1857), 8:245, cited in Verjus, *Le bon mari*, 261–62.

97. *Protestation d'un vrai soldat français*. The lawyer Ambroise Rendu also cited these passages in *Bulletin de Paris, ou relation historique des événements qui sont arrivés en France*, 155.

lamented that one class "did not share the general enthusiasm of the French: this class was the army. . . . A long absence had made it a stranger to the wishes and needs of the patrie."[98] In contrast, the contemporaneous *To the French Armies* heralded "Frenchmen of the army! The French army!" The repeated linking of the terms underscored that military men were members of the nation: "You are men, you are French, nothing will make you forget that you are French, meaning that you know how to combine courage and sensitivity, all the military virtues and those that make good citizens."[99] But Frenchness still required domesticating and transforming veterans into "good citizens."

To do so, pamphleteers confronted other associations of citizenship. These included civic productivity and the comparative usefulness of combatants and civilians. Royalists in 1814 denounced Napoleon's desire and those of his supporters to reduce the French people to a nation of warriors. *What Do Soldiers Who Seem to Miss War Want?* asked if those who longed for war wanted in "all professions, beginning with the farmer and the artisan, that there would be only one occupation, that of killing men and being killed?"[100] Similarly, *The Return of Peace, or France Saved*, declared that "fathers should teach their children that one can be as useful to the country in cultivating arts, commerce, and agriculture, as in shedding one's blood in the deluded ambition of conquest."[101]

Such claims echoed earlier insistence that civilians could be as patriotically useful as soldiers. But they went further, implying that civilians were more useful than military men, at least when war was fought for the wrong cause. Citizenship was not, and should not, be based only—or even primarily—on military service.

Conclusion

Looking at pamphlets reveals the very particular challenges of 1814–15, as contemporaries sought to come to terms with a peace that was far from victorious, where hundreds of thousands of men returned to a changed nation, and where a king had claimed the throne only with the help of foreign powers. It shows deeply embedded tensions. Soldiers and former soldiers featured prominently as both villains and victims, as willfully corrupted champions of war and as desperate conscripts who would benefit most from peace. In assessing the agency of former combatants, royalist pamphleteers effectively inverted revolutionary and Napoleonic views of the relationship between civilians and the military, the values of suffering and social utility, and the meanings of patriotism.

98. *Aperçu sur la révolution de 1815*, 7.

99. *Aux armées françaises par M. D.*, 3.

100. *Que vouloient ceux de nos braves qui ont paru regretter la guerre?*, 10.

101. F. M.***, *Le retour de la paix ou la France sauvée*, 21. He also argued against the "glamour of a frivolous education" for girls in favor of one that instilled virtue.

These tracts reveal that the transition to a postwar order was influenced not only by the ways individuals and families experienced war, but also by ways of talking about that experience and the possibilities of peace. They illuminate the vexed processes of remembering and forgetting in 1814 and 1815. Contemporaries emphasized or denied aspects of the recent past and struggled to attribute responsibility for the events they had just experienced, and determine how much men could, or would, start afresh. Writers adopted innovative strategies in figuring out how to negotiate these tensions, from lambasting ambitious soldiers as neglectful of their families to insisting on the youth of conscripts. They used familial metaphors, from portraying Napoleon as a heartless father and Louis XVIII as a benevolent patriarch to equating the status of serving soldiers with the legal submission of married women. Pamphleteers also invoked the real families of military men to argue that they should accept peace—not only for themselves, but also and especially for those at home. Even as they denounced Napoleon's ambition and that of the men who served him, they revealed the difficulties of disentangling military service and masculinity in the wake of war.

In the next chapter, we turn to other aspects of this postwar transition, and to seemingly less polemical cultural works, including theater, art, and music. Doing so uncovers hidden continuities with the Napoleonic era in the ways that men and women celebrated peace—and the challenges they faced. It also allows us to look more closely at the experiences and images of women in the aftermath of war.

CHAPTER EIGHT

Gender and the Cultural Politics of Peacemaking

MEN AND WOMEN WELCOMED peace and heralded—or contested—royalist rule in many arenas in the early Restoration.[1] If, as we saw in the previous chapter, pamphleteers wrote seemingly endless political tracts, playwrights, artists, songwriters, and poets also took up their quills and paintbrushes to make sense of a postwar order. For all, peace marked a dramatic break. It marked the reestablishment of royalist power after the Revolution and the cessation of hostilities after two decades of war and militarization—punctuated by the uncertainty of Napoleon's Hundred Days. It also entailed return of thousands of veterans, who had been heralded as virile heroes under Napoleon but were now associated with a defeated regime. Cultural works also reveal unexpected continuities in a period of political transformation. Artists and writers recycled plots and images created to celebrate peace during the Revolution and Napoleonic era and used them to laud a new regime. Such tools offered convenient ways of celebrating the end of war and templates for making sense of rapid change, but carried challenging associations.

Contemporaries decried the men and women who adapted older rhetoric and imagery to serve a new regime as *girouettes*, a term that can be translated as weathervanes, or more damningly as turncoats.[2] Historians have tended to view their adaptations as hypocrisy or pragmatic choices for surviving a world in turmoil.[3] Such cultural recycling, however, did not simply reflect the strategies of individual artists or writers. It also shaped the ways men and women

1. This chapter draws on material first published as Heuer, "No More Fears, No More Tears?"

2. Most famously, in *Dictionnaire des girouettes*.

3. Spitzer, "Malicious Memories"; Serna, *La république des girouettes*; Fureix and Lyon-Caen, eds., "1814–1815: Expériences de la discontinuité."

imagined soldiers' homecomings, negotiated gender roles in the aftermath of war, and viewed the power of the state.

To uncover both the power and challenges of these reuses, we turn first to popular theater. Traditions of ending plays celebrating peace with a marriage and general rejoicing worked well in a new order. But plays' embrace of martial masculinity did not fit easily with denouncing conscription. Portraying the homecomings of soldier-heroes required addressing the masculinity both of returning combatants and of those who had refused to fight. Was fear of injury or death a sign of cowardice or a sensible response to a regime that had reduced men to cannon fodder? Were those who came back from war brave and handsome men who deserved reward, as standard plots presumed—or were they mutilated and morally corrupt, incapable of resuming civilian life? How could you portray Napoleon's wars as wrong while still using frameworks that celebrated the men who fought those wars?

Restoration officials also revived earlier practices of honoring rosières and arranging state-sponsored marriages. Napoleonic authorities had transformed these rituals from older forms of philanthropy and theatrical fantasies of peace into tools for legitimating warfare. Restoration authorities adapted them in turn, using them to promote state power while trying to limit their associations as rewards for military service.

New representations would ultimately prove easier to use than older plots and rituals. The image of mothers grateful to a king who had ended conscription and saved their children was particularly useful. Images of stoic women who sent their sons to war, or choked back their tears at news of death, had bolstered governments requiring wartime sacrifices. Images of tearfully thankful mothers corresponded to the opposite exigencies. They legitimated peace and the king who had brought it. The idea that women were desperate for the end of war reflected their importance in anticonscription resistance, protecting draft dodgers and deserters from gendarmes who sought to arrest them. It built on Napoleonic visions of women upset by the threat of war posed to their menfolk and men who proved their virility by overcoming feminine tears.[4] But the image of peace-loving mothers in 1814 and 1815 was not simply a response to the devastation of war or a continuation of Napoleonic gender roles. Nor was it a timeless image of mothers distraught by warfare. Instead, it served specific purposes in a period of dramatic political transition.

Looking closely at these representations allows us to uncover new aspects of the history of emotion. As we have seen in previous chapters, revolutionaries and their successors sought to balance sensitivity and stoicism, and use emotionally charged displays for political ends. One of the most influential historians of emotion in the period, William Reddy, has argued that these dynamics had changed by 1814, as interest increasingly replaced sentimentalism as a

4. Hughes, *Forging Napoleon's Grande Armée.*

hegemonic principle for describing emotions and their impact.[5] Yet royalists still promoted highly sentimental scenes in certain contexts, especially those of reconciliation between the king and his people and of the comforts of peace.[6] These scenes were gendered in ways that were distinctive to the moment. Their emphasis on gratitude and relief distracted from other potential emotions, especially grief, suffering, and uncertainty.

While Restoration writers focused most on mothers grateful for peace, they also revisited the question of women soldiers. In the last days of the Empire and the Hundred Days, some Bonapartist writers revived images of women warriors seeking vengeance for their sons. Royalist authorities in turn appropriated aspects of these models. But when it came to recognizing actual women veterans, they distinguished women soldiers from men deemed worthy of true military awards.

Recycling Napoleonic Culture to Celebrate the End of Napoleonic Wars

Myriad popular plays heralded the peace brought by Louis XVIII's return.[7] Prints and engravings, poetic tributes, and newspapers similarly lauded peace, and royalist songs proliferated.[8] Many works were of dubious aesthetic merit and inherently short-lived. They represent some of the most visible productions of popular political culture in the aftermath of war, but reveal little of lived experience, a theme we will explore in the next chapter.

For most of these writers and artists, peace and Louis XVIII's triumphant return to France went hand in hand.[9] But they retook the plots, characters, and iconography of revolutionary and Napoleonic works to welcome this royalist peace. Some deliberately adapted their repertoire to the new regime. For

5. Reddy, *The Navigation of Feeling.*

6. Scholz, "La monarchie sentimentale" and "Past and Pathos."

7. At least nine plays, performed between April and June 1814, welcomed peace, as did at least five in 1815. Playwrights also added lines or scenes heralding peace to many existing plays.

8. The *Journal de l'Imprimerie* lists the names, prices, and publication dates of prints and engravings; see also Rosset, ed., *Un siècle d'histoire de France par l'estampe.* There was an explosion of songbooks in 1815 and 1816 with titles like *Chansonnier des amis du roi et des Bourbons, Le chansonnier des Bourbons,* and *Le bouquet des lis*; versions with the same title could be published in different places and contain different songs. The editor of *Le chansonnier du royaliste, ou Suite du chansonnier du roi et des Bourbons* (Lille: Chastiaux, 1815–16) claimed that when Bonaparte disembarked at Cannes in March 1815, royalists initially kept silent, but soon responded with many new songs. The range of songbooks seems to bear this out.

9. Such performances seem to have been exclusively royalist: none heralded Napoleon's return during the Hundred Days. See O. Bara, "1814–1815: Construction dramatique des événements"; and Astbury, "Répertoires traditionnels et répertoire nouveau."

example, one of the most prolific writers, Balisson de Rougemont, wrote, or cowrote, plays celebrating peace in 1807 and 1809, and Napoleon's wedding in 1810. He then composed plays for the return of the Bourbons in 1814, and for key events of the Restoration monarchy, including the duc de Berry's wedding in 1816 and the birth of the duke's son in 1820.

Playwrights and theatrical troupes also sometimes simply used existing works. The playwright Maurin had composed *The Peace at Home*, for performances at the Grand Théâtre de Lyon in 1809. The piece was subsequently put on in both Toulouse and Metz in 1814.[10] The plot and much dialogue remained the same, as did the principal characters, including an allegory of the peace, a gardener, and his wife. The 1809 version featured a German baron who did not believe that peace was possible or that the French had conquered Vienna; the 1814 version substituted a Spanish notable, now appropriately named Guerromann (Warman). Both characters served the purpose of expressing doubts about the reality of peace that were ultimately assuaged. Maurin made a few other changes to adapt the work to new political realities. He substituted praise for Louis XVIII for that of Napoleon. He also heralded the end of conscription in terms that echoed contemporary works: "Children next to their mothers / Will grow up without fearing war / No more replacements, no more conscripts / Vive, Vive, King Louis!"[11] But he made no secret that he was reusing an earlier play.

Contemporaries denounced the ability of playwrights like Balisson de Rougemont and Maurin to adapt to changing circumstances. The 1815 *Dictionnaire des girouettes* unmasked "politicians, writers, generals, artists, musicians, bishops, prefects, journalists, ministers, and others" who had praised the Revolution or Bonaparte and were now lauding Louis XVIII.[12] Others similarly listed turncoats or riposted with lists of "antigirouettes," political stalwarts.[13]

10. Maurin, *La paix en ménage, allégorie en un acte* and *La paix en ménage, allégorie analogue à la paix*. He had also produced a different work for the 1801 Peace of Lunéville, *La paix ou le triomphe de Mars*.

11. Maurin, *La paix en ménage, allégorie analogue à la paix*,19.

12. The *Dictionnaire des girouettes* was published anonymously but has been attributed to the comte de Proisy d'Eppe. It featured playwrights prominently, juxtaposing lines written to celebrate Napoleon and his son in 1810 and 1811 with praise of the Bourbon regime in 1814 and 1815.

13. Works included *Dictionnaire des protées modernes* (Paris: David and Locard, 1815); *Almanach des girouettes ou nomenclature d'une grande quantité de personnages marquans dont la versatilité d'opinions donne droit à l'Ordre de la girouette* (Paris: L'Ecrivain, 1815?); and Charles Doris, *Le censeur du "Dictionnaire des girouettes" ou les honnêtes gens vengés* (Paris: Mathiot, 1815). Counterdictionaries include *Dictionnaire des immobiles, par un homme qui jusqu'à présent n'a rien juré et n'ose jurer de rien* (Paris: Beuchot, 1815) and *Dictionnaire des braves et des non-girouettes* (Paris: Lévêque, 1816).

Yet recycled plays were popular. Cultural continuities provided a bridge in which references used to make sense of one world could be applied to another. There was also a physical continuity. Many of the same theaters staged shows and some of the same actors performed. Perhaps more surprisingly, given the Bourbon regime's fear of Bonapartism (especially after the Second Restoration), the same individuals continued to police the messages deemed appropriate onstage. Three out of the four censors active at the end of the Napoleonic Empire continued during the Restoration.[14] Although the definition of political subversion changed with the new regime, censors applied many of the same criteria to judge the literary and moral qualities of scripts.

The very system of censorship encouraged playwrights and theatrical troupes to reuse familiar plots and characters. Fifteen days before the opening of a play, a theater director was obliged to provide two copies of the script to censors. These did not include the names of the director or playwright. Plays could simply be accepted or rejected, although few works were completely refused. Censors asked for changes to passages they found offensive or politically sensitive, or to names that were too recognizable as real people. Theaters were given only two days to make the desired changes, unless they wanted the expense of postponing the performance.[15] Writers in the early Restoration, like those in the Napoleonic era, thus tended to recycle material readily to hand.

HANDSOME SOLDIERS, BRAVE CIVILIANS, OR COWARDLY CONSCRIPTS?

Throughout the late Revolution and Napoleonic era, playwrights imagined wedding bells ringing with the peace, claiming that it had been impossible for young women to find suitable mates while war continued. Balisson de Rougemont's 1809 *The Peace* is typical; it featured three young women singing, "during the war, we suffered from a famine of husbands. But now that peace is signed, we will see all these Frenchmen fly from the chariots of glory to the temple of marriage."[16] Topical plays in 1814 took the idea of "a famine of husbands" to the next level. They featured communities decimated by the departure of able-bodied men. *Live the Peace! Or Return to the Village*, first performed at the Théâtre de l'Ambigu Comique on May 4, 1814, depicted women, in the absence of men, acting as guards, mayors, and priests. A character asks, "Can a village survive without men? Can wives do without husbands? Can our young women be deprived of their lovers?"[17]

14. Joseph-Alphonse Esménard, Jean-Charles-Dominique Lacretelle, and Pierre-Edouard Lemontey. See Krakovitch, *Les pièces de théâtre soumises à la censure*; and Goldstein, "France," in *The Frightful Stage*.

15. Krakovitch, "La censure théâtrale," 22.

16. Balisson de Rougemont, *La paix*, 23.

17. Coupart and Varez, *Vive la paix! Ou le retour au village*, 17.

FIGURE 8.1. *The Ridiculous Rival,* from *The New Game of Marriage, or the Dowry,* 1815. Bibliothèque Nationale de France.

The playwrights, Coupart and Varez (the former also one of the three censors regulating theater) milked the situation for comic potential. As we have seen, war meant that women took on agricultural or business tasks done by men in other circumstances, but they did not serve as mayors or priests. The character lamenting men's absences is less concerned with general devastation than with the lack of dances in the village square. Representations like these amused audiences even while suggesting social disorder that needed to be changed.

Accounts of the shortage of men did reflect the reality that in parts of France, young men were far and few between. In September 1813, the prefect of the Ariège protested the weight of another draft because there was literally no one left: "I've taken everyone. From the years [of those reaching draftable age] of 1813 and 1814, there is no longer anyone capable of procreating. This measure is disastrous. I will put it into effect but it is my duty to tell you that these two years are deprived by this means of all men capable of working or marrying."[18] The prefect of the Doubs similarly reported in November that "Agriculture is suffering from lack of workers; large families are exhausted; the current round of conscription is removing the last few unmarried men able to bear arms. I can vouch for this, having seen with my own eyes on a journey of seventy leagues I have just made to revise the recruitment lists; the dearth of men is so great that women are doing all the work in the fields."[19]

Although conscription was supposed to be imposed equally throughout France, in proportion to population, certain departments—and certain regions, towns, or villages within those departments—were hit harder than others. The Ariège was particularly affected. But the prefects' complaints reflect a general absence of young men, especially in 1813 and early 1814. The number of incorporated men rose steadily under the Empire from 25,000 in 1804 to 270,000 in 1812; 350,000 in 1813; and almost half a million men in 1814—equivalent to 40 percent of that age group.[20]

Playwrights in 1814 and 1815 thus easily adapted earlier claims of a scarcity of eligible young men during war, in terms that likely made sense to contemporaries. They struggled more to appropriate another Napoleonic plot: young women loyal to absent soldier loves but pushed to marry other men. Audiences in 1814–15 would not have been surprised to encounter unsavory or ridiculous characters hoping to marry women whose hearts belonged to the valorous. In the early Restoration, theatrical rivals to returning soldiers or conscripted men included cripples, conniving old doctors, and babbling idiots. And as with earlier plays, young women ended up with brave veterans with names like Belle France or Good Heart.

But if early Restoration plots retook comic figures, playwrights hesitated about whether to portray civilian suitors as unworthy or soldiers as more heroic than men who had remained at home. Some writers still suggested that the only men left in France during wartime were not real men. In the 1814 *A Short Voyage of Vaudeville*, the hunchbacked pastry-maker—the rival to a brave soldier for the heroine's hand—tells her that "Handsome boys, well made and tall / the fine flower of families / once made beautiful children in marrying our daughters / now the handsome boys are gone, but on the other

18. AN F / 9 / 158, Lettre du préfet de l'Ariège au Directoire général de la conscription, 19 septembre 1813. Quoted in Forrest, *Conscripts and Deserters*, 41.

19. AN F / 1 / c / III Doubs 8, pièce 11, Debry à Montalivet, 10 novembre 1813.

20. Pigeard, *La conscription au temps de Napoléon*, 271; and Crépin, *Histoire de la conscription*, 146.

hand we are here / The lame and the hunchbacked are left / To make handsome men."[21] The song portrays the devastation of war; it also hints that handsome boys might come home with the end of war.

The vision of returning soldiers as handsome men was belied by other accounts. As we have seen, pamphlet literature questioned the desirability of veterans as husbands and their ability to return to domestic life. For example, the 1814 *Corsican Ogre*, a thinly disguised account of Bonaparte's life, contended that most former combatants were unattractive mates: "Young women find it disagreeable to have to dance with the one-armed and the lame, and to only be able to marry wigged [i.e., old] men."[22] It implied that even if war ended, the men who came limping home en masse had been destroyed by their service.

Several theatrical performances solved the tension between lauding heroic young men and depicting the horrors of war by claiming that there were still one or two young men left who would make good marital prospects, but who were about to be conscripted. The end of the war freed them to marry their girlfriends. Such men could thus be brave, virile, and handsome—without being mutilated or corrupted by battle. A few plays took this further. Their protagonists not only escaped war thanks to the miraculous return of the king, but also acknowledged a reluctance to fight. In the *Return of the Fleur-de-Lys*, first performed on May 2, 1814, at the Théâtre des Variétés in Paris, the would-be conscript admits that "I imagine myself disabled . . . I am not eager to lose my legs / It's in vain they try to sugarcoat the pill / I'd rather sing, long live Louis!" The conscript's mother connives to get a doctor to certify that he is unfit and should stay home; the doctor refuses, but only because he wants to marry the conscript's girlfriend.[23]

This depiction of attractive young men as wary of war was new. In Napoleonic theater, only cowardly fools avoided military service. War-adverse men made audiences uneasy even in 1814. The *Journal des arts, des sciences, et de la littérature* complained that a verse in the play *The Keys of Paris*, which proclaimed that "freed from a bloody law, a young man can henceforward be sure to close his mother's eyes" would have been better said not by a young man but by his grandmother, "for whom bravery is not an obligation."[24]

Unease became acute when audiences included foreign sovereigns. The journalist Jean-Gabriel Peltier noted his discomfort with *Long Live Peace*, performed in the presence of the king of Prussia and other foreign dignitaries in the audience. He critiqued "the obligation to have a cowardly and naïve peasant, a role that appears to the point of satiety in our comedies. If this character can be amusing on its own, this is not the moment when it will please

21. Barré, Radet, and Desfontaines, *Un petit voyage du vaudeville*, 6.

22. Rougemaître, *L'ogre de Corse*, 84.

23. Désaugiers and Gentil de Chavagnac, *Le retour des lys*.

24. *Journal des arts, des sciences, et de la littérature*, no. 291, April 25, 1814, 113–14.

brave men, especially when the elite of the warriors of Europe are called to see the French nation at home."[25] It was one thing to depict comic characters; it was another to challenge the courage of French warriors.

The mixed reaction to the *Return of the Fleur-de-Lys*, featuring a conscript loath to risk mutilation, was even more striking. Reading the draft script, the censors noted approvingly that "The scourge of conscription is artfully portrayed. It is the liveliest and most natural means to communicate the joy of our new situation." Nonetheless, they objected to the full title proposed by the playwright, *Return of the Fleur-de-Lys, or the End of Mars*. They noted that the "end of Mars" could signify either "the prize of Paris" (the golden apple of Greek mythology) or military decadence. The play was approved on April 29, 1814, on the condition that the authors change the subtitle and remove controversial passages.[26]

One of the authors, Marc-Antoine Désaugiers, had written earlier plays celebrating peace, but his depiction of the conscript in 1814 was unprecedented. There is no sense in his previous works that real French men might not want to fight.[27] In contrast, *Return of the Fleur-de-Lys* suggested that men had good reason for avoiding combat. A critic noted that the audience at the first performance, at the Théâtre des Variétés in Paris, applauded "as if the theater was full of the authors' friends."[28] But the reaction in Strasbourg a little over a month later, on June 12, 1814, was quite different. The play led to an uproar, precisely because it portrayed the conscript as fainthearted and frail. The prefect of Bas-Rhin reported, "It was not the subject of the piece that upset the large number of military men, and especially officers, who were at the performance, but the ridiculous character of the conscript." The curtain came down early, with a hurried rendition of the closing couplets and cries of "Vive le roi!" The prefect noted with relief that there was no further unrest.[29]

As well as depicting conscripts who did not want to leave home, popular theater featured men who wanted to quit the troops. One of the earliest such plays is *The Conscript's Return, or the Reestablishment of Louis XVIII on*

25. *Mémorial dramatique*, 181–82; *L'ambigu ou variétés littéraires et politiques*, vol. 45, no. 401 (May 20, 1814), 459.

26. AN F / 21 / 987, *Retour de la fleur de lys*. See also Krakovitch, "La censure théâtrale," 64.

27. In Désaugiers's 1801 *La paix ou il était temps*, Thérèse has three suitors; she is committed to marry the one who announces peace first, and connives to have her lover report the news. The 1807 *Un dîner par victoire* presents a farmer going bankrupt because he hosts a feast every time the French win a battle; fortunately, peace comes and his daughter weds the officer who brought the news. The *Famille Moscovite* (performed in December 1812, before the failed Russian invasion was fully known) depicts an impoverished Russian family who finds hope in the generosity of French soldiers. Désaugiers featured prominently in the *Dictionnaire des girouettes*.

28. *Mémorial dramatique*, 57.

29. AN F / 7 / 3733, Département du Bas Rhin, Rapport du préfet, 14 juin 1814.

His Ancestors' Throne, by Alexandre Delannoy. The play is set in Boulogne (in northern France) in early April.[30] The central character is Victor, who deserted because of the captain of his company, described as "a hard, bizarre, and imperious man," in an allusion to Napoleon. The captain was mistreating the unfortunate; Victor killed him in defending them, and was forced to flee, helped by his fellow soldiers, who also hated the captain.

Deserters had been popular protagonists in late eighteenth-century theater. *The Conscript's Return* echoed Mercier's *The Deserter*, performed regularly in the 1770s and 1780s. In both versions, the protagonist flees because he has attacked an imperious commander, although *The Conscript's Return* played up the captain's brutality more.[31] Theaters occasionally presented shows featuring deserters throughout the revolutionary and Napoleonic eras.[32] But the image of men leaving the troops with or without permission particularly resonated with demobilization in 1814.

The Conscript's Return intensified its picture of desperation by adding a mother whose son has been conscripted and is about to be "torn from her arms to join in combat that his soul detests." The play ends with the happy news that the senate has deposed Napoleon and made Louis XVIII king. The king decrees an amnesty for deserters; Victor is reunited with his girlfriend, and the mother embraces her conscript son. Concluding lines call for general rejoicing: "children, reassure yourselves, you will not be conscripts; mothers, too long unhappy, your children will no longer be taken from you."[33]

Theatrical troupes also revived works that had been censored earlier because of their depiction of military service. One of the most interesting is *Herman and Verner, or the Soldiers*, by Edmond de Favières.[34] The play is set in German lands in 1745; it features a young man, Verner, who has volunteered for three years. He longs to return home to marry his sweetheart and support his aging mother, but his new colonel is not party to the original agreement and insists that Verner stay on after the expiration of the three years. The work ends happily: Verner rejoins his fiancée after she and his mother beg for mercy and his devoted friend Herman offers himself as a replacement.

Favières had written a version of the story in 1790, as a libretto for the opera *Officer of Fortune*. The opera was scheduled for the summer of 1792 but

30. Delannoy, *Le retour du conscrit, ou le rétablissement de Louis XVIII sur le trône de ses ancêtres*. It is set on April 6, 1814, two days after the Provisional Government ended conscription.

31. Mercier, *Le déserteur*.

32. Sedaine, *Le déserteur*. Versions would be published in 1807 and on October 14, 1814. Gardel, *Le déserteur, ballet d'action*. A new version was performed at the Porte Saint-Martin in Year XII: Dauberval, *Le déserteur, ballet d'action*. See also Ferrand, *La diligence du Havre à Rouen*.

33. Delannoy, *Le retour du conscrit*, 34.

34. Favières, *Herman et Verner, ou les militaires*.

never performed. After war was declared, it was not a good moment to feature military commanders ceding to the tearful entreaties of village women and men more eager to return home than defend their country. Favières was able to resurrect the work during the Peace of Amiens. His timing, however, remained bad. The play was first performed at the Théâtre-Français on May 16, 1803. Hostilities between France and England resumed two days later.[35]

Censors who reconsidered the play in April 1814 noted that it had been banned because "it could inspire young conscripts with disgust for the severity of military life."[36] However, in the early Restoration, the play appeared eminently acceptable, precisely because of the disgust it inspired for the harshness of Napoleon's reign. Who better to represent abused innocence than a young woman telling a military official: "Monsieur the Colonel, I beg for his mother, for me, take pity on his situation, our future, our happiness depends on it. To take away the son of this virtuous mother is to condemn her to die, and me too." By implication, the king who ended conscription saved the lives of young men who would have been destroyed by war and the women who waited desperately at home.

Popular theater in 1814 and 1815 thus took up existing models for celebrating peace. It showcased young women able to wed with the end of war, who still chose soldiers or conscripts over less suitable rivals. Playwrights also drew on older ways for presenting men who had familial motives for wanting to leave the troops. But theatrical troupes struggled to adapt these plots and their associations of martial masculinity to emphasizing why men might want to stay home.

PUBLIC WEDDINGS AND POLITICAL PROPAGANDA

Popular theater was not the only site of cultural recycling in the early Restoration. Officials also experimented with recognizing rosières and holding state-sponsored marriages. As we have seen, Napoleonic officials viewed public weddings between veterans and poor young women as a tool for promoting war. To do so, they adapted Old Regime models of philanthropy and revolutionary celebrations of peace and employed these to new ends. Royalists similarly adopted state-sponsored marriage for their own purposes. They sought to legitimate royal power, while downplaying the associations of such weddings as rewards for injured veterans.

State-sponsored marriages had become rare in the last days of the Empire. To my knowledge, Napoleon did not sponsor weddings during the Hundred

35. Another work entitled *L'officier de fortune*, by Joseph Patrat and Antonio Bartolomeo Bruni, was performed in 1792, but had a very different plot. Bartlet, "Grétry and the Revolution," 52–56.

36. AN F / 21 / 966.

Days, presumably because his rule was too short to make them a priority. But the idea had not disappeared. An April 1815 petition from the veteran Jean Vasseire gives one indication of its continued resonance. He had married in Year IV (sometime in 1795–96), then obtained a divorce on the grounds of her "scandalous adultery." He now wanted to remarry, and his fiancée insisted on a church wedding. The local priest refused to wed them, claiming that as Vasseire's first marriage was a sacrament, the divorce was meaningless. Vasseire sought permission for a second marriage and a reward for his services. He had fought for twenty-four years, in the Rhine, the Vendée, Spain, Italy, and Egypt. In his view, he should be compensated for his sacrifices by having the state support his marriage and honor his new wife. Doing so would make up for his earlier domestic unhappiness: "the new *rozière* [sic] of Saint Flour will be under your auspices, a true compensation for the harm done to him by his first wife, who abandoned him secretly and left a child in his charge."[37]

Political theorists during the Hundred Days suggested that state-sponsored marriages would benefit both veterans and France as a whole. In *On Recruitment*, Charles Girou de Buzareingues imagined courage as well as physical strength as traits that could be inherited. He portrayed marriage as a reward for veterans and a tool for selective breeding. State-sponsored marriages would encourage volunteers and entice veterans to reenlist, foster bravery, and compensate combatants for their sacrifices. They would lead "military men, whose task it is to conserve and increase the race, to marry."[38] While acknowledging that ugly men should be allowed to wed and that France should let all babies live, he wanted to entice the bravest and handsomest men to reproduce most, "those destined by nature to be the glory and the support of their patrie."[39] He proposed giving veterans sufficient land to sustain a family of five. Men who received this support would choose "their wives among the most beautiful and most virtuous (*plus sage*) young women, and as much as possible, among the daughters of military men, so that this national largesse will be at once the prize of courage and of virtue and beauty."[40]

Girou was clearly inspired by Napoleonic state-sponsored weddings, but his treatise also echoed Old Regime plans for settling veterans. He addressed recurrent concerns that state support would oblige future generations to take up arms. Even if courage was passed on, children of soldiers were to be excused from obligatory military service. Here Girou combined concepts of individual and familial citizenship. He did not want to force a man to pay off his debt to

37. AN BB / 15 / 207, Vassiere (R2, 5892), 11 avril 1815.

38. Girou de Buzareingues, *Du recrutement*, 6. The work was registered on June 2, 1815.

39. Girou de Buzareingues, *Du recrutement*, 3.

40. Girou de Buzareingues, *Du recrutement*, 7.

the patrie both directly and through his sons. Sons who volunteered to fight, however, would advance more rapidly through the ranks.

Girou's tract was not well received. The satiric Napoleonic newspaper *Nain Jaune* mocked his desire to ensure that France's army should consist of handsome men and his obsequiousness to the Russian emperor.[41] The Restoration government was not opposed to veterans' marriages, as officials hoped that former combatants might disappear into domestic obscurity. But the government was little interested in arranging their weddings or supporting their future households.

ROYALIST ROSIÈRES

The royalist government did recognize rosières in various cultural works, initially for very limited purposes. In 1814, and again in the aftermath of the Hundred Days in 1815, the theme of the king crowning a virtuous young woman appeared as a means of legitimating royal rule. The 1814 *Fulfillment of the Rosière's Wishes* portrayed Louis XVIII in Germanic lands in 1794. The king awarded the crown to the "plus sage" girl of the canton; Napoleon's government had used the same term, to justify choosing young women as recipients of state-sponsored dowries. As Louis XVIII bestowed the crown, she responded, "My prince, God gives it back to you."[42] The same engraving appeared in May 1815 during the Hundred Days, with the tile of *Napoléon on Elba*. Napoleon now crowned the woman; she responded with "Sire, God and the French people return it [the crown] to you."[43] Subsequent Restoration artwork would return to the images of the king honoring a young, presumably virginal girl in anticipation of his own renewed coronation. The Paris salon of 1817 thus included Jean-Charles Tardieu's *Louis XVIII Crowning the Rosière of Mittau, 1799*.[44] It depicted the king's stay in modern-day Latvia not as a cold and uncertain exile, but as a bucolic familial scene, in which his eventual return to France was foreseen.

Theatrical performances also occasionally featured both rosières and royally blessed weddings. In *The Bearnais or Henri IV on a Voyage*, first presented at the Opéra-Comique on May 21, 1814, King Henri IV—generally portrayed as Louis XVIII's glorious predecessor—arrives incognito in a part of France where he spent his first few years. His good peasants recognize him. In return for their loyalty, he provides a dowry for the heroine of the piece, who is distained by her prospective father-in-law because she is a poor peasant. The play ends by promoting peace and exhorting the public to forget the recent

41. *Nain Jaune*, no. 375, June 25, 1815, 370.
42. Rosset, ed., *Un siècle d'histoire de France par l'estampe*, 3.
43. Rosset, ed., *Un siècle d'histoire de France par l'estampe*, 3.
44. Landon, *Salon de 1817*.

past, while giving the groom his longed-for titles of nobility.[45] Royal rosières appeared more explicitly in the titular *Rosières of Hartwell*, first performed at the Théâtre du Vaudeville on August 24, 1816; Hartwell refers to the English town where Louis XVIII settled after leaving Mittau.[46] Like Tardieu's painting, it focuses on the king's beneficence in crowning a local woman. In this case, the chosen girl, Louise, is a French émigré. The father of her beloved George, a British merchant named Miller, refuses their marriage because he does not want his son to marry a French woman. It turns out that Miller had been saved from poverty by the king's discrete charity; when Miller learns the identity of his benefactor, joyous reconciliation follows.[47]

Associations of state-sponsored weddings as a reward for both rosières and veterans resurfaced when the Restoration government organized state-sponsored weddings for real individuals on at least two occasions: the marriage of the duc de Berry to the princess Caroline in 1816 and the birth of his son, "the duc de Bordeaux," in 1820, shortly after the duc de Berry's assassination. Both these weddings and associated plays emphasized the role of the state in making marriages possible. They also reveal a growing ambivalence about the connections between manliness and military service.

THE WEDDING OF THE DUC DE BERRY

In June 1816, the duc de Berry wed Princess Caroline. The duke's marriage echoed, in a subdued form, the theatrical trappings that had accompanied Napoleon's wedding to Marie-Louise. All the major Parisian and some provincial theaters commemorated the occasion.[48] Celebrations for the duke's nuptials also renewed the tradition of government-sponsored dowries for selected couples.

Playwrights celebrating the marriage used strategies they had adopted to celebrate peace in 1814, denouncing conscription and praising a paternal monarch who saved the young. In *The Village Wedding* (performed at the Gaîté on June 15, 1816), the character Mother LaGaule—herself married to

45. Sewrin, Kreutzer, and Boieldieu, *Les Béarnais, ou Henri IV en voyage.*

46. One journal observed that "A very pretty engraving in which the king is represented crowning a rosière who tells him, 'My prince, God will give it back to you!' provided the basis for the play." Une très-jolie gravure dans laquelle le roi est représenté couronnant une rosière qui lui dit: Mon prince, Dira vous la rende! a fourni le sujet de la pièce." *Mercure de France*, vol. 68, August 1816, 234.

47. d'Artois, *La rosière d'Hartwell.*

48. These included *Charles de France, ou Amour et gloire*, at l'Opéra-Comique; *Le Chemin de Fontainebleau* at l'Odéon; *Les deux mariages*, at Variétés; *L'union des lis*, at Porte Saint-Martin; *Le mariage sous d'heureux auspices*, at l'Ambigu; *La noce de village*, at the Gaîté; *Le mariage de Robert de France* at the Théâtre-Français; and *Le dix-sept juin*, at the Théâtre de la Cour. Outside of Paris, the most important performance was *L'impromptu de Provence*, in Marseille, in Caroline's presence.

a former soldier turned farmer—sang that "While cruel wars / Harvested all our children / We heard from mothers / only tears and moans / Now it's completely different / When a child grows up / A good mother will have reason / To embrace him and cry / He's here; it's the king who's saved him." The next verse proclaimed that "Now, each young man will stay in his village, and on the day of her marriage, each girl will say, 'Without the king, I would not be here.'"[49]

Celebrations of Napoleon's marriage had praised the emperor's role in encouraging marriages to create new soldiers, not end war. While heralding peace, theater in 1816 sometimes undermined such celebrations of peace by suggesting that women would birth future warriors. In *Henry IV's Soldier*, the village heroine declared, "I will not be single all my life / and this hope is flattering / I will be able to give to my country / more than one defender."[50] Similarly, a character in *June Seventeenth* proclaimed succinctly, "If the duty of man is to serve the country / the duty of woman is to furnish the soldiers."[51]

Such declarations, however, emphasized women's role in reproducing future soldiers—loyal to the monarchy—more than rewards for military valor. Indeed, plays commemorating the duc de Berry's marriage revealed hesitation about rewarding veterans. In many plays in summer 1816, the future husbands of theatrical heroines were still soldiers, but healthy young men in the royal guard, not wounded veterans of the *grande armée*. This was also true for the fifteen real couples who received government dowries to celebrate the duke's marriage. Parisian administrators required eligible women to be natives of the city, be younger than twenty-five, have a profession, and have lost at least one parent. These criteria replicated Napoleonic requirements. Suitable grooms in 1816 were still defined by military service, but now much more elastically. Candidates included "royal volunteers, former soldiers known for their attachment to the King and the loyalty of their sentiments, or, finally, young men exercising a useful profession, registered on the roles of the National Guard, and performing their service with zeal and exactitude."[52] Even men who did not meet these conditions could be acceptable if they were known for their morals and devotion to the king. In laying out these requirements, the prefect of the Seine stressed the need to ensure that potential husbands pleased the rosières in question. His concern echoed Napoleonic administrators' unease about whether selected couples wanted to wed, but framed the primary honorees and people choosing partners as women, not wounded veterans.

49. Brazier and Dubois, *La noce de village*, 37.

50. Maréchalle, Barba, and Hocquet, *Le soldat d'Henri IV*, 4.

51. Gentil de Chavagnac and Désaugiers, *Le dix-sept juin*, 17.

52. Archives de Paris VD / 4/ 8, Dotation des jeunes filles à l'occasion du mariage du duc de Berri, 1 mai 1816.

SOLDIERS' MARRIAGES IN 1821

Five years later, another set of weddings celebrated the miraculous birth of the son of the duc de Berry after his father was assassinated.[53] The birth took place in changed political circumstances, following both the duke's assassination and new laws on military recruitment; we will look more closely at those dynamics later. Here it is worth noting that plays celebrating the child's birth still adapted plots about the marriages of combatants or veterans. In *Three Good Turns for One or the Two Baptisms*, performed free at the Gaîté on April 30, 1821, M. Gervais, a veteran and farmer, is baptizing his son on the same day as the local countess is baptizing hers. (The countess was Caroline de St.-Yberr, an anagram of Berry.) Gervais hopes to receive the cross of the Legion of Honor for his services and to use the accompanying pension for his niece Charlotte's dowry to marry his nephew (on different sides of the family). Charlotte's beloved hears rumors that Charlotte is in love with another man, Saint-Jules. Overcome with jealousy, he leaves his military post, jeopardizing his own standing and his uncle's medal. All ends well: Gervais receives a decoration for his services, Charlotte a dowry, and Saint-Jules, realizing his carelessness, intervenes with Henri's commander, to arrange a leave for the young man to wed Charlotte.[54]

In *The Baptism, or the Double Festival*, the protagonist is a veteran whose son was born the same day as the duc de Bordeaux.[55] The play presents a version of an old plot. Caroline, the infant's godmother, is in love with the young sergeant Charles, but an old miser wants to marry her. She is prevented from marrying her true love because her father is in prison for debt. Charles offers his savings to pay the debt, but thanks to the king's beneficence, Caroline's father is released from prison and gives his daughter's hand to her generous suitor.

If these plays featured military men as grooms, they proclaimed that good French men did not need to fight. In *The Village Baptism*, performed at the Vaudeville, Francœur frets, "if I have one worry, it is not to be able to shed my blood for the service of the king." The father of Francœur's beloved assures him: "My son, you only became a volunteer out of love for your Prince and for France; fortunately, you have done your studies, so you can be useful to your country in other ways."[56] He gives himself as an example; after seventeen campaigns, he was discharged by his general and has happily retired. Francœur

53. *Trois bienfaits pour un*, at the Gaîté; *Le baptême ou la double fête* at l'Ambigu Comique; *Les suites d'un bienfait*, at the Théâtre de la Porte Saint-Martin; *Le Château de Chambord*, at the Théâtre du Gymnase Dramatique; *Le baptême du village* at the Vaudeville; *Hôtel des Invalides ou la députation*, at the Théâtre-Français; and *Le garde-chasse de Chambord* at Variétés. Outside of Paris, topical plays included *L'a-propos alsacien* in Colmar.

54. Dubois, *Trois bienfaits pour un, ou les deux baptêmes*. The censors' judgment is in AN F / 21 / 976.

55. Coupart and Varez, *Le baptême, ou la double fête*.

56. Gentil de Chavagnac, de Bury, Ledoux, and de La Croisette, *Le baptême de village*, 8.

protests that to be able to accept rest cheerfully, it is necessary to set up a household; Maurice responds with enthusiasm at the idea of seeing Francœur and Thérèse wed.

Similarly, *The Alsatian A-Propos*, authored in part by a veteran living in Colmar, featured three military men engaged to be married. Praise for their brides echoed that for rosières under Napoleon: one, Louise, was designated "as the most virtuous and the worthiest of creating the happiness of a Brave (e.g., a soldier), and was named Rosière of the Canton." But the goal was not to create a new generation of warriors. Louise's fiancé pledges that "Finally, after long wars / We will live in peace in our foyers / We can all in our cottages / Rest on our laurels." He adds: "I have an assurance that I will no longer need to make war."[57]

Finally, *Hotel of the Invalides or the Deputation*, performed at the Théâtre-Français, shows that plays promised not only that war was definitively over, but also that injury was increasingly a sign of belonging to the past, not of virility or entitlement to reward.[58] It opens with military corps being invited to the celebrations for the baptism. Veterans at the Invalides lament that they have been left out and a drummer boy reports their unhappiness to a royal guard. The guard talks to his captain, who in turn talks to the governor of the Invalides. Eight veterans are chosen by lot to attend the ceremonies; felicitous chance leads to one veteran from each major battle. The play features a dowry; in this case, one of twelve provided by the city. But the lucky groom is not one of the wounded veterans—as would have been the case in both Napoleonic theater and state-sponsored marriages. Instead, the reward goes to the royal guard who called attention to their unhappiness. He weds the camp cook, to general rejoicing.

To celebrate the duke's baptism, the city of Paris actually provided dowries for fourteen girls, one in each of the twelve arrondissements, and two at the discretion of the prefect. Military service, even that of a young royal guard, was no longer the criterion for choosing eligible husbands. One of the first chosen in Paris was a tailor, whose bride was a seamstress.[59] The Municipal Council of Lyon similarly decided on October 12, 1820, to bestow dowries on six girls, without publicizing the role of such marriages in rewarding soldiers.[60]

New Icons: Grateful Mothers

While Restoration culture struggled with adapting older references and rituals, writers and artists also turned to a newly important image: mothers grateful to the king who had brought peace and saved their sons from conscription. Contemporaries acknowledged that the image of mothers desperate for

57. Antoine and Broulard, *L'a-propos alsacien*, 15.

58. Dubois, *Hôtel des Invalides ou la députation*.

59. Archives de Paris VD / 4 / 8, Dotation des jeunes filles à l'occasion de la naissance du duc de Bordeaux, 11 octobre 1820.

60. Archives Municipales Lyon, *Délibérations des corps municipaux*, vol. 5.

peace presented a strong contrast to the revolutionary vision of stoic Spartan women. In August 1814, the journalist Peltier described a scene in the café du Palais Royal. A thin man dressed in black proclaimed that the end of war had ruined him. He was an official poet for Napoleon; he would have made his fortune with one or two more battles. Yet while men had applauded his oratory even in the last days of the war, women had seen through his speeches. The poet related his failed attempt to inspire the mothers of conscripts:

> One day, I began to speak near the Marché des Innocents, next to a battalion of conscripts torn by a "paternal" sénatus-consulte from the hands of their weeping mothers. These women had never read the history of Sparta; their cries pierced the air. I felt the need to strengthen their courage and began to address them with a few philosophical and heroic sentences in a solemn tone. They became furious, and without the admirable speed of my feet, like a new Orpheus, I would have been torn to pieces. . . . Since this point I have only addressed myself to men.[61]

The image of weeping mothers echoed Napoleonic visions of women distressed by the departure of loved ones. Songs from the Empire featured men showing their bravery by triumphing over feminine tears and marching off to war.[62] But Peltier used the anecdote for very different purposes, suggesting that women opposed to conscription were more insightful than men who had continued to swallow heroic rhetoric.

The image of mothers grateful for the end of conscription reflected real relief of parents that their sons would not have to fight or would come home. It reflected the role of women in resisting conscription. But it was also a deeply political image. The mothers who appeared most were passive, the recipients of royal generosity rather than the agents of change. They were young women whose sons would stay home, rather than older mothers of veterans or men who had died. Focusing on the mothers of boys deflected attention from returned soldiers and highlighted the king's role in preserving families. It also sidestepped the problem of grief, emphasizing hopes for the future rather than mourning for the dead.

"THE CRY, UNDER THE EMPIRE, OF 'NO MORE CONSCRIPTION!' SO ENERGETICALLY PUT FORTH BY MOTHERS"

The belief that women, particularly mothers, had been especially active in opposing conscription was recurrent in the nineteenth century. In 1833, for example, the founders of the Lyonnais newspaper the *Conseiller des femmes*

61. *L'ambigu ou variétés littéraires et politiques*, vol. 46, no. 410 (August 20, 1814), 374.
62. Hughes, "Making Frenchmen into Warriors."

reminded readers of "the cry, under the empire, of 'No more conscription!' so energetically put forth by mothers, who contributed powerfully to the fall of the despotic system of the sword."[63]

Women did oppose conscription. Individuals hid family members who had deserted. They signed on for paper marriages so that potential conscripts might appear as heads of household and thus escape the draft. Women participated in collective resistance, attacking gendarmes to protect young men sought by the government or liberate those arrested for desertion or draft dodging.[64] In reporting these uprisings, police used vague expressions, invoking a "mob" or "crowd" of women, or offered rough numbers, like "about twenty women." Men and women sometimes worked together; for example, in 1806, a crowd of about forty people tried to free a condemned deserter in Amiens.[65] Descriptions of these mixed groups were similarly imprecise, often just mentioning "a mob of men and women."[66] Such reports suggest that women were frequently involved in opposition to conscription, even if that involvement is difficult to quantify.

Studies of resistance to the gendarmerie indicate that women were more engaged in opposing conscription than in other acts of civil disobedience. Aurélien Lignerneux has calculated that women participated in 46 percent of incidents connected to resistance to conscription, while they appeared in only 29 percent of other rebellions against the gendarmerie.[67] Women, especially mothers and sisters of conscripts, stirred up their families and neighbors to save young men or attacked authorities themselves. Their actions map onto the general chronology and geography of resistance to conscription.[68]

63. Prospectus, *Conseiller des femmes*, October 1, 1833, 2.

64. Many records are in AN BB / 18 / 1 through 85, Dossiers des délits relatifs à la conscription et au recrutement (an VII–1814); F / 7 / 8397 through 8724, Rapports faits au ministre par les diverses autorités locales: préfets, commissaires de police, généraux (an X–1814); and F / 9 / 150 through 261, Recrutement: correspondance générale. Because these series are organized geographically and there is no finding guide to women's involvement in resisting conscription, I consulted files concerning women noted in general studies of conscription, then relied on selective sampling. This analysis does not yield good statistical data, but it does provide a sense of women's activities, their recurrent presence in the archives, and the language used to describe them. For some incidents, see Bergès, *Résister à la conscription;* and Forrest, *Conscripts and Deserters*.

65. AN BB / 18 / 76.

66. Expressions include "attroupements des femmes," AN F / 7 / 8232, pièce 6909, Nièvre, Rébellion contre la gendarmerie dans la commune de Brisson ; "un attroupement se forme; les femmes du village," AN BB / 18 / 31, Ministre de la guerre, Paris, le 11 déc. 1813; "une vingtième de femmes assaillent à coup de pierres," AN BB / 18 / 76, reg. A2, pièce 2351, Courcelles; and "attroupement d'hommes et de femmes," AN BB / 18 / 76, reg. A1, pièce 7309, Omniécourt.

67. Lignereux, *La France rébellionnaire*, 40. Statistics are approximative.

68. Crépin, "La France plurielle," 13–26.

Such cases received little publicity either during or after the Empire. Napoleonic police dossiers noted feminine cries rallying those around them to defend young men from the gendarmes. But apart from reports of exceptional violence or the discovery of women disguised as men or vice versa, officials rarely made detailed commentaries.[69] Newspapers and other media also rarely covered protests. Administrators may have believed that the defense of a young man torn from his home corresponded to the traditional parameters of feminine action. The government also had little interest in calling attention to resistance, except in the case of exemplary punishments. For officials, it was better to suggest that all supported the regime. Cultural works—particularly those sanctioned by the government—could depict girlfriends and mothers bewailing men's departure, especially when men proved their courage by leaving. The image of women actively working to keep men home was a different matter.

For very different reasons, the Bourbon government was wary of identifying itself with stone-throwing peasant women. Representations of mothers appalled by conscription but helpless in the face of the law were far more resonant in 1814 than those of women defending deserters or draft dodgers. Peltier's women may have responded aggressively to the Palais Royal poet, but many of those facing Napoleonic authorities were depicted only as desperate. The 1814 *Fragments of a Work on Conscription* by the viscount Félix de Conny captures such scenes well. Conny claimed to have written the tract in 1807 but to have been prevented from publishing it; the book went through several editions starting in March 1814.[70] During the author's walk in the Bernaise region, he came across a village in an uproar. Armed officials were seizing young men, while women threw themselves at the feet of authorities and threatened suicide if their sons were taken. Conny's description of pleading mothers resonated with readers, and a critic in the *Mercure de France* began a review of the book by quoting it approvingly.[71]

This image of frantic mothers reinforced a general theme of royalist propaganda. It portrayed the French people as victims of Napoleon's tyranny and the king as their benevolent savior. But the mothers who featured most in royalist writings were not only passive; they were also young, the mothers of boys saved from future conscription by the return of their king.

69. For a woman disguised as a man who attacked a brigade in 1803 with her husband and brother, see AN AF / IV / 1327, and for men disguised as women in 1809, F / 7 / 8232, Rébellion contre la gendarmerie de Solre-le-Château.

70. Conny, *Fragmens d'un ouvrage sur la conscription*. The work has been attributed to J. Delahaye, but his authorship seems unlikely, as Delahaye was the division head for the minister of war in Westphalia. The Bernaise region was symbolically freighted; it had been home to Henri IV, the king whom Louis XVIII would hail as his predecessor.

71. Conny, *Fragmens*, 15; *Mercure de France*, vol. 60, July 1814, 127–29.

YOUNG MOTHERS AND THEIR HAPPY SONS

This emphasis on mothers and young sons in early Restoration celebrations of peace is striking. It complemented political rhetoric depicting Napoléon's armies as destroying the young. Artwork and songs promised that peace would allow mothers to keep their sons home. Pauline Auzou's painting *View from the Windows of Paris on the Day of Louis XVIII's Entry*, displayed at the November 1814 salon, is typical.[72] As one commentator described the painting: "A mother, weakened by illness and hardships, drags herself to the window to see him in whom she puts all her hopes. She clutches her son against her heart, knowing that he will not be taken from her. Her daughter, aged fifteen, seems to invite her to dry her tears. The youngest raises his small hands and cries, Vive le Roi!"[73]

Works from the Second Restoration conveyed analogous messages, like the September 1815 song "Return of Louis XVIII": "Under the reign of this good father, a horrible law will no longer take adolescent sons from their mothers every year . . . no more tyrants and no more war."[74] An engraving from December 1815 depicts a mother holding a paper in one hand and her arms around two young sons; she is seated before a bust of the king. The title makes the message clear: "The Good Mother: My children, I will keep you; Louis has freed us from conscription."[75]

The focus on mothers and boys bears relatively little relation to the social composition of the military. A few boys were trained in the camps through the system of enfants de troupe. Recruitment officers did not look closely at the age of potential conscripts in the last desperate days of the Napoleonic Empire. The Jourdan Law regulating conscription did not aim at adolescents, but rather at men aged over twenty, or eighteen in the case of volunteers. No subsequent draft changed official age requirements.

As we have seen, the emphasis on the young underscored Napoleon's savagery, the "Minotaur" who demanded a tribute of youth or the "Saturn" who devoured his children. Conversely, it suggested both the innocence of

72. *Vue des croisées de Paris, le jour de l'entrée de S. M. Louis XVIII*, reproduced in Fraser, *Delacroix*, 57. The original has disappeared, but a lithograph by Féréol Bonnemaison survives. Two years earlier, Auzou had painted *L'arrivée de l'impératrice Marie-Louise dans la galerie du château de Compiègne, le 27 mars 1812*, depicting the empress surrounded by young girls, women in white, and a nervous-looking Napoleon.

73. Rosset, ed., *Un siècle d'histoire de France par l'estampe*, 31.

74. "Le retour de Louis XVIII" by M. L. Damin, avocat, in Jaquelin and Rougemont, *Le chansonnier des Bourbons*, 79. The song is titled "L'heureux retour" in *Chansonnier des amis du roi et des Bourbons* (Paris), 54.

75. "La bonne mère: Mes enfans, je vous conservai; Louis nous a délivré de la conscription." The image is accompanied by "Le bon père," captioned "Mes enfans, je vous marierai: Louis nous a donné la paix." Fraser attributes these to Forget, based on a composition by Charles. *Delacroix*, 56.

FIGURE 8.2. Féréol Bonnemaison (lithographer), after a painting by Pauline Auzou, *View from the Windows of Paris on the Day of Louis XVIII's Entry*, 1814. Bibliothèque Nationale de France.

the French people as a whole and Louis XVIII's role in protecting families. It helped celebrate a monarch whose return was controversial, and legitimate his claims to be the father of the French. The ironically titled "Praise of Bonaparte" put it bluntly: "we are all the king's children / He is our father / The friend of our young men / and especially of mothers."[76] Depicting the king as

76. "Les éloges de Bonaparte," in *Chansonnier des amis du roi et des Bourbons* (Lille), 10.

a particular friend of mothers reinforced sentimental scenes of reconciliation between the king and his people.[77]

It also sidestepped questions of the virility of French soldiers in a time of defeat. The focus was less on the return of soldiers than on the joy of mothers who knew that their sons would be safe. Playing up women's emotions meant celebrating peace without addressing the masculine virtues of demobilized soldiers—and indeed, without addressing their place in a new order at all.

NO MORE ANGUISH, NO MORE TEARS

Focusing on women's relief and gratitude also sidestepped the persistence of grief. Playwrights, songwriters, and poets reassured audiences that their suffering had ended, thanks to the king. For example, the song "The Happy Return" promised "French, no more anguish, no more alarms" and asked Louis XVIII to "Heal our wounds, dry our tears." Similarly, the "Bumblebee of Notre Dame" welcomed the monarch as "wiping away our tears."[78]

While songs and speeches promised general rejoicing, they were directed most to soldiers' mothers, sweethearts, and wives. The play *The General Establishment of Peace,* performed in Dijon in June 1814, thus ended with the joyful announcement that "There will be no more alarms for wives / mothers you will dry your tears."[79] In the same vein, the song "The Renaissance of the Fleur-de-Lis" assured listeners: "Your happy days will soon be reborn / he unbinds you from slavery / from the cry of war and forever / the cruel law is abolished / Keep your children / mothers, no more anguish, no more tears."[80]

Such promises did not actually end anguish and tears. People welcomed the end of war, but still mourned a missing son or spouse or agonized over the fate of those who had disappeared. Royalists occasionally acknowledged public grief. Charles Nodier, for example, reported in April 1814 on a performance of the play *The Renaissance of the Fleur-de-Lis*, noting that "One woman near me, alone amid public joy, wept bitter tears, and nonetheless the fleurs de lis in her hairdo seemed to indicate that she had come with the intention of sharing public rejoicing. This woman was no doubt a mother of a soldier, and the child left to her, still quite young, watched her cry without understanding."[81] Similarly, a M. Dardouville reproached boisterous celebrations in the early Second Restoration, on the grounds that the costs of war made public joy

77. Scholz, "La monarchie sentimentale" and *Die imaginierte Restauration.*

78. Antignac, "L'heureux retour," in *Le chansonnier des Bourbons*, 22; and Jaquelin and Rougemont, *Le chansonnier des Bourbons,* 22, 94. See also Scholz, *Die imaginierte Restauration*, 84–92.

79. Chambelland, *La pacification générale*, 31.

80. "La renaissance des lis," in *Le lis et la violette*, 168.

81. *Journal des débats politiques et littéraires,* April 14, 1814, 1–2. Description reproduced in *L'ambigu ou variétés littéraires et politiques*, vol. 45, no. 399 (April 30, 1814), 218.

inappropriate. Mothers deprived of their sons by Bonaparte deserved respect. The editors of the *Journal de Paris* riposted that joy was fitting because it expressed gratitude to the king who had ended suffering; the public should respect the joy of mothers who had conserved their sons.[82]

These observations bring us back to another tension in royalist propaganda. Royalists decried the suffering Napoleon had caused, both to the wounded and dying on the battlefields and to their bereft loved ones. Pamphleteers dwelled on anguish at most length, but playwrights and songwriters also insisted on the human costs of war. Constant's song "Two Orphans of 1815" is typical; he laments: "How many wives abandoned, to satisfy his pride, how many young women, whose lovers are in their coffins. And you, tender and sensitive mothers, he sacrificed your children."[83]

Yet the regime provided few means for mourning those deaths or acknowledging sorrow. The Restoration organized public ceremonies for those deemed to be victims of the Revolution, and commemorations of the executions of Louis XVI and Marie Antoinette cast French people as mourners, not regicides. But there were no commemorative practices for the war dead.[84] This was in part because there were few obvious sites of memory. Most soldiers were buried on the battlefield (or in more gruesome cases, burned or thrown into water), rather than brought home.[85] Yet revolutionaries had built cenotaphs to the missing and absent dead.[86] The greater problem was that soldiers, who had both waged war and fallen victim to it, were too difficult to mourn in a new regime. Restoration writers cursed Napoleon's destructiveness, but focused on the happy mothers of young children whose sons would remain home.[87]

VICTIMS OF CONSCRIPTION

Comparing Restoration depictions of mothers to those in other wartime and postwar eras reveals further distinctive features of the period. In the Restoration vision of peace, French women were victims of conscription, not victims of war itself. The distinction is not trivial. The reality of rape as an instrument of war is all too well known. In many cases, real or threatened violence to women and children has been invoked to galvanize hatred of enemies, or

82. *Journal de Paris*, no. 208, July 27, 1815, 2.

83. Constant, *Les deux orphelins de 1815*.

84. While the king and some supporters promoted reconciliation by ignoring the past, hard-liners insisted on public reparation. Petiteau, "Portée de la politique symbolique" and *Lendemains d'empire*.

85. Hantraye, "Les sépultures de guerre."

86. Clarke, "Cenotaphs and Cypress Trees."

87. There were rare exceptions, like Lenoir-Leroche, *Description du calvaire des lauriers*. Lenoir-Leroche was a mystic; the Calvary cross she constructed was personal rather than official.

to recount national suffering and grievance.[88] In February and March 1814, Bonapartist newspapers like the *Journal de Paris* and the *Gazette de France* described atrocities that the Cossacks and other foreign soldiers committed against French women. This reflected real violence. Rape was a means for occupiers in France in 1814–15 to demonstrate power over the territory and people of France and was understood as a violation of the French nation.[89] Stories of violence served to stir up resistance, especially as newspapers emphasized violence against girls and the elderly.[90] But if Bonapartist newspapers reported brutalities, the theme of violence against women was rare in royalist works from 1814 and 1815. For them, the enemy was the usurper "Buonaparte," not foreign allies. They thus denounced Napoleon Bonaparte's particular crimes against French families: conscription, rather than the general violence of war.

The attention paid to mothers of young sons was similarly distinctive to the period. In the aftermath of World War I, widows, and especially mothers, represented public grief for both victorious and defeated nations. While widows could be young, the dominant cultural image was of older women beset by sorrow.[91] Governments also strategically invoked maternal grief during and after World War II. Nazi propaganda, for example, emphasized the sacrifices of bereaved war mothers over the suffering of war widows. This appeased pro-mother sentiment, while limiting the state's obligation to assist young mothers in the work force.[92]

In early Restoration France, the emphasis was quite different. The focus was on young mothers grateful to have their sons remain home, rather than older women who had lost their children. It was thus on hopes for the future, rather than grief for the past—even as the Bourbon monarchy trumpeted the Restoration of an old order.

Counterimages of Women and War

Such attention to grateful young mothers appears to show a broad cultural shift from seeing women as revolutionary heroines to the passive recipients of royal beneficence. This emphasis, however, represents a specific moment—the immediate aftermath of war—rather than a definitive long-term shift. It was also deeply partisan and instrumental. Looking at men's appropriation

88. For later examples, see Jolluck, "The Nation's Pain and Women's Shame"; Harris, "The 'Child of the Barbarian'"; and Gullace, *The Blood of Our Sons*.

89. Hantraye, *Les cosaques aux Champs-Élysées*, 41–42; and Haynes, *Our Friends, the Enemies*, 90–93.

90. Fahmy, *La France en 1814*, 12–13.

91. Evans, *Mothers of Heroes, Mothers of Martyrs*; Kuhlman, *Of Little Comfort*.

92. Heineman, "Whose Mothers?"

of women's voices and at counterimages of "new amazons" in the social and political unrest of 1814–15 suggests its limits.

Male pamphleteers and songwriters adopted women's voices to call for peace. The 1814 song "Women's Petition," by the blind troubadour Duverny, ends with the plea: "Give, if there is still time, the lover back to his beloved, the father to his children, the son to the tearful mother. Give peace to the entire world; the fair sex begs you. Cease war, and forever, cease to go against nature."[93] Similarly, a pamphlet from the Hundred Days, the *Daily Mirror*, was subtitled "The Address of Dames and Mothers of Parisian Families as Defenders of Mothers of Families of All Nations," claiming to speak in the name of peace-loving women.[94] The petitioners cry out that "Wives, mothers, sisters, friends, compatriots, implore and beseech you with all the force of their souls, their hearts heavy, burdened with grief, and their eyes filled with tears, to put an end to all their hardships and yours."[95]

Duverny's petition reflects his penchant for experimenting with characters' voices for playful or dramatic effects. In another song, "A Grenadier's Return to Justine," for example, a woman tells her lover that he has been replaced during his absence; it transpires that his "replacement" is his six-year-old son.[96] While the subtitle of the *Daily Mirror* suggests a collective address by women, it was only signed by a man, Sauvage, *typograph*, himself associated with three other pamphlets, all published at the beginning of the Second Restoration; none mention women.[97] Yet the choice to use women's voices in such texts suggests that they appeared convincing champions of peace.

Women did not necessarily present themselves in this role. If a few created striking images of maternal desire for peace, like Auzou's *View from the Windows of Paris on the Day of Louis XVIII's Entry*, these were rare. Similarly, women did not produce extensive texts heralding a royalist peace. In an overview of poets and writers praising the Bourbon regime, Corinne Legoy has identified only eleven women among 583 writers.[98] While later activists, like contributors to the 1833 *Conseiller des femmes*, used women's opposition

93. Jacques-Gilles Duverny, *Pétition des femmes. Air: de la soirée orageuse* (n.p., n.d). The tune came from a popular 1792 vaudeville featuring the protagonist's farewells to his wife and friends. Duverny probably composed his version during the late Napoleonic era, before the Restoration government had become a real possibility, as it makes no mention of Louis XVIII.

94. Sauvage, *Le miroir du jour.*

95. Sauvage, *Le miroir du jour.*

96. Jacques-Gilles Duverny, *Retour d'un grenadier auprès Justine* (n.p., n.d.).

97. Sauvage, *L'orage de vingt-cinq ans, passé, ou la tyrannie aux abois, couplets allégorique* (Paris: P.-N. Rougeron, n.d.), *Le masque tombé, ou dénouement d'une tragédie qui semblait être éternelle* (Paris: Laurens aîné, 1815), and *Notre père de Gand, ou adieux de Bonaparte aux français, dialogue entre des français et Bonaparte* (Paris: Laurens ainé, n.d.).

98. Legoy, *L'enthousiasme désenchanté.*

to the "despotic system of the sword" to claim a political voice, criticism of war was not a widespread means for women to assert public roles in 1814 or 1815.

The image of peace-loving women also associated peace with female royalism—women grateful for the end of war and the government that had brought it. Especially during the Hundred Days, Bonapartists refuted such associations, sometimes putting forth a more militant vision of civic motherhood than during the Empire. Madame L. D., author of *Conversation between a Bourbonist Woman and a Bonapartist Woman,* was thus outraged that royalists had claimed that women supporters of Napoleon were not true mothers. Such women were mothers "more than anyone . . . they are citizenesses until the posterity of their last nephews. They alone among women merit a patrie."[99]

"NEW AMAZONS"

A few works in 1814 and 1815 invoked not peace-loving women, but "new amazons."[100] While the royalist image of mothers seeking peace has relatively little direct connection to women's antiwar activism, real incidents inspired tracts featuring armed women. Several newspapers reported in late May 1815 that between two hundred and five hundred women dressed as men were "fulfilling the functions of soldiers." Papers printed an anonymous letter from someone in the city of Nancy, which claimed that "a dame of our acquaintance was a sergeant-major" in these troops. This was Mme Pellet d'Epinal; her husband, Jean-François, was a lawyer and poet, who had been involved in the defense of the city in 1814.[101] Cadot, the author of the 1815 *Voluntary Departure of New French Amazons,* was inspired by the story—as he had been by stories of women who took up arms during the Empire.[102]

There was also a long literary tradition of depicting women soldiers to rouse or titillate audiences. Restoration-era works echoed those from the Revolution and Empire. The title of the 1815 "Voluntary Enlistment and Departure of Young Women" likely reminded readers of revolutionary songs, including the 1793 "Departure in the First Requisition of Young Women for

99. Madame L. D., *Conversation entre une dame bourboniste et une dame buonapartiste,* 20.

100. Among others, see *L'enrôlement volontaire et départ des jeunes filles pour l'armée; Jeanne d'Arc aux jeunes françaises; Les filles et les femmes traitées comme elles le méritent;* and Cadot, *Départ volontaire des nouvelles amazones françaises.*

101. *Départ volontaire* cites the *Indépendant* from May 29, 1815. Versions of the letter appeared in the *Moniteur*, no. 140, May 20, 1815; and the *Journal de Lyon, ou Bulletin administratif* on May 23, 1815. On the Epinals, see Charton, "Souvenirs de 1814 à 1848," 263.

102. Cadot was also the author of *Virginie Ghesquière, ou la nouvelle héroïne française* (Paris: Croisey, 1812), inspired by a report in the *Journal de l'empire* of October 31, 1812. Ghesquière, or Chesquière, was real; see Hopkin, "The World Turned Upside Down," 82–83; and J.-C. Martin, *La révolte brisée,* 116–23.

the Army of the North," or Napoleonic pamphlets, such as the *Army of Bellone, Voluntary Enlistment of Two Hundred Thousand Young Women.*[103]

These texts all used the language of voluntary engagement. The 1812 *Armée de Bellone* reinforced its subtitle of *Voluntary Enlistment* with the deliberately gender-bending lines that "We have no engagements; we are girl volunteers; we leave our lovers until the end of the war and then we will marry, after having made conquests of all these good young men." Those in 1815 employed similar constructions. Not only did the title of the 1815 *Voluntary Departure of New French Amazons* emphasize the choice to take up arms; so did the narrators' proclamation that they would imitate "these patriotic women who devote themselves voluntarily to the noble profession of soldier."[104]

Yet images of armed women could make audiences uneasy even when authors were at pains to distinguish women volunteers from male conscripts. The intent of the *Armée de Bellone* was comic, including proposals to stock stores with oranges, lemons, and pastries for female troops and to appoint special officers to distribute love letters. The pamphlet still provoked real fears. The mayor of Bordeaux reported in December 1812 that in its wake, several women had received anonymous letters convoking them as if they were conscripts. Popular distress was sufficient to make the minister of police suppress the pamphlet after its initial authorization.[105]

Plays in the last days of the Napoleonic Empire also presented the well-worn theme of women defending besieged cities. In February 1814, *The Heroines of Belfort* alluded to the recent battle in the city and adapted the common plot of a young woman—here the daughter of a mutilated veteran—courted by rival suitors, including a brave soldier and a cowardly pastry maker. It also showed women dressed as men defending the ramparts, led by Madame Thomas, "braver than her husband."[106]

Tracts during the Hundred Days also tended to draw inspiration from prerevolutionary heroines. The 1815 pamphlet *Girls and Women Treated as They Deserve* is actually an overview of women's historical roles in defending cities from invaders.[107] In his 1815 *Voluntary Departure,* Cadot invoked women warriors in contemporary Alsace as well as during the medieval siege of Caen.[108] Such tracts revived the image of stoic women encouraging their menfolk to fight

103. Vingtrinier, *1789–1902: Chants et chansons des soldats,* 53–54; *L'armée de Bellone.*

104. Cadot, *Départ volontaire des nouvelles amazones françaises.*

105. AN F / 7 / 4286; and Hopkin, "The World Turned Upside Down."

106. The name in the title sometimes appears as Béfort. The play was not printed. See Lecomte, *Napoléon et l'empire racontés par le théâtre,* 264–65; *Magasin encyclopédique,* 1814, 1:415–16.

107. The author described women joining men on the ramparts, before concluding with a milder call for women to inspire men. *Les filles et les femmes traitées comme elles le méritent.*

108. Cadot, *Départ volontaire des nouvelles amazones françaises.*

and seeking vengeance for the loss of their husbands and sons. In March 1814, the *Journal de Paris* invoked Joan of Arc, Jeanne Hachette, and other French heroines, and proclaimed, "Let this martial spirit, of which women gave so many examples in the past, guide us again today! Let us find among today's women, heroines like those that the patrie names only with gratitude. Let the mother breathe only vengeance!"[109] The anonymous June 1815 pamphlet *Joan of Arc to Young French Women* claimed that for women not to fight, "It would be necessary not to be a mother! To have forgotten the exploits of our husbands, our lovers, our sons, our brothers!" The tract promised: "You will be avenged, mothers who are still crying on the tombs of your children."[110]

This invocation of maternal vengeance is striking because it was in the name of a quintessentially virgin heroine, and in this pamphlet, in a work addressed to young women. The theme of women joining husbands or lovers or inspiring them to fight had been common during the Revolution and continued occasionally into the Napoleonic era, despite the ban on women in the military after 1793. But calls for mothers to arm themselves were unusual—particularly for a regime that had depicted women as wary of violence. They were shaped by the defensive nature of war in the period, combined with a revival of republican vocabulary during the Hundred Days. They also implicitly opposed a royalist version of weeping peace-loving mothers.

In turn, royalists appropriated Bonapartist imagery. An engraving from the Hundred Days, *Oath of the French Amazons*, depicted women soldiers gathering around a figure of Joan of Arc to defend the Empire. Royalists used the same image but left hats and flags white; areas indicating where red and blue were to be added in the original were scratched out. It became an illustration of the royalist heroine, the duchesse d'Angoulême, the "amazon of Bordeaux," who tried to inspire the city's garrison to fight against Napoleon in May 1815.[111] Napoleon's supporters riposted that comparing the duchess to a true woman warrior, the Maid of Orleans, was the most damning possible judgment.[112]

The duchess in question, Marie-Thérèse Charlotte de France, was Louis XVI's daughter. Royalists saw her as the most sympathetic member of the royal family when the Bourbons returned in 1814 and described her as the new Antigone for her loyalty to her uncle, Louis XVIII. Songs and artwork praised her as the heroine, as well as the amazon, of Bordeaux. Yet they lauded her as

109. Quoted in the *Conservateur impartial*, no. 120, March 10, 1814, 108. The *Conservateur* mocked this call to arms, invoking Théroigne de Méricourt, Susanne Labrousse, and other women it defined as crazy.

110. *Jeanne d'Arc aux jeunes françaises*, 2.

111. Becquet, "Royauté, royalismes et révolutions."

112. *Nain Jaune*, no. 367, May 15, 1815, 187–88. See also Rosset, ed., *Un siècle d'histoire par l'estampe*, 165.

an inspirational presence rather than as a woman who took up arms. In contrast, Napoleon reportedly called her the "only man in the family."[113]

Joan of Arc remained a heroine of the early Restoration. The Maid's association with French opposition to the English was especially welcome during the Allied occupation of France from 1815 to 1818. While she continued to be a multivalent figure, she often figured less as a warrior than as a symbol of France's royalism and Catholicism.[114]

WOMEN VETERANS IN A NEW ORDER

The Restoration government also confronted the question of real women veterans, who, like male veterans, continued to seek recognition and financial support. In September 1814, the royalist heroine Renée Bordereau published her memoir to considerable popular attention.[115] Bordereau had enrolled in 1793 to fight against the republicans in the Vendée. She presented herself as the soldier Langevin, different from other soldiers only by the extent of her heroism, rather than as a woman in the war. When required to allude to her gender, she portrayed herself as a virtuous woman who wanted to avenge her family, claiming that she had seen forty-two of her relatives killed, and watched her father being massacred for his royalism. Bordereau compared herself implicitly to Joan of Arc throughout her memoirs, and like her republican counterparts in the Revolution, reiterated that her virtue, honesty, and courage were recognized by her comrades.[116] When asking for a pension in December 1814, she stressed her courage and exceptionality as a woman, describing herself as "the only peasant still alive, who, disguised in men's clothing, fought in all the wars with honor and bravery."[117] Like many veterans, she enumerated her injuries, including a bullet in her right leg, a blow from a saber on her right leg, and a bullet below her left eye.

Contemporary reviews lauded her authenticity while criticizing her literary style. They presented her as a heroine, but focused on her humanity rather than her courage and violence.[118] Rather than dwell on the twenty men Bordereau had allegedly killed, for example, the journalist Peltier insisted on her devotion to defending those in need.[119]

113. A lithograph, *Le seul homme de la famille: La duchesse d'Angoulême faisant son regard significatif*, was recorded on August 21, 1830; I have not been able to determine if it appeared earlier.

114. Haynes, *Our Friends, the Enemies*, 244–45.

115. Bordereau, *Mémoires*.

116. Cron, "Les mémoires des 'Vendéennes.'"

117. Reproduced in *L'intermédiaire des chercheurs et des curieux*, October 25, 1891, 821.

118. Nodier, *Le spectateur français*, 359–67.

119. *L'ambigu ou variétés littéraires et politiques*, vol. 47, no. 417 (October 30, 1814), 75–81.

Bordereau was awarded a pension in 1815, but she was an exception. The Restoration government generally minimized women's military courage. It contested the idea that women had earned military awards. In April 1817, the grand chancelier of the Legion responded to a query about the forty-year-old Catherine Claire Picard, accused of wearing the cross without being entitled to do so. Picard declared that she had received it after she replaced her husband during the battle of Wagram in 1809. (Her story echoes that of the revolutionary heroine Liberté Barreau, who picked up her husband's weapons after his death.) The chancelier declared that no woman had been admitted into the Legion of Honor.[120]

While the Restoration government was particularly distrustful of women associated with Napoleon, administrators rejected the requests of royalist women for the Cross of St. Louis, an award created by Louis XIV to reward military merit and loyalty to the sovereign.[121] In July 1817, the minister of war considered Louise De Bennes, "the chevalier de Haussay," who, along with her husband, had fought with the émigré armies at the battle of Quiberon in 1795. At least in certain accounts, she had been arrested and condemned to death, escaping only by reverting to women's clothing. While she received her husband's pension as his widow, the government denied her a pension in her own right. She did not meet the formal qualifications for a military pension—she neither was amputated nor had thirty years of service—but authorities also appeared skeptical of her claims as a woman soldier and her eligibility for the award. Similarly, Rose-Ursule Cailleau (born Urson) sought the cross for her service in the Vendée, particularly for saving the life of Mme de la Rochefoucault. Cailleau asked for "the decoration of St. Louis; nothing in the world would be more agreeable and would be the happiness of her life."[122] She was given a medal with an effigy of the king but turned down for the cross.

Indeed, no woman would be awarded the Cross of St. Louis or the Legion of Honor until the mid-nineteenth century. The first woman admitted to the Legion of Honor would be Angélique Duchemin (Brulon) who served as a vivandière and then as a sergeant from 1791 to 1798. Duchemin was not recognized until 1851, when she was aged seventy-nine; Napoleon III's government finally paid tribute to her "seven years of service, seven campaigns, and three wounds."[123]

In the later nineteenth century, a few other women sought to support themselves with tales of their adventures during the Napoleonic era. The Dutch writer and actress Ida Saint-Elme's memoirs, published in eight parts,

120. AN BB / 18 / 972, dossier 3245, Poursuites contre une femme Picard qui prétend avoir été décorée de la légion de l'honneur à Wagram.

121. Goupil-Travert, *Braves combattantes*, 136–37.

122. SHD 1 Yi 12, Urson / Cailleu.

123. S. Steinberg, *La confusion des sexes*, 260.

from 1827 to 1828, were scandalous largely because of her claim to have been the mistress of numerous officers.[124] The most famous memoirs of the era, those of Madame Saint-Gêne and Marie Thérèse Figueur, appeared in 1842.[125] But there were no women in the Restoration army itself. One woman disguised as a male soldier appears in the records, but she was quickly discovered. The Restoration government also limited the numbers of vivandières, and purged the troops of those whose sympathies were not clearly royalist.[126]

Conclusion

Men and women used revolutionary and Napoleonic tools to herald a royalist peace, even as they attacked the political orders that had produced those tools. Playwrights, artists, and songwriters recycled familiar ways of imagining soldiers' homecomings and celebrating peace. Officials adapted Napoleonic rituals, like state-sponsored weddings, to mark major events in a royalist order. While these references provided convenient and tempting blueprints, they were difficult to use. Fantasies of the romantic return of handsome soldier-heroes clashed with the realities of mass demobilization and Restoration denunciation of conscription. Celebrating rosières and state-sponsored weddings promised to bolster royal power, but only if weddings could be separated from rewards for military service and heroic injury.

Royalists did not want to abandon models of martial masculinity completely. One solution to reconciling virility with loyalty to a peacetime king was to proclaim that all French men were warriors, but only in defense of the throne. Songs in 1815 included lines like "If it's necessary to defend a father / the French are all soldiers," and "To combat tyranny, All French are good soldiers."[127] Such language asserted masculine militancy but emphasized soldiers' role in defending their father-king rather than in quests for personal glory. Since France was at peace in 1815 (after the Hundred Days), lines also suggested a readiness to take up weapons without requiring men to fight, focusing on imagined future heroism, rather than on veterans.

Some songs also celebrated the return of love to a postwar world. The song "Glory to Henri" called on a soldier to "come down from your ramparts, kneel by your mistress. . . . Cherish peace without weakness, on the field of love and the camp of honor." "Laments of a Troubadour" similarly proclaimed, "When the god of war terrified the earth, the gentle troubadour no longer sang of love. . . . With the return of the Bourbons, we can begin again . . . peace in its turn will

124. Under the title *Mémoires d'une contemporaine.*

125. Sutter, *Les campagnes de Mademoiselle Thérèse Figueur.*

126. Cardoza, "'Habits Appropriate to Her Sex,'" 199.

127. "Soyons tous soldats" and "La nouvelle Marseillaise," in *Le chansonnier royal, ou passetemps des bons français*, 40, 70; "Soyons tous soldats" also appears in *Chansonnier des amis du roi et des Bourbons contenant les chansons les plus piquants*, 69.

bring back love."[128] Such constructions presented romance as reward for military glory, while suggesting that love might ultimately substitute for glory.

Other postwar cultural works push us to reconsider what might seem to be a universal symbolism of mothers mourning for their lost sons. Images of mothers desperate for peace in early nineteenth-century France reflected real anguish and drew on established repertoires for confronting war. They also served ideological purposes and instrumentalized displays of emotion distinct to the period. In contrast to images of mothers during and after World War I, these did not embody collective suffering. While royalists painted Napoleon's regime as an unnatural order, in which mothers feared to have sons or hoped that boys would be born too weak to be conscripted, they quickly turned attention away from anguish to joy in a postwar world. They drew attention from problematic veterans to happy civilians. If images of a militantly patriotic women helped legitimate war and revolutionary state power, those of grateful peace-loving women served instead to celebrate the end of war and the return of royalist power.

At the same time, the Restoration state still had to confront the question of women who had taken up arms, whether in defense of Revolution or the royalist cause. Here too we can see forms of cultural recycling, as those in shifting regimes adapted earlier references to women warriors. The royalist government heralded the courage of certain royalist women warriors, but distinguished women veterans from male soldiers seen as deserving true recognition. As the decision to limit the recognition given to veterans suggests, these cultural frameworks had real impacts and uses. In the next chapter we turn from these cultural struggles to the lived experiences of the aftermath of war.

128. "Plaintes d'un troubadour" appeared in *Le chansonnier des amis du roi et des Bourbons, contenant les chansons les plus piquants*, 25–26; and *Le chansonnier royal, ou passetemps des bons français*, 73–75.

CHAPTER NINE

Wishing for the Death of the Woman Who Saved His Life: Living with the Aftermath of War

IN MARCH 1815, a farmer in northern France proclaimed his desire to marry a woman neighbor; the proposed match met with approval from both their families. There was only one problem.[1] The farmer had married in 1799 to escape the then new laws on conscription. Aged nineteen, he had wed a seventy-six-year-old woman; the marriage had saved him from becoming part of Napoleon's war machine. The couple never lived together. She soon moved to another village, and their "ghost marriage" ended when she died in December 1812. But the woman he now wanted to marry was the granddaughter of his former wife and technically his own granddaughter; the law banned their union.[2]

Another case from the archives reveals a young woman from southern France who petitioned the king in June 1814. She had only one brother, known for his skill making knives; both she and her widowed mother depended on his support. While her brother had initially been exempted because of his status as the only son of a widow, he was called up in 1813. To save her sibling, Marguerite Bladinières persuaded a local girl to marry him; the girl consented only on the grounds that Marguerite render the same service to another young man. Now that peace had come, both Marguerite and her brother regretted their hasty marriages.[3]

1. An early version of this chapter first appeared as Heuer, "Réduit à désirer la mort d'une femme."

2. AN BB / 15 / 205, Pas de Calais, Condette, 24 mars 1815, Ficheux.

3. AN BB / 15 / 205, Lot, Puy l'Eveque, 11 juin 1814, Bladinières.

Indeed, because marriage promised an escape from Napoleon's war machine, couples often wed precipitously and made wildly mismatched alliances. Young men married widows or spinsters in their eighties or even nineties, sometimes purchasing their consent. They also turned to middle-aged women whose poor health or questionable sanity had kept them single. Girls were pressured by their parents and neighbors into loveless matches, perhaps reassured by the idea that they were rescuing a fellow villager from death on the battlefields.

These couples anticipated that they would separate once peace finally arrived. Yet the strictures of the Napoleonic Civil Code made divorce difficult for them, while the abolition of divorce on May 8, 1816, would make it impossible. Annulment was of limited use. It was primarily associated with religious marriages. In most of these cases, couples' bonds were civil and remained legal whether or not they wed in church. Even those whose marriages had ended sometimes found themselves bound to their paper partners, like the farmer in love with his legal granddaughter. Thwarted in their efforts to separate, many turned to the government in hopes of a special dispensation that would end their predicament.

Their stories reveal how desperately some families sought to escape military service, as well as the unintended consequences of their strategies. In this chapter, we turn from the cultural negotiations of a postwar order to the lived experience of the aftermath of war. We touch on myriad practical challenges, from the legal difficulties that could face veterans seeking marriage to the challenges of establishing the fate of missing family members. Deserters struggled to regularize their status, while contemporaries argued about whether those who had contracted for a replacement to fight in their stead were required to honor those contracts once peace had arrived.[4] Like the pamphlets and plays we examined in previous chapters, such struggles show us just how much the reverberations of war continued after formal peace treaties were signed, and how much they affected those seemingly far from battle.

We focus most, however, on these paper marriages. They allow us to test what happened when the rhetoric of the Bourbon regime we saw in previous chapters—that of peacemakers healing the woes caused by Napoleon's war machine, and of a beneficent father-king restoring liberty to French families—was challenged by petitioners trying to use such language for their own purposes. In denouncing their false marriages, men and women passed judgment on revolutionary and Napoleonic wars and their legacies, linking the hardships of the home front to the battlefield, and the rash acts of the "usurper and tyrant" of the Empire to domestic disorder. Looking closely at their stories reveals what love, the free choice of a partner, and personal liberty could mean in an order that both enshrined and distrusted such principles. It also

4. On replacements, see Heuer, "Neither Cowardly nor Greedy?"

reveals how legal and social negotiations affected postwar gender relations, as authorities reconsidered the degree to which masculinity required military zeal, the limits of paternal control, and the appropriate relationships between domestic and military power.

The Practical Challenges of Postwar Order

Negotiating the aftermath of war came with myriad practical challenges for individuals and their families or potential families. One of the most pressing challenges was deciding whether the weddings of former veterans—so heralded by poets and playwrights—could actually take place. The imperial decree of June 16, 1808, had reinstated Old Regime measures mandating that soldiers and noncommissioned officers who wanted to marry had to obtain permission from the minister of war or the administrative council of their corps. On December 21, 1808, this was extended to *réformés*, officers released from active duty. The law intended to prevent officers from making unsuitable marriages that could lessen the respect owed to their station. Since officers who were not in active duty could still be called back, the same restriction applied.[5] These measures remained in place as the Empire ended.

As veterans returned home in 1814, many claimed that because peace had arrived, they should be allowed to marry. Local administrators often appeared convinced by their arguments. The public prosecutor in the Somme, for example, pleaded for an urgent response from central authorities on August 18, 1814, arguing that existing dispositions seemed only to be "the necessary consequences of the state of perpetual war that Napoleon devoted himself to." Since that war had finally ended, restrictions on marriage should too. Other administrators made similar requests. The mayor of Charenton-le-Pont argued in September 1814 that an "infinity of soldiers" were returning and wanted to marry. None had been domiciled in the same place for six months, a legal prerequisite for marriage; and almost none had permission from their superiors to wed. For those who had been released from prisoner-of-war camps, permission could be impossible to obtain, as their corps had often been dissolved. The mayor asked that formalities be set aside, at least for those who had been born in the commune, had family there, and were legally adult. An enforced wait would hurt both public morality and the interests of the state. Soldiers might also be prevented from making good marriages. The unstated implication was that women would find other partners in the interim.[6]

5. *Bulletin des lois,* no. 220, law no. 4032, Avis du conseil d'état sur les formalités pour le mariage des officiers reformés. See also Duval, *Étapes de la citoyenneté,* 54–55.

6. AN BB / 15 / 206, Lettre du maire de Charenton-le-Pont au ministre de la justice, 11 septembre 1815.

In the short term, the minister of justice responded that only those who formally retired could be dispensed from formalities.[7] In postwar confusion, local authorities sometimes expedited marriages anyway, and questions of sufficient residence soon became less critical. Yet subsequent measures continued to constrain veterans' relationships. A circular from February 15, 1815, retook Napoleonic stipulations and required authorities in the domicile of the future bride to verify her morality and economic status and what she could expect to inherit from her family; decrees from November 1817 and March 1818 further restricted procedures.[8] Individual circumstances compounded legal complications. The status of deserters remained murky, and individuals were uncertain of their rights. Former prisoners of war who wanted to wed French women could be considered deserters by their homelands, unable to acquire the paperwork to arrange their marriages. Conversely, French combatants who had married in war-torn areas outside of France could face challenges to the validity of their own liaisons.[9]

If men and women struggled to negotiate the legal complexities of family life for veterans, former deserters, and prisoners of war in France, many families also desperately sought to discover the fate of those missing in action. The archetypical figure is the title character in Balzac's novel *Colonel Chabert*, written in 1832 but set in the immediate aftermath of the Napoleonic wars. Chabert had been reported dead; but he—or possibly an imposter—returned home seeking to resume his prewar life. Chabert was fictional and serious identity fraud rare, but doubts about whether veterans had survived were common. Natalie Petiteau has used the phrase "impossible mourning" to describe the situations of families worried that their sons, brothers, or spouses had died, but unable to get confirmation.[10] While the prolonged silence of men in the troops had long been a concern, the absence of news became pressing with mass demobilization, when most men were released from service, prisons, and hospitals and allowed to return home, or at least to contact their families. Parents and siblings could remain in prolonged limbo, unable to fully grieve, or to divide up inheritances and deal with familial business without knowing what had happened to a missing man.

Joseph Baudlier's plea captures this sense of frustration well. His son had been called up in 1813 and disappeared sometime in 1815. In December 1817, Baudlier tried to sort out inheritances for his children, and lamented how impossible it could be to confirm the fates of former combatants: "There are

7. See various cases in AN BB / 15 / 206.

8. *Circulaire ministériel du 15 février 1815, aux lieutenants-généraux, relative aux formalités à remplir par les officiers qui désirent obtenir des permissions de mariage,* in Durat-Lasalle, *Droit et législation des armeés de terre et de mer,* 3:29.

9. For cases touching on all these themes, see the dossiers in AN BB / 15 / 207.

10. Petiteau, *Lendemains d'empire,* 114. On the challenges of confirming deaths, Hantraye, *Les cosaques aux Champs-Élysées,* 256–64.

undoubtedly many parents in my position, after the system of war consecrated by the monster who caused so much harm to our patrie. Must their youngest children be deprived of the benefits of law because their older brothers perished in some ambush or were massacred or mutilated mercilessly and in the most barbarous manner?"[11]

The government sought uneasily to expedite the process for confirming deaths, without wanting to make it easier to dissolve or deny family bonds. The Restoration government put into place short-term measures in 1814, as combatants began to return. A law issued on July 3, 1816, regularized procedures for declaring absent or legally dead soldiers, administrators, and employees of the armed forces who had disappeared between the declaration of war on April 20, 1792, and the peace treaty of November 15, 1815.[12] A January 13, 1817, law elaborated on these procedures. Following the Civil Code, presumptive heirs or spouses could request that men's absence be formally established. A man could be declared dead if it was proven that he had been missing without news for two years if his unit had served in Europe or four years if the corps had served farther afield. The measure applied to personnel associated with the troops.[13]

The archives contain proportionately more cases of parents and siblings seeking to learn the fate of their relatives than those of wives. This reflects the renewed constraints on military marriage after 1808, and the general decline in the number of married men in the troops after the radical Revolution. But the fate of women—tied to missing spouses by potentially indissoluble bonds—was particularly vexed. As one lamented, they were financially and socially limited, and doomed to "perpetual celibacy" unless they could prove their spouses' deaths.[14]

"TO SAVE MYSELF FROM CONSCRIPTION . . . I'LL MARRY YOU FOR SHOW"

Men and women who had married to avoid conscription could find themselves in similar situations. They were partners only on paper, but those paper bonds appeared indissoluble. Restoration writers turned from general denunciations of the horrors of conscription that we saw in the previous chapter to specific complaints about the ill-assorted marriages it provoked.

11. AN C / 2027, Baudlier.

12. *Obligations qu'auront à remplir les pères et mères de famille qui voudront faire déclarer l'absence.*

13. *Bulletin des lois,* no. 131, law no. 1530, Loi relative aux moyens de constater le sort des militaires absents, le 13 janvier 1817.

14. AN C / 2036, Gazet, la dame, demande que les femmes de militaires absens depuis longtemps et qui n'ont point donné de leurs nouvelles, puissent se remarier.

For example, the naturalist and fervent royalist Mouton-Fontenille de Laclotte contended that

> The young men destined to the odious sacrifice of conscription sought to use the bonds of marriage to avoid the law that threatened them. The union that should have been the happiness of their lives became a source of endless calamities. These marriages of circumstance, forced in the majority of cases, in which love, friendship, and tenderness were never consulted, often present the monstrous alliance of decrepitude with youth. . . . Others, more compatible in terms of age, were not by affinity. All was disparate, all disproportionate: age, tastes, temperament, character, social status.[15]

De Laclotte implied that the Napoleonic regime had been marked by both national and domestic disorder, and that the returned monarch would bring back harmony.

If polemical tracts denounced rushed marriages, individuals' stories reveal both how contemporaries actually viewed such marriages and the strategies they adopted to persuade authorities to end their alliances. Not surprisingly, couples contended that they had never lived together and had no children. Such claims reflect long-held understandings of the purpose of marriage. But petitioners also made arguments specific to the circumstances of the early Restoration. They linked individual marriages to the ravages of war and portrayed themselves as victims of a tyrant, supplicants who could only be rescued by a paternal monarch. They also connected their personal stories to larger affronts to religious and social order and constraints on liberty.

In the rest of this chapter, we look first at the strategies men and women adopted to negotiate paper marriages and present them as valid under Napoleon, the extent to which officials were aware of such marriages, and the measures they took to crack down on such arrangements. Historians have long noted that marriage rates in France rose with conscription drafts, especially in the desperate days of 1813. This phenomenon is often treated as a historical curiosity, or more seriously, as one aspect of draft evasion. Military historians, demographers, and specialists in the administrative power of the Napoleonic state have been most interested in these marriages; scholars of family, gender, and social history have paid less attention.[16] Scholars who have considered marriages as draft evasion have drawn primarily on the records compiled by

15. Mouton-Fontenille de Laclotte, *La France en délire*, 59–60.

16. For anecdotal accounts, see Dänzer-Kantof, *La vie des français*, 170; and Marchioni, *Les mots de l'empire*, 35. Studies of efforts to avoid service include Forrest, *Conscripts and Deserters;* Woloch, *The New Regime* and "Napoleonic Conscription"; Bergès, *Résister à la conscription;* Pigeard, *La conscription au temps de Napoléon*; and Crépin, "La France plurielle."

officials during wartime.[17] Such documents illuminate the extent of desertion and resistance to recruitment, and the differing responses to the military across France. They also reveal strategies that officials adopted to uncover fraud or to respond to evidence of it. Yet they give little sense of the men and women who married to escape conscription, the ways they circumvented official investigation, or their fates after their precipitous weddings.

A series of previously unexploited petitions between 1814 and 1819, as well as associated court cases, legislative debates, and administrative correspondence, provide more information about these couples.[18] Their petitions reveal both family dynamics and popular understandings of marriage. They show a particular hybrid of revolutionary and antirevolutionary rhetoric in the wake of political upheaval and war. Petitioners insisted on mutual consent and free choice in marriage, in terms that echoed revolutionary transformations of family. They also invoked central preoccupations of the Bourbon regime, including religion, honor, and respect for legitimate authority. But they did so to further a cause that seemed counter to such preoccupations: the dissolution of marriage. Melding these arguments required careful—if often unsuccessful—efforts to reframe liberty and social order in terms that would be acceptable to restored Catholic monarchy.

In most cases, central authorities dismissed petitioners and told them to try their luck in the courts. To explore what happened when individuals brought cases to trial, we turn to the town of Cahors, in the department of the Lot, where the surviving records are particularly rich. In late 1815 and 1816, the lower court in Cahors, the Tribunal of First Instance, regularly nullified such liaisons. Local judges put forth strong arguments about the importance of consent in marriage. They cited technical grounds for dissolving marriages, from the inability of underage women to commit to a union to the fact that a wedding had taken place without sufficient publicity. But local authorities also clearly considered that if a marriage had been undertaken to avoid conscription and the couple had not lived together, it was not a binding contract, regardless of other circumstances. Chastised by central authorities for their apparent disrespect for the sanctity of marriage, local officials sometimes reversed their approach to deny most demands for legal annulment. Higher administrators, appalled that the court had dissolved marriages at all, continued to complain. They sought to overturn earlier annulments, and ultimately took a case to the Supreme Court.

17. Bergès notes retrospective accounts of *mariages blancs* but focuses on the Aquitaine region. Bergès, *Résister à la conscription*, 212–13. Apparently inspired by one of early articles, Cédric Istasse has considered Belgian requests to have marriages annulled after Napoleonic rule. Istasse, "Les fraudeurs."

18. The richest cache of petitions is in AN BB / 15 / 205. Others are in AN C / 2026 through C / 2059, petitions to the Chambre des députés from 1814 to 1818. Individual petitions are scattered in the AN BB / 16 series.

THE PETITIONERS

Supplicants identified themselves with "a great number of honest families" and "an infinity of spouses, if one can use the term for individuals who did not really want to marry."[19] Both petitioners and administrators sometimes provided numbers. A notary reported twelve hundred petitions in the region of Picardie in August 1814.[20] The prefect of the Loire claimed in September 1814 that at least three hundred men and women had been affected in his department. A group from the same department declared that there were about fifty cases in their arrondissement, one of three in the Loire, and that if "terror had had the same results across the kingdom," there were at least thirty thousand people "married without really being married."[21]

It is impossible to get definitive numbers of how many people had wed to avoid military service. Because acceptance or resistance to conscription had varied so much across France, extrapolating from any given community does not provide an accurate total. The Loire, for example, had a relatively high percentage of deserters and draft dodgers, but fewer than the Gironde or Lozère.[22] Recourse to paper marriages as a strategy for avoiding conscription also depended partly on local demography and how cognizant or tolerant authorities were of such liaisons.

Those who had wed out of expediency but decided to make the best of a bad match or to wait for the death of an elderly partner, or who had quietly circumvented legal circumstances, did not come to authorities' attention. Men and women who had arranged paper marriages during the Napoleonic era had tried to disguise the extent to which both they and others in their communities had engaged in fraudulent marriages; during the Restoration, they sought instead to play up the number of people affected. Doing so made their requests seem part of a social problem worthy of governmental attention, rather than individual foolishness or selfishness.

The archives reveal petitions and queries from at least half the departments in France, especially in the southwest, the Rhône Alpes, and the north. Corresponding to general patterns of acceptance of, or resistance to, conscription, there were fewest cases in the northeast and the Ile-de-France.[23] Regardless of the exact numbers, the phenomenon was far from insignificant. It was also endemic.

19. AN BB / 15 / 205, Lozère et Calvados; C / 2073, Allain.

20. AN BB / 15 / 205, R2, 2004.

21. AN BB / 15 / 205, R2, 2225.

22. Forrest, *Conscripts and Deserters*, 2.

23. For regional reactions, see the above works by Forrest, Woloch, Bèrges, and Pigeard. See also Lannoy, "Préfets et conscription dans la Manche"; and Daly, "Conscription and Corruption."

The problem of deciding whether marriages should exempt men from military service had long bedeviled authorities. It had become a constant preoccupation after the first official law on conscription, the 1798 Jourdan Law. Officials charged with executing conscription reported a variety of doubtful marriages. They were most concerned by obvious fraud and by cases where priests or local authorities had conspired to antedate marriages, but also called attention to obviously mismatched liaisons and ones that seemed suspiciously rushed.

At the time of the Jourdan decree, the 1792 law still governed marriage, and allowed for far easier separation than would the Napoleonic Civil Code. Couples could realistically believe that they would be able to divorce once peace arrived. The extent to which this assumption permeated popular culture is suggested by a play performed in Douai in March 1801, *The Preliminaries of Peace or the Lovers Reunited*, intended to celebrate the Treaty of Lunéville between France and Austria. The play features a hapless peasant who courts a young girl only out of cowardice; as he explains in an aside, "To save myself from conscription / by a legitimate means / I'll make my declaration / and marry you for show / But once the danger's passed / I'll get divorced."[24]

As we have seen, the 1801 treaty brought only a short-lived peace. Mobilization under the Napoleonic Empire led to new attempts to evade conscription. While the 1804 Civil Code made divorce more difficult to obtain, it did not ban it, and a paper marriage could still appear an attractive means of escaping military service. The practice seems to have become especially common after supplementary drafts were introduced in 1809.[25] Conscripts who had initially drawn lottery numbers that would keep them from service, but who were afraid that they would be convoked for a supplementary draft, sought desperately to secure their fates.

Many authorities were suspicious of mismatched marriages, like the prefect of the department of the Nord, who complained in November 1809 about eighteen marriages between youths and elderly women—the oldest of whom was ninety-nine.[26] Such marriages, like fraud, self-mutilation, desertion, and other strategies for avoiding military service, made recruitment harder. But paper marriages seemed particularly immoral. On October 13, 1813, the prefect of the department of the Aisne denounced "monstrous marriages that are the height of the most shameful cowardice." Men who arranged such marriages were not simply craven weaklings who refused to fight. They were worse: inhuman beasts "who rebel against the voice of the patrie and of honor, and profane, under the protection of the laws, the most sacred of all bonds." He labeled marriages between young men and women over fifty as particularly "contrary to nature and good morals" and concluded that when subterfuge was

24. Courtois, *Les préliminaires de paix ou les amans réunis*, 38.

25. Woloch, *The New Regime*, 421.

26. AN AF / IV / 1124, Rapport du ministre de la guerre à l'Empereur, 19 juillet 1809.

indisputable, conscripts should be sent to fight even if their marriages were theoretically valid.[27]

The most serious accusation was that avoiding military service through a fake marriage did not reduce the number of people the state took to fight. It simply shifted the burden. Fake marriages forced the departure of men needed at home in their role as sons supporting infirm parents or orphaned siblings.[28] This was especially true in departments like the hard-hit Aisne, where the prefect explained that he had been prevented from fulfilling conscription quotas by mismatched marriages and had ultimately sent off twenty conscripts who were technically, but not realistically, wed.[29]

Young men—often at their parents' behest—continued to try to use fake marriages to escape the military, although they became more creative in their arrangements as authorities intensified efforts to track down draft dodgers. As petitioners from the department of the Somme later explained, potential conscripts in their town initially married women over fifty. This worked until the Draft of 300,000 Men in February 1813. At that point, so many marriages took place that recruitment authorities concluded that mismatched alliances should not excuse recruits from military service. Young men did not abandon marriage as a strategy for evading conscription but sought to become less obvious. They tied their fates to women who were only in their thirties or forties, but whose infirmities or poor health made them otherwise unlikely candidates for marriage.[30]

In other cases, young women appeared to have been pressured into marriage, often as teenagers. These unions would have appeared more plausible to authorities. Normally, a fifteen- or sixteen-year-old girl would not wed, but under the Napoleonic Civil Code, she could legally do so. Such matches did not raise the red flags that accompanied unions between eighteen-year-old men and eighty-year-old women. But their seeming legitimacy could mask desperation or coercion.

Most supplicants in the early Restoration who sought a divorce or annulment of paper marriages had been wed in 1813. The reasons for this were twofold. The military debacles of 1813 brought strong pressure to find more soldiers.[31] As men of conscription age sought to avoid new drafts, the marriage rate soared across France. André Armengaud has charted a jump from a national average of fewer than 14 marriages per 1,000 inhabitants in 1811 to

27. AN F / 7 / 3583, Aisne.

28. Forrest, *Conscripts and Deserters*, 50–52; and AN F / 7 / 3583, Lettre du Ministère de la guerre au monsieur le conseilleur d'état chargé du 1er arrondissement de la police générale, 23 octobre 1813.

29. AN F / 9/ 151, Lettre de préfet de l'Aisne au ministre de l'intérieur, 2 janvier 1814.

30. AN C / 2027, Beaumetz.

31. For reports on different measures, see AN F / 7 / 3583; for an overview of conscription in 1813, Woloch, "Napoleonic Conscription."

almost 27 in 1813. The numbers plunged again after 1813. Similar numbers appeared more locally. For example, in Toulouse, there were 21.8 new spouses for every 1,000 inhabitants in 1813; the rate fell to 13.5 the following year, after war ended.[32]

Legal constraints also left many of those who married in 1813 desperate to separate. It was usually impossible for them to petition for divorce for cause: in most cases, neither partner had committed adultery or harmed the other through outrageous conduct, ill usage, or grievous injuries. Moreover, divorces for cause required living together, which most of these couples did not do. The logical option would appear divorce for mutual consent. But that was only an option if a man was over twenty-five and a woman over twenty-one; men who had married to escape conscription were often far younger. Most couples who petitioned in 1814 or 1815 had also been married for less than the two years required before they could legally divorce. When rumors began to circulate in spring 1816 that divorce would be abolished, they became increasingly desperate, and pled with authorities for a special exemption if divorce was outlawed.

Strategies for Overturning Paper Marriages

Many different writers pleaded for an end to paper marriages. While authorship can be difficult to determine, petitions include letters from not only individual men and women, but also their parents, groups from the same village or region, and concerned priests and local authorities. Some individuals clearly composed letters themselves. In other cases, supplicants were illiterate or unprepared to draft persuasive pleas to central authority; as for many revolutionary petitioners, their stories were filtered through intermediaries trained in legal discourse and literary devices. Petitioners sometimes submitted versions of their petitions to multiple authorities, whether out of uncertainty about who to appeal to or in hopes of finding a more sympathetic ear. For example, Antoinette Poncet, an illiterate servant of a Lyonnais dyer, beseeched both the duchesse de Berry and the duc d'Angoulême because they had passed through her home city and might be powerful intermediaries.[33] Groups of petitioners could also be unsure of the best venue for pleading their cause. For example, several couples in the commune of Saint-Sauveur, in the department of the Manche, petitioned the Chamber of Deputies in November 1815; they turned to the minister of justice in January 1816.[34]

The petitions also show the extent to which paper marriages reflected familial arrangements. Many were written by parents on behalf of their sons,

32. Armengaud, "Mariages et naissances." For a year-by-year table of marriages in Paris showing the 1813 peak, see Pigeard, *La conscription au temps de Napoléon*, 141.

33. Ultimately forwarded to the minister of justice; AN BB / 15 / 205, Poncet.

34. AN C / 2047 and BB / 15 / 205.

and a roughly equal number on behalf of their daughters. In a sharp contrast to revolutionary patterns of divorce, more men than women petitioned the government to dissolve their marriages.[35] When women did petition, they tended to be girls who had been persuaded to sign marriage records by their parents or neighbors, not indigent or infirm older women whose consent had often been purchased rather than coerced.

Those seeking the end of their marriages made several kinds of arguments. Not surprisingly, couples contended that they had never lived together and had no children. They sought to prove that their marriages were purely civil and not religious, disparaging both the bonds of civil marriage and the procedures of divorce as perverse revolutionary inventions. But they also adapted aspects of revolutionary discourse to portray their marriages as forced bonds, rather than freely made unions, and identified such bonds as scandalous affronts against nature. At the same time, they played heavily on the returned monarchy's denunciation of conscription, arguing that the ultimate force behind their marriages was Napoleon's despotic government. Cowardliness or cruelty were both real and the product of a tyrant's power, which had led men and women to behave in ways that would not have happened in peacetime or under a more benevolent regime.

A REGISTRATION, NOT A MARRIAGE: RELIGION, SCANDAL, AND SOCIAL ORDER

Almost every petitioner sought to establish that his or her marriage was a civil bond, but not a religious one. While the 1791 constitution had made marriage into a purely civil contract, few in the early Restoration seemed to accept this concept. Many petitioners added qualifications to paint civil bonds as fictive, referring to "what one calls civil marriage," "pretend marriage," or "sham marriage." Others sought terms that would distinguish their contracts from true marriage, like "registration" or "civil act."[36]

If possible, supplicants provided evidence of their belief in the centrality of religion. A farmer in the Tarn-et-Garonne thus insisted that his marriage contract had specified that church ceremonies would follow; since the ceremonies had not taken place, his marriage should be considered illegitimate.[37] Others included testimony from neighbors about their religious convictions

35. Women during the Revolution petitioned for divorce one and a half times more often than men. Phillips, *Family Breakdown*, 57. The proportion of women petitioners under the Civil Code of 1804 was similar to under the 1792 law.

36. Examples include AN C / 2047, Saint-Sauveur; C / 2038, Jean B15–205, Marguerite Blandières, and the petition for the mayor of Vernon; and C / 2028, Marie Françoise Bouvet.

37. AN BB / 15 / 205, R2, 3824.

or asked priests to write on their behalf.[38] A few supplicants reported being shocked to discover that their civil marriages were binding; for example, an 1817 petition on behalf of another couple in the Tarn-et-Garonne, Antoine Cavaille and Marie Maynard, described the two as planning their weddings to other partners only to discover to their amazement that the civil marriage they had registered in 1810 bound them to each other.[39]

In the early Restoration, such arguments seemed likely to fall on receptive ears. The Chamber of Deputies regularly received petitions proposing that the laws be changed so that marriage would only be considered legitimate when sanctioned by the church.[40] Even under Napoleon, priests had sought to hold religious ceremonies to wed couples who had previously been married only civilly. Restoration "missionaries," fervent religious men who sought to re-Christianize France after the experiences of the Revolution and the Empire, intensified efforts to convert civil marriages into religious bonds. In some cases, devout priests refused burial to men and women who had been married civilly, but who had not sanctified their bonds by church ceremonies.[41]

In trying to discredit the bonds of their marriages, petitioners also sought to appeal to Restoration officials' horror of scandal. Those seeking to abolish divorce in the early Restoration denounced civil marriages as an abomination. For example, the conservative newspaper *L'ami de religion* rejoiced in March 1816 that divorce would soon be abolished and anticipated an end to "scandalous marriages that religion does not consecrate."[42]

Petitioners used similar terms. They referred to these marriages as "the most scandalous disorder," "truly scandalous unions," "the scandal of society," and so forth.[43] Here they echoed Napoleonic officials, who had similarly denounced marriages, especially unions between young men and old women, as affronts to nature and morals.[44] But for Napoleonic authorities, scandal had been the fraud and selfishness of men who resorted to such measures.

38. See the 1814 petition from the curé Jaunes for his parishioners in the Vendée in AN C / 2038; and the July 1816 petition from the curé of Saint-Jean-des-Bois in Orne, for a young man in his parish, in AN BB / 15 / 205.

39. AN C / 2038, Lentillac.

40. For example, AN C / 2032, Courtois, curé de Pilon, Meuse, voudroit qu'on déclarait illégitimes tous les mariages contractés civilement sans avoir été sanctionnés par la bénédiction du prêtre; and AN C / 2039, Leeussan, maire du Moraux, Dept. du Lot et Garonne, demande que la législation ne reconnaisse de mariage, qu'après la sanctification suivant la loi de la religion des époux. The first is undated but precedes the 1816 abolition of divorce; the second is from March 1, 1816.

41. AN F / 7 / 3742 and F / 7 / 3743.

42. *L'ami de la religion: Journal ecclésiastique, politique, et littéraire*, no. 163, March 2, 1816, 87.

43. AN C / 2042, Montmession; C / 2028, Bouvier; and C / 2038, Jaunes.

44. For example, in October 1813, the minister of war denounced unions between young men and old women as scandalous. AN F / 7 / 3583.

For petitioners, the scandal was one of loveless marriages, made permanent even though they were unsanctified by the church and could never produce children. In such circumstances, allowing marriages to continue was a scandal; divorce or annulment was not.

Petitioners also contended that ending their marriages was in the interests of the state. This is particularly clear in a petition from inhabitants of the department of the Somme. They proclaimed that to escape "the most monstrous of military systems, . . . we separated ourselves from the masses of unfortunate men that war has since mowed down." Like others, they lamented the "bonds formed by necessity," but also hinted at risks of allowing paper marriages to continue: "Celibacy in marriage is often the source of the greatest crimes." They insisted, "ill-assorted marriages [were] condemned by nature and the principles of a paternal government." They concluded by appealing to a king's desire to increase his subjects, depicting themselves as eager "to become fathers of families and pay the sacred debt they owe to France and to their king."[45]

Complaints about scandal and the unnaturalness of their unions required petitioners to separate their cases from valid marriages, which they acknowledged should be permanent. Many petitioners derided divorce as a revolutionary abomination and congratulated the monarchy on abolishing it. Two men in the Loire thus explained in early 1816 that they had both anticipated divorcing by mutual consent but had decided not to do so because "divorce was repugnant to their consciences." More pragmatically, they feared they would not have time to complete the formalities. Similarly, in March 1817, Antoine Cavaille in the Tarn-et-Garonne commended the Chamber of Deputies: "You have abolished the law that authorized divorce. All good Frenchmen have applauded this measure ordered by morality and safety."[46]

Petitioners' insistence on religious benediction of marriages suggests that the secularization of the Revolution had limited effects, at least in more remote regions. But petitioners' rhetoric also reveals more instrumental references to honor and religion. They sought to use the regime's moralizing language for their own purpose, expressing their horror at divorce for real marriage while beseeching the government to end the scandal of their own unnatural and unsanctified bonds.

LOVE AND TYRANNY

If petitioners insisted on the secular and scandalous nature of their paper marriages, they also equated their marriages to slavery. "Chained by a sterile bond," doomed to "ghastly slavery," eager to bless a government that would

45. AN C / 2045, Les soussignés, habitants de la commune de Prouville, arrondissement de Doullens, département de la Somme.

46. AN C / 2027, Barbeis; AN C / 2030, Cavaille.

"break the yoke of his captivity"; such phrases appear in almost every petition.[47] In itself, comparing unhappy marriage to slavery was scarcely new. Champions of divorce during the Revolution constantly invoked liberty and captivity.[48] Men and women seeking divorce or legal separation during the Napoleonic era were more likely to refer to specific causes of marital distress, but still used the rhetoric of slavery.

Such metaphors took on new valences in the early Restoration, as petitioners sought to demonstrate that their marriages were invalid not because of individual misbehavior or the oppressive nature of unbreakable contracts, but because of particular historical circumstances. The constraints of Napoleon's war machine had enslaved them. In this logic, the emperor's tyranny had subjugated good French men; forcing men and women to remain with their paper spouses perpetuated this slavery.

Not surprisingly, supplicants invoked any evidence that might demonstrate their lack of consent, as did Marie Mazet, who claimed that her contract was invalid because she had been capable of signing and had not done so.[49] Petitioners sometimes claimed to have been wed without their advance agreement or knowledge of the arrangements. Pierre Blanc, for example, maintained that his father had informed him of the marriage on the day of his wedding; he did not know his bride, the daughter of a local papermaker.[50] Even those who had technically chosen their own spouses argued that they had been too rushed to make a real choice: Pierre LaBeauté contended that he had married a seventy-four-year-old woman only because he did not have time to select a real wife.[51]

Individual stories of coerced and precipitous marriages echoed contemporary rhetoric about the domestic and social disorder caused by Napoleon Bonaparte. For example, *France in 1814 and 1815*, a tract published anonymously by a returned émigré, sought to discredit Napoleonic rule by describing the rush for marriage as soon as a draft was announced. The terrified parents of a young man, and their no less panicked son, immediately began a hunt for "a woman willing to sacrifice herself to guarantee the young man's exception from military conscription." The family began their quest at noon; they asked one woman, then a second, a third, a fourth, without finding a willing victim. At midnight, the exhausted parents left their son with relatives and continued the search; they finally found a partner at six in the morning. Based on this contract, the conscript was able to secure his exemption. The couple passed

47. AN C / 2038, Landes; C / 2028, Ronsin; BB / 15 / 205, Jean Sol.

48. On liberty and slavery in revolutionary rhetoric about divorce, see Ronsin, *Le contrat sentimental*; Théry, *Le démariage;* Desan, *The Family on Trial;* and Ruffier-Méray, "La hiérarchie au sein du couple."

49. AN C / 2038, Landes.

50. AN BB / 15 / 205, Blanc.

51. AN BB / 15 / 205, LaBeauté.

each other a few days later without recognizing one another.[52] The émigré's account exaggerated the rush to marriage in some circumstances—families could predict that conscripts would face the draft at least once after their twentieth birthday, and act accordingly—but extraordinary drafts and rumors of possible new drafts did provoke frenzied responses.

Perhaps most often, petitioners pled ignorance of the effects of their civil bonds, suggesting that they had not made free contracts because they had not understood the effects of the law. It is difficult to tell how much ignorance was genuine. Administrative testimony does suggest real confusion, especially in remote areas. But ignorance was also a useful plea for those who did not want to be seen as having chosen their bonds.

Supplicants contended generally that they had been forced by the tyranny of war and Napoleon's state. It was impossible to make a free choice in such conditions. Petitioners referred to conscription as a tyrannical law.[53] Their language echoed many contemporary pamphlets, such as the polemical 1814 *Tombs of the Great Army*. The author identified conscripts as helpless youth and Napoleon as a monster, lamenting the fate of conscripts "under a tyrannical law devoted to the new Minotaur, far hungrier than that of Athens."[54]

For petitioners, such rhetoric not only attacked Napoleon Bonaparte's regime; it also implied that disobedience to tyranny was justified. It directly linked the costs of war on the battlefield and on the home front. A petition for Marie-Anne Eustache, in the department of Hérault, shows these connections with particular eloquence. Eustache explained to the Chamber of Deputies in 1816:

> Conscription has long been the curse of France. On one hand, it destroyed numerous victims on the battlefield; on the other hand, it has placed a mass of individuals under the constraint of disastrous marriages, making them suffer all the burdens of marriages without enjoying its pleasures. It is conscription that has produced these deplorable marriages, which have given birth only to despair and tears; it is conscription that dictated the vows that the mouth pronounced and the heart rejected; it alone formed these knots that the laws recognize but that religion never consecrated, these knots that have never truly been tied but cannot be dissolved.[55]

Eustache's petition portrayed mismatched couples not as actors who had made free decisions about their personal lives, but as innocent victims of a

52. *La France en 1814 et 1815 . . . Lettre de M.D.M à M.W. Bew* (n.p., 1815). The original is in the Lyon Public Library. Extracts, including the above passage, appeared in *L'ambigu ou variétés littéraires et politiques*, vol. 53, no. 471 (April 30, 1816), 180–81.

53. AN BB / 15 / 205; see especially R2, 2145; R2, 2818; and R3, 3144. For a brief analysis of this theme in women's petitions, see Krakovitch, "Les pétitions, seul moyen d'expression."

54. Hapdé, *Les sépulcres de la grande armée*, 41.

55. AN C / 2038. For a second petition by Eustache, AN BB / 15 / 205, Eustache.

cruel system, as much fatalities of a tyrannical law as those killed on the battlefield. She indirectly called attention to the sterility of such marriages, which produced despair rather than children. Eustache added an emotional dimension: for a bond to be legitimate, it had to be accepted by the heart. Many petitioners hinted at the importance of love in legitimating marriages, but for most, the role of tyranny in forcing paper unions promised to be a more effective argument for dissolving their bonds than the absence of affection.

As petitioners insisted that their marriages were one product of Napoleon's despotic rule, they also contended that the new government should restore real liberty. Petitioners sometimes conflated multiple senses of liberty in order to claim that their marriages were symbols of national oppression rather than individual choice. For example, a March 1816 petition on behalf of the inhabitants of Beaumetz acknowledged, "One can ask why they did not marry seriously, rather than having chained their liberty." But, the supplicants continued, the answer is clear "if one considers that on one hand, most had neither a profession or a fortune, and on the other hand, they all were comforted by the hope that they would soon see the end of the despotism under which we suffered, and thus recover their liberty."[56]

When trying to establish that their marriages were forced, petitioners sometimes complained about parental coercion. According to the Civil Code, men under twenty-five and women under twenty-one needed parental permission to marry. Although some older men married as a precaution—especially during the drafts of 1813 that threatened to take many previously exempted—most men seeking to avoid conscription were under twenty-five. Following the Jourdan Law, conscription drafts affected those from twenty to twenty-five. Conscripts' parents were thus usually aware of their sons' plans for marriage and could actively promote such unions. In calling for an end to their bonds, some men invoked parental pressure to show that their consent had been forced; women were even more inclined to do so. More precisely, women who wed in their old age did not refer to parental compulsion, but young women who had registered marriages with conscripts regularly argued that such bonds were not of their choosing.

A petition on behalf of Marie Rose Blanc is typical of many pleas, though she married later than most—on May 24, 1815, during the Hundred Days. She lamented the violence employed to make her marry civilly at the age of fifteen and a half. She had been legally old enough to marry; article 144 of the Civil Code authorized men to marry at age eighteen and women at fifteen. But fifteen was still young; the average age for women to wed was 25.6 in the decade between 1810 and 1819, and 26.4 in 1815.[57] Marie Rose insisted that she

56. AN C / 2027, Beaumetz.

57. Lyons, *Napoleon Bonaparte and the Legacy*, 47; Houdaille, "Marriage under the French Revolution and the First Empire."

had been both too ill and immature to marry but had been forced by ambitious parents who sought to save a young man pursued by the conscription authorities. Afflicted with tuberculosis, she had initially obtained a grace period of four years before she was to live with her new husband, but now wanted only to go to a convent.[58]

Similarly, Marie Françoise Bouvet beseeched the Chamber of Deputies in January 1816 to turn a "paternal regard on my sad situation. I say paternal because my own father betrayed me; I implore you under his name."[59] Bouvet insisted that she had repeatedly voiced her aversion to her proposed husband and protested the marriage. She had ultimately been unable to resist the argument that she would be responsible for her future husband's life if she refused him.

Like Bouvet, many petitioners sought to appeal to the paternal benevolence of authorities.[60] This was a part of a very long tradition of identifying the king as father. It was reinforced by the Bourbon government's depiction of itself as a paternal regime, and Napoleon's rule as the perversion of parental authority. But it had particular relevance in this case, given the role of parental approval of marriage. If parents had been unable to oversee their children's marriages properly, then the father of the French people should take care of his children and remedy this situation.

Yet many petitioners hesitated to disparage their own parents' influence, choosing to emphasize Napoleon's unjust rule over parental force. As we have seen, Bouvet insisted that her marriage was against her will. However, she also depicted her father as a well-intentioned man now full of regrets: "My father has seen my sorrow and regret and laments having been the cause of my own misfortune; he feels it entirely, he reproaches himself bitterly for having forced me to sign an act to which my heart was missing."

Indeed, the theme of parental regrets, like that of parental authority, appears regularly both in the petitions of couples seeking divorce and in those by their parents.[61] For example, Pierre Jean-Baptiste Blanc claimed that he married only because of his father's pressure: "Paternal power trumped all other considerations." In a separate petition, his father acknowledged that he had urged his son to marry, and asked that Pierre, and others in similar situations, be given back "a liberty that they have lost without reflection, most often because of the power of obedience to their parents."[62]

Many parents were truly shocked when they realized that their efforts to save their sons or neighbors' sons had doomed their children to unhappiness,

58. AN BB / 15 / 205, R3, 7837.

59. AN C / 2028, Bouvet.

60. For another striking example, see AN C / 2047, Saint-Sauveur.

61. See especially AN BB / 15 / 205.

62. AN C / 2028, Blanc, le s. demande une loi qui annulle les mariages contractés seulement devant l'officier civil pour s'exempter de la conscription.

ending hopes of grandchildren and family legacies. Yet emphasizing their good intentions was also a strategic choice in appealing to a regime that enshrined paternal authority. It allowed young men, and especially young women, as well as those writing on their behalf, to claim that their marriages were not free choices, while insisting that the real tyranny was Napoleon's war machine.

If these petitioners disparaged revolutionary concepts when praising religious marriage, when equating marriage to slavery, they adopted key elements of revolutionary discourse. Yet their invocations of liberty echoed contemporary attempts to associate rushed and coerced marriages with revolutionary and especially Napoleonic tyranny. These petitions also reveal distinctive aspects to how men and women depicted consent and liberty in the period. In many circumstances, women identified marriage with slavery to argue that they were constrained by unequal legal bonds.[63] Both men and women in paper marriages defined their marriages as enslavement. Yet they had to tread carefully when moving from general claims that they were forced to marry by conscription law to describing immediate parental pressure to wed; they thus presented parental power as well-intentioned rather than despotic.

MADWOMEN AND BRUTES, COWARDS AND HEROES

If petitioners invoked religion, honor, and liberty, they also struggled with the legacies of martial masculinity, especially the stakes of refusing to fight for Napoleon's army. Here petitioners rarely touched on themes raised by those reluctant to fight earlier, like economic responsibilities to family. Instead, they hesitated whether to label this reluctance as cowardice or courage. Women sometimes disparaged their husbands' weakness—but also excused that weakness by linking it to Napoleon's illegitimate power. This ambivalence parallels petitioners' attempts to decry parental pressure while accepting the legitimacy of parental power. It is captured by a petition for Etinnette Vial, who presented herself as married in December 1813 at the age of fifteen years and twenty-three days. She had been legally old enough to marry, but by less than a month. Vial beseeched the king as "the friend, the protector, the father of the French" to help her. She described her husband, André Grand, as a coward and as having a "sour character, a black soul, and a hard heart." He was "sufficiently scheming" that he "succeeded odiously in escaping the kidnapping and abduction of young men from the breast of their families, when hideous despotism nurtured fury and insanity among your unfortunate subjects."[64] The rhetoric of the petition simultaneously disparaged her husband's "odious scheming" and suggested that this scheming was legitimate because it was a means to

63. Offen, "How (and Why) the Analogy of Marriage."

64. AN BB / 16 / 658, 1818, 19 juin (R4, 1862), dépt du Rhône, canton Riverie, Etinnette Vial.

escape "kidnapping and abduction." Vial's mixed message reflected a common strategy among women of decrying a bad marriage while depicting a spouse as fellow victim of Napoleon's tyranny.

In contrast, some men portrayed their decision not to fight as an act of loyalty to the monarchy. This was exemplified by François Barrière Bienvenu, who presented himself as ready to do anything for his true monarch: "he preferred to sacrifice his fortune and pay for a replacement, than be obliged himself to carry arms against his legitimate king."[65] Similarly, Pierre Labeauté explained in October 1814 that he had paid for two replacements and when those failed to guarantee his freedom from military service, he had married in 1813, since "it was repugnant, Sire, to his sentiments to shed his blood for a cause so opposed to the interests of your Majesty."[66]

Arguing that one had sent a replacement could be a claim of support for a regime, rather than resistance to it. As we have seen, in the mid-1790s, men and women argued that the replacements they had arranged for themselves or their children in February 1793 were proof of their devotion to the Republic. They or their families had sacrificed twice when, despite their replacements, young men were required to fight in August 1793. When the government reauthorized replacement in 1799, contemporaries sought to downplay its unsavory aspects by portraying substitutes as helping families in need. Pamphleteers during the early Restoration presented the cost of replacements as another example of Napoleon's exploitation of the French people, but the use of substitutions did not prove royalist loyalty.

In general, it was difficult to establish that a petitioner had avoided conscription out of courageous devotion to an absent monarch—especially for a generation who had not been alive when the last king ruled. When petitioners did marshal evidence, it was often on the level of an 1814 memoir for Pierre Jean-Baptiste Blanc in the department of the Aude. Blanc sought to demonstrate his loyalty by pointing out that his father, a former mayor, had arranged for a funeral mass for Louis XVI on March 4, 1793. While a dangerous act under the Jacobins, it seems a thin proof of his son's devotion to the Bourbon regime when faced with conscription twenty years later.[67]

Men's and women's different approaches to cowardice and loyalty correspond to other differences between their petitions. Both disparaged their marriages, in hopes of persuading authorities not only that their bonds were illegitimate, but also that paper marriages could never become real. Yet men were more likely to lament the physical state of their spouses—as decrepit old women, as ugly and unhealthy, or as subject to fits of insanity—while young women, who presumably had married spouses closer to their own age and condition, more often bewailed

65. AN BB / 15 / 205, François Barrière Bienvenu.
66. AN BB / 15 / 205, Pierre Labeauté.
67. AN BB / 15 / 205, Pierre Jean-Baptiste Blanc.

their husbands' cruelty and deception. A practical reason lurked behind this distinction. If couples could not get divorced or annul their marriages, they might be able to obtain a legal separation. The legal grounds for separations were limited to violence, cruelty, or grievous insults. Women may have been more subject to abuse; they also had more hopes of invoking it as grounds for separation.[68]

Overall, petitioners played on the Restoration's rhetoric of peace and denunciations of the effects of Napoleon's war. They contended that apparent cowardice or cruelty were real—and legitimate grounds for the dissolution of a marriage. But they also argued that such behavior was beyond individual control, the product of a perverse regime that had victimized everyone.

Official Responses

Petitioners in the early Restoration had good reason to hope that the government would respond favorably. One of the more prominent officials of the new regime, the abbé de Montesquiou, Minister of the Interior, not only shared in the general denunciation of conscription, but also specifically condemned marriages made to avoid military service. On July 24, 1814, he bewailed the "disorder and immortality" of "marriages concluded with haste and imprudence."

Part of Montesquiou's agenda was to emphasize the devastation wrought by war. He presented a table showing that 1.3 million men had been called up since the beginning of 1813, although he acknowledged that not all of these measures had been executed. Like some of his contemporaries, he felt compelled to discuss, and reject, the idea based on Malthus that conscription had actually led to demographic growth through marriages.[69] He insisted that conscription was bad both for individuals and for the population as a whole. He claimed that "We have even seen men, quickly grown weary of a state that they had only embraced in order to avoid conscription, throw themselves into the very danger they sought to avoid and offer themselves as replacements in order to escape misery they had not anticipated and break horribly mismatched bonds."[70]

Montesquiou's rhetoric had a grain of truth to it. Replacements in 1813 did include married men. There may have been a larger percentage of such men than there had been earlier in the Empire, given both the high demand

68. Reddy, "Marriage, Honor, and the Public Sphere."

69. Thomas Malthus's work had been translated into French: *Essai sur le principe de population* (Paris: Paschoud, 1809).

70. Montesquiou-Fezensac, *Rapport de S. Exc. le Ministre de l'Intérieur*, 5. The abbé de Montesquiou was the minister of the interior throughout the First Restoration, from May 13, 1814, to March 20, 1815.

for replacements in 1813 and the premium that replacements could ask, and presumably, give to their families.[71]

But there is little evidence that those unhappily married were particularly inclined to volunteer. Many married men who left in 1813 and 1814 were forced to do so by officials who did not see their marriages as viable excuses, especially if they did not have children. Conversely, many, perhaps most, of those who married only to avoid conscription did not live together. Certainly, it was in the interest of petitioners to insist that they had never cohabited in order to prove the fictional nature of their bonds. Couples who had set up household only to find themselves ill-matched had fewer hopes of a special exemption, and none at all if they had had children. The extreme disparity of many of these unions still suggests that cohabitation was likely rare.

Montesquiou's speech was printed in many newspapers and collections of political tracts.[72] At least one petitioner cited it explicitly. Writing to the Chamber of Deputies in August 1814, a Mr. Perrier quoted Montesquiou's lines about newly married men turning to military service to escape their precipitous marriages. Perrier observed that conscription had been abolished and the divorce procedure filled with obstacles. The government should thus help the great number of young men who had married in 1813 only to escape Bonaparte's extraordinary draft and make it possible for them to divorce or at least to separate.[73]

The legislature cast Perrier's petition aside, as it did thousands of other petitions on topics deemed inappropriate for, or unworthy of, government attention. The government of the First Restoration did, however, briefly consider what to do about such marriages in the fall of 1814. Debate was provoked by another petition, this one from a Parisian living on the Rue Saint-Honoré. Saint Félix addressed the Assembly because he had read in the newspapers that the deputy Mauray proposed abolishing divorce for any cause. After congratulating Mauray on the apparent happiness of his own marriage, Saint Félix argued that even under the Napoleonic Civil Code, it was difficult to prove cause, except when a wife openly tried to murder her husband.

Like petitioners, Saint Félix called attention to the "precipitous marriages during these last years by young men and women who wanted to escape

71. On the rise in replacements and their cost in 1813, Maureau, "Le remplacement militaire."

72. These include the *Journal de Lyon, ou Bulletin administratif et politique du département du Rhône*, no. 43, July 19, 1814; *Mercure de France*, vol. 59, June 1814, 556; *L'ambigu ou variétés littéraires et politiques*, vol. 46, no. 407 (July 20, 1814), 154; *Le conservateur impartial*, no. 60 (July 28, 1814), 344; *Journal de Paris*, vol. 38, no. 184, July 13, 1814, 3; and M. Malte Brune, *Le spectateur ou variétés historiques, littéraires, critiques, et morales* (Paris: Poulet, July, August, and September 1814), 2:313. It was reprinted in later tracts; among others, see *Les yeux ouverts pour tout le monde*, 154.

73. AN C / 2044, Perrier. The petition is dated August 30, 1814.

Bonaparte's bloody laws."[74] But his argument differed from many of those who had married to avoid conscription. He called for divorce based on mutual incompatibility or on the request of one partner. He invoked mismatched marriages as a particular reason for this form of divorce, rather than arguing that marriages to avoid conscription were in a case by themselves and should be dissolved even if divorce was not tolerated in general.

On November 12, 1814, the head of the Commission on Petitions, Victor Avoyne de Chanteryene, responded to Saint Félix's petition and to several others. He argued that divorce for mutual incompatibility had been rejected in the discussion of the Civil Code. The new government had no intention of multiplying divorces or making them easier to arrange than they had been under Napoleon. While imprudent marriage bonds might be a misfortune for some families, it would be a far greater misfortune to encourage citizens to break the "contract whose stability is a concern for all of society."[75] The legislature dismissed the idea of divorce based on mutual incompatibility and refused to consider an exception for marriages made to avoid conscription.

Petitioners continued to send hopeful requests to the legislature, as well as to the minister of justice and other authorities, throughout the First Restoration and the early years of the Second Restoration. In most cases, the Chamber of Deputies simply dismissed supplications. In some cases, petitions provoked brief discussion. For example, on October 17, 1815, Barthelémi Blanc, a farmer and mayor of the hamlet of Moussoulens in the department of the Aude, petitioned for a special law that would dissolve his son's 1813 marriage and those of others in similar positions.[76] On November 11, 1815, the deputy Focaut reported to the legislature on Blanc's proposition as well as twenty-one other petitions on various subjects. The *Moniteur* reported that "The chamber dismisses as completely contrary to morality and public order the request made by M. Blanc, mayor, for a law that would release from their bonds a crowd of young men who only married in front of the civil officer to avoid conscription."[77]

Petitioners continued to hope for an exemption or new law even after divorce was abolished in May 1816. On January 20, 1817, Baysselance, a notary in the town of Bergerac in the Dordogne, asked for an exception to the ban on divorce for those who had only contracted a civil marriage to escape conscription.[78] He got nowhere. Similarly, in November 1818, two couples from the

74. AN C / 2047, Saint Félix à Messieurs les députés des départements.

75. *Moniteur universel*, no. 516, November 12, 1814, 1275. See also Ronsin, *Le contrat sentimental*, 236–37.

76. AN C / 2028.

77. *Moniteur universel*, no. 314, November 10, 1815, 1239.

78. He proposed that article 2 of the project of the law on divorce be modified in favor of those who had contracted a civil marriage only to escape conscription law. *AP*, series 2 (January 1817), 18:211. See also Ronsin, *Le contrat sentimental*, 253.

department of the Lot, Jean Landes and Marianne Cassagne from Lentillac, and Jean-Pierre Larribe and Marie Mazet, in Frayssinhes, sought exceptions for themselves. They marshaled considerable supporting testimony from their priests and local officials about the fictive nature of their bonds and the lack of religious ceremonies. The legislature dismissed their claims, noting that since civil bonds legitimated a marriage, the absence of a church wedding did not void their union.[79]

Overall, the policy of the central government was clear. Napoleon's militarized regime had led to social and domestic disorder. But dissolving legal marriages—even those of couples brought together by force—would also lead to disorder, potentially on a far more serious scale. There could be no systematic nullification of marriages made to escape conscription.

The Courts

Petitioners to the minister of justice fared little better than those who addressed the legislature. The minister told petitioners that they should take their cases to the courts. This response ignored their claims that their situations did not fit existing legal categories. It also ignored the fact that petitioners often turned to the central government because they had already tried to annul their bonds in local courts—and failed to do so. For example, we have seen the case of Marguerite Blandières, whose brother decided to marry to avoid military service if she also wed a conscript. She petitioned the minister of justice in June 1814 only after having sought in vain to end her marriage in a local court.[80]

Because there were no formal grounds for invalidating marriages undertaken to avoid conscription, many petitioners turned to technical arguments. They claimed that the official who had performed their marriage could not legally do so; that the marriage was "clandestine," and thus invalid; or that one partner had been too young to marry legally. The range of arguments and the extent to which they hid petitioners' true motives mean that it is difficult to trace cases through the courts. But cases that do surface suggest that people often failed to prove that their marriages had not been properly formalized. For example, the domestic servant Antoinette Poncet brought her case before the Tribunal of First Instance of Lyon in January 1816. Her lawyer argued her marriage was invalid because it had been performed by the civil official of a commune in which neither she nor her supposed husband had resided. The court ruled that this was insufficient grounds for ending the marriage. The legal inability of an official to marry nonresidents of his jurisdiction could only

79. For their petitions, see AN C / 2038; and *AP*, series 2 (November 1818), 22:135.

80. AD Lot 3U1 325, pp. 288–89, 395–96. Financial considerations played a role; Marguerite's family had promised money to her putative husband in the marriage agreement.

negate a marriage if the ceremony had been performed clandestinely. In this case, the marriage had been appropriately publicized.[81]

Some of the most revealing court cases come from the department of the Lot, in southwestern France. This is one of the areas with the strongest tradition of resistance to conscription under Napoleon.[82] Supplicants in the region seeking to end their marriages initially fared much better than their counterparts in many other locales, especially in late 1815 and early 1816. The Cahors Tribunal of First Instance heard at least fifteen cases for annulment in the first half of 1816. It ruled repeatedly that marriages that had been undertaken only to avoid conscription did not represent real contracts and should be nullified. On March 30, 1816, the court thus judged that the October 1813 marriage between Jean Vincents and Jeanne Costeraste had to be annulled because "One cannot consider as free and as is what is required by a contract as important as conjugal union, the consent given to escape the risk of military service." In April 1816, they considered the case of a local weaver and his supposed wife, and concluded:

> Nothing concerns society more than the authenticity and publicity of marriages; it is in the essence of marriage that the consent given by both spouses be perfectly free and have no other object than conjugal union. The facts put forward by Jean Raynal prove the clandestine nature of his marriage with Antoinette Cavaillac and prove as well that the marriage had no other purpose than to shield Jean Raynal from military service, which is to say from imminent danger of an almost certain death.[83]

To establish that marriages were simply paper arrangements and should be dissolved, the court invoked grounds for annulment in the Napoleonic Civil Code. It repeatedly ruled that marriages were illegitimate because they had been contracted in a private home, rather than in the town hall or other public space; had taken place without parental consent; or had been arranged against the will of one or both of the parties. Judges added the standard arguments that there had been no religious celebration and that the parties had never lived together or considered themselves as husband and wife. They also noted specific evidence. For example, Jeanne Costeraste and Jean Vincents claimed that their marriage had taken place behind the closed doors of a shoemaker's shop; such a clandestine union could not be seen as adequately publicized.[84] Marie Fontanelle described herself as so opposed to her proposed marriage that she fled her parents' house and spent the night hiding in an

81. AD Rhône Ucl 45 1816 and Uciv 67 1816.

82. Bergès, *Résister à la conscription*; Crépin, "La France plurielle."

83. AD Lot 3U1 327, pp. 205, 288–89.

84. AD Lot 3U1 327, pp. 144–45.

oven. Her parents dragged her out over her tears; she continued to insist that the arranged marriage was against her wishes.[85]

As Fontanelle's story suggests, the men, and especially the women, who made their cases in the local courts could be more explicit about parental coercion than petitioners who appealed to the paternalistic authority of the central state. Yet young women, especially those who had been minors at the time of their marriages, appeared in the courtroom with their fathers. They continued to denounce the pressures of Napoleon's regime and to emphasize their families' good intentions.

Whatever litigants' arguments, the situation soon changed. In July 1816, Seguy, a new public prosecutor in the Cahors Tribunal, wrote his superior, the prosecutor general at the royal court of Agen. He denounced the ease with which the Cahors court was ending marriages. Seguy was well aware that these marriages had been undertaken to avoid conscription. He noted that in some cases judges acknowledged that couples had wed so that a man would not have to fight. In other records, "one does not find the words conscription or military service." This did not mean that such logic was absent. On the contrary, this phrasing was "simply the way they [the judgments] were written. The goal or the cause was always to avoid military service."[86]

Unlike his contemporaries in the Cahors courtroom, Seguy did not see the goal of avoiding military service as a valid reason to dissolve marriages. He was distressed by the ways that the technical grounds used to end marriages encouraged fraud. The court's decision that a marriage was invalid because it had been clandestine often depended on false testimony. Because the parties involved both sought separation, and were usually supported by their community, it was easy to find witnesses willing to lie.

But the public prosecutor was bothered by something more fundamental. The Tribunal had annulled marriages in the months leading up to the official abolition of divorce on May 8, 1816—and continued to do so afterward. The prosecutor objected that the judgment that there was no "free consent, because conscription had forced this step" made it too easy to end marriage. If this logic were followed, "the most solemn, the most important, and the most indissoluble act of society would be broken without opposition." Couples, aided by the courts, could use this "pretext of conscription to break marriage, and revive by this means the law of divorce that the state has just abolished." In his view, divorce for mismatched marriages was the first step to destroying marriage entirely.[87]

The prosecutor general passed on these complaints to the minister of justice, along with copies of five judgments the Tribunal of First Instance of Cahors had

85. AD Lot 3U1 327, p. 413.
86. AN BB / 15 / 208, Cahors, 31 août 1816, au ministre de la justice.
87. AN BB / 15 / 208, Lot, Cahors, R3, 3380.

rendered in April and May of 1816. In September 1816, the minister drafted a response, proclaiming that the easy dissolution of marriage was a "violation that attacks the very foundations of society."[88]

The Cahors Tribunal seems to have accepted this logic. It rejected the requests of several men and women seeking the nullification of their marriages in late 1816 and 1817. The story of Antoinette Soulié is particularly revealing. She brought a case in July 1816 arguing that her parents had used violence to force her to marry a farmer, Antoine Marraux. The court acknowledged: "there can be no marriages without consent; it is necessary to have free consent on the part of both spouses and violence is the exclusion of freedom." But they also ruled that since divorce had required detailed proof, nullification should require similar evidence.[89] When she reappeared before the courts in March 1817, the Tribunal hesitated, unsure whether law now allowed a married woman to bring a case, since a wife could not engage in legal proceedings without her husband's permission or special approval from the courts. Soulié continued to pursue her cause. But when in August 1817 she again appeared before the Tribunal, she had had a child. She admitted that her putative husband was not the father, but the court refused to accept her testimony. According to the Civil Code, a child born to a couple during their marriage was deemed to be the husband's. Offspring legally proved that the two had cohabitated; cohabitation was proof that they had consented to the marriage and could not annul it.[90]

Since the courts consistently judged cohabitation as evidence of consent, the case would probably have been overturned earlier—although if the court had nullified the marriage in 1816, pregnancy would presumably not have been an issue. In other cases, however, the courts clearly applied new standards. In considering the bond between Marie Emeric and Bernard Jongla in June 1817, the court ruled that since the registers of civil status were open to the public, the couple could not claim that there had been inadequate publicity to validate their marriage. Such judgments made it much harder to argue that a marriage had been clandestine and thus subject to nullification.

Another judgment set an even more limiting precedent. Rosetta Barthelemi, supported by her father, contested her marriage in May 1817. Her father sought to establish that she had been too young to marry in April 1813. But the very attempt to document her age was taken as proof that the family had been aware of the marriage, and that neither the couple nor their respective parents had challenged its validity until April 1815. The courts invoked article 183 of the Civil Code, which stated that if no one contested the legitimacy of a marriage within a year, it was valid. The Cahors Tribunal had ignored the article

88. AN BB/15/208, Lot, Cahors, R3, 3380.

89. AD Lot 3U1 327, pp. 634–35.

90. AD Lot 3U1 328, pp. 152, 582.

in earlier cases. Invoking it now made it essentially impossible for those who had married to avoid conscription to contest their marriages. Concerned with protecting men from military service, few had rushed to void their marriages within the requisite year.

The story, however, does not end there. The prosecutor general at the Royal Court of Agen was so outraged by such marriages that he decided not only to make it impossible to obtain annulments in the future, but also to reverse earlier annulments rendered by the Tribunal of First Instance of Cahors. He focused on one of the five cases that the public prosecutor had brought to his attention, that of Pierre Laborie and Perette Coudère, who had married on July 20, 1813. Pierre had brought a suit on April 29, 1816, declaring that his marriage had been celebrated clandestinely; the couple had not celebrated their marriage religiously or lived together. After verifying these claims, the Tribunal annulled the marriage on May 16, 1816.[91] On February 10, 1817, Laborie remarried; all the appropriate formalities were observed. But the very next day, February 11, the prosecutor general notified Laborie that he was contesting the annulment of the first marriage, using his powers as a public official entitled to oppose affronts to public order.

A little less than a year later, on January 18, 1818, the Royal Court ruled that Laborie and Coudère's original marriage was valid. The prosecutor general argued during the trial that a public official could use the legal device of *réquisition* to challenge a depraved act against public interests. He reiterated that any legal loophole allowing men and women to end marriage fell into this realm of depravity:

> If the minister's action in such a case is not sufficiently authorized by the text of the law, it is nonetheless necessary to decide that it follows irresistibly from its spirit, as it is commanded by the interests of morals and public honesty; the contrary opinion could become the source of the greatest abuses, since it would not be rare to see careless or fickle spouses free themselves from the prohibition of the law on divorce and seek divorces, by framing them as requests for annulment for marriage.[92]

Laborie then appealed his case to the Supreme Court. It ruled on March 5, 1821, that the Royal Court of Agen had committed an abuse of power; the annulment of Laborie and Coudère's marriage stood. Since Laborie by then had two children with his second wife, this was no doubt welcome news.

It is striking, however, that conscription dropped out of the discussion. The Supreme Court made no reference to military service in forcing marriage. As we have seen, the courts tended to focus on technical causes for annulling or

91. AD Lot 3U1 327, pp. 338, 414.

92. *Journal du Palais présentant la jurisprudence de la cour de cassation* (Paris: Bureau du journal de Palais, 1821): 252–60.

dissolving marriages. But even when the lower courts had addressed the role of conscription in forcing marriages, lawyers and judges now set it aside, focusing instead on issues like publicity or the need for parental consent. The argument that the tyrannical law of conscription had destroyed families disappeared as grounds for discussing marriage and society.

Conclusion

Many couples were bound together for life. The story of Louis Charles Cavillou reveals the costs of this bondage with acuity. A conscript in 1807, he had drawn a lucky number; he then married in 1810 as a precaution against being conscripted in the future. His wife, at least on paper, was a seventy-nine-year-old woman whose consent he admitted that he had bought. In October 1815, he petitioned the authorities to end his marriage to this indigent old woman, asking if he would be "reduced to wishing for the death of the woman who saved his life, in order to be able to marry the one he loves and is his only happiness."[93] Like most of his counterparts, he was told to try his luck in the courts, where there was little hope of ending his marriage. Cavillou's fate was indeed to wish for the death of the woman who had saved his life.

Yet the stories of mismatched marriages show us far more than the doomed fates of a few individuals. They reveal the long-term consequences of war, not just in cultural works but also in lived experiences. We tend to think of the aftermath of war in terms of the challenges of veterans trying to readjust to civilian life or the lasting grief of families who lost loved ones. Yet the end of the Napoleonic wars also affected those who never went near the battlefields—including those who actively sought to avoid fighting.

These petitions also show the limits of the Restoration government's rhetoric of peacemaking. The Bourbons repeatedly denounced conscription, championing the returned king as the protector of families against the monster who had sought to destroy them. But the Restoration government would ultimately value the unbreakable bonds of legal marriage over individuals' accounts of military coercion and oppression, even oppression by a hated regime.

93. AN BB / 15 / 205, R2, 7351.

CONCLUSION

New Conscripts and Soldier-Farmers

ON MARCH 10, 1818, only four years after the Restoration government abolished conscription, it brought back mandatory military service. Legislators claimed that the law concerned recruitment rather than conscription and avoided using the term "conscripts." Proponents contended that recruitment was simultaneously civic, national, and royal—thus truly different from the depredations of the tyrant Napoleon. The 1818 law, amended in 1824 and 1832, would remain the basis of French recruitment until the Third Republic.[1]

The law is surprising for many reasons. It passed while foreign troops occupied France after the Second Restoration. As the minister of war observed, debate involved the extraordinary spectacle of a government discussing its forces while foreign armies remained on its territory.[2] It is even more surprising that a regime that had founded its legitimacy partly on ending conscription would reinstate a form of it so quickly.

The impetus was largely pragmatic: voluntary enlistment had failed to provide enough soldiers.[3] The army had shrunk to 117,000 troops, a number that could not provide even minimal defense. By 1817, it was forced to use 18,000 national guardsmen to fill its ranks.[4] The writer Charles Louis Lesur claimed that France had only a simulacrum of an army. Voluntary enrollments barely provided for the elite corps, while legions were emptied.[5]

1. Crépin, *La conscription en débat* and "Gouvion-Saint-Cyr et la loi refondatrice de 1818."

2. *Bulletin des lois*, no. 200, law no. 3695, Loi sur le recrutement de l'armée, 10 mars 1818.

3. Crépin, *Histoire de la conscription*, 157–63.

4. Forrest, *The Legacy of the French Revolutionary Wars*, 92–94.

5. Lesur, *Annuaire historique universel pour 1818*, 52.

The resulting 1818 Gouvion Saint Cyr law was a more moderate—and thus likely more acceptable—form of conscription than Napoleonic precedents. Most importantly, it was introduced during peace; those drafted now faced far less risk of death. Like the 1798 Jourdan conscription law, it began with volunteers, before establishing procedures for a draft.[6] The new law sanctioned exemptions and allowed for replacements. It capped the army at 240,000, with the aim of raising only about 40,000 troops each year, meaning that men facing a draft had a good chance of avoiding service. While the law maintained the principle that the nation had a right to call on all male citizens to fight, it affected far fewer people than earlier incarnations of national military service. Conversely, however, it mandated six years of service for those enlisted. It also created a reserve army of veterans, bringing personnel from revolutionary and Napoleonic troops into the Restoration army.[7]

If practical considerations prompted legislators to reinstate military service, the law was also shaped by ideological struggles. Proponents of conservatism, liberalism, constitutional monarchy, and republicanism used the measure to argue for competing visions of society.[8] They also quietly but repeatedly touched on what military service should mean for "citizen soldiers" and for their families. So too did the artists and writers responsible for promoting a new image of veterans in the 1820s, the *soldat laboureur* or soldier-farmer.

These developments suggest how contemporaries sought to move past the immediate experiences of the revolutionary and Napoleonic wars. But mass mobilization and peacemaking also had much larger impacts. Looking backward from the Restoration allows us to reconsider the dramatic changes of the revolutionary era, and to see how violence, citizenship, gender, and family were fundamentally entangled. It also helps us to make sense of the legacies of this tumultuous time.

Enlisting Young Men: Soldiers and Their Families

Some worried about the military not just because of the devastation associated with Napoleon's troops, but also because they saw it as a threat to paternal power. Throughout the revolutionary and Napoleonic eras, officials fretted about parents' roles in inspiring their sons to fight or keeping them from service. Some in the Restoration, however, were more concerned with the willfulness of sons. Local officials called for raising the age of majority to twenty-five, and

6. *Bulletin des lois*, no. 200, law no. 3695, Loi sur le recrutement de l'armée, 10 mars 1818.

7. Volunteers served eight years in the infantry and cavalry, six in other corps. Forrest, *The Legacy of the French Revolutionary Wars*, 93. See also *Historique des diverses lois sur le recrutement*, 15.

8. Hippler, "Conscription in the French Restoration" and "The French Army."

complained that the ability of young men to enlist allowed them to escape parental supervision. The Conseil General of the Somme thus argued in 1816 that since France needed businessmen and farmers, young men should remain under paternal authority until they had learned civilian work ethics, while those in the Hérault complained in July 1817 that even if young men were not conscripted, they could still challenge their fathers by volunteering at age eighteen.[9] In 1818, the deputy Jacques Claude Beugnot echoed such concerns by proposing that minors enlist only with permission from their father or guardian.

His opponents mocked this proposal. Charles Texier de Hautefeuille proclaimed, "to hear the gentleman, a young man who enlists embarks on the road to perdition." The largest number of potential recruits were between eighteen and twenty; requiring paternal permission would discourage them. Another deputy, René Marie Jollivet, insisted that there was no need for debate, as the age for volunteering had been established not by conscription law but by the Civil Code.[10] Jollivet's view prevailed, but left aside how the Code itself had been shaped by, and reinforced, Napoleon's war machine.

Like their predecessors, proponents of the 1818 law did not see military service as incumbent upon all citizens—or even all young men. Some still envisioned dividing the obligations of citizenship among family members. As the deputy Josse-Beauvoir proclaimed, "A father has to give one of his sons to the fatherland as the price of protection of his liberty, his property, and the conservation of his other children who will be exempted."[11] Legislators also debated whether the government should provide a blanket release for all oldest sons and only sons, because of their familial responsibilities. They ultimately limited exemptions to cases involving additional factors, such as the oldest son in families where both parents had died; the oldest or only son of a widow, a blind father, or a parent aged over seventy; the older of two brothers subject to the same draft; or younger men whose brothers were currently serving, had died in service, or had been released from duty because of injuries. The decision not to exempt all oldest and only sons reflected concerns that a general exemption would remove too many men from the pool. It also reinforced state power even as Restoration authorities lauded patriarchal order.

Other proponents of the law justified recruitment on the grounds of the paternalistic nature of a Bourbon army, in supposed contrast to Napoleon's troops. The former *commissaire des guerres*, Pierre-Agathange Odier, made the metaphor of family central to his overview of military legislation in December 1818.[12] It helped him argue that citizens (by which Odier specifically meant fathers) would "give their sons to the patrie" knowing that they would be well

9. AN BB / 16 / 866, Somme; and AN BB / 16 / 311, Hérault.

10. *Journal de Paris*, no. 28, January 28, 1818.

11. Josse-Beauvoir, *Opinion de . . . , sur le recrutement de l'armée*, 5–6. Quoted in Hippler, "Conscription in the French Restoration," 287n30.

12. Odier, *De la réforme dans la législation militaire*. He claimed to have written the book eighteen months earlier but been unable to publish it.

treated. In turn, the state would substitute for fathers, caring for all those who took up arms.[13]

Discussion of the familial dimensions of recruitment focused on fathers and sons. In contrast to the strategies used to legitimate military service during the Revolution, post-1818 recruitment propaganda rarely asked women to inspire men to fight. In the early Restoration, collective biographies devoted to Napoleonic heroes occasionally paid tribute to sacrificing mothers, like Marie Labée, who exhorted her sons to take up arms in 1799.[14] But such references were rare. Military recruitment after 1818 was not a levée en masse; authorities had little desire to mobilize society as a whole. It was difficult for a government that claimed to have rescued mothers by saving their sons from conscription to ask women to legitimate a new recruitment law.

A Renewed Rush to Marriage?

The new law raised familiar questions: should recruits marry, and if so, what would their marriages mean? In early 1818, one veteran dismissed the idea that the recruitment law would provoke bad marriages by those seeking to avoid service. He noted with indignation that "The titles of husband and father do not make him any less intrepid in defending the patrie, because the patrie contains all he holds most dear."[15] Yet others insisted that if the new draft was a civic obligation, soldiers had ceased to be citizens imbricated in both military and civilian life. In the 1818 *Military Eloquence,* Jacques-Gilbert Ymbert argued that the modern soldier was a new creation—not because of the civic duty of men to fight, but because of the separation of combatants from families. In ancient Rome, being a husband and father could be combined with military service, as men would return during peace. That had changed with standing armies. A soldier had to renounce marriage and abandon personal affections, a sacrifice that should only be asked of the young.

In practice, young men did sometimes rush to marriage in hopes of escaping conscription. According to the new law, French men who had reached the age of twenty in the previous year were subject to de facto conscription. For the first lottery, men who had turned twenty in 1816 or 1817 were included, unless they had married before the law was promulgated.[16]

Such marriages readopted an old strategy. Even as some sought to end paper marriages made to avoid conscription under Napoleon, other young men rushed to wed in hopes of escaping military service. Their weddings were provoked by rumors, like a report in January 1816 that Bonaparte had landed in Toulon.

13. Odier, *De la réforme dans la législation militaire,* 96, 176.

14. Including P. F. Tissot, *Les fastes de la gloire,* 1:22–23; Colau, *Le soldat laboureur,* 13–14; and Arnault, *Biographie nouvelle des contemporains,* 10:189.

15. Henri . . . , *Adresse au roi,* 12.

16. Article 7 of the March 10, 1818, law.

Distressed local officials complained about the motives and effects of these liaisons. The prefect of Charente complained in February 1816 that numerous young men were marrying, often before they reached physical maturity. The prefect of Saône-et-Loire similarly worried that "Premature and badly matched marriages are spreading. Parents say openly that their goal is to save their sons from conscription threatened by the return of the usurper."[17]

Divorce was not yet banned in early 1816, but as we have seen, contemporaries were aware that it would likely be outlawed. Hasty marriages continued after divorce was abolished in May 1816, when the memory of conscription was still fresh. Fear of Napoleon's war machine remained strong enough to outweigh both hopes that the Restoration government would permanently end war and the increased constraints of wedlock. As the threat of war receded, especially after Napoleon's death in 1821, waves of preemptive marriages would also disappear, to be remembered primarily only by those forced to live with their legacies.

Swords and Ploughshares: The Soldat Laboureur

At the same time as the Restoration government changed what it meant for men to take up arms, artists and playwrights promoted new ways of seeing veterans. Around 1818, they introduced the figure of the *soldat laboureur*, or soldier-farmer, a reference that would become widespread in the early 1820s.[18] The image combined classical allusions, revolutionary and Napoleonic visions of men who served the state as either farmers or soldiers, and attempts to persuade veterans to accept peace under a Bourbon king. It was popular, elegiac, and double-edged. It suggested that even as former warriors shed wistful tears for dead heroes, they had accepted the labors of peace. But the possibility that soldiers might take up arms again also challenged royalist postwar order.

The soldat laboureur appeared in paintings, engravings, and especially in the new medium of lithographs.[19] In 1820, Horace Vernet exhibited a painting that would become iconic.[20] Critics Etienne Jouy and Antoine Jay

17. On Charente and the Saône-et-Loire, see AN F / 7 / 3736, Bulletins du 19 février 1816 and 23 février 1816. More generally, see Ploux, *De bouche à l'oreille*, 158–59; and Hazareesingh, *The Legend of Napoleon*, 58.

18. Athanassoglou-Kallmyer, "Sad Cincinnatus"; Puymège, *Chauvin, le soldat-laboureur*; Hopkin, *Soldier and Peasant;* and Hornstein, *Picturing War in France.*

19. In 1818, Pierre Roche Vigneron's now lost images the *Soldat laboureur I & II* showed a man next to two horses and a plow, while in Nicolas-Toussaint Charlet's 1818 *Le soldat français*, a veteran is standing on top of a body. His leg is being bandaged; he is holding a rifle and biting down to contain pain (Metropolitan Museum, New York). See also Eugène Carrière, *Le soldat français*, 1818 (National Gallery of Victoria, Melbourne).

20. Horace Vernet, *Peace and War or the Soldat Laboureur*, 1820 (Wallace Collection, London). Imitations included Jean-Pierre-Marie Jazet, *Le soldat laboureur*, 1821 (Museum of Fine Arts, Houston); and Fleuret, *Le soldat laboureur*, 1822 (Grand Palais, Paris). See

FIGURE 9.1. Jean-Pierre-Marie Jazet, *The Plowing Soldier after Horace Vernet*, 1821. The Metropolitan Museum of Art, New York, The Elisha Whittelsey Collection, 1960.

observed that the painting was a follow-up to his 1818 *The Soldier of Waterloo*, which showed a wounded grenadier who had buried his fallen comrades. The same veteran now unearthed a rusted helmet while plowing and reflecting on the remains of his compatriots. The critics claimed that the two paintings

also Ivan Jablonka, "Le mythe du soldat-laboureur," *Histoire par l'image*, http://www.histoire-image.org/etudes/mythe-soldat-laboureur.

could be a poem entitled "The Life of the Soldier-Citizen," combining devotion to the country, tears for dead heroes, and regret for lost glory, with respect for laws and the labors of peace.[21]

Such images usually depicted a veteran alone, but a few suggested families as comfort. In Vernet's 1818 lithograph *In the Environs of a Ball*, a veteran with a wooden leg plays with a child.[22] Despite the visual isolation of Vernet's 1820 veteran, Jouy and Jay imagined him surrounded by loved ones: "As the sun sets, he thinks deeply about his success and failures, but at least he will rediscover his family, an adored companion will pour a generous glass of wine for him; he will embrace his mother and caress his young child, and the smile will return to his lips."[23]

By its nature, theater depicted social interactions; plays about veterans thus placed them more centrally in relation to family members than did artwork. Restoration playwrights also added a revived seignorialism. The 1819 *Soldat laboureur* by Henri Franconi featured Félix, an impoverished veteran longing to marry, who finds a coffer of gold in a field. The land belongs to his seigneur, who gives half the gold to the young man in exchange for cultivating his lands. Félix marries Marie, who will also work on the farm. The benevolent seigneur expedites their wedding, proclaiming that "I will serve as father; I am happy to bring virtue and courage together to the altar."[24]

The playwright reinforced these messages with the same characters in 1821. Félix's son Adolphe was now a second lieutenant; in typical theatrical fashion, Adolphe rescues his love—the seigneur's daughter—from brigands. The seigneur proclaims that there is a brave soldier in the heart of every farmer, and bestows his daughter's hand as a reward for her courageous lover.[25] Much in the play echoes revolutionary and Napoleonic narratives, including the long absence of a soldier, a well-timed dowry, and the union of virtue and courage. But money is not a direct reward for heroism or for women's patriotic choices; it comes instead from a local dignitary, binding a veteran to his seigneur's fields.

If Franconi's plays drew acclaim, the term "soldat laboureur" became most popular with a play that debuted in September 1821, *The Harvesters in Beauce, or, The Soldat Laboureur*.[26] The newspaper *L'album* reported that nothing in the theater's repertoire had been more successful.[27] In the play, Francœur

21. Jouy and Jay, *Salon d'Horace Vernet*, image 22, 96–98.

22. In Hornstein, *Picturing War in France*, 69–70.

23. Jouy and Jay, *Salon d'Horace Vernet*, 96.

24. Franconi, *Le soldat laboureur*, 19. Franconi's troops had performed military-inspired works during the Napoleonic Empire.

25. Franconi and Ponet, *Le soldat fermier, ou le bon seigneur*.

26. Dumersan, Francis, and Brazier, *Les moissonneurs de la Beauce, ou, Le soldat laboureur*. The setting invoked an area of northern France associated with Henri IV, the sixteenth-century king beloved by the Restoration monarchy.

27. The newspaper denied that partisanship had drawn crowds. Puymège, "Chauvin and Chauvinism," 53.

returns from war after twenty-six years to help his aged mother with a farm she rents and is about to lose. Fortunately, a retired colonel realizes that Francœur saved his life at Austerlitz. He gives the farm to Francœur's sister, who marries her previously impoverished sweetheart, to the dismay of a rich man who had sought her hand. The plot and characters echoed revolutionary and Napoleonic devices, including a prominent personage who rewards a soldier who has saved his life. But it recast those structures to emphasize the soldat laboureur's civilian industry and the paternal benevolence of the local nobility.

One of the three playwrights, Théophile Marion Dumersan, also published a novel entitled the *Soldat Laboureur*. An epigram presented the subject: "the sensible valor / of a soldier, French citizen / who accepts the peace / and proud of a rustic industry / Useful to his mother and his sister / knows that one can serve his country / at home, as on the field of honor."[28] Critics heralded it as a model. The *Revue encyclopédique* proclaimed, "this excellent work should be placed in the hands of all soldiers who can read, and who, returning to their homes, must be brought back to the ideas of peace and happiness if we do not want the habits that they have contracted to become dangerous to the state."[29]

If some commentators praised the return of soldat laboureurs to domestic virtue, others emphasized the soldier part of the equation. The Bonapartiste Pierre Colau dedicated his 1822 work, also entitled the *Le soldat laboureur*, to "Hero-farmers, or heroes who only have farmers for ancestors, who will not blush to tell the universe that you left the plow to race to the aid of your country."[30] In his construction, former soldiers were truly honorable and ready to rise again.

Royalists sometimes objected to the theme, even when it was not explicitly accompanied by Bonapartism. In reviewing a September 1821 performance, one critic noted that a "grand personage" had complained about the excessive number of military plays in Paris.[31] Administrators forbade the actor who played the soldat laboureur to appear on stage in the uniform associated with the role. As the playwright Charles-Guillaume Etienne complained, "Who would have believed that an actor, who played the role of the Soldat Laboureur with a talent worthy of the first Théâtre Français, would not be permitted to wear a costume that Horace Vernet gave his old warrior in one of his loveliest and most noble compositions?"[32] Censors debated whether to approve another play, *The Inn at Strasbourg*, which included a young woman whose father was killed in the army, and who was in love with a poor veteran-turned-teacher. They demanded to know if "Monsieur the Director General intends to authorize a fully military show with yet another soldat laboureur."[33] The piece

28. Dumersan, *Le soldat laboureur*, 1:vii.

29. *Revue encyclopédique*, 15:600.

30. Colau, *Le soldat laboureur*, v–vi.

31. Arge and Ragueneau de la Chainaye, *Histoire critique des théâtres de Paris*, 233.

32. Etienne, *Les plaideurs*, xvi.

33. AN F / 21 / 975, Auberge de Strasbourg. Edmond's former colonel stays at the inn and wins money from an English man that serves as a dowry for the teacher.

does seem to have been approved. Such complaints suggest that if the image of soldat laboureurs promised to return veterans to farm and family, its associations with Napoleonic warriors provoked continuing unease.

Struggles to define postwar forms of recruitment and mixed reactions to the soldat laboureur remind us how much the military and civilian experiences of war and its aftermath were intertwined throughout the late eighteenth and early nineteenth centuries. Indeed, if we look back from the Old Regime through the Revolution and the aftermath of the Napoleonic wars, we see both new connections and new tensions between these realms.

Lessons and Legacies?

VIOLENCE, GENEROSITY, AND USEFUL CITIZENS

War, by definition, is violent. David Bell has even contended that the French revolutionary and Napoleonic wars marked the birth of "warfare as we know it," with new and apocalyptic forms of violence. Aspects of these wars were particularly brutal—most infamously, civil war in the Vendée and guerilla warfare in Napoleonic Spain—but brutality spilled beyond the battlefields. There were regular reports of massacres, atrocities, and sexual violence across Europe.[34] When royalists denounced veterans as dangerous and debauched, they did so to discredit Napoleonic soldiers. But their accusations also reflected real challenges in returning men trained in killing to civilian life.

From the earliest stages of the Revolution through the Restoration, however, civilians also encountered accounts of soldiers' humanity, from giving money to the poor to saving drowning children.[35] As a character in one 1804 play proclaimed, "To bring victory on the fields of glory, a valiant soldier must risk his life, but he serves his patrie even better when he rescues someone in need."[36] Depictions of warriors as generous offset fears of their violence and distance from other citizens. Seeing men as embedded in familial networks reinforced this. It highlighted combatants' connections with their fellow citizens, even as contemporaries mused on whether soldiers were, or should, be a group apart. It is one reason why marriage appeared so often as a reward for veterans.

Insisting on soldiers' humanity was not unique to the era. But it reflects the specific emphasis on civic usefulness in revolutionary constructions of citizenship. Such concerns shaped public discussion about those who took up arms, as well as those who refused or ceased to fight. The practice of replacement—paying someone to fight in place of a conscript—called particular

34. Forrest, "Society, Mass Warfare, and Gender in Europe."

35. For examples, see the 1794 *Recueil des actions héroïques*, the 1798–99 *Bulletin décadaire,* and the 1808 *L'honneur français.* See also Clarke, "'Valour Knows Neither Age nor Sex'"; and Biard, "L'omniprésence de la guerre."

36. Roelandts, *Les dots ou la fête du 11 frimaire*, 32–33.

attention to the motives of those who avoided the obligation of military service. Initially tolerated, replacement was banned with the 1793 levée en masse, then relegitimated in 1799 in the wake of conscription law. Cultural tracts sought to make it acceptable by portraying the money paid to replacements not as a tainted exchange between the cowardly and the greedy, but as an act of generosity, in which young men offered themselves to families in need.[37] Similarly, petitioners in the early Restoration presented marriages undertaken to avoid conscription not as self-interested indulgences, but as choices showing patriotic devotion to their king or as acts forced upon them.

Those invested in war could also appear selfish. Plays featured characters who bet against peace, like war profiteers who wanted only to enrich themselves, and who lost out as romantic rivals to soldiers who welcomed the end of war. Such works portrayed military men as fighting to achieve a victorious peace, not out of innate brutality. Others—greedy civilians or barbaric enemies—were responsible for prolonging war. This vision became harder to sustain in Napoleonic wars of conquest but did not completely disappear.

In contrast, Restoration pamphleteers claimed that veterans were selfish in longing for a return to battle, placing personal ambitions over their families and country. But pamphleteers also argued that men had been forced into fighting, in an effort to make France into a nation of soldiers. The image of the soldat laboureur functioned to show that farmers were as important as warriors in postwar France, and that ex-combatants should be working to nourish their families and fellow citizens—even if they lacked the means to do so.

If war highlighted men's apparent selfishness or generosity, it also called attention to women's sacrifices, including in consenting to or resisting their loved ones' departures and in accepting the domestic hardships produced by war. By the Restoration, authorities downplayed women's agency in making these sacrifices, presenting them as proof not of individual citizenship, but rather of the overall costs of Revolution and war.

Accounts of military marriage particularly raised questions about women's patriotic altruism. Brides could appear as the passive embodiment of reward for masculine glory. This theme appeared in prerevolutionary works like Wille's 1781 painting *Double Reward for Merit*, where an officer was shown receiving both military honors and the hand of a general's daughter in marriage; it persisted into Restoration cultural productions, like Franconi's plays. Women, however, also actively chose, or rejected, grooms, and writers insisted on the importance of their choices. Authorities trying to arrange state-sponsored weddings confronted the question of whether real women would embrace—or reject—proposed veteran grooms, and how to ensure that couples wed without appearing coerced. Even when contemporaries emphasized the decision of both partners to wed, marriage appeared a reward for both. Revolutionary

37. Heuer, "Neither Cowardly nor Greedy."

and Napoleonic works rarely addressed the likelihood that caring for injured men might entail long-term hardship for their wives. At least in official views, marriage to ex-combatants rewarded virtuous women—even while charging women with the happiness of their husbands—rather than requiring them to sacrifice themselves.

THE POWER AND LIMITS OF MARTIAL MASCULINITY

If ideas of wartime selfishness, generosity, and sacrifice both influenced and were shaped by changing gender roles, other factors could also be critical. The revolutionary and Napoleonic eras left powerful legacies in models of martial masculinity. Associating virility with military prowess was scarcely new in the eighteenth century. But the Revolution forged new connections between masculinity, soldiering, and citizenship, making military service into something that could, at least in theory, be expected of all men. Authorities used domestic relations to reinforce these connections, both negatively—as officials associated desertion and draft dodging with effeminate cowardice—and positively, in promises that combatants' families would be supported and veterans rewarded with marriages. Yet looking at the connections between soldiers and their families or potential families also shows the limits of martial virility.

Indeed, even works that invoked family to celebrate martial masculinity hinted at these limits. Popular theater, for example, heralded returning soldiers as heroes, promising marriage as a reward both for combatants and for their loyal girlfriends. Yet plays suggested that veterans might be disfigured and weakened, not heroes to be imitated but objects of pity. Returned soldiers might have found partners elsewhere, or be too destructive or debauched to return to domestic life. While theaters reassured audiences that these fears were unwarranted, plays implicitly acknowledged their power.

The limits of martial masculinity and alternative models of citizenship appeared more explicitly when men avoided military service or sought to leave it. There were high rates of desertion and draft dodging in parts of France. Men sometimes asserted virility not by fighting for the state but by resisting forced recruitment. Yet even those who accepted—or claimed to accept—the civic obligation to take up arms challenged the universality of that obligation. They insisted that civilians, especially farmers, could be as useful as soldiers, that men were as responsible to their families as to their patrie, and that responding to need could be as important as military courage.

The end of the Napoleonic wars posed the most acute challenges to martial masculinity, as veterans returned to a defeated nation and to a government that despised the emperor who had led their troops. But alternatives to martial masculinity appeared from the earliest days of the Revolution. Understanding the power of these alternatives helps us to recover overlooked possibilities for defining citizenship, including those based around family responsibilities, economic productivity, and sensitivity to suffering.

Looking at challenges to martial masculinity also specifically helps us rethink the history of the body and of disability. Establishing that one was physically incapable of fighting was usually the surest, and often the only, way to secure release from military service. Those who were profoundly incapacitated were a distinct category, embodying the most visible forms of loss, whether they were paraded in the National Convention as heroes or reduced to begging on the streets. Many men, however, were weakened, but theoretically able to provide for themselves and their families—if less effectively than their able-bodied compatriots. Soldiers hoping to be discharged presented physical strain as a badge of honor. They sought to establish themselves simultaneously as incapable of further fighting and as capable of acting as productive civilians and responsible family members. Authorities arranging for state-sponsored marriages of veterans similarly struggled to weigh reward for service or compensation for injury against the need for households to be economically viable. Lurking in the background was the recurrent question of whether women would, or should, find scarred men and "peg legs" desirable partners.

It can be difficult for modern historians to see the extent to which contemporaries were concerned with men physically incapable of soldiering but still useful in civilian life. Historians of the Revolution have tended to pay more attention to the extraordinary displays of martyrs' corpses than to the ordinariness of battlefield injury and disease. The horrors of the world wars have overshadowed earlier impacts of injury on masculinity. Our conceptual difficulties also reflect postwar developments in the nineteenth century. In the immediate aftermath of the wars, the wooden leg–maker became a symbol of a war profiteer whose ambitions were dashed with Napoleon's fall. One anonymous caricature demonstrates the tenor of these images: it featured a woodworker, accredited by the devil Napoleon ("His Majesty Lucifer the 1st"), who did business on the Rue des Martyrs (Martyrs' Street). He reacted with despair to the end of his flourishing commerce in artificial legs, lamenting that "One more campaign, and my happiness would be assured!" Instead, he had to put his shop up for rent.

The wooden legs of soldat laboureurs called attention to sacrifices, while suggesting that veterans had become incapable of further service. As the nineteenth century progressed, the injured increasingly appeared as objects of pity or ridicule, a fate intensified by the Restoration government's refusal to allow veterans groups to organize. Scars and wooden legs became less signs of heroic sacrifice and romantic desirability than markers of age and infirmity, and reminders of a past royalists sought to expunge.

FIGURE 9.2. *Despair of the Wooden Leg Turner,* 1814. Musée Carnavalet, Paris.

WOMEN, STATE POWER, AND NEW MODELS OF CITIZENSHIP

Military service was overwhelmingly a masculine affair. The few women who took up arms—and the greater number who accompanied the troops as laundresses and vivandières—were exceptional. But the very exceptionality of their stories, from the choices that led them to take up arms to their forced demobilization after 1793, also illuminates the interconnections of gender, war, and citizenship. Such liminal figures reveal otherwise implicit expectations. Women soldiers also did not entirely disappear after their official expulsion, either as real individuals, whose demands for pensions and recognition unsettled multiple regimes, or as fictionalized figures whose stories would inspire, challenge, or titillate audiences long after the formal end of war.[38]

Revolution also combined with war to profoundly affect civilian women. Women took on unfamiliar labor and business arrangements in the absence

38. The 1818 *Manuel des braves* featured the 1794 exploits of the revolutionary heroine Liberté Barreau, while Louis-François Lejeune's 1819 painting of an 1812 battle in Spain showed a vivandière as a heroic warrior defending four wounded men. Hornstein, *Picturing War in France*, 54–55.

of men, while confronting the grief of losing loved ones. They also interacted repeatedly with different governments, in efforts that ranged from investigating the fate of brothers, husbands, or sons missing in action to trying to dissolve paper marriages made in hopes that a man could avoid conscription. These interactions often positioned women as supplicants seeking help, rather than as political actors asserting rights. Yet they still required women to negotiate legal and administrative structures in unprecedented ways, and to do so long after the Napoleonic Code reinforced patriarchal power. Women also defined themselves as citizens owed by the state, whether because of their own actions or because of their support of male combatants.

Indeed, if by 1818 military recruiters had ceased to ask women regularly to sacrifice their sons or inspire men to fight, this represented a real change from earlier practices. During much of the Revolution and Napoleonic era, women established their patriotism not just through their own actions but also through their support of male combatants. In the twenty-first century, we tend to think of citizenship in terms of individual rights. Revolutionary formulations remind us of how much citizenship, especially the duties of citizenship, could be viewed as a collective enterprise, one that required family members to consent to a man's departure or led to households dividing civic duties between men who fought and those who served at home.

Looking at military service and its end also calls attention to the roles of the state in private life and its limits. The ability to force men to leave their homes and take up arms, or conversely, to demobilize, was a profound, and in many ways, more lasting form of state power than the political experiments of the radical Revolution. Yet contemporaries found ways to challenge, circumvent, or reframe it. Revisiting these dynamics allows us to see how the state claimed authority, how gender roles were reshaped—and how people resisted that power.

EMOTIONAL ROLLERCOASTERS

The era of the French Revolution also appears a turning point in the history of emotion, but it was not a straightforward one. Revolutionaries associated certain emotions with citizenship—including patriotic courage, filial piety, and civic generosity—and expected men and women to use these emotions to display their commitment to the patrie. But they also expected citizens to suppress other emotions in the face of patriotic need. Archival records suggest persistent tensions between silencing complaints for the good of the nation (while being recognized for silencing those complaints) and mobilizing accounts of suffering for personal and political ends. They also show recurrent questions about not only which emotions were appropriate, but also how they could be used or combined. Did love augment or detract from military prowess? Was bravery uniquely masculine? How could sensitivity to suffering be reconciled with stoicism and hatred of revolutionary enemies? When did filial duty outweigh patriotic zeal? How could one balance the dictates of gratitude against those of romance—and the prospect of a lifetime commitment?

All of the regimes that governed France between 1789 and 1830 sought to direct strong public expressions of emotion—and faced challenges in doing so. Managing emotions around war was particularly challenging. Sending off recruits was supposed to be a joyous display of unity, but it was also a wrenching time of separation. Official recognition of those killed in battle had to be handled carefully to express appreciation and inspire vengeance, while avoiding calling attention to the severity of losses and the possibility of defeat.

If challenges were recurrent, strategies for handling public displays changed dramatically. Authorities in the radical Revolution sought to turn "sterile tears" into calls for action. Officials in the late 1790s retook this strategy, but at a point when people had become wary of gory spectacles. The mixed response to the 1799 Rastadt assassinations shows the growing difficulty of using martyrs to inspire outrage and recruit soldiers. Concern about displaying the war dead and grieving families also became more acute as war continued. If families of ordinary warriors were sometimes prominent in the early Revolution, the Directorial government and the Napoleonic state marked the deaths of heroic generals, but usually avoided collective funeral ceremonies for ordinary soldiers. By the Empire, processions of war widows and children had become rare. While bewailing the familial costs of war and the devastation wrought by the usurper Buonaparte, Restoration authorities also avoided ceremonies for the war dead. They sought either to forget the past or to commemorate those deemed to be victims of the Revolution, rather than war.

Historians of emotion have considered how displays of emotion could be gendered in times of war, but we have rarely explored the specific uses of displays of *women's* emotions. Images of mothers who repressed their own feelings to send their loved ones to war and accept their absences and deaths established the superiority of the mother country and its rightful demands on all citizens. Such images were most prominent at the height of the radical Revolution. They persisted afterward but were increasingly replaced in the Napoleonic period by images of girlfriends whose fretfulness contrasted with male courage. Restoration invocations of mothers' tearful gratitude to the king who had saved their sons functioned instead to support peacetime order and a postwar government. These various representations reflected changing gender roles, social realities, and conventions of expressing emotion. But they also served specific political purposes, helping to legitimate, at least in theory, the governments defined by war and by its end.

CULTURAL RECYCLING

Few would dispute that the eighteenth-century political and cultural universe was very different from the postrevolutionary world. But looking at gendered images and practices in relation to war reveals not only shifting emotional displays, but also cultural continuities across different regimes. Both authorities and "ordinary" individuals adopted familiar references and rituals and tried to reshape them for a new order. Revolutionaries claimed to have broken completely with the "Old" Regime, a break symbolized by replacing the Christian calendar with one beginning with the Republic. Years later, Restoration officials promised other forms of fresh starts; even as they sought to "restore" monarchical order, authorities also experimented with *union et oubli*, the strategic forgetting of recent history. Yet many who promoted new orders also turned to familiar references to make sense of the world.

Such recurrent cultural forms mask changes. Almost all governments imagined romance as a reward for military service. But they differed in how they depicted soldiers' rivals in love; the extent to which romance served not only as a reward for fighting but also as a compensation for injury; and the ways in which they used marriages of soldiers to legitimate civilian power. Napoleonic state-sponsored weddings of veterans drew on older French traditions, including royal philanthropy, celebrations of village "rose queens," and revolutionary festivals. But they also transformed these precedents, showcasing wounded veterans as deserving and desirable husbands. In adapting theatrical fantasies of soldiers' nuptials with the end of war, authorities also effectively turned a celebration of peace into a means of promoting long-term war.

Individuals also adapted older forms of rhetoric and reference to personal causes, while taking onboard the assumptions baked into those references. This may be clearest in the case of those seeking in the early Restoration to end marriages made to avoid conscription. They reshaped both antirevolutionary and revolutionary arguments to their own purposes, disparaging divorce as a perverse invention, while adapting revolutionary discourse to present their paper unions as forced bonds and affronts against nature. But they found themselves struggling with aspects of those arguments, as well as with an intransigent state. Such stories suggest ways that similar adaptions may haunt other moments of dramatic change, while carrying troublesome associations with them.

The Long-Term Resonances of the Soldier's Reward

Let us turn to one last play, the 1823 *Conscript*.[39] It too features a version of a soldat laboureur. The title explicitly invokes conscription, despite legislators' denial in 1818 that they were reinstating it. Charles, the conscript, is reluctant to leave his love Marie. She worries what will happen if he forgets her. Charles's mother wishes that she had the money to buy a replacement, but reassures Marie that there is "Nothing like war to form a man." He will return mustached, virile, and mature. Marie says that she likes him better as he is, but since Charles has drawn the unlucky number three, he has no choice. As he is

39. Merle, Simonnin, and Laloue, *Le conscrit*.

contemplating his farewells, Charles proclaims that Marie and his mother will both reign over his heart.

Meanwhile, Jacques, another young man in the village, is disappointed that he has not been chosen. Jacques volunteers to replace Charles; the latter hesitates because he is concerned that he will be viewed as a coward. Jacques tells him that he is needed by his mother and girlfriend. While "a farmer must be a good soldier," it is also possible for a farmer to be a good citizen by staying at home; Charles remains useful because he "cultivates the earth of the patrie."

Images of the soldat laboureur resonated differently as memories began to fade and circumstances changed. The lives of Napoleonic veterans gradually improved.[40] While liberals in the early 1820s imagined the soldat laboureur as a suffering but loyal veteran, by the later nineteenth century, this image would come to be associated with the apocryphal Chauvin, the eponym of chauvinism, identified retroactively as a volunteer in the armies of the Revolution and the Empire. It signified less the vexed fate of veterans than xenophobia and sexism. In the later nineteenth century, Chauvin would become closely associated with agrarianism, colonialism, and nationalism, and in the twentieth century, with the puppet leader of Vichy France, Pétain.[41] Yet if the particular image of the soldat laboureur would transform dramatically, we should not forget the lasting power of the "soldier's reward." The connections and contradictions between gender, war, and citizenship formed and reformed in the revolutionary era have profoundly shaped our contemporary world.

40. Petiteau, *Lendemains d'empire*; and Hazareesingh, *The Legend of Napoleon*.

41. Puymège, "Chauvin and Chauvinism" and *Chauvin, le soldat-laboureur.*

BIBLIOGRAPHY

Archival Sources

ARCHIVES NATIONALES (AN)

AD / 114 / A	Rastadt
AF / II / 273	Armée de l'Ouest
AF / II / 312 and 313	Personnel des armées, arrêtées individuels du Comité de salut public
AF / III / 144B	Guerre, objets divers
AF / III / 158	Guerre: Commission militaire des Conseil des Cinq Cents
AF / III / 313 / 1 to 77	Guerre: Demandes relatives à des réquisitions, congés et exemptions de service
AF / III / 444 and 450	Minutes des arrêtés, messages et lettres du Directoire
AF / III* / 270 and 271	Registres, réquisitions, an IV–an V
AF / IV / 1124	Conscription, 1809–1810
AF / IV / 1327	Police militaire, gendarmerie, an X–an XIII
AF / IV / 1449	Addresses au premier consul
BB / 15 / 205 to 208	Dispenses pour mariage
BB / 16 / 311 and 866	Correspondance gén. de la division civile, Hérault et Somme
BB / 18 / 1 to 85	Dossiers des délits relatifs à la conscription et au recrutement, an VII– 1814
BB / 18 / 972	Deuxième bureau de la Division criminelle, 1817
C / 459 and 568	Assemblées du Directoire
C / 2026 to 2059	Chambre des députés, pétitions 1814–1818
C / 2073	Chambre des députés, pétitions, 1824
D / III / 338	Minutes et pétitions adressées au Comité de Législation
F / 1 / a / 23	Circulaires, an V–an VIII
F / 1 / c / 1 / 113	Fêtes et cérémonies diverses, Rastadt
F / 1 / c / III Ain I to Zuyederzée 2	Esprit public et fêtes (par département)
F / 7 / 3491 to 3492	Théâtres de Paris: Police, an IV–1812
F / 7 / 3493	Théâtres des dépts: Police, an IV–1818
F / 7 / 3583	Conscription: Objets généraux, an XI–1815
F / 7 / 3732 to 3733	Bulletins de police, 1814
F / 7 / 3736	Bulletins de police, 1816
F / 7 / 3742 and 3743	Bulletins de police, 1816
F / 7 / 3781	Bulletins de police, 1813
F / 7 / 4286	Mélanges, 1791–1817
F / 7 / 8232	L'inspecteur géneral de la gendarmerie au ministre de la police générale
F / 7 / 8397 to 8724	Rapports faits au ministre par les diverses autorités locales, an X–1814
F / 9 / 54 Bis	Affaires militaires, Exécution du décret du 25 mars 1810, en ce concerne le mariage de 6000 militaires
F / 9 / 150 to 261	Recrutement: Correspondance générale

F / 9 / 286	Recrutement: Fraudes
F/ 9 / 288 to 289	Recrutement: Exemptions et dispenses
F / 15 / 2818	Comité de secours publics
F / 15 / 2835	Secours aux familles des militaires, 1792–an V
F / 21 / 966, 975, 976, and 987	Procès-verbaux de la censure à Paris: Classement par théâtres

ARCHIVES DÉPARTEMENTALES DE LA GIRONDE (AD GIRONDE)

1M 698

ARCHIVES DÉPARTEMENTALES DU LOT (AD LOT)

L225 and 3U1

ARCHIVES DÉPARTEMENTALES DU RHÔNE (AD RHÔNE)

1 M 111, Ucl 45 1816, and Uciv 67 1816

ARCHIVES DÉPARTEMENTALES DES YVELINES (AD YVELINES)

4M 17

ARCHIVES DE PARIS

VD / 4 / 8

SERVICE HISTORIQUE DE LA DÉFENSE (SHD)

1 M Mémoires
1 Yi 1 to 1 Yi 53 Femmes militaires

PERIODICALS (EIGHTEENTH- AND NINETEENTH-CENTURY)

L'ambigu ou variétés littéraires et politiques
L'ami de la religion: Journal ecclésiastique, politique, et littéraire
Archives parlementaires (abbreviated *AP)*
L'avant-coureur: Feuille hebdomadaire
Bulletin décadaire
Bulletin des lois
Bulletin officiel du Directoire helvétique et des autorités du Canton de Léman
Censeur dramatique, ou Journal des principaux théâtres de Paris et des départements
Courrier de l'égalité
Courrier des spectacles
Décade philosophique
L'esprit des journaux françois et étrangers
La feuille villageoise
Gazette nationale ou le Moniteur universel

Journal de Lyon, ou Bulletin administratif et politique du département du Rhône
Journal de Lyon, ou Moniteur du département de Rhône et Loire
Journal de Paris
Journal des arts, des sciences, et de la littérature
Journal des débats et des décrets
Journal des débats politiques et littéraires
Journal des défenseurs de la patrie
Journal du Palais présentant la jurisprudence de la cour de cassation
Journal encyclopédique
Magasin encyclopédique: ou Journal des sciences, des lettres et des arts
Mercure de France
Nain Jaune ou le Journal des arts, sciences, et de la littérature
Recueil des actions héroïques et civiques
Vedette ou journal du département du Doubs

Printed Primary Sources

A. de B***. *Aux armées (12 mars).* Paris: Herban, 1815.

Almanach des muses pour l'an VI. Paris: Chez Louis, an VI.

Amanton, Claude-Nicole. *Discours prononcé par le maire . . . d'Auxonne, le 2 décembre 1810, jour de la fête de l'anniversaire du couronnement de S. M. l'Empereur, en la grande salle de l'Hôtel de Ville, lors du couronnement de la rosière et de son mariage avec un militaire.* Dijon: Frantin, 1811.

Antoine, and P. Broulard. *L'a-propos alsacien, ou ventre-saint-gris quel beau jour pour la France.* Colmar: Decker, 1821.

Aperçu sur la révolution de 1815. Paris: Renard, 1815.

Appel aux français. Marseille: Antoine Ricard, 1815.

Arge, Auguste Philibert Chalons d', and Armand Henri Ragueneau de la Chainaye. *Histoire critique des théâtres de Paris pendant 1821.* Paris: Lelong and Delaunay, 1822.

L'armée de Bellone: Enrôlement volontaire de deux cent mille filles. Blois: Dezans, n.d.

Arnaud. *Réponse d'un parisien, ci devant soldat à l'armée de Sambre et Meuse, aujourd'hui vétéran, aux misérables et méprisables sortie des royalistes.* [Paris]: Delaguette, 1815.

Arnault, Antoine Vincent. *Biographie nouvelle des contemporains ou dictionnaire historique.* 20 vols. Paris: Émile Babeuf, 1820–25.

Aude, Joseph. *Le café d'une petite ville.* Paris: Barba, an X.

———. *La paix.* Paris: Barba, 1797.

———. *Le présent du gouvernement aux guerriers pacificateurs.* Paris: Leroi-neufvillette, 1798.

Aude, Joseph, and Charles-Louis Tissot. *Les bruits de la paix ou l'heureuse espérance.* Paris: Toubon, 1797.

Audras, Mathieu Tournay, and Jean-Baptiste-Charles Vial. *Les avant-postes, ou l'armistice.* Paris: Magasin de pièces de théâtre, an IX.

Aulard, François Alphonse. *Paris pendant la réaction thermidorienne et sous le Directoire.* 5 vols. Paris: Cerf, 1898–1902.

———. *Paris sous le consulat: Recueil de documents pour l'histoire de l'esprit public à Paris.* 4 vols. Paris: Maison Quantin, 1903–1909.

———. *Recueil des actes du comité de salut public.* 29 vols. Paris: Imprimerie nationale, 1893–1959.

Auvin, Charles Joseph Arnold Victor d'. *Mélanges de littérature et de politique pour servir à l'histoire.* Brussels: Les Marchands de Nouveautés, 1815.

Aux armées françaises par M. D. Paris: Dentu, 1815.

Azémar, Louis Guérin d'. *Les deux miliciens ou l'orpheline villageoise*. Paris: Duchesne, 1772.

Baillot, Denis. *L'heureux jour ou les cinq mariages*. Versailles: Jacob, 1810.

Balisson de Rougemont, Michel-Nicolas. *La paix, divertissement en vaudevilles*. Paris: Masson, 1809.

Bara, Jean-Baptiste. *Discours prononcé par Bara (des Ardennes), sur le départ des conscrits du même département*. Paris: Imprimerie nationale, an VII.

Barbier, Edmond. *Chronique de la régence et du règne de Louis XV (1718–1673) ou Journal de Barbier*. Paris: Charpentier, 1857.

Bardel, Auguste. *La paix ou le mariage de Rosine*. Grenoble: Chez Ferry, 1801.

Barré, Pierre-Yves, Jean-Baptiste Radet, and François-Georges Desfontaines. *Un petit voyage du vaudeville, divertissement en un acte pour le retour de la paix*. Paris: Fages, 1814.

Barrey, Pierre Edmond. *Le cri de l'indignation: Réponse à M Méhée de la Touche par le chevalier de Barrey, mousquetaire noir*. Paris: Patris, 1814.

Beauchamp, Alphonse de. *An Authentic Narrative of the Invasion of France in 1814*. London: Henry Holborn, 1815.

Belfort, Mme. *L'Artémise française ou les heureux effets de la paix*. Paris: Fages, 1801.

Berthre de Bourniseaux, Pierre-Victor-Jean. *Histoire de Louis XVI, avec les anecdotes de son règne*. 4 vols. Paris: Rosier et Mame, 1829.

Bibliothèque des souvenirs ou Anecdotes curieuses et faits historiques publiés depuis le 21 mars 1814. Paris: Pierre Blanchard, 1814.

Bié, Mathurin. *L'épousera-t-il? ou la prise de Vienne*. Paris: Cavanagh, 1805.

Bogez-Villeneuve. *Liberté Barrau ou les héroïnes républicaines*. Paris, 1794.

Boinvilliers, Jean-Etienne-Judith-Forestier. *Le cri de l'humanité, hymne funéraire demandé par l'administration municipale du canton de Beauvais, pour perpétuer le souvenir de l'assassinat commis par l'Autriche sur les ministres français, près de Rastadt*. Beauvais: Desjardins, an VII.

Bordereau, Renée. *Mémoires de Renée Bordereau, dite Langevin, touchant à sa vie militaire dans la Vendée*. Paris: Michaud, 1814.

Botte, Pierre. *Discours prononcé par le citoyen P. Botte. (Professeur de belles-lettres à l'Ecole Centrale du Département de L'Escaut, Le jour de la fête funéraire, dédiée aux mânes des citoyens Bonnier et Roberjot: Ministres de la République Française. Massacrés à Rastadt le 9 Floréal an VII, ordonnée dans tous les Cantons de la République par la Loi du XXII Floréal an VII*. Gand: Begyn, an VII.

Bottin, Sébastien. *Éloge funèbre des citoyens Bonnier et Roberjot, ministres plénipotentiaires de la république française au congrès de Rastadt, lâchement assassinés, le 9 floréal an VII, par les ordres de la maison d'Autriche*. Strasbourg: Levrault, an VII.

Bouilly, Jean-Nicolas, Jean-Guillaume-Antoine Cuvelier, and Hector Chaussier. *Le tombeau de Turenne, ou l'armée du Rhin à Saspach*. Paris: Barba, an VII.

Bourgoing, Jean-François. *Correspondance d'un jeune militaire, ou mémoires du Marquis de Luzigini et d'Hortense de Saint-Just*. 2 vols. Yverdun: chez l'auteur, 1778.

Boussanelle, Louis de. *Aux soldats*. P.-M. Delaguette, 1786.

———. *Le bon militaire*. Paris: Lacombe, 1770.

Boussemart, Louis. *Le républicain moustache en belle humeur, sur le succès de nos armes et la conquête de la Savoie*. Paris: Daniel, 1798.

Brazier, Nicolas, and Jean-Baptiste Dubois. *La noce de village, ou le tableau en miniature*. Paris: Barba, 1816.

Brémontier, Georges Thomas. *Discours prononcé . . . sur le départ des conscrits de la Seine-Inférieure. Séance du 24 frimaire an VII*. Paris: Imprimerie nationale, 1799.

Briois, Citoyen. *La mort du jeune Barra ou une journée de la Vendée*. Paris: Barba, an II.

Bulletin de Paris, ou relation historique des évènements qui sont arrivés en France en 1814 et 1815, et particulièrement pendant le siège de Paris, depuis le 22 juin jusqu'au 8 juillet, époque du roi dans sa capitale. Paris: Lerouge, 1815.

Cadiot, Marcellin. *Collection des principaux discours prononcés à la Tribune nationale depuis 1789 jusqu'à ce jour.* 2 vols. Paris: Rue Saint-André des Arts, 1826.

Cadot, Daphnis. *Départ volontaire des nouvelles amazones françaises.* Paris: Badouin, n.d.

Caffiaux, Philippe-Joseph. *Défenses du beau sexe ou mémoires historiques, philosophiques, et critiques pour servir d'apologie aux femmes.* 4 vols. Amsterdam: Aux dépenses de la compagnie, 1753.

Cambronne, Auguste. *La paix et l'hymen ou le guerrier récompensé.* Valenciennes: Prignet, 1801.

Cerfvol, de. *Mémoire sur la population dans lequel on indique le moyen de la rétablir et se procurer au corps militaire toujours subsistant et peuplant.* London, 1768.

Chambelland, Claude-Antoine. *La pacification générale ou l'hôtellerie de Calais.* Dijon: Carion, 1814.

Chansonnier de la paix pour l'an X (1802), contenant les meilleures ariettes nouvelles qui ont été chantées dans les spectacles du Vaudeville et des Italiens. Paris: Les libraires associés, an X.

Chansonnier des amis du roi et des Bourbons. Paris: Chez Guyot et Depelafol, 1815.

Chansonnier des amis du roi et des Bourbons. Lille: Castiaux, 1815.

Chansonnier des amis du roi et des Bourbons, contenant les chansons les plus piquants, faites depuis le retour de Buonaparte en France. Lyon: Chambet, 1815.

Chansonnier républicain et le décadaire. Paris: Dufart, 1793–94.

Chansonnier républicain et le décadaire. 2nd ed. Paris: Dufart, an III.

Le chansonnier royal. Rennes: Vve Frout, 1815.

Le chansonnier royal, ou passetemps des bons français. Dédiés aux gardes nationales. Paris: J.-G. Dentu, 1815–1816.

Charavay, Etienne, ed. *Correspondance générale de Carnot.* Vol. 2. Paris: Imprimerie nationale, 1844.

Chateaubriand, François-René de. *De Buonaparte, des Bourbons, et de la nécessité de se rallier à nos princes légitimes, pour le bonheur de la France et celui de l'Europe.* Paris: Laurent Fournier, 1814.

Chauchet Bourgeois, Richard. *Discours prononcé par Chauchet, en présentant au Conseil une adresse de l'administration centrale des Ardennes, relative au départ des conscrits.* Paris: Imprimerie nationale, an VII.

Chénier, Marie-Joseph. *Discours prononcé par M.-J. Chénier, de l'Institut national, à la cérémonie funèbre célébrée au Champ de Mars le 20 prairial an VII de la république française, en l'honneur de nos ministres plénipotentiaires assassinés par l'Autriche.* Paris: Laran, an VII.

Cheppe, Charles A. de. *Harangue sur la tyrannie, par A.-C. de C***.* Paris: Potey, 1814.

Clément, J. *Journal littéraire.* 4 vols. Paris: Forget, 1797.

Cochin, Charles-Nicolas. *Réponse de M. Jérôme, râpeur du tabac, à M Raphael.* Paris, 1769.

Colasin. *Dialogue entre un conscrit et un royaliste dans un café près l'Arsenal.* [Paris], n.d.

Colau, Pierre. *Le soldat laboureur, ou les héros cultivateurs; choix d'actions mémorables, pour faire suite aux invincibles et aux grenadiers français.* Paris: Vauquelin, 1822.

Collection de différentes pièces relatives à la déchéance de Napoléon Bonaparte et au rétablissement de Louis XVIII. Paris: Les Marchands de Nouveautés, 1814.

Collection des lois et décrets: Approuvée et encouragée par le Comité de Salut Public. 12 vols. Douai: Lagarde, n.d.

Collections des livrets des anciennes expositions depuis 1673 jusqu'en 1800. Paris: Liepmannssohn, 1871.

Collot, Jean-François-Henri. "Invalides." In *Encyclopédie, ou dictionnaire raisonné des sciences, des arts et des métiers, etc.*, edited by Denis Diderot and Jean le Rond d'Alembert. University of Chicago: ARTFL Encyclopédie Project (Autumn 2022 edition), edited by Robert Morrissey and Glenn Roe, https://encyclopedie.uchicago.edu, 17:801–4.

Colombier, Jean. *Préceptes sur la santé des gens de guerre ou hygiène militaire*. Paris: Chez Lacombe, 1775.

Conny, Félix de. *Fragmens d'un ouvrage sur la conscription*. N.p., n.d.

Constant. *Les deux orphelins de 1815 ou la tendresse maternelle*. N.p., n.d.

Conversation de Va de Bon Cœur et de Lavaleur, grenadiers français. Paris: Nouzou, 1814.

Coriolis d'Espinouse, Charles Louis Alexandre. *Le tyran, les alliés, et le roi*. Paris: Le Normant, 1814.

Correspondance de Napoléon Ier. 32 vols. Paris: Bibliothèque des introuvables, 2006.

Coupart, Antoine, and E. F. Varez. *Le baptême, ou la double fête, vaudeville en 1 acte, à l'occasion du baptême de S.A.R. Monseigneur le Duc de Bordeaux*. Paris: Fages, 1821.

———. *Vive la paix! Ou le retour au village*. Paris: Corbeaux, 1814.

Courtois. *Les préliminaires de paix ou les amans réunis, comédie en trois actes représenté à Douai le 12 ventôse an 9*. Douai: Carpentier, an IX.

———. *Le retour de la paix, divertissement allégorique en un acte et en vaudevilles*. Douai: Carpentier, an IX.

Cri de l'Europe contre l'assassinat des plénipotentiaires français massacrés à Rastadt par les ordres de l'Autriche. N.p.: Lachave, an VII.

Cubières-Palmézeaux, Michel de. *Au peuple français, sur l'assassinat de ses plénipotentiaires à Rastadt, poème dithyrambique*. Paris: Laran, an VI.

Cuvelier de Trie, Jean-Guillaume-Antoine. *Fête de l'Être Suprême*. Paris: Imprimerie des écoles républicaines, 1794.

———. *La fille hussard, ou le jeune sergent*. Paris: Barba, 1796.

Darracq, François-Balzathar. *Discours prononcé . . . sur le départ des conscrits des Landes. Séance du 29 frimaire an VII*. Paris: Imprimerie nationale, 1799.

D'Artois, Archille. *La rosière d'Hartwell*. Paris: Huet-Masson,1816.

Dauberval, Jean. *Le déserteur, ballet d'action en trois actes*. Paris: Barba, [1804)].

David, Jacques-Louis. *Rapport sur la fête héroïque pour les honneurs du Panthéon à décerner aux jeunes Barra et Viala, séance du 23 messidor an II*. Paris: Imprimerie nationale, n.d.

Debry, Jean. *Discours prononcé par Jean Debry . . . séance du 1er prairial an VII*. Paris: Imprimerie nationale, an VII.

Les décades républicaines: ou histoire abrégée de la République. 6 vols. Paris: Imprimerie de la Société Typographique des Trois Amis, an II.

Déclaration individuelle sur l'assassinat des ministres français à Rastadt, avec le plan topographique de Rastadt et de ses environs exécuté sur la carte allemande. Paris: Dabin, an VII.

De la fausse gloire de Buonaparte et de la vraie gloire des armées françaises. Lyon: Penzin, 1814.

Delannoy, Alexandre. *Le retour du conscrit, ou le rétablissement de Louis XVIII sur le trône de ses ancêtres*. Boulogne: LeRoy-Berger, 1814.

Désaugiers, Marc-Antoine, and Michel-Joseph Gentil de Chavagnac. *Le retour des lys. A propos en un acte et en vaudeville, à l'occasion de l'entrée de Sa Majesté Louis XVIII à Paris*. Paris: Les Marchands de Nouveautés, 1814.

Des causes des malheurs de la France sous Napoléon Bonaparte ou quelques aveux de Napoléon, échappés aux remords de sa conscience. Vannes: Mahé-Bizette, 1814.

Deschodt, Cornil-François. *Discours prononcé le 20 prairial an VII dans le temple décadaire de la commune d'Hazebrouck*. Hazebrouck: Dabecker Itzweire, 1799.

Desennes, J. *Code général français*. 22 vols. Paris: Ménard et Desenne fils, 1818–1825.

Desfontaines, François-Georges. *La fille soldat, fait historique*. Paris: Théâtre du Vaudeville, 1794.

Desfontaines, François-Georges, Pierre-Yves Barré, Jean-Baptiste Radet, Jean-Baptiste-Denis Després, and Jean Marie Deschamps. *Le Pari. Divertissement en un acte, en prose et en vaudevilles, à l'occasion de la paix*. Paris: Migneret, 1797.

Des pamphlets, de leur nature, et de leur danger, par un observateur impartial. Paris: Didot jeune, 1814.

Deux mots de vérité: Buonaparte jugé par lui-même, nécessité d'une constitution. [Paris]: Charles, 1814.

Le diable prophète, ou petit entretien amical entre Astarot et Napoléon. Paris: Le Normant, 1814.

Dialogue entre un paysan, un ancien soldat de Bonaparte et un bourgeois de Loret. Orléans: Guyot ainé, 1816.

Dictionnaire des girouettes ou nos contemporains peints d'après eux-mêmes. Paris: Eymery, 1815.

Discours d'un brave militaire à ses frères d'armes. Paris: Cellot, 1814.

Discours prononcé à la fête de la reconnaissance et des victoires par le président de l'administration municipale de Versailles, le 10 prairial l'an IV. Versailles, [1796].

Discours prononcé dans la Chapelle du Lazaert de Marseille, le 3 juillet 1814. Marseille: Mossy, 1814.

Doche-Delisle, René. *Discours par Doche-Delisle, représentant du peuple, sur le départ des conscrits du département de la Charente. Séance du 11 frimaire an VII*. Paris: Imprimerie nationale, an VII.

Dorfeuille, Antoine. *Commissaire des représentants du peuple aux volontaires des armées de la république*. Roanne: Cabot, 1793.

Dorvigny. *La parfaite égalité ou les tu et toi*. Paris: Barba, 1794.

Dubois, Jean-Baptiste. *Hôtel des Invalides ou la députation*. Paris: Barba, 1821.

——. *Les lauriers rose ou le tribut de village*. Paris: Barba, 1810.

——. *Trois bienfaits pour un, ou les deux baptêmes*. Paris: Quoy, 1821.

Dubroca, Louis. *Réponse aux faiseurs de pamphlets et d'anecdotes contre Buonaparte*. Paris: Les Marchands de Nouveautés, 1814.

Ducolombier, Jean-Pierre, *La victoire et la paix, comédie pour être représentée à l'occasion de la fête de la paix, célébrée à Gap, le 6 prairial an 5*. Gap: Allier, 1797.

Dulaurent, C. *Le bon père: Discours prononcé dans la Section des Tuileries, le décadi 20 frimaire, à la fête de la Raison et de la Vérité*. Paris: Imprimerie nationale, an II.

Dulaurent, Citoyen. *La bonne mère*. Paris: Imprimerie nationale, an II.

Dumersan, Théophile Marion. *Le soldat laboureur*. 3 vols. Paris: Barba, 1822.

Dumersan, Théophile Marion, M. Francis, and Nicolas Brazier. *Les moissonneurs de la Beauce, ou, Le soldat laboureur comédie villageoise, mêlée de couplets*. Paris: Boulet, 1821.

Dupaty, Emmanuel. *La fête de Meudon*. Paris: L'auteur, 1810.

Dupont-de-Lille. *La paix ou le retour du bon fils*. Paris: Fages, 1801.

Durat-Lasalle, Louis. *Droit et législation des armées de terre et de mer*. 10 vols. Paris: L'auteur, 1842-1857.

Duval, Alexandre, and Louis Benoit Picard. *La vraie bravoure*. Paris: Lepetit, 1793.

Duviquet, Pierre. *Discours . . . sur le départ des conscrits de la Nièvre. Séance du 29 frimaire an VII*. Paris: Imprimerie nationale, an VII.

L'enrôlement volontaire et départ des jeunes filles pour l'armée. Paris: Imprimerie de J. Mornoval, n.d.

Épitre au roi par un garde national. Paris: Sétier, 1814.

Épitre du Diable à Bonaparte, signé: Lucifer, et plus bas, par ordre: le duc de Frioul. N.p., mai 1814.

Essai sur les sentiments qu'on doit au Buonaparte. Paris: Crapelet, 1815.

Etienne, Charles-Guillaume. *Les plaideurs sans procès.* Paris: Théâtre Français, 1821.

Eude, Jean François. *Discours . . . sur le départ des conscrits du département de l'Eure.* Paris: Imprimerie nationale, an VII.

Explication des ouvrages de peinture et dessins, sculpture, architecture et gravure des artistes vivans. Paris: Imprimerie des sciences et des arts, 1802.

Extrait des réclamations du département de la Manche, contre les prétendues loix des 4 janvier 1793 & 17 nivôse, relatives aux successions. Paris: Gorsas, 1794–1795.

F. M.*** *Le retour de la paix ou la France sauvée.* Paris: Les Marchands de Nouveautés, 1814.

Favières, Edmond de. *Herman et Verner, ou les militaires, fait historique.* Paris: Huet, an XI.

Ferrand, Olivier. *La diligence du Havre à Rouen ou le conscrit déserteur.* Rouen: Bertholet, 1802.

Ferrière, Claude Joseph de. *Nouvelle introduction à la pratique, ou dictionnaire des termes de pratique, de droit, d'ordonnances, et de coutumes.* 2 vols. Paris: Prudhomme, 1734.

Les filles et les femmes traitées comme elles le méritent, ou conseil aux filles, aux épouses, aux mères de famille à toutes les femmes en général. Paris: Poulet, 1815.

Fortia de Piles, Alphonse-Toussaint-Joseph-André-Marie-Marseille de. *Conversation entre le Gobe-Mouche Tant Pis et le Gobe-Mouche Tant Mieux.* Paris: Eymery, 1814.

———. *Quatrième conversation entre le Gobe-Mouche Tant Pis et le Gobe-Mouche Tant Mieux.* Paris: Eymery, 1815.

———. *Seconde conversation entre le Gobe-Mouche Tant Pis et le Gobe-Mouche Tant Mieux* Paris: Eymery, 1814.

———. *Troisième conversation entre le Gobe-Mouche Tant Pis et le Gobe-Mouche Tant Mieux.* Paris: Eymery, 1815.

Franconi, Henri. *Le soldat laboureur: Mimodrame en un acte.* Paris: Fages, 1819.

Franconi, Henri, and Louis Portellete Ponet. *Le soldat fermier, ou le bon seigneur.* Paris: Martinet, 1821.

Garat, Dominique Joseph. *Discours prononcé par Garat, après la lecture du message sur l'assassinat des ministres à Rastadt. Séance du 16 floréal an VII.* Paris: Imprimerie nationale, an VII.

Gardel, Maximilien. *Le déserteur, ballet d'action en trois actes.* Paris: P.R.C. Ballard, 1786.

Gentil de Chavagnac, Michel-Joseph, Fulgence de Bury, Paul Ledoux, and Ramond de La Croisette. *Le baptême de village ou le parrain de circonstance.* Paris: d'Evrat, 1821.

Gentil de Chavagnac, Michel-Joseph, and Marc-Antoine Désaugiers. *Le dix-sept juin, ou l'heureuse journée.* Paris: Ballard, 1816.

Girou de Buzareingues, Charles. *Du recrutement.* N.p., 1815.

Godard d'Aucourt de Saint-Just, Claude. *L'heureuse nouvelle, opéra impromptu à l'occasion de la paix.* Paris: Feydeau, an VI.

Gouges, Olympe de. *L'entrée du Dumourier à Bruxelles ou les vivandiers.* Paris: Regnaud, 1793.

Grande conspiration des ainés de famille contre les cadets, ou la loi du 17 nivôse justifiée dans son effet rétroactif. Paris: Robiot, 1795.

Guéau de Reverseaux de Rouvray. *La paix de l'Europe avec la France, et la paix de la France avec elle-même.* Paris: Nouzou, 1814.

Guibert, Jacques Antoine Hippolyte de. *Essai général de tactique, précédé d'un discours sur l'état actuel de la politique et de la science militaire en Europe, avec le plan d'un ouvrage intitulé: La France politique et militaires.* 2 vols. London: Chez les libraires associés, 1772.

Guillemain, Charles-Jacob. *L'enrôlement supposé*. Paris: Cailleau, 1781.

Hapdé, Jean-Baptiste Augustin. *Les sépulcres de la grande armée ou tableau des hôpitaux pendant la dernière campagne de Buonaparte*. Paris: Eymery, 1814.

Henri . . . ancien grenadier de Ste Foy. *Adresse au roi par un grenadier de la vielle armée*. Paris: Plassan, 1818.

Herbin, P. *Éloge funèbre du citoyen Joubert*. Tours: L'héritier-Vauquer, n.d.

Hespelle, Auguste. *La seule véritable religion démontrée contre les athées, les déistes et tous les sectaires*. 3 vols. Paris: Veuve Hérissant, 1774.

Historique des diverses lois sur le recrutement depuis la révolution jusqu'à nos jours. Paris: Imprimerie nationale, 1902.

Hoffman, François-Benoît. *Lisistrata ou les athéniennes, comédie en 1 acte et en prose, mêlée de vaudevilles, imitée d'Aristophane, dont les représentations ont été suspendues par ordre*. Paris: Huet, 1802.

Les hommes se plaignent! Que dirons-nous donc? Ou lettres des chevaux de France à Buonaparte. [Paris]: Mornoval, 1814.

Ivernois, Francis d'. *Napoléon administrateur et financier*. Paris: J. J. Paschoud, 1814.

Jacques, dit le Boiteux, cultivateur, à son fils, Henry. Capitaine dans le . . . de Ligne. Paris: Belin, 1814.

Jaquelin, Jacques-André, and Michel-Nicolas Balisson de Rougemont. *Le chansonnier des Bourbons: Dédié à S.A.S Madame la duchesse douairière d'Orléans*. Paris: Rosa, 1815.

Jardin. *Le déjeuner des volontaires*. Paris: Pollet, an II.

Jarry. *Discours prononcé par le citoyen Jarry, président de l'administration municipale de Besançon, à la fête funéraire en mémoire des citoyens Bonnier et Roberjot, ministres de la république française, au congrès de Rastadt*. Besançon: Jean-François Daclin, an VII.

Jaucourt, Chevalier de. "Milice." In *Encyclopédie, ou dictionnaire raisonné des sciences, des arts et des métiers, etc.*, edited by Denis Diderot and Jean le Rond d'Alembert. University of Chicago: ARTFL Encyclopédie Project (Autumn 2022 edition), edited by Robert Morrissey and Glenn Roe, https://encyclopedie.uchicago.edu, 10:505.

Jeanne d'Arc aux jeunes françaises ou appel aux femmes courageuses de la capitale par la Pucelle d'Orléans. Paris: Lanoe, n.d.

Joigny. *Cécile et Julien ou le siège de Lille*. Paris: Deperne, an II.

Josse-Beauvoir, Auguste Guillaume. *Opinion de . . . , député de Loir et Cher, sur le recrutement de l'armée, prononcée dans la séance du 14 janv. 1818*. Paris: Imprimerie nationale, 1818.

Jouy, Etienne de. *La paix et l'amour*. Lille: Vanackere, 1797.

Jouy, Etienne de, and Antoine Jay. *Salon d'Horace Vernet: Analyse historique et pittoresque des quarante-cinq tableaux exposés chez lui en 1822*. Paris: Ponthieu, 1822.

Kéralio, Louis-Félix Guinement. *Encyclopédie méthodique: Art militaire*. 4 vols. Paris: Panckoucke; Liège: Plomteux, 1784–1797.

L. D., Madame. *Conversation entre une dame bourboniste et une dame buonapartiste*. Paris: Chaumerot Jeune, 1815.

L. D. M. Y. *Lettre d'un général à son fils, colonel à l'armée française*. Paris: Dentu, 1815.

Lacretelle, Charles. *Histoire de France, pendant le dix-huitième siècle*. 3 vols. Paris: Buissons, 1812.

Laissac, de. *De l'esprit militaire, nouvelle édition*. La Haye, 1785.

Landon, C. P. *Salon de 1817*. Paris: Chaignieau ainé, 1817.

Landreau de Maine-au-Picq. *Digression sur le célibat des prêtres et des militaires, dans l'intérêt de la politique, des mœurs et de la religion*. 3 vols. Geneva and Paris: l'auteur, 1787.

Larue de Mareilles, A.-M.-J. de. *Aux armées. Il fut: Que-sera-t-il? Et quelle peut être l'avenir de son influence dans le monde politique?* Paris: Maugeret, 1814.

Ledrut, A. L. *Honneur aux militaires ou examen impartial de cette question: Buonaparte est-il un héros?* Paris: Les Marchands de Nouveautés, 1814.

Legal-Lalande, J. G. M. *Le retour du soldat de l'armée d'Italie ou le fête de la paix au village.* Quimper: Barazer, 1797.

Lehodey de Saultchevreuil, Etienne. *Histoire de la régence de l'impératrice Marie-Louise.* Paris: Petit, 1814.

Lemercier, Népomucène-Louis. *Réflexions d'un français sur une partie factieuse de l'armée.* Paris: Dentu, 1815.

Lenoir-Leroche, Claire Réguis. *Description du calvaire des lauriers, monument élevé au nom des mères, des veuves . . . et des orphelines des guerriers français.* Paris: Huzard-Courcier, 1820.

Lesbroussart-Dawaele, Philippe. *Réponse à l'ouvrage de M. de Châteaubriand, intitulé "De Buonaparte, des Bourbons, et des alliés."* Paris: Les Marchands de Nouveautés, 1814.

Lestrade, Louis François. *Opinion d'un ancien militaire sur la Constitution, la France, et les français.* Paris: Michaud frères, 1814.

Lesur, Charles-Louis. *Annuaire historique universel pour 1818.* Paris: Rignoux, 1818.

Lettre d'un ancien capitaine d'infanterie à MM. Les comédiens du théâtre français. Paris: Palais-Royal, 1814.

Lettres du grenadier Lafranchise au grenadier Lavaleur. [Paris], 1815.

Lettres d'un voyageur à Paris à son ami Sir Charles Lovers, demeurant à Londres, sur les nouvelles étampes de Greuze. Paris: Chez Hardouin, 1779.

Lévy, Jean Baptiste Michel de. *Journal historique ou Fastes du règne de Louis XV, surnommé le bien aimé.* Paris: Prault, 1766.

Liberté, patrie, Napoléon, l'Honneur, l'ami et le soldat de son pays à ses concitoyens. Saint-Brieux: Beurel, 1815.

Le lis et la violette, chansonnier royal, par un ami du roi, contenant divers poèmes, chansons, et couplettes satiriques sur Buonaparte, suivis des chants patriotiques sur le retour des Bourbons en France. Paris: Caillot, 1816.

Lombard de Langres, Vincent. *Contes militaires.* Paris: Patris, 1810.

M. C. A. *Entretiens d'un père de famille sur les événements de 1814 et 1815.* Rouen: Periaux, 1815.

Macors? *Le siège ou l'héroïne républicaine, par un citoyen de Ville Affranchie.* Ville Affranchie, 1793.

Maignet, Etienne-Christophe. *Rapport et projet de décret sur les secours à accorder aux pères, mères, femmes, et enfans des citoyens-soldats qui sont dans le besoin.* Paris: Imprimerie nationale, 1792.

Maréchalle, Alexandre-Marie, Jean-Nicolas Barba, and Hocquet. *Le soldat d'Henri IV.* Paris: Barba, 1816.

Masson de Pezay, Alexandre-Frédéric-Jacques. *La rosière de Salency.* Paris: Fages, 1771.

Maurin. *La paix en ménage, allégorie analogue à la paix.* Toulouse: Caunes, 1814.

———. *La paix en ménage, allégorie en un acte et en vers.* Lyon: Pelzin et Drevon, 1809.

———. *La paix ou le triomphe de Mars.* Bordeaux: Laguillotière, 1801.

Mayeur de St. Paul, François Marie. *Jeanne Hachette ou le siège de Beauvais* signé Mlle. M. F. A. G***. Cad. Paris: Brunet, 1784.

Mémorial dramatique: ou Almanach théâtral pour l'année 1815. Paris: Hoquet, 1815.

Mercier, Louis-Sébastien. *Le déserteur.* Paris: Le Jay, 1770.

———. *Le Nouveau Paris.* 6 vols. Paris : Fuchs, 1800.

———. *Tableau de Paris.* 12 vols. Amsterdam, 1782–1788.

Merle, Jean Toussaint, Antoine-Jean-Baptiste Simonnin, and Ferdinand Laloue. *Le conscrit.* Paris: Quoy, 1823.

Michel, Jean-André. *Discours sur l'amour de la patrie.* Coutances: Agnès, 1792.

Mirabeau, Honoré Gabriel. *De la monarchie prussienne, sous Frédéric le Grand.* 4 vols. London, 1788.

Mittié, Jean. *La paix ou les amans réunis.* Paris: Marais, an VI.

Montesquieu, Charles de Secondat Baron de. *The Spirit of the Laws.* Originally published 1748. Translated by Thomas Nugent. Kitchener: Batoche Books, 2001.

Montesquiou-Fezensac, François-Xavier-Marc Antoine. *Rapport de S. Exe. Le Ministre de l'Intérieur, sur la situation de la France, lu à la séance du 12 juillet 1814.* Paris: Hacquart, 1814.

Moreau de Vormes, Jacob-Augustin-Antoine. *Discours . . . sur le départ des conscrits du département de l'Yonne.* Paris: Imprimerie nationale, an VII.

Mouton-Fontenille de laclotte, Marie-Jacques-Philippe. *La France en délire, pendant les deux usurpations de Buonaparte.* Paris: Guyot, 1815.

Naquet, Alfred. *Le divorce.* Paris: Dentu, 1877.

Nettement, Philippe. *Le second retour des Bourbons ou la fin de la révolution, par M. Nettement, ancien secrétaire de légation à Londres.* Paris: Gueffier, 1815.

Neufchâteau, François de. *Ordre de la marche et des cérémonies qui seront observées, au Champs de Mars, le 20 prairial pour la fête funéraire ordonnée par le Corps législatif en mémoire des ministres plénipotentiaires de la République, assassinés près de Rastadt, le 9 floréal, par les troupes autrichiennes.* Paris: Imprimerie de la rue du Chantre-Honoré, an VII.

Nodier, Ch. *Le spectateur français depuis la restauration du trône de St Louis et Henri IV.* Paris: Censeurs, 1815.

Noël, J.-M. *Poltronet ou Marions nos filles.* Paris: Dufay, 1801.

Norvins, Jacques Marquet de Montbreton. *Portefeuille de mil huit cent treize: ou, tableau politique et militaire, avec le récit des événements de cette époque.* 2 vols. Paris: Mongie, 1825.

Nos malheurs sont finis ou histoire de deux amants mariés pendant les fêtes du couronnement. Paris: Masson, 1805.

Obligations qu'auront à remplir les pères et mères de famille qui voudront faire déclarer l'absence ou constater en justice le décès des militaires, administrateurs ou employés aux armées, disparus depuis la première déclaration de guerre du 21 avril 1792 jusqu'au traité de paix du 20 nov. 1815. Paris: Baudouin, n.d.

Odier, Pierre-Agathange. *De la réforme dans la législation militaire.* Paris: Testu, 1818.

P. G. *Que d'heureux tu vas faire, vaudeville en un acte, analogue à la paix générale.* Bordeaux: Pagaud et Baudin, 1802.

La paix est faite! Chantons. Paris: Tigre, 1815.

Palasne de Champeaux, Antoine-Julien-Pierre. *L'heureuse journée.* Paris: Logerot-Petiet, 1801.

Parquin, Denis Charles. *Souvenirs de gloire et d'amour du lieutenant-colonel Parquin.* Paris: Tallandier, 1911.

Patrat, Joseph. *L'officier de fortune ou les deux militaires.* Paris: Delavigne fils, 1792.

———. *La petite ruse.* Paris: Balard Huet, 1797.

———. *Le petit homme rouge.* Paris: Becket, 1814.

Pétion, Jérôme. *Essai sur le mariage, considéré sous des rapports naturels, moraux et politiques; ou Moyens de faciliter & d'encourager les mariages en France.* Geneva, n.p., 1785.

Le petit voyage du grand homme ou itinéraire de Bonaparte de Fontainebleau à l'Ile d'Elbe. Lyon: Chambet, 1814.

Petites vérités au grand jour, sur les acteurs, les actrices, les peintres, les journalistes, l'institut, le portique républicain, Bonaparte, . . . par une société d'envieux, d'intrigans et de cabaleurs. Paris, an VIII.

Pezzani, J. A. *Traité des empêchements du mariage ou commentaire sur le chapitre 1er du titre 5 du Code civil.* Paris: Videcoq, 1838.

Philipon de La Madelaine, Louis, and François-Pierre-Auguste Léger. *Le dédit mal gardé.* Paris: Théâtre du Vaudeville, 1794.

Picard, Louis-Benoît, and François Devienne. *Rose et Aurèle.* Paris: Huet, 1794.

Pillet, Fabien. *Année théâtrale pour l'an X, contenant une notice sur chacun des théâtres de Paris, les acteurs, les pièces nouvelles et les débuts.* Paris: Courcier, 1801.

Plumptre, Anne. *A Narrative of Three Years Residence in France, Principally in the Southern Departments, from the Year 1802 to 1805.* 3 vols. London: Mawman, 1810.

Plutarch. *Oeuvres morales de Plutarque.* Translated by Abbé Ricard. 16 vols. Paris: Vve Desaint, 1783.

Pompadour, Jeanne Antoinette Poisson. *Mémoires de Madame la marquise de Pompadour.* 2 vols. Paris: Maume et Delaunay, 1830.

Pradel, Eugène de. *Le bouquet de violettes ou la réunion des braves au café Montansier.* Paris: Les Marchands de Nouveautés, 1815.

Précis de ce qui s'est passé lors de la rentrée dans le royaume de France de S. M. Louis XVIII, dit le Désiré. Paris: Ancelle, 1815.

Procès-verbal de la fête célébrée à Nevers pour le dernier départ des conscrits. Nevers: Lefebvre, an VII.

Procès-verbal de la fête de la victoire et la reconnaissance. Metz: Lamort, [1796].

Procès-verbal de la fête des victoires et la reconnaissance célébrée dans la commune de Bruxelles. Brussels: Huyghe, an IV.

Procès-verbal de la fête funèbre célébrée par l'administration municipale du 12e arrondissement du canton de Paris, dans le temple de la Piété filiale, le 20 prairial an VII de la république. [Paris]: Ballard, n.d.

Proclamation du Conseil général du département de la Seine et du Conseil municipal de Paris. Paris: Le Normant, 1814.

Profession de foi d'un militaire français. Paris: Les Marchands de Nouveautés, 1815.

Protestation d'un vrai soldat français, contre le dernier attentat de Napoléon Buonaparte. Brest: Michel, 1815.

Que vouloient ceux de nos braves qui ont paru regretter la guerre? Paris: Le Normant, 1814.

R . . . *Épitre aux armées françaises.* Paris: Delaunay, 1814.

Radet, Jean-Baptiste, François-Georges Desfontaines, and Pierre-Yves Barré. *Enfin nous y voilà.* Paris: Brunet, 1801.

Recueil des actes du Directoire exécutif, procès-verbaux, arrêtés, instructions, lettres et actes divers. 4 vols. Paris: Imprimerie nationale, 1910–1911.

Recueil des actions héroïques et civiques des républicains français. Paris: Imprimerie nationale, an II.

Recueil des proclamations et arrêtés des représentants du peuple français, envoyés près les armées du Nord et de Sambre et Meuse. 2 vols. Brussels: Huyghe, 1794.

Réflexions d'un officier supérieur, retiré, sur la position actuelle de la France.[Paris]: Moreaux, 1815.

Réflexions d'un soldat à ses camarades sur la chute de Buonaparte et le rétablissement de la famille des Bourbons sur le trône de France, par un officier du 58e régiment de ligne. Paris: Dentu, 1814.

Réflexions joyeuses d'un garçon de bonne humeur, sur les tableaux exposés au salon en 1781. Paris: Vatel, 1781.

Réflexions sur la catastrophe des ministres de la république à Rastadt. N.p., 1799.

Réflexions sur le corps de la maréchaussée, adressées, en forme de lettre, à l'auteur du livre intitulé: "Défense du système de guerre moderne, etc." Geneva, 1781.

Règlement provisoire concernant le service intérieur, la police, et la discipline des troupes d'infanterie, 1 juillet 1788. Paris: Imprimerie royale, 1788.
Revue encyclopédique ou analyse raisonnée des productions les plus remarquables dans la littérature, les sciences, et les arts. 69 vols. Paris: Revue Encyclopédique, 1819–1833.
Rézicourt. *Les vrais sans-culottes ou l'hospitalité républicaine*. Paris: Sourds-Muets, 1793.
Robespierre et Bonaparte, ou les deux tyrannies. Paris: Les Marchands de Nouveautés, 1814.
Robinet, Jean-Baptiste. *Dictionnaire universel des sciences morale, économique, politique et diplomatique; ou Bibliothèque de l'homme d'état et du citoyen*. London: Librairies associés, 1782.
Rocheplate, Alphonse de. *La conscription: Ode*. Paris: Poulet, 1814.
Roelandts, Jean. *Les dots ou la fête du 11 frimaire*. Gand: Samuel Berthoud, 1804.
Rougemaître, C-J. *L'ogre de Corse*. Paris: Louis, 1814.
Roujoux, Louis-Julien. *La paix, divertissement*. Quimper: G. J. L.-Derrien, 1797.
Sauvage. *Le miroir du jour, ou adresse des dames et mères de famille parisiennes au nom et comme défenderesses des mères de famille de toutes les nations du monde, aux Représentans de la Nation Française, sur la paix*. Paris: Rougeron, 1815.
Sedaine, Michel-Jean. *Le déserteur*. Paris: Hérissant, 1769.
Servan, Joseph. *Le soldat citoyen, ou vues patriotiques sur la manière la plus avantageuse de pourvoir à la défense du royaume*. Neufchâtel, 1780.
Seville, Charles-Victor-Armand. *Le dernier bulletin ou la paix*. Paris: Tigre, 1806.
Sewrin, Charles-Augustin. *Les nouvelles réjouissances ou l'impromptu de Nanterre*. Paris: Neuve Saint Marc, 1811.
Sewrin, Charles-Augustin, Rodolphe Kreutzer, and François Adrien Boieldieu. *Les Béarnais, ou Henri IV en voyage*. Paris: Vente, 1814.
Soulavie, Jean-Louis. *Mémoires historiques et anecdotes de la cour de France, pendant la faveur de la marquise de Pompadour*. Paris: Arthus Bertrand, 1802.
Soulié, Melchior. *L'officier français à Milan*. Foix: Pomiés l'ainé, 1798.
Sutter, Thérèse. *Les campagnes de Mademoiselle Thérèse Figueur, aujourd'hui Madame Vve Sutter, ex-dragon aux 15e et 9e régiments, de 1793 à 1815*. Paris: Dauvin et Fontaine, 1842.
Tableau comparatif des demandes contenues dans les cahiers des trois ordres, remis à MM les Députés aux États généraux. N.p., 1789.
Tissot, Charles-Louis. *Les salpêtriers républicains*. Paris: Toubon, 1794.
———. *Tout pour la liberté*. Paris: Toubon, 1792.
Tissot, Pierre François. *Les fastes de la gloire ou les braves recommandés à la postérité*. 5 vols. Paris: Raymond, 1818–1822.
Tournay, Mathieu. *Le congé ou la fête du vieux soldat*. Paris: Masson, 1802.
Un grand nombre de citoyens de la Commune du Laon, département de l'Aisne, aux membres du Conseil des Cinq-Cents. Paris: Imprimerie nationale, Floréal an VII.
Vadé, Jean-Joseph. *Les racoleurs, opéra-comique*. Paris: Duchesne, 1756.
Vée, and Barral. *L'héroïne de Mithier*. Paris: Libraire du vaudeville, 1794.
La vérité est toujours vérité. Paris: Renard, 1815.
Vermorel, A., ed. *Oeuvres de Robespierre*. Paris: Cournel, 1867.
Viel-Castel, Théodore. *Réflexions politiques en juillet 1815*. Versailles: J.-A. Lebel, 1815.
Villiers, Nicole. *Barra, ou la mère républicaine*. Dijon: Causse, an II.
Villiers, Pierre-Antoine, and P. G. A. Bonel. *La guinguette, ou réjouissances pour la paix*. Paris: Barba, an IX.
Winckler, Théophile Frédéric. *Le répertoire du vaudeville: ou Recueil des meilleures pièces*. Iena: Frédéric Fromann, 1800.
Les yeux ouverts pour tout le monde. Paris: Place André des Arts, 1816.
Ymbert, Jacques-Gilbert. *Éloquence militaire, ou l'art d'émouvoir de soldat*. Paris: Magimel, 1818.

Secondary Sources

Aaslestad, Katherine. "Citizenship in Action: Hanseatic Women's Wartime Associations." In *Gender in Urban Europe: Sites of Political Activity and Citizenship*, 1750–1900, edited by Krista Cowman, Nina Javette Koefoed, and Asa Karlsson Sjögren, 124–40. New York: Routledge, 2014.

———. "Identifying a Postwar Period: Case Studies from the Hanseatic Cities Following the Napoleonic Wars." In *Decades of Reconstruction: Postwar Societies, Economies, and International Relations from the 18th to the 20th Centuries*, edited by Ute Planert and James Retallack, 158–78. Cambridge: Cambridge University Press, 2017.

———. "Republican Traditions: Patriotism, Gender, and War in Hamburg, 1770–1815." *European History Quarterly* 37, no. 4 (2007): 582–602.

Aaslestad, Katherine, Karen Hagemann, and Judith A Miller. "Introduction: Gender, War and the Nation in the Period of the Revolutionary and Napoleonic Wars—European Perspectives." *European History Quarterly* 37, no. 4 (2007): 501–6.

Alès, Anatole. *Les femmes décorées de la Légion d'honneur et les femmes militaires*. Paris: Melet, 1886.

Alzas, Nathalie. *La liberté ou la mort: L'effort de guerre dans l'Hérault pendant la révolution*. Aix en Provence: Université de Provence, 2006.

Armengaud, André. "Mariages et naissances sous le consulat et l'empire." *Revue d'histoire moderne et contemporaine* 17, no. 3 (1970): 373–90.

Astbury, Katherine. "Répertoires traditionnels et répertoire nouveau à Paris sous les Cent-Jours." In *Fièvre et vie du théâtre sous la révolution française et l'empire*, edited by Thibaud Julian and Vicenzo De Santis, 195–212. Paris: Classiques Garnier, 2019.

Athanassoglou-Kallmyer, Nina. "Sad Cincinnatus: Le Soldat Laboureur as an Image of the Napoleonic Veteran after the Empire." *Arts Magazine* 60, no. 9 (1986): 65–75.

Atkins, Stephen. "Restoration Policies towards Books and Pamphlets, 1814–1830." *Proceedings of the Annual Meeting of the Western Society for French History* (1986): 153–16.

Baecque, Antoine de. *The Body Politic: Corporeal Metaphor in Revolutionary France, 1770–1800*. Translated by Charlotte Mandell. Stanford: Stanford University Press, 1997.

Bara, Olivier. "1814–1815: Construction dramatique des événements et modes théâtraux de symbolisation du présent." *Revue d'histoire du XIXe siècle* (2014): 109–22.

Baraud, A. "Les rosières de la Roche-Sur-Yon depuis 1809." *Revue du Bas Poitou et des provinces de l'Ouest* 23 (1910): 62–66.

Barker, Emma. *Greuze and the Painting of Sentiment*. Cambridge: Cambridge University Press, 2005.

Bartlet, Elizabeth C. "Grétry and the Revolution." In *Grétry et l'Europe de l'Opéra-Comique*, edited by Philippe Vendrix, 47–81. Mardaga: Conseil de la Musique de la Communauté française de Belgique, 1992.

Becquert, Noël. "Les 'mariages de l'empereur' en 1810 dans l'arrondissement de Nontron." *Bulletin de la Société historique et archéologique du Périgord*, 112, no. 3 (1975): 222–29.

Becquet, Helene. "Royauté, royalismes et révolutions: Marie-Thérèse-Charlotte de France (1778–1851)." PhD diss., Université de Paris 1, 2009.

Bell, David. *The Cult of the Nation in France: Inventing Nationalism, 1680–1800*. Cambridge, MA: Harvard University Press, 2001.

———. *The First Total War: Napoleon's Europe and the Birth of Warfare as We Know It*. Boston: Houghton Mifflin, 2007.

Bell, David, Annie Crépin, Hervé Drevillon, Olivier Forcade, and Bernard Gainot. "Autour de la guerre totale." *Annales historiques de la révolution française* 366 (2011): 153–70.

Bergès, Louis. "A l'origine de la conscription nationale: Le débat autour de la loi Jourdan-Delbrel." *Mémoires de la Société pour l'histoire du droit et des institutions des anciens pays bourguignons, comtois et romands* 49 (1992): 155–61.

———. *Résister à la conscription, 1798–1814: Le cas des départements aquitains*. Paris: CTHS, 2002.

Bertaud, Jean-Paul. "L'armée et le brevet de virilité." In *Histoire de la virilité*, vol. 2, *Le triomphe de la virilité, le XIXe siècle*, edited by Alain Corbin, Jean-Jacques Courtine, and Georges Vigarello, 63–82. Paris: Seuil, 2011.

———. *Quand les enfants parlaient de gloire: L'armée au cœur de la France de Napoléon*. Paris: Flammarion, 2006.

———. *La révolution armée: Les soldats-citoyens et la révolution française*. Paris: Laffont, 1979.

———. "La révolution et la politique sociale en faveur des militaires." *Revue du Nord* 75, no. 299 (1993): 181–91.

———. "Le théâtre et la guerre." In *Armée, guerre et société à l'époque napoléonienne: Actes du colloque organisé par l'Institut Napoléon et la Bibliothèque Marmottan les 17 et 18 novembre 2000*, edited by Jacques-Olivier Boudon, 177–88. Paris: Éditions SPM, 2004.

———. "La virilité militaire." In *Histoire de la virilité*, vol. 2, *Le triomphe de la virilité, le XIXe siècle*, edited by Alain Corbin, Jean-Jacques Courtine, and Georges Vigarello, 157–202. Paris: Seuil, 2011.

Bertaux, Louis. *Notice sur la rosière de Suresnes*. Saint Cloud: Belin, 1851.

Bianchi, Serge. *Héros et héroïnes de la révolution française*. Paris: Comité des travaux historiques et scientifiques, 2012.

Biard, Michel. "L'omniprésence de la guerre." In *Révolution, consulat, empire, 1789–1815*, edited by Michel Biard, Philippe Bourdin, and Silvia Marzagalli, 464–515. Paris: Belin, 2009.

Biard, Michel, and Claire Maignon. *La souffrance et la gloire*. Paris: Vendémiaire, 2018.

Blaufarb, Rafe. *The French Army, 1750–1820: Careers, Talent, Merit*. Manchester: Manchester University Press, 2003.

Blum, Carol. *Strength in Numbers: Population, Reproduction, and Power in Eighteenth-Century France*. Baltimore: Johns Hopkins University Press, 2002.

Bonneuil, Noël. "Démographie de la nuptialité au XIX siècle." In *La société française: Tradition, transition, transformations*, edited by Jacques Dupaquier and Denis Kessler, 83–119. Paris: Fayard, 1992.

Bordes, Philippe. "La patrie en danger par Lethière et l'esprit militaire." *Revue du Louvre* 4–5 (1986): 301–6.

Bordes, Philippe, and Alain Chevalier. *Catalogue des peintures, sculptures, et dessins: Musée de la Révolution Française*. Vizille: Musée de la Révolution Française, 1996.

Borély, A. E. *Histoire de la ville du Havre: De 1789 à 1813*. 5 vols. Le Havre: Lepeletier, 1880–1885.

Boudon, Jacques-Olivier. "Le retour des prisonniers de guerre dans l'Europe de 1814." In *Rien appris, rien oublié? Les restaurations dans l'Europe postnapoléonienne (1814–1830)*, edited by Jean-Claude Caron and Jean-Philippe Luis, 183–97. Rennes: PUR, 2015.

———. *Le sexe sous l'empire*. Paris: Vuibert, 2019.

Bouhet, Patrick. "Les femmes et les armées de la révolution et de l'empire: Un aperçu." *Guerres mondiales et conflits contemporains* 50, no. 198 (2000): 11–29.

Bourke, Joanna. *Dismembering the Male: Men's Bodies, Britain, and the Great War*. Chicago: University of Chicago Press, 1996.

———. "Love and Limblessness: Male Heterosexuality, Disability, and the Great War." *Journal of War and Culture Studies* 9, no. 1 (2016): 3–19.

Bouteiller, Jules Edouard. *Histoire complète et méthodique des théâtres de Rouen.* 4 vols. Rouen: Giroux et Renaux, 1880.

Bouzard, Thierry. *Anthologie du chant militaire français.* Paris: Grancher, 2000.

Brice, Raoul. *La femme et les armées de la révolution et de l'empire (1792–1815).* Paris: L'édition moderne, 1913.

Broers, Michael. "Civilians in the Napoleonic Wars." In *Daily Lives of Civilians in Wartime Europe, 1618–1900*, edited by Linda Frey and Marsha Frey, 133–74. Westport, CT: Greenwood Press, 2007.

———. "The Concept of 'Total War' in the Revolutionary–Napoleonic Period." *War in History* 15, no. 3 (2008): 247–68.

Brown, Howard. *War, Revolution, and the Bureaucratic State: Politics and Army Administration in France, 1791–1799.* Oxford: Clarendon Press, 1995.

Brown, Michael, Anna Maria Barry, and Joanne Begiato, eds. *Martial Masculinities: Experiencing and Imagining the Military in the Long Nineteenth Century.* Manchester: Manchester University Press, 2019.

Cabanes, Bruno, and Guillaume Piketty. *Retour à l'intime au sortir de la guerre.* Paris: Tallandier, 2009.

Cage, E. Claire. *Unnatural Frenchmen: The Politics of Priestly Celibacy and Marriage, 1720–1815.* Charlottesville: University of Virginia Press, 2015.

Calvet, Stéphane. *Les officiers charentais de Napoléon au XIXe siècle : Destins de braves.* Paris: Indes Savants, 2010.

———. "The Painful Demobilization of the Napoleonic Grande Armée." *Journal of Military History* 80, no. 1 (2016): 77–92.

Carbonnières, Philippe de. *Lesueur: Gouaches révolutionnaires. Collections du Musée Carnavalet.* Paris: Musée Carnavalet, 2005.

Cardoza, Thomas. "'Habits Appropriate to Her Sex': The Female Military Experience in France during the Age of Revolution." In *Gender, War and Politics: Transatlantic Perspectives 1775–1830*, edited by Karen Hagemann, Jane Rendall, and Gisela Mettele, 188–205. Basingstoke: Palgrave Macmillan, 2010.

———. *Intrepid Women: Cantinières and Vivandières of the French Army.* Bloomington: Indiana University Press, 2010.

———. "Stepchildren of the State: Educating 'Enfants de Troupe' in the French Army, 1800–1845." *Paedagogica Historica* 37, no. 3 (2001): 551–68.

———. "'These Unfortunate Children': Sons and Daughters of the Regiment in Revolutionary and Napoleonic France." In *Children and War: A Historical Anthology*, edited by James Alan Marten, 205–15. New York: New York University Press, 2002.

Cardoza, Thomas, and Karen Hagemann. "History and Memory of Army Women and Female Soldiers." In *The Oxford Handbook of Gender, War, and the Western World Since 1600*, edited by Karen Hagemann, Stefan Dudink, and Sonya O. Rose, 176–200. Oxford: Oxford University Press, 2020.

Caron, Pierre. *Paris pendant la terreur: Rapports des agents secrets du ministre de l'intérieur.* 6 vols. Paris: Picard, 1910–1978.

Catros, Philippe. "Tout français est soldat et se doit à la défense de la patrie (Retour sur la naissance de la conscription militaire)." *Annales historiques de la révolution française* 348 (2007): 7–23.

Chappey, Jean-Luc. "L'assassinat de Rastadt et les enjeux du 'cri de vengeance' sous le second Directoire." In *La voix et le geste: Une approche culturelle de la violence sociopolitique*, edited by Philippe Bourdin, Mathias Bernard, and Jean-Claude Caron, 69–96. Clermont-Ferrand: Presses Universitaires Blaise Pascal, 2005.

Charters, Erica, Eve Rosenhaft, and Hannah Smith. *Civilians and War in Europe, 1618–1815.* Liverpool: Liverpool University Press, 2012.

Charton, Charles. "Souvenirs de 1814 à 1848." *Annales de la Société d'émulation du département des Vosges* 13, no. 3 (1870): 239–73.

Chassin, Charles-Louis, and Léon Clément Hennet. *Les volontaires nationaux pendant la révolution*. 3 vols. Paris: Léopold Cerf, 1899–1906.

Chauvin-Madeira, Paul. "Mœurs et droit des militaires: Trois siècles de débats autour de l'autorisation de mariage." *Droits* 63, no. 1 (2021): 17–38.

Chickering, Roger. "Total War: The Use and Abuse of a Concept." In *Anticipating Total War: The German and American Experiences, 1871–1914*, edited by Manfred F. Boemeke, Roger Chickering, and Stig Förster, 13–28. Washington, DC: Cambridge University Press, 1999.

Chickering, Roger, and Stig Förster, eds. *War in an Age of Revolution, 1775–1815*. Washington, DC: Cambridge University Press, 2010.

Ciotti, Bruno. *Du volontaire au conscrit: Les levées d'hommes dans le Puy-de-Dôme pendant la révolution française*. Clermont-Ferrand: Presses Universitaires Blaise Pascal, 2001.

———. "Les 'embusqués de Vénus' dans le Puy de Dôme: Premiers aperçus sur la course au mariage sous la révolution." In *La plume et le sabre: Hommages offerts à Jean-Paul Bertaud*, edited by Michel Biard, Annie Crépin, and Bernard Gainot, 227–35. Paris: Sorbonne, 2002.

Claeys, Prosper. "Dotations et mariages de rosières." In *Pages d'histoire locale gantoise*, 3:97–109. Gand: Vuylsteke, 1894.

Clarke, Joseph. "Cenotaphs and Cypress Trees: Commemorating the Citizen-Soldier in the Year II." *French History* 22, no. 2 (2008): 217–40.

———. *Commemorating the Dead in Revolutionary France: Revolution and Remembrance, 1789–1799*. Cambridge: Cambridge University Press, 2007.

———. "'Valour Knows Neither Age nor Sex': The Recueil des Actions Héroïques and the Representation of Courage in Revolutionary France." *War in History* 20, no. 1 (2013): 50–75.

Clifford, Dale. "Can the Uniform Make the Citizen? Paris 1789–1791." *Eighteenth-Century Studies* 34, no. 3 (2001): 363–82.

Cohen, Deborah. *The War Come Home: Disabled Veterans in Britain and Germany, 1914–1939*. Berkeley: University of California Press, 2001.

Connelly, Owen. *The French Revolution and Napoleonic Era*. San Francisco: Holt, Rinehart, and Winston, 1991.

Conner, Susan. "Les Femmes Militaires: Women in the French Army." *Proceedings: Consortium on Revolutionary Europe, 1750–1850*, vol. 12 (1982): 290–302.

———. "Up from the Footnotes: Amazons, Miscreants, Marginal and Not-So-Marginal Women in Napoleonic Social History." *Consortium on Revolutionary Europe* (1997): 213–20.

———. "La Vraie Madame Sans-Gêne: Women Soldiers in the French Revolutionary and Napoleonic Armies, 1792–1815." *Napoleonic Scholarship* no. 2 (2010): 14–19.

Connors, Logan. "Total Theatre for Total War: Experiences of the Military Play in Revolutionary France." *Theatre Survey* 62 (2021): 51–66.

Corbin, Alain, Jean-Jacques Courtine, and Georges Vigarello, eds. *Histoire de la virilité*. 3 vols. Paris: Seuil, 2011.

Corvisier, André. *L'armée française de la fin du XVIIe siècle au ministère de Choiseul: Le soldat*. Paris: PUF, 1964.

Crépin, Annie. "1812: Fin d'une époque de la conscription." *Revue historique des armées* 12, no. 267 (2012): 33–42.

———. *La conscription en débat, ou le triple apprentissage de la nation, de la citoyenneté, de la république*. Arras: Artois Presses Université, 1998.

———. *Défendre la France: Les français, la guerre et le service militaire, de la guerre de sept ans à Verdun*. Rennes: PUR, 2005.

———. "La France plurielle devant la conscription." In *Armée, guerre et société à l'époque napoléonienne: Actes du colloque organisé par l'Institut Napoléon et la Bibliothèque Marmottan les 17 et 18 novembre 2000*, edited by Jacques-Olivier Boudon, 13–30. Paris: Éditions SPM, 2004.

———. "Gouvion-Saint-Cyr et la loi refondatrice de 1818." In *La plume et le sabre: Volume d'hommages offertes à Jean-Paul Bertaud*, edited by Michel Biard, Annie Crépin, and Bernard Gainot, , 313–25. Paris: Sorbonne, 2002.

———. *Histoire de la conscription*. Paris: Gallimard, 2009.

———. *Révolution et armée nouvelle en Seine-et-Marne (1791–1797)*. Paris: Comité des travaux historiques et scientifiques, 2008.

———. "Soldats et citoyens, soldats parce que citoyens: Les hommes de l'armée nouvelle." In *La révolution française: Une histoire toujours vivante*, edited by Michel Biard, 197–208. Paris: Tallandier, 2009.

———. *Vers l'armée nationale: Les débuts de la conscription en Seine-et-Marne, 1798–1815*. Rennes: PUR, 2011.

Crépin, Annie, Jean-Pierre Jessenne, and Hervé Leuwers, eds. *Civils, citoyen-soldats et militaires dans l'état-nation (1789–1815)*. Paris: Société des études robespierristes, 2006.

Cron, Adélaïde. "Les mémoires des 'Vendéennes': Un récit de guerre au féminin?" *Itinéraires* (2011): 45–63.

Coutanceau, Henri. *La campagne de 1794, à l'armée du Nord*. 5 vols. Paris: Chapelot, 1903–1908.

Daly, Gavin. "Conscription and Corruption in Napoleonic France: The Case of the Seine-Inférieure." *European Review of History: Revue européenne d'histoire* 6, no. 2 (1999): 181–97.

———. "Napoleon's Lost Legions: French Prisoners of War in Britain, 1803–1814." *History: Journal of the Historical Association* 89 (2004): 361–80.

Dänzer-Kantof, Boris. *La vie des français au temps de Napoléon*. Paris: France Loisirs, 2004.

Davidson, Denise. *France after Revolution: Urban Life, Gender, and the New Social Order*. Cambridge, MA: Harvard University Press, 2007.

———. "'Happy' Marriages in Early Nineteenth-Century France." *Journal of Family History* 37, no. 1 (2012): 23–35.

———. "Making Society 'Legible': People-Watching in Paris after the Revolution." *French Historical Studies* 28, no. 2 (2005): 265–96.

———. "The New (Emotional) Regime: Bourgeois Reactions to the Turmoil of 1814–1815." *French Historical Studies* 42, no. 4 (2019): 595–621.

———. "Women at Napoleonic Festivals: Gender and the Public Sphere during the First Empire." *French History* 16, no. 3 (2002): 229–332.

Davis, Natalie Zemon. *Fiction in the Archives: Pardon Tales and Their Tellers in Sixteenth-Century France*. Stanford: Stanford University Press, 1987.

Déon-Bessière, Danièle. *Les femmes et la légion d'honneur depuis sa création*. Paris: Les éditions de l'officine, 2002.

Desan, Suzanne. *The Family on Trial in Revolutionary France*. Berkeley: University of California Press, 2004.

———. "Pétitions des femmes en faveur d'une réforme révolutionnaire de la famille." *Annales historiques de la révolution française* 344 (2006): 27–46.

———. "Théroigne de Méricourt: Gender and International Politics in Revolutionary Europe." *Journal of Modern History* 92 (2020): 274–310.

———. "'War between Brothers and Sisters': Inheritance Law and Gender Politics in Revolutionary France." *French Historical Studies* 20, no. 4 (1997): 597–635.

Deschamps, Léon. "Les femmes soldats dans la Sarthe." *La révolution française: Revue d'histoire moderne et contemporaine* 47 (1904): 326–35.

DiCaprio, Lisa. *The Origins of the Welfare State: Women, Work, and the French Revolution.* Urbana: University of Illinois Press, 2007.

Dock, Terry Smiley. *Women in the Encyclopédie: A Compendium.* Madrid: Porrúa Taranzas, 1983.

Dodman, Thomas. "1814 and the Melancholy of War." *Journal of Military History* 80, no. 1 (2016): 31–55.

———. "Ordinary Radicalization: Becoming a Citizen-Soldier during the French Revolution." *Journal of Modern History* 94, no. 4 (2022): 751–89.

———. *What Nostalgia Was: War, Empire, and the Time of a Deadly Emotion.* Chicago: University of Chicago Press, 2018.

Domine, Jean-François. "Le chant du départ de Marie Joseph Chénier et Etienne Méhul." *Annales historiques de la révolution française* 329 (2002): 89–100.

Drévillon, Hervé, Bertrand Fonck, and Michel Roucaud, eds. *Guerre et armées napoléoniennes: Nouveaux regards.* Paris: Bibliothèque Napoléon, 2013.

Dudink, Stefan. "After the Republic: Citizenship, the Military, and Masculinity in the Making of the Dutch Monarchy, 1813–1814." *Representing Masculinity: Male Citizenship in Modern Western Culture,* edited by Stefan Dudink, Karen Hagemann, and Anna Clark, 89–108. New York: Palgrave Macmillan, 2007.

———. "Citizenship, Mass Mobilization, and Masculinity in a Gendered Perspective, 1770s–1870s." In *The Oxford Handbook of Gender, War, and the Western World Since 1600,* edited by Karen Hagemann, Stefan Dudink, and Sonya O. Rose, 201–26. Oxford: Oxford University Press, 2020.

Dudink, Stefan, Karen Hagemann, and Anna Clark, eds. *Representing Masculinity: Male Citizenship in Modern Western Culture.* New York: Palgrave Macmillan, 2007.

Dudink, Stefan, Karen Hagemann, and John Tosh, eds. *Masculinities in Politics and War: Gendering Modern History.* Manchester: Manchester University Press, 2004.

Dunne, John. "Napoleon's 'Mayoral Problem': Aspects of State-Community Relations in Post-Revolutionary France." *Modern & Contemporary France* 8, no. 4 (2000): 479–91.

Duplessis, Georges. *Inventaire de la collection d'estampes relatives à l'histoire de France léguée en 1863 à la Bibliothèque nationale par M. Michel Hennin.* 5 vols. Paris: Champion, 1878–1884.

Duval, Eugène-Jean. *Étapes de la citoyenneté des militaires, 1789–1999.* Paris: Éditions d'écrivains, 2000.

———. *Régards sur la conscription, 1790–1997.* Paris: Fondation pour les études de défense, 1997.

Dwyer, Philip. "'It Still Makes Me Shudder': Memories of Massacres and Atrocities during the Revolutionary and Napoleonic Wars." *War in History* 16, no. 4 (2009): 381–405.

———. "Public Remembering, Private Reminiscing: French Military Memoirs and the Revolutionary and Napoleonic Wars." *French Historical Studies* 33, no. 2 (2011): 231–58.

———. "Violence and the Revolutionary and Napoleonic Wars: Massacre, Conquest and the Imperial Enterprise." *Journal of Genocide Research* 15, no. 2 (2013): 117–31.

———. "War Stories: French Veteran Narratives and the 'Experience of War' in the Nineteenth Century." *European History Quarterly* 41, no. 4 (2011): 561–85.

Dziembowski, Edmond. *Un nouveau patriotisme français: La France face à la puissance anglaise à l'époque de la guerre de sept ans.* Oxford: Voltaire Foundation, 1998.

Evans, Suzanne. *Mothers of Heroes, Mothers of Martyrs: World War I and the Politics of Grief.* Montreal: McGill-Queen's University, 2008.

Fahmy, Scandar. *La France en 1814 et le gouvernement provisoire.* Paris: Nizet et Bastard, 1934.

Fauré, Christine. "Doléances, déclarations, et pétitions: Trois formes de la parole publique sous la révolution." *Annales historiques de la révolution française* 344 (2006): 5–25.

Favret, Mary. *War at a Distance: Romanticism and the Making of Modern Warfare*. Princeton: Princeton University Press, 2009.

Feilla, Cecilia. *The Sentimental Theater of the French Revolution*. Burlington, VT: Ashgate, 2013.

Finch, Alison. *Women's Writing in Nineteenth-Century France*. Cambridge: Cambridge University Press, 2000.

Foissy-Aufrère, Marie-Pierre, and Jean-Clément Martin, eds. *La mort de Bara: De l'évènement au mythe autour du tableau de Jacques-Louis David*. Avignon: Fondation du Musée Calvet, 1989.

Forray-Carlier, Anne, and Jean-Marie Bruson. *Au temps des merveilleuses: La société parisienne sous le Directoire et le Consulat*. Paris: Association Paris-Musées, 2005.

Forrest, Alan. "L'armée de l'an II: La levée en masse et la création d'un mythe républicain." *Annales historiques de la révolution française* 335 (2004): 111–30.

———. "Citizenship and Masculinity: The Revolutionary Citizen-Soldier and His Legacy." In *Representing Masculinity: Male Citizenship in Modern Western Culture*, edited by Stefan Dudink, Karen Hagemann, and Anna Clark, 111–29. New York: Palgrave Macmillan, 2007.

———. "Citizenship and Military Service." In *The French Revolution and the Meaning of Citizenship*, edited by Renée Waldinger, Philip Dawson, and Isser Woloch, 153–65. Westport, CT: Greenwood Press, 1993.

———. "Citizenship, Honour, and Masculinity: Military Qualities under the French Revolution and Empire." In *Gender, War and Politics: Transatlantic Perspectives, 1775–1830*, edited by Karen Hagemann, Jane Rendall, and Gisela Mettele, 93–109. Basingstoke: Palgrave Macmillan, 2010.

———. *Conscripts and Deserters: The Army and French Society during the Revolution and the Empire*. New York: Oxford University Press, 1989.

———. "Le départ du conscrit dans la représentation et la mémoire." In *Les européens dans les guerres napoléoniennes*, edited by Natalie Petiteau, Jean-Marc Olivier, and Sylvie Caucanas, 35–47. Toulouse: Privat, 2012.

———. *The French Revolution and the Poor*. Oxford: Blackwell, 1981.

———. *The Legacy of the French Revolutionary Wars: The Nation-in-Arms in French Republican Memory*. Cambridge: Cambridge University Press, 2009.

———. "The Military Culture of Napoleonic France." In *Napoleon and Europe*, edited by Philip Dwyer, 43–58. Harrow: Longman, 2001.

———. *Napoleon's Men: The Soldiers of the Revolution and Empire*. London and New York: Hambledon, 2002.

———. "Napoleonic Veterans and the Challenge of Peace." In *A History of the European Restorations*, vol. 2, *Culture, Society, and Religion*, edited by Michael Broers, Ambrogio A. Caiani, and Stephen Bann, 168–76. London: Bloomsbury, 2020.

———. "'La Patrie en Danger': The French Revolution and the First Levée en Masse." In *The People in Arms: Military Myth and National Mobilization since the French Revolution*, edited by Daniel Moran and Arthur Waldron, 8–32. Cambridge: Cambridge University Press, 2003.

———. "Propaganda and the Legitimation of Power in Napoleonic France." *French History* 18, no. 4 (2004): 426–45.

———. "Society, Mass Warfare, and Gender in Europe during and after the Revolutionary and Napoleonic Wars." In *The Oxford Handbook of Gender, War, and the Western World Since 1600*, edited by Karen Hagemann, Stefan Dudink, and Sonya O. Rose, 158–75. Oxford: Oxford University Press, 2020.

———. *The Soldiers of the French Revolution*. Durham: Duke University Press, 1990.

Forrest, Alan, Etienne François, and Karen Hagemann, eds. *War Memories: The Revolutionary and Napoleonic Wars in Modern European Culture*. Basingstoke: Palgrave Macmillan, 2012.

Forrest, Alan, Karen Hagemann, and Jane Rendall. "Introduction: Nations in Arms, People at War." In *Soldiers, Citizens, and Civilians: Experiences and Perceptions of the Revolutionary and Napoleonic Wars, 1790–1820*, edited by Alan Forrest, Karen Hagemann, and Jane Rendall, 1–22. Basingstoke: Palgrave Macmillan, 2009.

Fournial, Etienne, and Jean-Pierre Gutton, eds. *Cahiers de doléances de la province de Forez pour les états généraux de 1789*. 2 vols. Saint-Etienne: Centre d'études foresiennes, 1974–75.

Fournier, Stéphanie. "Le vaudeville ou l'art de s'adapter aux circonstances." In *Fièvre et vie du théâtre sous la révolution française et l'empire*, edited by Thibaud Julian and Vicenzo De Santis, 83–98. Paris: Classiques Garnier, 2019.

Fraser, Elisabeth. *Delacroix, Art, and Patrimony in Post-Revolutionary France*. Cambridge: Cambridge University Press, 2004.

Frederking, Bettina. "'Il ne faut pas être le roi de deux peuples': Strategies of National Reconciliation in Restoration France." *French History* 22, no. 4 (2008): 446–68.

Frey, Linda, and Marsha Frey, eds. *Daily Lives of Civilians in Wartime Europe, 1618–1900*. Westport, Conn.: Greenwood Press, 2007.

Frey, Linda, and Marsha Frey. *The History of Diplomatic Immunity*. Columbus: Ohio State University Press, 1999.

Fumeaux, Holly. *Military Men of Feeling: Emotion, Touch, and Masculinity in the Crimean War*. Oxford: Oxford University Press, 2016.

Fureix, Emmanuel. "L'iconoclasme politique: Un combat pour la souveraineté (1814–1816)." In *Révolutions et mythes identitaires: Mots, violence, mémoire*, edited by Annie Duprat, 173–93. Paris: Nouveau Monde, 2009.

———. "Police des signes, ordre et désordre en temps de crise (1814–1816)." *Histoire urbaine* no. 43 (2015): 157–76.

Fureix, Emmanuel, and Judith Lyon-Caen, eds. "1814–1815: Expériences de la discontinuité." Special issue, *Revue d'histoire du XIX siècle* 49 (2014).

Füssell, Marian. "Between Dissimulation and Sensation: Female Soldiers in Eighteenth-Century Warfare." *Journal for Eighteenth-Century Studies* 41, no. 4 (2018): 527–42.

Gainot, Bernard. *1799, un nouveau Jacobinisme? La démocratie représentative, une alternative à brumaire*. Paris: Comité des travaux historiques et scientifiques, 2001.

———. "Le dernier voyage: Rites ambulatoires et rites conjuratoires dans les cérémonies funéraires en l'honneur des généraux révolutionnaires." In *La voix et le geste: Une approche culturelle de la violence socio-politique*, edited by Philippe Bourdin, Mathias Bernard, and Jean-Claude Caron, 97–113. Clermont-Ferrand: Presses Universitaires Blaise Pascal, 2005.

———. "Persistance d'une culture de l'héroïsme républicain sous le Directoire: Le recueil des actions héroïques ou le livre du soldat francais, du général Championnet (1789–1799)." In *Héros et héroïnes de la révolution française*, edited by Serge Bianchi, 179–94. Paris: Comité des travaux historiques et scientifiques, 2012.

———. "Rites et contexte dans les cérémonies funèbres en l'honneur des généraux de la République (1796–1800)." In *Représentation et pouvoir: La politique symbolique en France (1789–1830)*, edited by Natalie Scholz and Christina Schröer, 83–91. Rennes: PUR, 2007.

Gautier, Théodore. *La période révolutionnaire, le consulat, l'empire, la restauration, dans les Hautes-Alpes*. Gap: Guillaume, 1895.

Germani, Ian. *Dying for France: Experiencing and Representing the Soldier's Death, 1500–2000*. Montreal: McGill-Queen's Press, 2023.

———. "Dying for Liberty in the French Revolutionary Wars." *French History and Civilization* (2020): 97–108.

———. "Mediated Battlefields of the French Revolution and Emotives at War." In *Battlefield Emotions, 1500–1800: Practice, Experience, Imagination*, edited by Erika Kuijpers and Cornelis Van der Haven, 173–94. London: Palgrave Macmillan, 2016.

———. "Staging Battles: Representations of War in the Theatre and Festivals of the French Revolution." *European Review of History: Revue européenne d'histoire* 13, no. 2 (2006): 203–28.

Germer, Stefan. "In Search of a Beholder: On the Relation between Art, Audiences, and Social Spheres in Post-Thermidor France." *Art Bulletin* 74 (1992): 19–36.

Germond de Lavigne, Alfred. *Les pamphlets de la fin de l'empire, des cent jours, et de la restauration*. Paris: Dentu, 1879.

Gildea, Robert. *Children of the Revolution: The French, 1799–1914*. Cambridge, MA: Harvard University Press, 2008.

Godineau, Dominique. "De la guerrière à la citoyenne: Porter les armes pendant l'ancien régime et la révolution française." *Clio: Histoire, femmes, et sociétés* 20 (2004): 43–69.

Goldstein, Jan. *The Post-Revolutionary Self: Politics and Psyche in France, 1750–1850*. Cambridge, MA: Harvard University Press, 2005.

Goldstein, Robert Justin. "France." In *The War for the Public Mind: Political Censorship in Nineteenth-Century Europe*, edited by Robert Justin Goldstein, 125–73. Westport, CT: Praeger, 2000.

Goldstein, Robert Justin, ed. *The Frightful Stage: Political Censorship of the Theater in Nineteenth-Century Europe*. New York: Berghahn Books, 2009.

Goodman, Dena. "Marriage Choice and Marital Success: Reasoning about Marriage, Love and Happiness." In *Family, Gender, and Law in Early Modern France*, edited by Jeffrey Merrick and Suzanne Desan, 26–61. University Park: Penn State University Press, 2009.

Gougelmann, Stéphane, and Anne Verjus, eds. *Écrire le mariage en France au XIXème siècle*. St-Etienne: Publications de St-Etienne, 2017.

Goupil-Travert, Maria. *Braves combattantes, humbles héroïnes: Trajectoires et engagées volontaires de la révolution et de l'empire*. Rennes: PUR, 2021.

Grabilier, Léonce. "Jeanne Schellinck." *L'intermédiaire des chercheurs et des curieux* 40, no. 1225 (1909): 937–41.

Grieg, Matilda. *Dead Men Telling Tales: The Industry of Napoleonic War Writing, from 1808 to Today*. Oxford: Oxford University Press, 2021.

Grigsby, Darcy Grimaldo. "Revolutionary Sons, White Fathers, and Creole Difference: Guillaume Guillon-Lethière's *Oath of the Ancestors* of 1822." *Yale French Studies* 101 (2002): 201–26.

Guinier, Arnaud. *L'honneur du soldat: Éthique martiale et discipline guerrière dans la France des Lumières*. Paris: Champ Vallon, 2014.

Guiomar, Jean-Yves. *L'invention de la guerre totale: XVIIIe–XXe siècle*. Paris: Éditions du Félin, 2004.

Gullace, Nicoletta. *The Blood of Our Sons: Men, Women, and the Renegotiation of British Citizenship during the Great War*. London: Palgrave, 2002.

Hagemann, Karen. "Female Patriots: Women, War and the Nation in Prussia during the Anti-Napoleonic Wars." *Gender and History* 16, no. 2 (2004): 397–424.

———. "'Heroic Virgins' and 'Bellicose Amazons': Armed Women, the Gender Order and the German Public during and after the Anti-Napoleonic Wars." *European History Quarterly* 37, no. 4 (2007): 507–27.

———. "The Military and Masculinity: Gendering the History of the Revolutionary and Napoleonic Wars, 1792–1815." In *War in an Age of Revolution, 1775–1815*, edited by Roger Chickering and Stig Förster, 331–52. Washington, DC: Cambridge University Press, 2010.

———. "A Valorous Volk Family: The Nation, the Military, and the Gender Order in Prussia in the Time of the Anti-Napoleonic Wars, 1806–15." In *Gendered Nations: Nationalisms and Gender Order in the Long Nineteenth Century*, edited by Ida Blom, Karen Hagemann, and Catherine Hall, 179–205. Oxford: Berg, 2000.

Hagemann, Karen, Stefan Dudink, and Sonya O. Rose, eds. *The Oxford Handbook of Gender, War, and the Western World Since 1600*. Oxford: Oxford University Press, 2020.

Hagemann, Karen, Alan Forrest, and Jane Rendall, eds. *Soldiers, Citizens and Civilians: Experiences and Perceptions of the French Wars, 1790–1820*. Basingstoke: Palgrave Macmillan, 2009.

Hagemann, Karen, Jane Rendall, and Gisela Mettele, eds. *Gender, War and Politics: Transatlantic Perspectives 1775–1830*. Basingstoke: Palgrave Macmillan, 2010.

Haize, Jules. "Saint-Servan sous le premier empire: La fête du couronnement, les rosières." *Revue du Pays d'Aleth* (1908): 21–27.

Hantraye, Jacques. *Les cosaques aux Champs-Élysées: L'occupation de la France après la chute de Napoléon*. Paris: Belin, 2005.

———. "Les sépultures de guerre en France à la fin du Premier Empire." *Revue d'histoire du XIXe siècle* 30 (2005): http://journals.openedition.org/rh19/1007.

Harris, Ruth. "The 'Child of the Barbarian': Rape, Race, and Nationalism in France during the First World War." *Past and Present* 141 (1993): 170–206.

Harten, Elke, and Hans-Christian Harten, eds. *Femmes, culture, et révolution*. Paris: Des Femmes, 1989.

Haynes, Christine. "Making Peace: The Allied Occupation of France, 1815–1818." In *War, Demobilization, and Memory: The Legacy of War in the Era of the Atlantic Revolutions*, edited by Alan Forrest, Karen Hagemann, and Michael Rowe, 51–67. Basingstoke: Palgrave Macmillan, 2016.

———. *Our Friends, the Enemies: The First Allied Occupation of France (1815–1818)*. Cambridge, MA: Harvard University Press, 2018.

Haynes, Christine, Jennifer Heuer, and Denise Davidson. "Ending War: Revisiting the Aftermath of the Napoleonic Wars." Introduction to special issue, *Journal of Military History* 80, no. 1 (2016): 11–30.

Hazareesingh, Sudhir. *The Legend of Napoleon*. London: Granta Books, 2004.

Heimann, Nora. *Joan of Arc in French Art and Culture, 1700–1855*. Aldershot: Ashgate, 2005.

Heineman, Elizabeth. "Whose Mothers? Generational Difference, War, and the Nazi Cult of Motherhood." *Journal of Women's History* 12, no. 4 (2001): 138–64.

Hennet, Leon. "Une femme-soldat: Anne Françoise Pélagie Dulierre." *Annales révolutionnaires* 1, no. 4 (1908): 610–21.

Heuer, Jennifer Ngaire. "Celibacy, Courage, and Hungry Wives: Debating Military Marriage and Citizenship in Pre-revolutionary France." *European History Quarterly* 46, no. 4 (2016): 648–67.

———. "Citizenship, the French Revolution, and the Limits of Martial Masculinity." In *Gender and Citizenship in Historical and Transnational Perspective*, edited by Rachel Fuchs and Anne Epstein, 19–38. Basingstoke: Palgrave Macmillan, 2016.

———. *The Family and the Nation: Gender and Citizenship in Revolutionary France*. Ithaca: Cornell University Press, 2005.

———. "Hats on for the Nation! Women, Citizens, Soldiers, and the 'Sign of the French.'" *French History* 16, no. 1 (2002): 28–52.

———. "Neither Cowardly nor Greedy? Buying and Selling Escape from Conscription in Revolutionary and Post-Revolutionary France." *French History* 36, no. 2 (2022): 209–29.

———. "No More Fears, No More Tears? Gender, Emotion, and the Aftermath of the Napoleonic Wars in France." *Gender and History* 28, no. 2 (2016): 438–60.

———. "'Réduit à désirer la mort d'une femme qui peut-être lui a sauvé la vie': La conscription et les liens du mariage sous Napoléon." *Annales historiques de la révolution française* 348 (2007): 25–40.

———. "Rethinking Gender, Sexuality, and the French Revolution." In *The Cambridge History of the Age of Atlantic Revolutions*, edited by Wim Klooster, 272–99. Cambridge: Cambridge University Press, 2024.

———. "Soldiers as Victims or Villains? Demobilization, Masculinity, and Family in French Royalist Pamphlets, 1814–1815." *Journal of Military History* 80, no. 1 (2016): 121–44.

Hippler, Thomas. *Citizens, Soldiers, and National Armies: Military Service in France and Germany, 1789–1830*. New York: Routledge, 2008.

———. "Conscription in the French Restoration: The 1818 Debate on Military Service." *War in History* 13, no. 3 (2006): 281–98.

———. "The French Army, 1789–1914: Volunteers, Pressed Soldiers, and Conscripts." In *Fighting for a Living: Comparative History of Military Labour*, edited by Jan-Erik Zürcher, 419–46. Amsterdam: Amsterdam University Press, 2014.

———. "Service militaire et intégration nationale pendant la révolution française." *Annales historiques de la révolution française* 329 (2002): 1–16.

———. "Volunteers of the French Revolutionary Wars: Myths and Reinterpretations." In *War Volunteering in Modern Times from the French Revolution to the Second World War*, edited by Christine G. Kruger and Sonja Levsen, 23–39. Basingstoke: Palgrave Macmillan, 2011.

Holtman, Robert B. *Napoleonic Propaganda*. Baton Rouge: Louisiana State University Press, 1950.

Hopkin, David. "Female Soldiers and the Battle of the Sexes in France: The Mobilization of a Folk Motif." *History Workshop Journal* 56 (2003): 78–104.

———. "'My Gunners Will Burn Your Houses, My Soldiers Will Pillage Them': What French People Were Singing About When They Sang about Napoleon." *French History* 36, no. 1 (2022): 100–20.

———. *Soldier and Peasant in French Popular Culture, 1766–1870*. Woodbridge: Boydell Press for the Royal Historical Society, 2003.

———. "Sons and Lovers: Popular Images of the Conscript, 1798–1870." *Modern & Contemporary France* 9, no. 1 (2001): 19–36.

———. "The World Turned Upside Down: Female Soldiers in the French Armies of the Revolutionary and Napoleonic Wars." In *Soldiers, Citizens and Civilians: Experiences and Perceptions of the French Wars, 1790–1820*, edited by Karen Hagemann, Alan Forrest, and Jane Rendall, 77–98. Basingstoke: Palgrave Macmillan, 2009.

Hornstein, Katie. *Picturing War in France, 1792–1856*. New Haven: Yale University Press, 2018.

Houdaille, Jacques. "La France à l'époque napoléo nienne: Le problème des pertes de guerre." *Annales historiques de la révolution française* 42, no. 199 (1970): 46–62.

———. "Marriage under the French Revolution and the First Empire." *Population* 37, no. 1 (1982): 160–67.

Houdecek, François. "Le gouvernement de Louis XVIII et le retour des prisonniers de guerre français en Russie 1814–1816." *Napoleonica: La revue* 3, no. 21 (2014): 45–73.

Howard, Martin. *Napoleon's Doctors: The Medical Services of the Grande Armée*. Stroud: Spellmount, 2006.

Hufton, Olwen. *Women and the Limits of Citizenship in the French Revolution*. Toronto: University of Toronto Press, 1992.

Hughes, Michael J. *Forging Napoleon's Grande Armée: Motivation, Military Culture, and Masculinity in the French Army, 1800–1808*. New York: New York University Press, 2012.

———. "Making Frenchmen into Warriors: Martial Masculinity in Napoleonic France." In *French Masculinities: History, Culture, and Politics*, edited by Christopher Forth and Bertrand Taithe, 51–67. Basingstoke: Palgrave Macmillan, 2007.

———. "Military Values: Heroism and Masculinity." In *The Cambridge History of the Napoleonic Wars*, vol 3, *Experience, Culture, and Memory*, edited by Alan Forrest and Peter Hicks, 30–49. Cambridge: Cambridge University Press, 2023.

Hunt, Lynn. *The Family Romance of the French Revolution*. Berkeley: University of California Press, 1992.

———. *Inventing Human Rights*. New York: W. W. Norton, 2007.

Hurl-Eamon, Jennine. "Did Soldiers Really Enlist to Desert their Wives? Revisiting the Martial Character of Marital Desertion in Eighteenth-Century London." *Journal of British Studies* 53, no. 2 (2014): 356–77.

———. *Marriage and the British Army in the Long Eighteenth Century: "The Girl I Left Behind Me."* Oxford: Oxford University Press, 2014.

Huss, Marie-Monique. *Histoires de famille: Cartes postales et culture de guerre*. Paris: Noesis, 2000.

Ihl, Olivier. *Le mérite et la république: Essai sur la société des émules*. Paris: Gallimard, 2007.

Istasse, Cédric. "Les fraudeurs aux lois conscriptionnelles napoléoniennes: Les 'mariages simulés' de conscrits des départements belges en 1813–1815." In *Les européens dans les guerres napoléoniennes*, edited by Natalie Petiteau, Jean-Marc Olivier, and Sylvie Caucanas, 75–90. Toulouse: Privat, 2012.

Janin, Édouard. *Histoire de Montluçon: D'après des documents inédits*. Paris: Lechevalier, 1904.

Jarvis, Katie. *Politics in the Marketplace: Work, Gender, and Citizenship in Revolutionary France*. Oxford: Oxford University Press, 2019.

Jolluck, Katherine R. "The Nation's Pain and Women's Shame: Polish Women and Wartime Violence." In *Gender and War in Twentieth-Century Eastern Europe*, edited by Nancy Wingfield and Maria Bucur, 193–219. Bloomington: Indiana University Press, 2006.

Jones, Colin. *Charity and Bienfaisance: The Treatment of the Poor in the Montpellier Region, 1740–1815*. Cambridge: Cambridge University Press, 1982.

Jones, Peter. *The Peasantry and the French Revolution*. Cambridge: Cambridge University Press, 1988.

Jourdan, Annie. *Les monuments de la révolution, 1770–1804: Une histoire de représentation*. Paris: Honoré Champion, 1997.

Julian, Thibaud. "Les 'gratis' de Napoléon: Gloire et spectacles à Paris en temps de fête." *Studia Francesci* 191 (2020): 278–85.

Kaiser, Thomas. "From the Austrian Committee to the Foreign Plot: Marie-Antoinette, Austrophobia, and the Terror." *French Historical Studies* 26, no. 4 (2003): 579–617.

Kennedy, Emmet. "The Most Performed Plays of the Decade."In *Theatre, Opera, and Audiences in Revolutionary Paris: Analysis and Repertory*, by Emmet Kennedy, Marie-Laurence Netter, James P. McGregor, and Mark V. Olsen, 21–34. Westport, CT: Greenwood Press, 1996.

Kennedy, Emmet, Marie-Laurence Netter, James P. McGregor, and Mark V. Olsen, eds. *Theatre, Opera, and Audiences in Revolutionary Paris: Analysis and Repertory*. Westport, CT: Greenwood Press, 1996.

Key, Ellen. *War, Peace, and the Future: A Consideration of Nationalism and Internationalism and the Relation of Women to War*. New York: Putnam's Sons, 1916.

Kienitz, Sabine. "Body Damage: War Disability and Constructions of Masculinity in Weimar Germany." In *Home/Front: The Military, War and Gender in Twentieth-Century Germany*, edited by Karen Hagemann and Stefanie Schüler-Springorum, 181–205. Oxford: Berg, 2002.

Krakovitch, Odile. "La censure théâtrale sous le premier empire." *Revue de l'Institut Napoléon* 158–159 (1992): 9–105.

———. "Les pétitions, seul moyen d'expression laissé aux femmes: L'exemple de la restauration." In *Femmes dans la cité, 1815–1871*, edited by Alain Corbin, Jacqueline Lalouette, and Michèle Riot-Sarcey, 347–72. Paris: Créaphis, 1997.

———. *Les pièces de théâtre soumises à la censure (1800–1830): Inventaire des manuscrits des pièces (F18 581 à 668) et des procès-verbaux des censeurs (F21 966 à 995)*. Paris: Archives Nationales, 1982.

———. "Le théâtre de la république et la censure sous le Directoire." In *Le théâtre sous la révolution, politique du répertoire (1789–1799)*, edited by Martial Poirson, 169–92. Paris: Desjonquères, 2008.

Kroen, Sheryl. *Politics and Theater: The Crisis of Legitimacy in Restoration France, 1815–1830*. Berkeley: University of California Press, 2000.

Krul, Wessel. "Painting Plutarch: Images of Sparta in the Dutch Republic and Enlightenment France." In *Ancient Models in the Early Modern Republican Imagination*, edited by Wyger Velma and Arthur Weststeijn, 157–88. Leiden: Brill, 2017.

Kruse, Wolfgang. "Revolutionary France and the Meanings of the Levée en Masse." In *War in an Age of Revolution, 1775–1815*, edited by Roger Chickering and Stig Förster, 299–312. Washington, DC: Cambridge University Press, 2010.

Kruse, Wolfgang, and Romain Thomas. "La formation du discours militariste sous le Directoire." *Annales historiques de la révolution française* 360 (2010): 77–102.

Kuhlman, Erika. *Of Little Comfort: War Widows, Fallen Soldiers, and the Remaking of the Nation after the Great War*. New York: New York University Press, 2012.

Lacour, Léopold. *Trois femmes de la révolution: Olympe de Gouges, Théroigne de Méricourt, Rose Lacombe*. Paris: Plon-Nourrit, 1900.

Lamy, Jérôme, and Matthieu Mounier. "La chair et le canon: Problématiques pour une histoire des blessures de guerre." In *La blessure corporelle: Violences, souffrances, symboles et représentations*, edited by Pierre Cordier and Sébastien Jahan, 25–39. Poitiers: GERICO, 2003.

Landes, Joan B. "Republican Citizenship and Heterosocial Desire: Concepts of Masculinity in Revolutionary France." In *Masculinities in Politics and War: Gendering Modern History*, edited by Stefan Dudink, Karen Hagemann, and John Tosh, 96–115. Manchester: Manchester University Press, 2004.

———. *Visualizing the Nation: Gender, Representation, and Revolution in Eighteenth-Century France*. Ithaca: Cornell University Press, 2001.

Lannoy, François. "Préfets et conscription dans la Manche sous le consulat et l'empire (1800–1814)." *Annales de Normandie* 50, no. 4 (2000): 511–22.

La Sicotière, M. de. "Les rosières en Basse Normandie." *Bulletin de la Société historique et archéologique de l'Orne*, 3–4 (1884): 397–451.

Lecomte, Louis-Henry. *Histoire des théâtres de Paris: Le Théâtre national, le Théâtre de l'égalité, 1793–1794*. Paris: Daragon, 1907.

———. *Napoléon et l'empire racontés par le théâtre*. Paris: Jules Raux, 1900.

———. *Napoléon et le monde dramatique, étude après des documents inédits*. Paris: Daragon, 1912.

Legoy, Corinne. *L'enthousiasme désenchanté: Éloge du pouvoir sous la restauration*. Paris: Société des études robespierristes, 2010.

Lemaire, Jean-François. *Les blessés dans les armées napoléoniennes*. Paris: Lettrage, 1999.

———. "Les blessures de la guerre." In *Armée, guerre et société à l'époque napoléonienne: Actes du colloque organisé par l'Institut Napoléon et la Bibliothèque Marmottan les 17 et 18 novembre 2000*, edited by Jacques-Olivier Boudon, 151–64. Paris: Éditions SPM, 2004.

Lesueur, Frédéric, ed. *Département de Loir-et-Cher: Cahiers de doléances du bailliage de Blois et du bailliage secondaire du Romorantin pour les états généraux de 1789*. 2 vols. Paris: Rivière, 1907.

Lévêque, Guillaume. "Les mariages impériaux de 1810 dans le département de l'Indre." *Revue de la Haute Auvergne* 63 (2001): 313–28.

Lignereux, Aurélien. *La France rébellionnaire: Les résistances à la gendarmerie (1800–1859)*. Rennes: PUR, 2008.

Livesey, James. *Making Democracy in the French Revolution*. Cambridge, MA: Harvard University Press, 2001.

Lok, Matthijs. "La culture du silence sous la restauration: Une étude comparative des politiques de l'oubli en France et aux Pays-Bas." In *Rien appris, rien oublié? Les restaurations dans l'Europe postnapoléonienne (1814–1830)*, edited by Jean-Claude Caron and Jean-Philippe Luis, 213–22. Rennes: PUR, 2015.

———. "Un oubli total du passé? The Political and Social Construction of Silence in Restoration Europe (1813–1830)." *History and Memory* 26, no. 2 (2014): 40–75.

Lok, Matthijs, and Natalie Scholz. "The Return of the Loving Father: Masculinity, Legitimacy, and the French and Dutch Monarchies (1813–1815)." *BMG: Low Countries Historical Review* 127, no. 1 (2012): 19–44.

Lottin, Denis. *Recherches historiques sur la ville d'Orléans*. Orléans: Imprimerie Jacob, 1840.

Loubinoux, Gérard. "Ambitions mal placées et extravagance dans le théâtre de Joseph Aude." In *Le théâtre sous la révolution, politique du répertoire (1789–1799)*, edited by Martial Poirson, 247–58. Paris: Desjonquères, 2008.

———. "Les figures du théâtre de Joseph Aude." In *Les arts de la scène et la révolution française*, edited by Philippe Bourdin and Gérard Loubinoux, 419–38. Clermont-Ferrand: Presses Universitaires Blaise Pascal, 2004.

Louis, Jérôme. "La dissolution de l'armée impériale, 1814–1824." *Revue historique des armées* 4 (1997): 29–34.

———. *Reading Culture and Writing Practices in Nineteenth-Century France*. Toronto: University of Toronto Press, 2008.

Lynn, John A. *The Bayonets of the Republic: Motivation and Tactics in the Armies of Revolutionary France, 1791–94*. Urbana: University of Illinois Press, 1984.

———. *Women, Armies, and Warfare in Early Modern Europe*. Cambridge: Cambridge University Press, 2008.

Lyons, Martyn. *Napoleon Bonaparte and the Legacy of the French Revolution*. New York: St. Martin's Press, 1994.

Mabo, Solenn. "Des Bretonnes en résistance: Genre, religion, et contestation politique." *La révolution française: Cahiers de l'institut d'histoire de la révolution française* (2020): https://journals.openedition.org/lrf/4306#ftn3.

———. "Femmes engagées dans la chouannerie: Motivations, modalités d'action, et procès de reconnaissance (1794-1830)." *Genre & histoire* (2017): https://journals.openedition.org/genrehistoire/2687.

———. "Genre et armes dans les conflictualités locales en Bretagne (1789–1799)." *Annales historiques de la révolution française* 393 (2018): 77–98.

Maës, Gaëtane. *Les Watteau de Lille: Louis Watteau (1731–1798), François Watteau (1758–1823)*. Paris: Arthena, 1998.

Mainardi, Patricia. *Husbands, Wives, and Lovers: Marriage and Its Discontents in Nineteenth-Century France*. New Haven: Yale University Press, 2003.

Mainz, Valerie. *Days of Glory? Imaging Military Recruitment and the French Revolution*. Basingstoke: Palgrave Macmillan, 2016.

Mansker, Andrea. "'Marriages by the Petites Affiches': Advertising Love, Marital Choice, and Commercial Matchmaking in Napoleon's Paris." *French Historical Studies* 41, no. 1 (2018): 1–31.

Mannucci, Erica Joy. "Le militaire dans le théâtre de la Révolution française." In *Les arts de la scène et la révolution française*, edited by Philippe Bourdin and Gérard Loubinoux, 381–95. Clermont-Ferrand: Presses Universitaires Blaise Pascal, 2004.

Mansel, Philip. *Louis XVIII*. London: Blond and Briggs, 1981.

Marchioni, Jean. *Les mots de l'empire*. Paris: Actes Sud, 2004.

Marsden, Kathryn. "Married Nuns in the French Revolution: The Sexual Revolution of the 1790s." PhD diss., University of California Irvine, 2014.

Martin, Brian Joseph. "Military Mates: From Revolutionary Fraternity to Napoleonic Intimacy in the Memoirs of Sergeant Faucheur." *Journal for Eighteenth-Century Studies* 41, no. 4 (2018): 543–58.

———. *Napoleonic Friendship: Military Fraternity, Intimacy, and Sexuality in Nineteenth-Century France*. Durham, NH: University Press of New England, 2011.

Martin, Jean-Clément. "Femmes et guerre civile, l'exemple de la Vendée, 1793–1796." *Clio: Femmes, genre, histoire* 5 (1997): https://journals.openedition.org/clio/410.

———. *La révolte brisée: Femmes dans la révolution française et l'empire*. Paris: Armand Colin, 2008.

———. "Travestissements, impostures, et la communauté historienne: A propos des femmes soldats de la révolution et de l'empire." *Politix: Revue des sciences sociales du politique* 19, no. 74 (2006): 31–48.

Maureau, Alain. "Le remplacement militaire de l'an VIII à 1814, d'après les registres de notaires d'Avignon aspect juridique et sociale." *Revue de l'Institut Napoléon* 131 (1975): 121–44.

Maza, Sarah. *Private Lives and Public Affairs: The Causes Célèbres of Prerevolutionary France*. Berkeley: University of California Press, 1993.

———. "The Rose Girl of Salency: Representations of Virtue in Prerevolutionary France." *Eighteenth-Century Studies* 22, no. 3 (1989): 395–412.

Mazeau, Guillaume. "Émotions politiques: La révolution française." In *Histoire des émotions: Des Lumières à la fin de XIXème siècle*, edited by Alain Corbin and Jean-Jacques Courtine, 98–142. Paris: Seuil, 2016.

Meyer, Jessica. "'Not Septimus Now': Wives of Disabled Veterans and Cultural Memory of the First World War in Britain." *Women's History Review* 13, no. 1 (2004): 117–38.

Mihaely, Gil. "L'effacement de la cantinière ou la virilisation de l'armée française au XIXe siècle." *Revue d'histoire du XIXe siècle* 30 (2005): 2–17.

Mikaberidze, Alexander. *The Napoleonic Wars: A Global History*. Oxford: Oxford University Press, 2020.

Morieux, Renaud. "Patriotisme humanitaire et prisonniers de guerre en France et en Angleterre pendant la révolution française et l'empire." In *La politique par les armes: Conflits internationaux et politisation, XVe–XIXe siècles*, edited by Laurent Bourquin, 301–16. Rennes: PUR, 2014.

Nancey, P. M. "Fêtes à l'occasion du mariage de l'empereur et voyage de Napoléon 1er et de Marie Louise à Dunkerque." *Mémoires de la Société dunkerquoise, pour l'encouragement des sciences, des lettres et des arts* 4 (1904): 5–63.

Nielsen, Wendy C. *Women Warriors in Romantic Drama*. Newark: University of Delaware Press, 2013.

Nochlin, Linda. *Representing Women*. New York: Thames and Hudson, 1999.

Offen, Karen. "How (and Why) the Analogy of Marriage with Slavery Provided the Springboard for Women's Rights Demands in France, 1640–1848." In *Women's Rights and*

Transatlantic Antislavery in the Era of Emancipation, edited by Kathryn Kish Sklar and James Stewart, 57–81. New Haven: Yale University Press, 2007.

———. "Women's Memory, Women's History, Women's Political Action: The French Revolution in Retrospect, 1789-1889-1989." *Journal of Women's History* 1, no. 3 (1990): 211–30.

Osman, Julia. *Citizen Soldiers and the Key to the Bastille*. Basingstoke: Palgrave Macmillan, 2015.

Outram, Dorinda. *The Body and the French Revolution: Sex, Class and Political Culture*. New Haven: Yale University Press, 1989.

Ozouf, Mona. *Festivals and the French Revolution*. Cambridge, MA: Harvard University Press, 1988.

Padiyar, Satish, Philip Shaw, and Philippa Simpson, eds. *Visual Culture and the Revolutionary and Napoleonic Wars*. London: Routledge, 2018.

Parker, Geoffrey. *The Cambridge History of Warfare*. Cambridge: Cambridge University Press, 2005.

Parker, Lindsay A. H. "Veiled Emotions: Rosalie Jullien and the Politics of Feeling in the French Revolution." *Journal of Historical Biography* 13 (2013): 208–30.

Pasco, Allan. *Revolutionary Love in Eighteenth- and Early Nineteenth-Century France*. Surrey: Ashgate, 2009.

Perry, Heather. *Recycling the Disabled: Army, Medicine, and Modernity in WWI Germany*. Manchester: Manchester University Press, 2014.

Petiteau, Natalie. *Guerriers du premier empire: Expériences et mémoires*. Paris: Les Indes savantes, 2011.

———. *Lendemains d'empire: Les soldats de Napoléon dans la France du XIXe siècle*. Paris: La boutique de l'histoire, 2003.

———. "Les mariés de l'an 1810 en Vaucluse: Mannes impériales et réalités sociales." *Provence historique, mélanges offerts à Noël Coulet* (1998): 397–410.

———. "La mémoire royaliste de 1814–1815." In *Rien appris, rien oublié? Les restaurations dans l'Europe postnapoléonienne (1814–1830)*, edited by Jean-Claude Caron and Jean-Philippe Luis, 169–81. Rennes: PUR, 2015.

———. "La portée de la politique symbolique à l'égard des armées napoléoniennes." In *Représentation et pouvoir : La politique symbolique en France (1789–1830)*, edited by Natalie Scholz and Christina Schröer, 147–56. Rennes: PUR, 2007.

———. "La restauration face aux vétérans de l'empire." In *Repenser la restauration*, edited by Jean-Yves Mollier, Martine Reid, and Jean-Claude Yon, 31–44. Paris: Nouveau Monde, 2005.

———. "Le retour de guerre: Destins de vétérans après 1815." In *Armée, guerre et société à l'époque napoléonienne: Actes du colloque organisé par l'Institut Napoléon et la Bibliothèque Marmottan les 17 et 18 novembre 2000*, edited by Jacques-Olivier Boudon, 87–104. Paris: Éditions SPM, 2004.

———. "Survivors of War: French Soldiers and Veterans of the Napoleonic Wars." In *Soldiers, Citizens and Civilians: Experiences and Perceptions of the French Wars, 1790–1820*, edited by Karen Hagemann, Alan Forrest, and Jane Rendall, 43–58. Basingstoke: Palgrave Macmillan, 2009.

Petiteau, Natalie, ed. *Voies nouvelles pour l'histoire du premier empire: Territoires, pouvoirs, identités*. Paris: La boutique de l'histoire, 2003.

Phillips, Roderick. *Family Breakdown in Late Eighteenth-Century France: Divorces in Rouen, 1792–1803*. Oxford: Clarendon Press, 1981.

Pichichero, Christy Lauren. *The Military Enlightenment: War and Culture from Louis XIV to Napoleon*. Ithaca: Cornell University Press, 2017.

Pigeard, Alain. *La conscription au temps de Napoléon, 1798–1814*. Paris: Giovanangeli, 2003.

———. "La conscription sous le premier empire." *Revue du Souvenir Napoléonien* 430 (1998): 3–20.
Ploux, François. *De la bouche à l'oreille: Naissance et propagation des rumeurs dans la France du XIXe siècle*. Paris: Aubier, 2003.
Plumauzille, Clyde. *Prostitution et révolution: Les femmes publiques dans la cité républicaine (1789–1804)*. Paris: Champ Vallon, 2016.
Plumauzille, Clyde, and Guillaume Mazeau. "Penser avec le genre: Trouble dans la citoyenneté révolutionnaire." *La révolution française* (2015): https://journals.openedition.org/lrf/1458.
Pomery, Sarah. *Spartan Women*. Oxford: Oxford University Press, 2002.
Poulet, Henry Jean. *Les volontaires de la Meurthe aux armées de la révolution, levée de 1791*. Paris: Berger-Levrault, 1910.
Puymège, Gérard de. *Chauvin, le soldat-laboureur: Contribution à l'étude des nationalismes*. Paris: Gallimard, 1993.
———. "Chauvin and Chauvinism: In Search of a Myth." *History & Memory* 6, no. 1 (1994): 35–72.
Rapport, Mike. *The Napoleonic Wars: A Very Short Introduction*. Oxford: Oxford University Press, 2013.
Rawson, Elizabeth. *The Spartan Tradition in European Thought*. Oxford: Clarendon Press, 1969.
Reddy, William. "Marriage, Honor, and the Public Sphere in Post-Revolutionary France: Separations de Corps, 1815–1848." *Journal of Modern History* 65 (1993): 437–72.
———. *The Navigation of Feeling: A Framework for the History of Emotions*. Cambridge: Cambridge University Press, 2001.
———. "Sentimentalism and Its Erasure: The Role of the Emotions in the Era of the French Revolution." *Journal of Modern History* 72, no. 1 (2000): 109–52.
Reynolds, Sian. *Marriage and Revolution: Monsieur and Madame Roland*. Oxford: Oxford University Press, 2012.
Roberts, Meghan. *Sentimental Savants: Philosophical Families in Enlightenment France*. Chicago: University of Chicago Press, 2016.
Ronsin, Francis. *Le contrat sentimental: Débats sur le mariage, le divorce de l'ancien régime à la restauration*. Paris: Aubier, 1990.
Rosenfeld, Sophia. "Thinking about Feeling, 1789–1799." *French Historical Studies* 32, no. 4 (2009): 697–706.
Ross, Mary Ellen. "La femme militaire de la révolution française: Motifs, modèles, et tactiques littéraires." *French and Francophone Women Facing War*, edited by Alison Fell, 47–68. New York: Peter Lang, 2009.
Rosset, Anne-Marie, ed. *Un siècle d'histoire de France par l'estampe, 1770–1871, Restauration et les cent-jours*. Vol. 5. Paris: Bibliothèque nationale, 1938.
Rouvière, F. "Les rosières du premier arrondissement du Gard." *Revue du Midi* 29 (1901): 36–46.
Rowe, Michael. "Civilians and Warfare during the French Revolutionary Wars." In *Daily Lives of Civilians in Wartime Europe, 1618–1900*, edited by Linda Frey and Marsha Frey, 93–132. Westport, CT: Greenwood Press, 2007.
Roy, Donald, and Victor Emaljanow. *Romantic and Revolutionary Theatre, 1789–1860*. Cambridge: Cambridge University Press, 2003.
Ruffier-Méray, Jahiel. "La hiérarchie au sein du couple et de la famille—le divorce à Toulon, 1792–1796." In *Hiérarchies, subordinations, et insubordinations en Roussillon et en Provence*, 17–52. Perpignan: Presses Universitaires de Perpignan, 2019.
Salvante, Martina. "The Wounded Male Body: Masculinity and Disability in Wartime and Post WWI Italy." *Journal of Social History* 53, no. 3 (2019): 644–66.

Sautel, Gérard. "Droit de pétition, doctrine sociale et perspective révolutionnaire (mai 1791)." In *Histoire du droit social*, edited by Jean-Louis Harouel, 483–92. Paris: PUF, 1989.

Schmidt, Rüdiger. "'Le théâtre se militarise': Le soldat-citoyen dans le théâtre de la Révolution française." In *Représentation et pouvoir: La politique symbolique en France (1789–1830)*, edited by Natalie Schölz and Christina Schröer, 63–82. Rennes: PUR, 2007.

Schnapper, Bernard. *Le remplacement militaire en France: Quelques aspects politiques, économiques, et sociaux du recrutement au XIXe siècle*. Paris: SEVERN, 1968.

Scholz, Natalie. *Die imaginierte Restauration: Repräsentationen der Monarchie im Frankreich Ludwigs XVIII*. Darmstadt: Wissenschaftliche Buchgesellschaft, 2006.

———. "La monarchie sentimentale: Un remède aux crises politiques de la Restauration?" In *Représentation et pouvoir: La politique symbolique en France (1789–1830)*, edited by Natalie Scholz and Christina Schröer, 185–98. Rennes: PUR, 2007.

———. "Past and Pathos: Symbolic Practices of Reconciliation during the French Restoration." *History & Memory* 22, no. 1 (2010): 48–80.

Schröer, Christina. "La représentation du Nouveau Régime: Les élites politiques et sociales dans les gravures du Directoire." In *Représentation et pouvoir: La politique symbolique en France (1789–1830)*, edited by Natalie Schölz and Christina Schröer, 39–61. Rennes: PUR, 2007.

Schwab, Léon. "Variétés: Les femmes aux armées." *La révolution dans les Vosges* 6 (1912–13): 108–15.

Seigan, Kobo. "La propagande pour la conscription, l'armée et la guerre dans le département de la Seine-Inférieure, du Directoire à la fin de l'Empire." In *La plume et le sabre: Hommages offerts à Jean-Paul Bertaud*, edited by Michel Biard, Annie Crépin, and Bernard Gainot, 271–81. Paris: Sorbonne, 2002.

Seriu, Naoko. "Déserteur et femme-soldat en marge de l'institution militaire au milieu du XVIII siècle." In *Combattre, gouverner, écrire: Études réunies en l'honneur de Jean Chagniot*, 709–22. Paris: Economica, 2003.

———. "Du féminin dans les discours militaires au XVIIIème siècle." *Genre & histoire* (2007): https://doi.org/10.4000/genrehistoire.103.

Serna, Pierre. *La république des girouettes*. Sessel: Champ Vallon, 2005.

Serna, Pierre, Antonino de Francesco, and Judith A. Miller, eds. *Republics at War, 1776–1840: Revolutions, Conflicts and Geopolitics in Europe and the Atlantic World*. Basingstoke: Palgrave Macmillan, 2013.

Seznec, Jean, and Jean Adhémar, eds. *Diderot: Salons*. 4 vols. Oxford: Clarendon Press, 1957–1967.

Shaw, Philip. "Longing for Home: Robert Hamilton, Nostalgia, and the Emotional Life of the Eighteenth-Century Soldier." *Journal for Eighteenth-Century Studies* 39, no. 1 (2016): 25–40.

Shusterman, Noah. "Bearing Arms and Arming Citizens in the French Revolution." https://ageofrevolutions.com/2016/10/19/bearing-arms-and-arming-citizens-in-the-french-revolution/.

Smart, Annie. *Citoyennes: Women and the Ideal of Citizenship in Eighteenth-Century France*. Newark: University of Delaware Press, 2012.

Smith, Jay Michael. *The Culture of Merit: Nobility, Royal Service and the Making of Absolute Monarchy in France, 1600–1789*. Ann Arbor: University of Michigan Press, 1996.

Spang, Rebecca. "The Frivolous French: 'Liberty of Pleasure' and the End of Luxury." In *Taking Liberties: Problems of a New Order from the French Revolution to Napoleon*, edited by Judith Miller and Howard Brown, 110–25. Manchester: Manchester University Press, 2002.

Spitzer, Alan B. "Malicious Memories: Restoration Politics and a Prosopography of Turncoats." *French Historical Studies* 24, no. 1 (2001): 37–61.

Steinberg, Ronen. *The Afterlives of the Terror: Facing the Legacies of Mass Violence in Post-Revolutionary France*. Ithaca: Cornell University Press, 2019.

Steinberg, Sylvie. *La confusion des sexes: Le travestissement de la Renaissance à la révolution*. Paris: Fayard, 2001.

Stoker, Donald, ed. *Conscription in Napoleonic Europe: A Revolution in Military Affairs, 1789–1815*. New York: Routledge, 2008.

Taylor, George. *The French Revolution and the London Stage, 1789–1805*. Cambridge: Cambridge University Press, 2000.

Théry, Irène. *Le démariage: Justice et vie privée*. Paris: Odile Jacob, 1993.

Thoral, Marie-Cecile. *From Valmy to Waterloo: France at War, 1792–1815*. Basingstoke: Palgrave Macmillan, 2010.

Tintou, J. "En Haute Vienne, mariages de militaires ordonnés par Napoléon." *Lemouzi*, no. 67 (1978): 192–200.

Tissier, André. *Les spectacles à Paris pendant la révolution: Répertoire analytique, chronologique, et bibliographique*. Geneva: Droz, 1992–2022.

Tocqueville, Alexis de. *The Old Regime and the French Revolution*. Chicago: University of Chicago Press, 1988.

Tozzi, Christopher. "Home Fronts and Battlefields: Experiencing the Revolution through a Military Lens." In *Living the French Revolution*, edited by Mette Harder and Jennifer Ngaire Heuer, 103–24. London: Bloomsbury, 2020.

———. *Nationalizing France's Army: Foreigners, Jews, and Blacks in the French Military, 1715–1831*. Charlottesville: University of Virginia Press, 2016.

Triomphe, Pierre. *1815, la Terreur blanche*. Toulouse: Privat, 2017.

Tuttle, Leslie. "Celebrating the Père de Famille: Fatherhood in Eighteenth-Century France." *Journal of Family History* 29, no. 4 (2004): 66–381.

———. *Conceiving the Old Regime: Pronatalism and the Politics of Reproduction in Early Modern France*. Oxford: Oxford University Press, 2010.

Valade, Pauline. "Public Celebrations and Public Joy at the Beginning of the French Revolution (1788–1791)." *French History* 29, no. 2 (2015): 182–203.

Vallée, Gustave. *La conscription dans le département de la Charente (1798–1807)*. Paris: Recueil Sirey, 1936.

———. "Le remplacement militaire dans la Charente sous le régime de la conscription." *La révolution française, revue d'histoire moderne et contemporaine* 80 (1927): 222–35, 312–30.

Verdier, Gabrielle. "From Reform to Revolution: The Social Theater of Olympe de Gouges." In *Literate Women and the French Revolution of 1789*, edited by Catherine Montfort, 189–221. Birmingham, AL: Summa Publications, 1994.

Verjus, Anne. *Le bon mari: Une histoire politique des hommes et des femmes à l'époque révolutionnaire*. Paris: Fayard, 2010.

———. *Le cens de la famille: Les femmes et le vote 1789–1848*. Paris: Belin, 2002.

Verjus, Anne, Claire Cage, Jennifer Heuer, Andrea Mansker, and Meghan Roberts. "Regards croisés sur le mariage à l'époque révolutionnaire et impériale." *Annales historiques de la révolution française* 398 (2017): 144–71.

Verjus, Anne, and Denise Zara Davidson. *Le roman conjugal: Chroniques de la vie familiale à l'époque de la révolution et de l'empire*. Paris: Champ Vallon, 2011.

Verjus, Anne, Jennifer Heuer, and Françoise Orazi. "Introduction: Féminismes en Europe." *Annales historiques de la révolution française* 411 (2023): 3–24.

Vidalenc, Jean. *Les demi-soldes: Étude d'une catégorie sociale*. Paris: Rivière, 1955.

Viennot, Éliane. *Et la modernité fut masculine: La France, les femmes et le pouvoir, 1789–1804*. Paris: Perrin, 2016.

Vincent-Buffault, Anne. *The History of Tears: Sensibility and Sentimentality in France.* Translated by Teresa Bridgeman. Basingstoke: Macmillan, 1991.

Vingtrinier, Joseph. *1789–1902: Chants et chansons des soldats de France.* Paris: Méricant, 1902.

Vonau, Jean-Laurent. "Les événements tragiques du printemps 1799: L'assassinat des plénipotentiaires français au congrès de Rastatt." *L'Outre-Foret: Revue du Cercle d'histoire et d'archéologie de l'Alsace du Nord* 111 (2000): 32–41.

Vovard, André. "Les rosières de l'empereur." *Revue philomathique de Bordeaux et du sud-ouest* 17–18 (1914): 138–48.

Wahnich, Sophie. *Les émotions, la Révolution française et le présent: Exercices pratiques de conscience historique.* Paris: CNRS, 2009.

Waquet, Jean. "Un essai d'action psychologique: L'assassinat des plénipotentiaires français au congrès de Rastadt (22 avril 1799) et l'appel des conscrits de l'an VII aux armes." *Revue internationale d'histoire militaire* 30 (1970): 181–93.

Waresquiel, Emmanuel de, and Benoît Yvert. *Histoire de la restauration, 1814–1830: Naissance de la France moderne.* Paris: Perrin, 2002.

Weens, Clément. "Quand la politique d'assistance aux parents des défenseurs de la patrie cesse d'être une mesure de salut public." *Histoire de la justice* 32 (2021/2): 141–53.

Welschinger, Henri. *La censure sous le premier empire.* Paris: Charavay, 1882.

Wicks, Charles Beaumont. *Charles Guillaume Etienne: Dramatist and Publicist, 1777–1845.* Baltimore: Johns Hopkins University Press, 1940.

Woloch, Isser. *The French Veteran from the Revolution to the Restoration.* Chapel Hill: University of North Carolina Press, 1979.

———. "Napoleonic Conscription: State Power and Civil Society." *Past and Present* 111 (1986): 111–29.

———. *The New Regime: Transformations of the French Civic Order, 1789–1820s.* New York: W. W. Norton, 1994.

———. "'A Sacred Debt': Veterans and the State in Revolutionary and Napoleonic France." *Disabled Veterans in History*, edited by David A. Gerber, 117–44. Ann Arbor: University of Michigan Press, 2000.

———. "War Widows Pensions and Social Policy in Revolutionary and Napoleonic France." *Societas: A Review of Social History* 6, no. 4 (1976): 235–54.

Wrede, Martin. "Le portrait du roi restauré ou la fabrication de Louis XVIII." *Revue d'histoire moderne et contemporaine* 53, no. 2 (2006): 112–38.

Wrigley, Richard. *The Politics of Appearance: The Symbolism and Representation of Dress in Revolutionary France.* Oxford: Berg, 2002.

INDEX

Page numbers in italics refer to illustrations. All geographic locations are in France, unless otherwise specified.

A NOTE ON THE TYPE

THIS BOOK has been composed in Miller, a Scotch Roman typeface designed by Matthew Carter and first released by Font Bureau in 1997. It resembles Monticello, the typeface developed for The Papers of Thomas Jefferson in the 1940s by C. H. Griffith and P. J. Conkwright and reinterpreted in digital form by Carter in 2003.

Pleasant Jefferson ("P. J.") Conkwright (1905–1986) was Typographer at Princeton University Press from 1939 to 1970. He was an acclaimed book designer and AIGA Medalist.

The ornament used throughout this book was designed by Pierre Simon Fournier (1712–1768) and was a favorite of Conkwright's, used in his design of the *Princeton University Library Chronicle.*